The
Atomic Components
of Thought

The Atomic Components of Thought

John R. Anderson
Christian Lebiere

Carnegie Mellon University

*With the collaboration of
Daniel Bothell, Michael D. Byrne,
Marsha Lovett, Michael Matessa,
Dario D. Salvucci, and
Christian D. Schunn*

LAWRENCE ERLBAUM ASSOCIATES, PUBLISHERS
1998   Mahwah, New Jersey   London

Lawrence Erlbaum Associates, Inc., Publishers
10 Industrial Avenue
Mahwah, NJ 07430

Cover design by Kathryn Houghtaling Lacey

Library of Congress Cataloging-in-Publication Data
Anderson, John R. (John Robert), 1947–
The atomic components of thought / John R. Anderson, Christian Lebiere.
      p. cm.
Includes bibliographical references and indexes.
ISBN 0-8058-2816-8 (hardcover : alk. paper). — ISBN 0-8058-2817-6 (pbk. : alk. paper)
   1. Cognition. 2. Human information processing. 3. Cognitive psychology. I. Lebiere, Christian. II. Title.
BF311.A58944   1998
153—dc21
                                                                97-51871
                                                                     CIP

Books published by Lawrence Erlbaum Associates are printed on acid-free paper, and their bindings are chosen for strength and durability.

Printed in the United States of America
10 9 8 7 6 5 4 3 2

Contents

Preface

This book achieves a goal that was set 25 years ago when Anderson and Bower (1973) published the HAM theory of human memory. That theory reflected one of a number of then current efforts to create a theory of human cognition that met the twin goals of precision and complexity. Until that time, the standard for precision had been the mathematical theories of the 1950s and 1960s. These theories took the form of precise models of specific experiments along with some informal verbally stated understanding of how they could be extended to new experiments. They seemed to fall far short of capturing the breadth and power of human cognition that was being demonstrated by the new experimental work in human cognition.

HAM represented an effort to create a computer simulation system that overcame the shortcomings of this earlier generation of mathematical models. These computer simulation systems were efforts to create computationally powerful models of human cognition that actually performed a wide range of tasks. Performing simulations instead of formal analyses offered the promise of dealing with complexity without sacrificing precision. Like other initial efforts of the time, HAM fell short of the aspirations set for it. First, it was only a theory of human memory and so failed to address many critical phenomena in human cognition. Second, although there was a running program, the sense in which it actually performed the tasks in question was weak. There was a lot of accompanying verbal theory to explain how it really applied to many tasks and in many cases it just became a mathematical model.

The next 10 years saw two major efforts on our part to address the problems of scope. In 1976, the ACT theory (Anderson, 1976) was first described. It included a production rule system of procedural memory to complement HAM's declarative memory. This provided a computationally adequate system that was indeed capable of accounting for all sorts of cognition. In 1983, Anderson published the ACT* system, which extended

ACT with a neurally plausible model of subsymbolic processing and a theory of production rule learning. Perhaps the highlight of that era was a simulation of child language acquisition in the 1983 book.

Each of these versions of ACT came with computer simulation code but still much of the modeling took the form of mathematical models of the simulations and informal assumptions about their application. It is perhaps telling that we no longer have access to any of the code that underlay HAM or these early versions of ACT. The theory still survived more as mathematical models held together by a verbal story than as a simulation. The last piece of code to disappear was the GRAPES production system (Sauers & Farrell, 1982), which implemented the procedural aspect of ACT*. This survived into the 1990s largely because it served as a basis for some of our intelligent tutoring systems. It disappeared when we finally abandoned the Franz LISP implementation of our LISP tutor.

In 1993, a new version of ACT was published called ACT-R. This system was an effort to summarize the theoretical progress we had made on skill acquisition in the intervening 10 years (e.g., Singley & Anderson, 1989) and tune the subsymbolic level of ACT with the insights of the rational analysis of cognition (Anderson, 1990). Accompanying that book was a computer disk containing the first comprehensive implementation of the theory. The fact that we could produce this implementation reflected both our growing understanding (derived from all the partial implementations we had produced) and that LISP, the implementation language of these theories, had become standardized.

The appearance of a generally available, full-function code set off a series of events that we hardly planned and that have resulted in this book. The catalyst for this was the emergence of a user community. When the book was first published, Werner Tack suggested that we hold a summer workshop. For years, this had been recommended for earlier versions of ACT but Anderson had always resisted the suggestion because he recognized that the theory was not ready. However, Lebiere insisted that assembling a critical mass of users was essential to the ultimate success of the theory and that a physical gathering was the only way to achieve that goal. We held what was to be the first ACT-R Summer School and Workshop in 1994. As a summer school, the first was a disaster but as a workshop it was the moment in which a real user community was born.

The creation of that user community resulted in a whole new dynamic to the theory. One dimension of change was to the language of the theory. The theory became a language spoken among all members of the community rather than a language spoken by authors of the theory to readers of the theory. This forced a greater standardization and consistency. We successfully worked on our problems with ACT-R education and later summer schools were much more successful. The goal of successful education created a pressure against unnecessary complexity and further pressure for standardization.

Another change was to the implementation of the theory. Inefficiencies and obscure features that the authors could tolerate were not acceptable to the community. A good example of this was the evolution of the older analogy mechanism into the current production compilation as described in Chapter 4. This was substantially driven by user frustrations. We also produced a much more efficient implementation of ACT-R. A development environment was created that supported learners. The development environment moved us away from our private language (LISP) to the public language (ACT-R).

A third change was to the level of detail at which we attempted to account for data. Different members of our community were interested in different aspects of data and we had no choice but to produce a theory that accounted for it all. The experimental psychology practice of computer-implemented experiments was the computational experience that was most common as a background for our community. As a consequence, we found ourselves moving to a system in which our ACT-R models interacted with experimental software just the way subjects did.

These influences bit by bit had an effect on the details of the theory. The tweakings of the details slowly built up and resulted in a net qualitative change in the theory. It reached the point where we realized that the symbolic knowledge units of the theory had acquired a new psychological reality. As the title of this book announces, they had become the atoms of thought.

The past books in this series had been planned as writing exercises that would stimulate and discipline the creation of advances in the theory. This book was written as a response to the events that had occurred. We needed to document and justify the new theory. In writing the book, we became seized by an aspiration that went beyond just describing the theory correctly. We decided to try to display what the theory could do by collecting together and describing some of its in-house applications. Originally, this was conceived as a loose collection of papers but the ever-increasing need for uniformity and consistency took over. All of these models are running on the World Wide Web and all use the same ACT-R software. The result is hardly everything that one could aspire for in terms of precision and scope, but it is more than Anderson dreamed of 25 years ago.

The book reflects tens of years of work in ACT-R accumulated over many researchers. The chapters are authored by the people who did that particular work. No doubt the reader will be impressed by the scope of the research and the quality of the individual work. However, less apparent but no less important was the effort that everyone put into achieving the overall consistency and technical integrity of the book. This is the first work in cognitive science to precisely model such a wide range of phenomena with a single theory. No one person could have done it alone and it could not have been done by a bunch of individuals working in isolation.

The Cognitive Science Program at ONR (Susan Chipman) and the Human Cognition and Perception Program of the NSF have continued their long-standing support of this research. We view the outcome as evidence of the importance of sustained funding of scientific research with a constant focus. Lawrence Erlbaum Associates has done much to facilitate this work in organizing an extensive set of reviews and coordinating with our web-based efforts. In addition to this, they continue to make available the prior books in this series including Anderson (1983), which they rescued from the premature abandonment by Harvard Press. This is another sort of sustained support critical to the growth of our science.

Many people have read and commented on these chapters. Wayne Gray, Todd Johnson, Clayton Lewis, Peter Pirolli, and Brian Ross each read all or most of the chapters. In addition, Stu Card and Hal Paschler provided expert comments on Chapter 6; Gordon Bower and Stephen Lewandowsky provided expert comments on Chapter 7; Jerry Busemeyer, Lynn Devenport, and Rob Nosofsky provided expert comments on Chapter 8; Mark Ashcraft, Jamie Campbell, and Jane Zbrodoff provided expert comments on Chapter 9; Keith Holyoak and Laura Novick provided expert comments on Chapter 10; and Gary Bradshaw and Jeff Shrager provided expert comments on Chapter 11. Anderson would also like to acknowledge Chris Schunn's assistance in reading the chapters in which Anderson is the first author. We want to acknowledge Stellan Ohlsson's general comments on the direction of the ACT project.

Finally, we want to thank the people who provide the support for the development of the total package. Mike Matessa has maintained the ACT-R home page and Dan Bothell is responsible for the ACT-R models running on the web. Peter Brusilovsky and Elmar Schwarz have developed the Web-based Interbook (Brusilovsky, Eklund, & Schwarz, 1997; Brusilovsky,

Schwarz, & Weber, 1996), which implements the ACT-R tutorial and the running models. Jon Fincham has developed the ACT-R environment including its tutorial components. Helen Borek has supported all of the manuscript preparation and coordination. Her work in tying all the pieces together has been nothing short of heroic.

1

Introduction

John R. Anderson
Christian Lebiere
Carnegie Mellon University

NEWELL'S DREAM

The challenge of science is to find the order that exists in the complexity of the world. Certainly, psychology faces one of the larger challenges: trying to understand the structure of human cognition, which is perhaps the most complex of all systems. Ever since modern cognitive psychology took form in the 1950s and 1960s, it has tended to adopt a divide-and-conquer approach to this challenge. This involves focusing on specific aspects of human cognition and trying to understand in detail what is happening in those aspects. The classic example of this was Sternberg's (1969) effort to study how people searched through a small number of elements in short-term memory. The reason for such a narrow focus was the respect for data that psychology had acquired from its earlier history—one needs to care about the exact response structure and temporal structure of behavior if one wants to understand it. It seemed impossible to be able to deal with data at that level of detail unless one focused on relatively circumscribed aspects of cognition. The assumption behind this divide-and-conquer strategy was that one would be able to understand all the pieces of cognition separately and then put them together into a single theory.

Twenty-five years ago at the 1972 Carnegie Symposium, Allen Newell (Newell, 1973a) raised the question of whether this strategy was really working in his famous "You can't play 20 questions with nature and win" paper. In it, he lamented the tendency of cognitive psychology to divide the world into little paradigms each with its own set of questions and logic. Each seemed to manufacture an endless stream of research without the overall picture of human cognition becoming any clearer. As he wrote prophetically:

> Suppose that in the next thirty years we continued as we are now going. Another hundred phenomena, give or take a few dozen, will have been discovered and explored. Another forty oppositions will have been posited and their resolution initiated. Will psychology then have come of age? Will

1

it provide the kind of encompassing of its subject matter—the behavior of man—that we all posit as a characteristic of a mature science? It seems to me that clarity is never achieved. Matters simply become muddier and muddier as we go down through time. Thus, far from providing the rungs of a ladder by which psychology gradually climbs to clarity, this form of conceptual structure leads rather to an ever increasing pile of issues, which we weary of or become diverted from, but never really settle. (Newell, 1973a, pp. 287–289)

Newell felt that the way to make progress was to work on unified theories that simultaneously addressed all aspects of cognition. Basically, Newell's point was one that will be familiar to a software engineer: There are numerous constraints among all the pieces and one needs to try to understand from the beginning how they fit into the whole.

In a companion piece at that symposium, Newell (1973b) introduced his answer to this dilemma. He described his first production system theory of human cognition. It was a single system to perform the diverse set of tasks that occupied cognitive psychology. As he described production systems:

A production system is a scheme for specifying an information processing system. It consists of a set of productions, each production consisting of a condition and an action. It has also a collection of data structures: expressions that encode the information upon which the production system works—on which the actions operate and on which the conditions can be determined to be true or false.

A production system, starting with an initially given set of data structures, operates as follows. That production whose condition is true of the current data (assume there is only one) is executed, that is, the action is taken. The result is to modify the current data structures. This leads in the next instant to another (possibly the same) production being executed, leading to still further modification. So it goes, action after action being taken to carry out an entire program of processing, each evoked by its condition becoming true of the momentarily current collection of data structures. The entire process halts either when no condition is true (hence nothing is evoked) or when an action containing a stop operation occurs.

Much remains to be specified in the above scheme to yield a definite information processing system. What happens (a likely occurrence) if more than one production is satisfied at once? What is the actual scheme for encoding information? What sort of collection of data structures constitutes the current state of knowledge on which the system works? What sort of tests are expressible in the conditions of productions? What sort of primitive operations are performable on the data and what collections of these are expressible in the actions of productions? What sorts of additional memories are available and how are they accessed and written into? How is the production system itself modified from within, or is this possible? How much time (or effort) is taken by the various components of the system and how do they combine to yield a total time for an entire processing? (Newell, 1973b, pp. 463–464)

Over the years, Newell explored a number of variations on his production system conception, concluding with his Soar theory of human cognition (Newell, 1990). There have been many other production system architectures of human cognition. Our work has been in the production system framework since the introduction of the ACT system (Anderson, 1976).

Like many good ideas, it has taken years of development and exploration for the production-system construct to reach its full potential.[1] Now it has reached a point where production system models can address phenomena in cognitive psychology in a way that is competitive with the narrow single-paradigm accounts. For most of this time, production systems have been out of the focus of attention of the cognitive psychology community. However, there has been quiet and steady progress. The field of production systems had become sufficiently rich by 1987 that Klahr, Langley, and Neches could publish a book reviewing no fewer than 26 (then past and present) production systems. In the last 10 years, production systems have begun to truly realize the potential that Newell had seen for them. They are the only modeling formalism capable of spanning a broad range of tasks, dealing with complex cognition, in complete detail, and with a high degree of accuracy.[2] Right now, there are at least four current and active production system theories: ACT-R (Anderson, 1993), 3CAPS (Just & Carpenter, 1992), EPIC (Meyer & Kieras, 1997), and Soar (Newell, 1991), with Kintsch's (1992) construction-integration theory being a close relative. The combined accomplishments of these theories is nothing less than staggering.

---

[1] The neural network framework is another example of the maturation process; that is, it took about 25 years from the early 1960s to the mid to late-1980s for the concept to become truly useful.

[2] Certainly, this claim is bound to raise certain hairs. The most obvious current alternatives to this claim are the various connectionist models, which have addressed a wide variety of phenomena, sometimes with a great deal of concern about correspondence to data. However, these models have not been greatly concerned with combinatorially complex tasks, such as studies of problem solving or human–computer interaction. Along with this neglect has been a neglect of a detailed accounting for the temporal structure of cognition. Connectionist cycles are typically loosely related to the time to do a task and learning "epochs" to the actual steps of learning a competence. Production system models, as was intended by Newell, are at their strongest when they are accounting for the control of complex cognition. This weakness of connectionist models may change with the appearance of *hybrid architectures*, which use symbolic structures to control connectionist components. ACT–R is basically a hybrid architecture that has a subsymbolic level performing connectionist-like computations (see Chapter 12 for details).

Chapter 12 of this book provides a comparison of these theories. However, the majority of this book is devoted to describing the accomplishments of the ACT–R theory. With obvious bias, we regard this theory as the one that has best achieved Newell's dream. The way we argue for this conclusion is not to disparage the other theories, which we admire, but rather to show what ACT–R can do.

We pursue this demonstration in the spirit of Newell's original idea by showing how it can address the details of some of the paradigms in cognitive psychology. Thus, we try to show that ACT–R offers a potential for some of the unity that Newell desperately wanted to see in psychology. Newell's 20-questions paper has often been criticized for not appreciating the depth of understanding that does exist in each of these domains. In later years, Newell's argument increasingly became that the well-understood empirical regularities in these domains had now set the stage for a new level of theory. This was basically the argument in his 1990 book. That book described Soar as a theory to unify the regularities in psychology. Like Soar, ACT–R is a theory that tries to deal with the rich empirical detail that has evolved in cognitive psychology.

We have written this book because ACT–R has passed a critical point of practicality in its development where it now offers a real potential of providing the unifying theory. A wide range of researchers can now use ACT–R to develop computer simulations of phenomena of interest to them. The function of this book is to provide a description of the theory at a level that will help researchers use it and understand its use by others. The book also provides examples of ACT–R's application to a wide range of phenomena in memory, problem solving, and skill acquisition. ACT–R is applied to tasks that range from recognizing whether an item is in a list to the cognitive processes underlying the design of a memory experiment. There have been a number of theoretical developments in ACT–R that have helped enable this practical breakthrough, and we describe these theoretical developments at appropriate places in the book. However, up front, in terms of what is new in this book, we want to highlight the fact that it describes a usable system for accurately modeling in detail a wide range of cognitive phenomena.

When we say ACT–R is now a practical system, we mean three things:

1. It is easy to learn to use the ACT–R modeling system.
2. It is natural to develop cognitive models in the ACT–R modeling system.
3. The models developed tend to be accurate models.

The degree to which these assertions are true of the ACT–R system described here is a relative matter. We claim they are much more true of the current ACT–R than previous versions of ACT and more true of the current ACT–R than competing formalisms. However, there is plenty of room for improvement, and it is a constant aspiration of our group to make ACT–R more practical.

This book and ACT–R participate in a set of technological developments that even Allen Newell would not have imagined 25 years ago. This book is really only an advance organizer to what is available as part of the ACT–R theory. Corresponding to this book is a World Wide Web site from which it is possible to obtain (a) the ACT–R software for developing ACT–R models, (b) extensive instructional material showing how to develop models in ACT–R, (c) running versions of all the models in the book, and (d) the data to which these models were fit. The book is written in the spirit of a (relatively) easy-to-follow highlight. The interested reader can branch from it to appropriate portions of the Web site. We have made a repository of ACT–R material available as a Web site because we conceive of this supporting material as a living document that will grow as new applications of ACT–R are developed. The ACT–R home page is to be found at the Web site http://act.psy.cmu.edu. There is an active research community around the world that is using ACT–R for cognitive modeling. The research described in this book is only a fraction of the research involving ACT–R. One can find pointers to this research and to other researchers from the ACT–R home page.

A BRIEF SKETCH OF ACT–R

Before progressing any further, it is necessary to place on the table a basic sketch of the ACT–R theory. ACT–R consists of a theory of the nature of human knowledge, a theory of how this knowledge is deployed, and a theory of how this knowledge is acquired. As elaborated later, ACT–R assumes that there are two types of knowledge—declarative and procedural. *Declarative knowledge* corresponds to things we are aware we know and can usually describe to others. Examples of declarative knowledge include "George Washington was the first president of the United States" and "Three plus four is seven." *Procedural knowledge* is knowledge that we display in our behavior but that we are not conscious of. Procedural knowledge basically specifies how to bring declarative knowledge to bear in solving problems.

Declarative knowledge in ACT–R is represented in terms of chunks (Miller, 1956; Servan-Schreiber, 1991), which are configurations of elements that encode various things that we know. Figure 1.1 is a graphical display of a chunk encoding the addition fact that $3 + 4 = 7$. This chunk can also be represented textually:

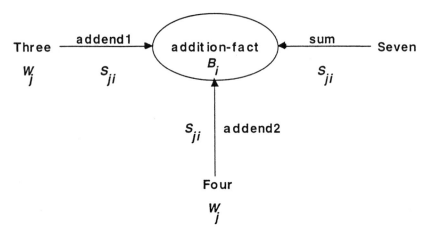

FIG. 1.1.   A network representation of an ACT–R chunk.

Fact3+4
          is a   ADDITION-FACT
     addend1   Three
     addend2   Four
        sum   Seven

In the preceding text, Fact3+4 is just an arbitrary name given to the chunk. It is followed by a series of slots and associated values. The first slot, isa, is special and gives the type of the chunk. The remaining slots (addend1, addend2, and sum) are associated with this addition-fact type and their values define the $3 + 4 = 7$ fact. Figure 1.1 reveals the structure of such a chunk. It serves essentially to interassociate the slot values of the chunk. The S_{ji} terms in Fig. 1.1 refer to associative strengths between slot values and chunks and the B_i refers to the base-level activation of the chunk. These quantities are relevant to calculating the activation levels of such chunks. These activation processes determine the availability of the knowledge, as Chapter 3 develops.

Production rules specify how to retrieve and use such declarative knowledge to solve problems. As an example of procedural knowledge Table 1.1 gives a production set for solving multicolumn addition problems. This and all other examples in the book can be retrieved by following the published models link from the ACT–R Web site. This production set consists of a set of productions where each production is a condition-action pair. The condition specifies what must be true for the production rule to apply, and the action specifies a set of things to do if the production applies. The conditions test for the state of the current goal and chunks in declarative memory, whereas the actions can change the goal state. The rules in Table

TABLE 1.1
The English Version of the Multi-Column Additional Rules

Start-Problem

IF	the goal is to do an addition problem but no column has been identified
THEN	set a subgoal to add the digits in the ones column
	and note that the tens column is the next one to work on

Read-Number 1

IF	the goal is to add the numbers in the column
	and the first number has not been encoded
THEN	encode the first number in the column

Read-Number 2

IF	the goal is to add the numbers in the column
	and the second number has not been encoded
THEN	encode the second number in the column

Add-Numbers

IF	the goal is to add the numbers in the column
	and another number is their sum
THEN	note that other number as the sum

Extract-Answer

IF	the goal is add the numbers in the column
	and the sum has been computed
	and the sum has a ones digit and a tens digit
THEN	note the tens digit as the digit to be carried
	and set the answer to the ones digit

Process-Carry

IF	the goal is to add the numbers in the column
	and there is an answer and a carry
THEN	change the answer to one more
	and remove the marking of the carry

Write-Answer

IF	the goal is to add the numbers in the column
	and there is no carry
	and the to-be-carried digit has been determined
THEN	write the answer in the answer row of the column
	and pop the goal

Last-Column-No-Carry

    IF   the goal is add the numbers in a column
              and an item has been read into the bottom number slot
              and that item is a +
              and there is no carry to be passed on
    THEN note the problem as finished
              and pop the goal

Last-Column-Carry

    IF   the goal is add the numbers in a column
              and an item has been read into the bottom number slot
              and that item is a +
              and there is a carry to be passed on
    THEN note the problem as finished write out the carry
              and pop the goal

Next-Column

    IF   the goal is to do an addition problem
              and the column to add has been determined
              and the carry is known
    THEN set a subgoal to add the digits in that column with the carry
              and note that the next column is the one to add

Stop-Problem

    IF   the goal is to do an addition problem
              and the problem has been flagged as finished
    THEN stop by popping the goal

1.1 are presented in an informal, English-like form. We delay presenting them in formal ACT–R syntax until the next chapter.

An important part of the ACT–R theory concerns how it organizes all of these small units of knowledge in order to achieve organized higher level cognition. For instance, Table 1.2 presents a trace of the productions in Table 1.1 working together to produce a coherent solution to the following problem:

$$\begin{array}{r} 239 \\ + \underline{125} \end{array}$$

The first production, **Start-Problem**, applies when the goal is to do an addition problem and no column is being focused on. It focuses attention on the ones column. It also sets a subgoal to process the numbers in that column. The next productions, **Read-Number 1** and **Read-Number 2**, read the numbers from the column (later Chapters 5 and 6 discuss the issue of how ACT–R can actually read information from a visual array). The fourth production, **Add-Numbers**, adds these numbers by retrieving the

Table 1.2
Trace* of Production Set in Table 1.1
Solving, 239 + 125

Cycle 0: Start-Problem
      Cycle 1: Read-Number1
      Cycle 2: Read-Number2
      Cycle 3: Add-Numbers
      Cycle 4: Extract-Answer
      Cycle 5: Write-Answer
4
Cycle 6: Next-Column
      Cycle 7: Read-Number1
      Cycle 8: Read-Number2
      Cycle 9: Add-Numbers
      Cycle 10: Process-Carry
      Cycle 11: Extract-Answer
      Cycle 12: Write-Answer
6
Cycle 13: Next-Column
      Cycle 14: Read-Number1
      Cycle 15: Read-Number2
      Cycle 16: Add-Numbers
      Cycle 17: Extract-Answer
      Cycle 18: Write-Answer
3
Cycle 19: Next-Column
      Cycle 20: Read-Number2
      Cycle 21: Last-Column-No-Carry
Cycle 22: Stop-Problem

*The indentation of this trace reflects the depth of the goal stack.

addition fact that $9 + 5 = 14$. The fifth production, **Extract-Answer**, identifies 4 as a number to be written out. Then the production **Write-Answer** writes this out and pops the goal of processing this column to return to the original goal of solving the whole addition problem. Then, **Next-Column** switches attention to the tens columns and on it goes.

We regard each production in the sequence as being a basic step of cognition. As we describe in more detail later, only a very limited amount of processing can be accomplished in these steps. The decisions about what the steps are carry substantial psychological significance. At each step, we can potentially record some action such as an utterance, a keystroke, or an eye movement. Thus, decisions in ACT–R about the grain size in which to model human cognition are much determined by the grain size of overt behavior. Another significance of this step size involves learning. Each of these rules is learned separately. Failures in competence can be understood as missing or incorrect rules. Thus, a student may not have the rule **Process-Carry** and so will fail to correctly process columns that require a carry.

These production rules also display the significance of goal structures in providing a higher level organization to control the running of production rules in ACT–R. At any point in time, there is a "stack" of goals that encodes the system's intentions.[3] ACT–R is always trying to achieve the goal that is on top of that stack. It can "pop" that goal, in which case the goal is removed from the stack and ACT–R focuses on the next goal. In the preceding example, this happened when it accomplished a column addition and returned to the goal of the overall addition. ACT–R can also push a new goal on the stack, in which case that goal takes over as the focus of attention. The ACT–R theory is a very fixed-attention architecture. At any point in time, it is focused on a single goal and at any point in time, a single production fires. Despite the focus, the architecture can support the distractibility and opportunism that is part of human cognition, as the next chapter discusses.

Figure 1.2 displays the information flow in the ACT–R system. There are essentially three memories—a *goal stack*, which encodes the hierarchy of intentions guiding behavior, a *procedural memory*, containing the production rules, and a *declarative memory*, containing the chunks. These are all organized through the *current goal*, which represents the focus of attention. The current goal can be pushed on the stack, or the current goal can be popped, in which case the next goal is retrieved from the stack. Productions are

---

[3]A stack is a concept for storing information in a first-in, last-out basis. It is analogous to a stack of trays at a cafeteria. The last tray placed on the stack is the first removed. In the case of goals, when one is "popped," or removed, the next most recent is retrieved. A goal stack records the hierarchy of intentions, in which the bottom goal is the most general and the goals above it are subgoals set in its service.

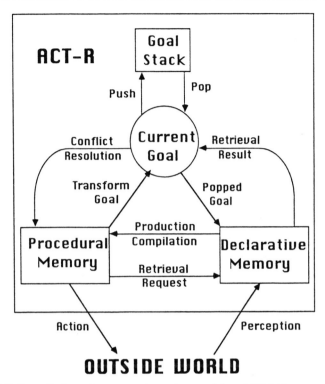

FIG. 1.2 Flow of information among the various modules of ACT–R.

selected to fire through a *conflict resolution* process, which chooses one production from among the productions that match the current goal. The selected production can cause actions to be taken in the outside world, can transform the current goal (possibly resulting in pushes and pops to the stack), and can make retrieval requests of declarative memory (such as, what is the sum of 3 and 4?). The retrieval result (such as 7) can be returned to the goal. The arrows in Fig. 1.2 also describe how new chunks and productions are acquired. Chunks enter declarative memory either as popped goals, reflecting the solutions to past problems, or as perceptions from the environment. Productions are created from declarative chunks through a process called *production compilation*. Figure 1.2 provides one overview of ACT–R and this book expands on each of the arrows in that figure.

ACT–R can be described as a purely symbolic system in which discrete chunks and productions interact in discrete cycles. However, ACT–R also has a subsymbolic level in which continuously varying quantities are processed, often in parallel, to produce much of the qualitative structure of human cognition. The B_i and S_{ji} terms like those in Fig. 1.1 are quantities that participate in neural-like activation processes that determine the speed and success of access to chunks in declarative memory. Similar quantities control access to production rules. Thus, even in the context of multicolumn addition, these quantities influence things like speed of retrieval of the number facts and choice among alternative strategies for doing multicolumn addition. ACT–R also has a set of learning processes that can modify these subsymbolic quantities. These learning processes serve to tune ACT–R to the statistical regularities in the environment. This subsymbolic level is described in detail in Chapters 3 and 4. As this book illustrates, ACT–R's behavioral predictions are more a function of its subsymbolic assumptions than they are of its symbolic assumptions.

This concludes the brief overview of the ACT–R theory. The goal in this brief overview was to place on the table the general conception of information processing in ACT–R. The remainder of this chapter attempts to highlight some of the significant features of the ACT–R theory.

AN ATOMIC LEVEL OF THOUGHT

ACT–R is a theory with over 20 years of history. There have been three relatively well-defined and distinct theories defined in that framework: ACTE (Anderson, 1976), ACT* (Anderson, 1983), and ACT–R (Anderson, 1993). ACTE introduced most of the basic concepts that have stayed part of all the ACT–R theories—declarative memory as a set of units (then called *propositions*), procedural memory as production rules, strengths in declarative and procedural memory, and declarative activation processes to link declarative and procedural memory. ACT* did much to work out a plausible neural-like calculus of activation and produced the first plausible theory of production learning. The evolution from ACT* to ACT–R was guided by the rational analysis of Anderson (1990), which was concerned with how cognition achieved its adaptive function. Guided by the rational analysis, ACT–R added further refinements to the activation calculus and provided a substantially different and more defensible theory of production learning. The theory being described here is just a variant of ACT–R as it was introduced in 1993. Its variant status is denoted by the use of version numbers. The 1993 theory was ACT–R 2.0 and the current theory is ACT–R 4.0.[4] The first section of Chapter 12 gives a detailed review of the assumptions of ACT–R 4.0 and where they differ from ACT–R 2.0. There are some new details, and they are discussed at appropriate points in the

---

[4]There was an ACT–R 1.0, which was a precursor to ACT–R 2.0, and an ACT–R 3.0, which was a more efficient implementation of ACT–R 2.0.

book. However, it seemed inappropriate to get into such details in an introductory chapter.

Here, we highlight what we see as the big theoretical news in ACT-R 4.0 and what we think was critical to passing the threshold of practicality such that ACT-R can now be used by many researchers to model a wide range of phenomena. The relatively small theoretical adjustments in ACT-R have conspired together to convey on the chunks and productions of ACT-R a profound sense of psychological reality. This has reached the point where we think we have identified the atomic components of cognition, as announced in the title of this book. We think now that we can claim that productions define the units with which thought progresses and chunks define the units with which knowledge is retrieved from declarative memory. As the experienced ACT-R reader will discover, this is not just a matter of anointing something already in the theory with the title "atomic". Over the past 5 years, there have been significant changes in the details of ACT-R's chunks and productions that have enabled this title.

In using the word atom we are calling on a metaphor to physical science, and we think it is an apt metaphor. Chunks and productions in ACT-R 4.0 are as far down as one can go in the symbolic decomposition of thought. On average every couple of hundred milliseconds, another production fires, a few declarative chunks are processed, and cognition advances another step. Each step of symbolic learning involves the acquisition of another chunk or production. Thus, ACT-R now captures the symbolic grain size of cognition.

Just as with the atomic level in the physical sciences, there are significant levels above and below that level. In ACT-R there is a level of goal structures above these elements that provide the chemical structure of thought and that fuse these elements into coherent cognition. There is a subsymbolic level of activation-based computations, which determines many of the continuously varying, qualitative properties of the symbolic cognitive elements. As the book develops, the statistical tuning of knowledge at this subsymbolic level underlies much of the adaptive character of thought.

Just as the identification of the atom was the enabling condition for much scientific progress at the subatomic and superatomic levels, so we believe that the current formulation in ACT-R enables similar progress in the study of cognition. That is, we are not so much announcing a scientific discovery; rather, we are describing an enabling condition for progress to be made. If the secret of science is carving nature at the joints, we propose ACT-R's chunks and productions as defining the critical cognitive limbs. This book contains a set of proposals for the properties of these cognitive atoms—these properties are largely assertions about the subsymbolic level. Undoubtedly, these will change somewhat with time, just as our understanding of the subatomic structure of matter has changed with time.

THE NO-MAGIC DOCTRINE IN ACT–R

The next three chapters describe the basic theory in terms of its assumptions about knowledge representation (Chapter 2), performance (Chapter 3), and learning (Chapter 4). The current ACT–theory maintains the predictive successes of the past ACT theories, although it often carries these to new levels of detail. These three chapters contain a number of brief examples to illustrate the theory and to show how ACT–R deals with domains and phenomena that reflect its past—problem solving, memory, and skill acquisition. The remainder of this book contains some detailed applications of the ACT–R theory, but they are more than just applications—they illustrate the new aspirations of the theory.

Emboldened both by the qualitative changes in ACT–R's success as a practical modeling system and the psychological reality of its basic chunks and production rules, we have increased our aspirations for the theory. We have tried to banish completely the looseness that has existed in all theoretical accounts in cognitive science, including our own past theories. Essentially, theories in psychology have always counted on a sympathetic audience to understand how the theories should be applied and evaluated. For instance, our theory of fact retrieval (Anderson, 1974) counted on understanding of how the experiment was broken into study and retrieval trials, how presentations of probes resulted in internal representation and instantiated the parameters of the model, which aspects of the data (i.e., latency, not accuracy) were addressed, and so forth. Although we cannot claim to have completely eliminated such looseness, we have striven to do so as much as possible. This is what we call the "no-magic" doctrine in ACT–R. We describe here six tenets of that doctrine and how they are realized in this book.

1. Experimentally Grounded.   Typically, theories of higher level cognition stop short of specifying how subjects interact with the physical world. Recently, Meyer and Kieras (1997) criticized this aspect of theories as exemplifying what they call "disembodied cognition." Such theories fail to properly represent the processing costs of extracting information from the environment, and they have unprincipled degrees of freedom in representing that information.

Almost all of the experimental tasks used in the history of ACT have involved subjects interacting with material presented on a computer screen. This includes both laboratory work and work with computer tutors (e.g.,

Anderson, Corbett, Koedinger, & Pelletier, 1995). Therefore, it has been of priority to specify how subjects access information from a computer screen and deal with a keyboard and mouse. Chapter 5 describes an extension to ACT–R called the "visual interface" that does this. It incorporates existing ideas of other researchers about visual attention and perception into a software system that is capable of dealing with the same experimental software that subjects do. It parses the screens as they do and enters key presses and mouse gestures into the computer event stream as they do. The data record it creates is indistinguishable, formally, from the data record that subjects create. For this limited domain, the gap has been bridged between the physical world and the theory.

In Chapter 6, Mike Byrne extends this effort more generally to deal with audition, speech, and other hand gestures. He has borrowed extensively from the Meyer and Kieras's EPIC work in this direction. However, there are critical differences between the ACT–R system and EPIC. In ACT–R, cognition remains serial at the level of production rule firings, whereas EPIC is parallel. Byrne compares the ACT–R and EPIC approach in the domain of the psychological refractory period where EPIC has been developed the most. He shows that ACT–R offers a superior account. This domain provides a good test of ACT–R's scheme for which aspects of perception and action can be carried out in parallel with cognition. In developing this extension to ACT–R, Byrne has brought ACT–R's theory of mental timing to a new level of precision.

The experimental grounding of ACT–R has created a relatively unique situation. In many modeling formalisms, such as some connectionist formalisms, it is possible to create models whose correspondence to actual cognition is unclear.[5] In contrast, every ACT–R model corresponds to a subject performing in some particular experiment. The fact that one can look at any ACT–R model and think about the experiment it implies and the behavior it predicts has created a new level of reality in cognitive modeling. No longer are we plagued with models that might or might not be neat ideas, but we just cannot tell for sure because their mappings to reality are not defined.

2. Detailed and Precise Accounting of Data.   Many cognitive theories of a phenomenon specify only general aspects of the data that come from studies of the phenomenon. This is not necessarily because they are imprecise, but because they are specified at a level of abstraction such that it is not clear what their commitments are on certain aspects of the data. Thus, a theory of free recall might specify how much a subject will recall, but

---

[5] See earlier Footnote 2.

not the order and latency of recall. A theory of analogy might predict which analogy a subject will make, but not specify the time course of how the analogy develops. Such abstraction means that these theories fail to achieve the specificity of mechanism that we aspire to in psychological theory.

Because of its experimental grounding, ACT–R is not allowed such freedom from detail. ACT–R makes predictions about every aspect of the empirical phenomena that the experimental software registers. In particular, ACT–R must make predictions about both response choice and response latency and for any variation of an experimental paradigm that one might devise. Chapter 7 attempts to do this with respect to list memory experiments, accounting for a wide range of results concerning accuracy and latency. In such memory experiments, response choice is typically measured in terms of accuracy, but in fact, response choices can be richer than just right or wrong. Marsha Lovett, in Chapter 8, addresses choice generally, both in problem solving and in simpler situations, both for humans and for other organisms.

3. Learnable Through Experience.   Most ACT–R models assume a system that starts out with substantial relevant knowledge, as is the case for the typical undergraduate subject. This raises the question of whether the knowledge is learnable through experience. ACT–R does contain mechanisms for learning. It is an aspiration in ACT–R to have all knowledge (chunks and production rules) learnable through experience. This substantially reduces our degrees of freedom in proposing a model for a task. For instance, Chapter 9 on cognitive arithmetic, examines what happens when ACT–R is given the mathematical experience of a typical American child. We see that it grows its basic arithmetic knowledge from kindergarten to college as it has been documented to evolve in American students. Given the extensive research that has been done on cognitive arithmetic, this is an ideal domain for addressing the issue of whether our ACT–R can model the development of knowledge over an extensive period.

4. Capable of Dealing With Complex Cognitive Phenomena.
ACT has had a history of modeling complex learning phenomena including the cognitive models for intelligent tutors (Anderson et al., 1995). This ability to model complex cognition is one of the great strengths of production systems over other modeling formalisms. There has been a perception that this may be something ACT–R has lost with its new emphasis on the detail of cognition and atomic components of thought. The last two chapters illustrate that this is not the case. Rather ACT–R is now better able to model complex cognition. Chapter 10, by Dario Salvucci, on learning by analogy to examples, models, in exquisite detail, the process of learning to solve physics problems. It brings the understanding of analogical learning to an unprece-

dented level of precision. Chapter 11, by Chris Schunn, raises the bar of complexity and detail to a new level he provides an ACT–R model for how a cognitive scientist designs and interprets experiments to test a theory.

5. Principled Parameters.   At the subsymbolic level, numerous parameters govern the behavior of ACT–R. In the past, reviewers have complained about what seemed theoretical sleights of hand as parameter values jumped around from experiment to experiment to fit the data. This book reflects a considerable effort to constrain and understand the effects of parameter variation in ACT–R. The new atomic constraints on productions and chunks are critical to achieving an understanding of parameter variation. Moreover, to communicate both the models and their parameter choices, running simulation models are available over the Web, so that readers can explore the parameter space dynamically and see how the behavior of the model varies.

6. Neurally Plausible.   Ever since ACT* in 1983, there has been the goal to have the computation in ACT be plausible, given what was known about the brain. For practical purposes, it never made sense to actually implement ACT as a brain model, as this would get in the way of being able to efficiently simulate higher level cognitive processes. However, we had always intended that correspondences could be made between ACT and the brain. Since 1983, the developments in cognitive neuroscience have been dramatic and they have influenced the current version of ACT–R. The third section of the last chapter, Chapter 12, briefly describes a system called ACT–RN which is a connectionist implementation of ACT–R. Its basic structure was determined not only by an understanding of connectionist computation, but also by knowledge of how the brain organizes human cognition. That system was completed (Lebiere & Anderson, 1993) shortly after the completion of ACT–R 2.0 and has served as one of the forces guiding the revisions that led to ACT–R 4.0.

Production systems have suffered from the perception that they were computer-like and not brain-like in their computation. In part, this is because they are computer simulation models. However, this was never more than a superficial reason because there are many computer simulations of brain processes. The greater difficulty has been that it has not been clear how production systems map onto specifications of brain processes. Hopefully, ACT–RN will make this neural mapping clearer. ACT–R can be regarded as an abstraction of neural computation that is useful for modeling higher level cognition.

The major goal of ACT–R is to provide a system for modeling human cognition that is easy to learn and use and that naturally leads to accurate models. Each of these no-magic principles can be seen as furthering that goal.

2

Knowledge Representation

John R. Anderson
Christian Lebiere
Carnegie Mellon University

The function of this chapter is to specify how knowledge is represented in ACT–R. However, to do this, we also need to specify something about how ACT–R processes this knowledge. The process assumptions in ACT–R can be organized according to the 2 x 2 x 2 system illustrated in Table 2.1. There are assumptions about how the system performs and how the system learns. Within each topic, one can distinguish between assumptions that are relevant to declarative memory and assumptions that are relevant to procedural memory. One can further divide the assumptions according to whether they apply to ACT–R at the symbolic level or at the subsymbolic level. This and the next two chapters discuss all aspects of the theory (i.e., all eight cells in Table 2.1). Table 2.1 indicates where each aspect of the theory is discussed. Table 2.1 also indicates the units in the ACT–R Web tutorial that correspond to these topics. This Web tutorial can be accessed by following the <u>tutorial</u> link from the ACT–R Web site http://act.psy.cmu.edu. In our ACT–R classes, we typically devote 1 week to each tutorial unit. There are nine tutorial units. Students appear to require all 9 weeks (at 5–10 hours per week) to come to mastery of the material. So a word to the wise: The material in these chapters is not to be taken lightly.

As can be seen from Table 2.1, this chapter on knowledge representation also discusses the performance assumptions of ACT–R at the symbolic level. This is because assumptions about how knowledge is represented are not meaningful until they are tied to how the knowledge is used. The symbolic performance assumptions in this chapter are not the only consequences of the ACT–R representational assumptions. They are just the most immediate consequences. These representational assumptions also serve as the framework for the other ACT–R process assumptions.

TABLE 2.1
Process Assumptions of the ACT-R Theory

Performance		
	Declarative	*Procedural*
Symbol	Chapter 2	Chapter 2
	Tutorial Units 1 & 2	Tutorial Units 1 & 2
Subsymbolic	Chapter 3	Chapter 3
	Tutorial Units 4 & 5	Tutorial Unit 3
Learning		
	Declarative	*Procedural*
Symbol	Chapter 4 & 5	Chapter 4
	Throughout	Tutorial Unit 8
Subsymbolic	Chapter 4	Chapter 4
	Tutorial Unit 6	Tutorial Unit 7

This chapter contains sections to discuss the procedural-declarative distinction, which is the most fundamental assumption in the ACT–R theory, the representation of declarative knowledge as chunks, the representation of procedural knowledge as productions, and the critical role of goal structures in organizing behavior. At all points in the development of the ACT–R theory, we maintain an intimate relationship with data. Therefore, the chapter ends with a discussion of the Tower of Hanoi task and the ACT–R model for it. This is a task that depends on performance assumptions at the symbolic level.

THE PROCEDURAL–DECLARATIVE DISTINCTION

The distinction between declarative and procedural knowledge has been part of the ACT–R theory since its inception in 1976. At that time, the procedural-declarative distinction was somewhat in disrepute in artificial intelligence (e.g., Winograd, 1975) and was largely ignored in cognitive psychology. About the only authority we could point to for support of the distinction was the philosopher Ryle (1949). Reflecting this intellectual climate, the series of production systems associated with Allen Newell eschewed a long-term declarative knowledge system and only had a long-term repository of procedural knowledge in the form of production rules.

The insistence on a parallel, long-term, declarative repository in the ACT theories reflects their origins in the HAM theory (Anderson & Bower, 1973), which was a theory of human declarative memory. Thus, ACT–R sharply contrasts in this regard with the Soar production system, which does not make such a distinction.

Since the 1970s, there has been quite a revival of the procedural-declarative distinction in cognitive psychology. There is the now well-known cognitive neuroscience evidence pointing to such a distinction (Phelps, 1989; Squire, 1992). This includes the evidence that damage to the hippocampal area results in the loss of ability to form new declarative memories, but not new procedural memories.[1] Also, research on implicit learning (Curran & Keele, 1993; Lewicki, Hill, & Bizot, 1988; Nissen & Bullemeyer, 1987) indicates that it is possible to create situations where normal subjects appear to learn new procedural skills without accompanying declarative knowledge. Thus, it seems that ACT was right in its 1976 postulation of a procedural-declarative distinction—that these two types of knowledge are implemented neurally in fundamentally different ways. Recently (Knowlton, Mangels, & Squire, 1996), there has been evidence that the basal ganglia play a critical role in the establishment of procedural knowledge. Damage to this area results in loss of ability to acquire procedural knowledge, but not of the ability to acquire declarative knowledge.

Recent research reported by Rabinowitz and Goldberg (1995) nicely illustrates some of the behavioral differences between declarative and procedural knowledge.[2] They used a variant of the alphabet arithmetic task developed by Logan and Klapp (1991). Rabinowitz and Goldberg presented subjects with problems of the form letter + number = ? and subjects had to respond with the letter that is that many numbers advanced in the alphabetic sequence. Thus, given C + 3 = ?, the subject should respond F. In one condition, subjects were practiced on answering just a certain 12 of these letter-number combinations, whereas in another condition, they received practice on many more (72). Rabinowitz and Goldberg proposed that over time, subjects came to respond in the first condition by just retrieving the examples from declarative memory, whereas in the second condition, they continue to use and practice a general procedure for doing alphabet addition. Thus, we can call the first group the declarative subjects and the second group the procedural subjects.

---

[1]The hippocampal area is not the locus of these declarative memories because old declarative memories are not lost. It is thought that both procedural and declarative memories are stored cortically, but that the hippocampus plays a role in supporting new declarative memories.

[2]We have reported similar research: Anderson and Fincham (1994) and Anderson, Fincham, and Douglass (1997).

In ACT–R terms, initially, both groups of subjects would have to rely on general productions for performing alphabet arithmetic. Thus, to a problem like C + 3 = ?, the following production would apply:

IF   the goal is to answer *letter* + *number* = ?
THEN   set a subgoal to increment *letter number* times
and then report the answer

Other productions would then count up the alphabet. Initially, both groups of subjects took longer to answer problems with larger addends, suggesting they were indeed counting up the alphabet.

However, with practice, the declarative subjects would have productions like the following to retrieve the repeated facts from declarative memory:

IF   the goal is to answer *letter* + *number* = ?
and *letter* + *number* = *newletter*
THEN   respond with *newletter*

This would mean that they should become very good at solving the specific 12 problems and become unaffected by the size of the addend. However, these declarative subjects would cease to practice their general productions for alphabet arithmetic.

Rabinowitz and Goldberg found that the declarative subjects performed the task more rapidly than the procedural subjects and became unaffected by the size of the digit being added to the letter. On the other hand, the declarative subjects did worse than the procedural subjects when transferred to a task where they had to answer problems they had never seen before. This indicates that they had memorized specific facts rather than practiced general procedures. Rabinowitz and Goldberg also used a transfer task of going from addition to subtraction. That is, after training on C + 3 = ?, subjects would then switch to F – 3 = ? Declarative subjects showed much better transfer than did the procedural subjects when tested for subtraction on the same problems that they had studied. This shows that they were able to reverse their declarative knowledge in a way they were not able to reverse their procedural knowledge. Procedural knowledge differs from declarative knowledge in that it is committed to a direction of use.

Although ACT–R is compatible with the general results of Rabinowitz and Goldberg, whether it can account for the detailed data is another matter. This gets into issues of ACT–R's subsymbolic assumptions and other aspects of the theory. Johnson (1997a) has undertaken the task of developing such a model and with considerable success. His work should be consulted for details.

The Structure of Chunks

Chunks encode small independent patterns of information as sets of slots with associated values. The type of the pattern is given in an isa[3] slot, whereas other slots of a chunk indicate the information that is being configured together. For instance, consider the following two possible chunks:

    Fact3+4
        isa ADDITION-FACT
        addend1 Three
        addend2 Four
        sum Seven

    Object1
        isa WORD
        part-of Sentence1
        value The
        position First

The first is the perhaps now familiar addition fact with its slots of addend1, addend2, and sum. The second is a chunk encoding that the word *the* occurred first in a particular sentence.

Chunks have origins from one of two sources—either as encoding of goals or as encoding of objects in the environment. Thus, the $3 + 4 = 7$ chunk, Fact 3+4, is a record of some completed goal to find out what the sum of 3 and 4 is (which was possibly accomplished by some simple algorithm like counting). Other chunks have their origin in the encoding of objects in the environment. The most common chunks of this sort in this book encode words, but any object can result in a chunk encoding. Chapter 5 discusses the role of visual attention and perception in creating such chunks.

Corresponding to the two sources for chunks, there tend to be two styles of slot structures. Slots that encode goals involve specification of a relation (like ADDITION-FACT) and a set of arguments (like Three, Four, and Seven). The second kind of chunk structure comes from encoding of perceptual objects. As illustrated in the preceding example, these contain slots to provide the type of the object, pointers to the larger structure in which the object is found, and the position of that object in the larger structure. Although object chunks and goal chunks tend to have different sorts of slots, the two types of chunks are syntactically identical and are identically processed by the production system.

---

[3]The *isa* slot is qualitatively different than other slots and really serves to classify the pattern formed by the other slots.

The claim that all chunks have their origins either as goals or as encodings of objects in the environment is a strong one that we are still trying to digest in the ACT–R community. Our experience so far is that it is a quite workable constraint and a useful one because it provides needed guidance in how to represent knowledge. It is interesting to see how it plays out in specific examples. As one example, consider comprehending a printed sentence. The physical sentence is encoded by a series of chunks, such as Object1 shown earlier encoding the words of the sentence. This encoding is delivered by the visual interface (see Chapter 5). A goal is set to comprehend the sentence, and if this goal is successfully popped, it will have a representation of the sentence like:

    Proposition1
        isa COMPREHENSION-GOAL
        relation Give
        agent Mary
        object Fido
        recipient John

This claim about the origins of declarative knowledge has strong connections to well-worn philosophical issues about the origins of knowledge (see Anderson & Bower, 1973, for a discussion). The chunks that come from the environment represent the empiricist claim that knowledge originates from experience. The chunks that are popped goals represent the rationalist claim that people construct their own knowledge. As often is the case, a good scientific theory proclaims both sides of a philosophical controversy to be right.

Although, syntactically, chunks in ACT–R 4.0 are much the same as the chunks in ACT–R 2.0 (described in Anderson, 1993), they do display one major simplification over the ACT–R 2.0 chunks. They do not allow for lists of elements to be the values of slots.[4] The values of slots are either chunks or features. Even in 1993, we lamented the use of lists as slot values, but permitted them in ACT–R to support programming practices that can be traced back to the GRAPES production system (Sauers & Farrell, 1982). However, as we tried to systematize the theory, lists became a price too great to pay. Basically, it is not possible to place a coherent psychological interpretation on these list structures. The decision to jettison lists as slot values was key to the emergence of the chunk as an atomic structure.

---

[4]More precisely, ACT–R 4.0 does not have facilities for processing list structures with the exception of certain slots for dependency types—see the second section of Chapter 4.

PRODUCTION RULES

Production rules involve a more complex set of representational assumptions than do chunks. Therefore, we develop their representation in two passes. The first subsection provides a general description of their features, and the second subsection provides the detailed syntax.

General Features of Production Rules

Production rules are supposed to correspond, intuitively, to steps of cognition. One of the important developments from ACT–R 2.0 to ACT–R 4.0 is a more precise interpretation of what is meant by a "step of cognition." The basic structure of a production in ACT–R 4.0 is:

goal condition + chunk retrieval → goal transformations

This "goal condition" involves some tests on the goal state. If these tests succeed and the production is chosen, then the retrieval is performed. The retrieval involves the matching of one or more chunk patterns to declarative memory in order to retrieve information. On the basis of the goal and the retrieved information, ACT–R then makes some transformations to the goal state. These transformations can involve changing the state of the current goal, popping the current goal, or creating and pushing subgoals. A subgoal can be achieved either by firing more productions or by performing some motor program. Thus, creating and pushing a subgoal can amount to performing an action. By changing the goal state, production rules can refract themselves and so avoid loops where the same production rule fires over and over again.[5]

Conflict Resolution is the term used in production systems to refer to the process by which a production is selected. ACT–R can filter out most production rules by the tests on the goal.[6] However, these tests do not always identify a unique production rule, and the next chapter discusses how ACT–R chooses among multiple productions that match a goal. When it selects a production, there may also be more than one alternative chunk it can retrieve to match each chunk pattern. Again, the next chapter discusses how ACT–R decides which chunk to retrieve. Both of these choices are determined by subsymbolic processes.

---

[5]ACT–R does not have a scheme whereby production rules automatically refract, as did some of the earlier production systems, including ACT* (Anderson, 1983) and OPS (Forgy & McDermott, 1977).

[6]That is, ACT–R selects only productions involving a goal of the same type as the current goal with matching slot values.

The image of cognition being painted by ACT–R is one in which some production fires to change the goal state every few hundred milliseconds (the range in latency is from about 50 msec to, at most, about 1 sec) and thought progresses serially by these goal transformations. Lest this seem an overly serial image of cognition, it should be noted that at the subsymbolic level, millions of parallel computations are taking place to support this level of cognition. Lest this seem an overly microscopic image of cognition, it should be noted that the goal structures are organizing these individual steps into a coherent whole.

As developed in Anderson (1993), there are four significant claims associated with the use of production rules:

1. Modularity. The modularity claim is that production rules are the units in which procedural knowledge is acquired and deployed. This amounts to the claim that they are the procedural atoms. Much of the 1993 book provided evidence for the modularity of production rules. Basically, it showed that the learning of complex skills could be decomposed into the learning of many production rules. Figure 2.1 shows some more recent data making the same point from Corbett, Anderson, and O'Brien (1995) from the LISP tutor. Students are asked to write a number of LISP functions and the figure shows their error rate at each point in each function across the early material. Students show a lot of jumps and drops in their error rates at different points. The figure also shows the predictions of a model that assumes that each production rule has its own learning curve. Figure 2.2 averages together those points where the same production rule is applying. As Fig. 2.2 illustrates, there is smooth learning over these points. Thus, the reason for the rises and falls in Fig. 2.1 is the fact that new production rules are being introduced at different points in the curriculum. The success in accounting for complex behavioral profiles like Fig. 2.1 is, for us, the most compelling support for the production rule as the unit of skill acquisition.[7]

2. Abstraction. The next two claims were those of production abstraction and goal factoring. These claims serve to provide the critical distinctions between production rules and the stimulus-response bonds of the earlier behaviorist era. The abstraction feature of production rules refers to the fact that a production rule can apply in many different situations producing different actions in these situations. Thus, the production rule for **Add-Column** in Table 1.1 would apply no matter what numbers were

---

[7]Much of the tutor modeling involves the larger ACT–R 2.0 production rules, but in the case of Fig. 2.1, there would be only one critical unit of ACT–R 4.0 knowledge (production or chunk) that needs to be acquired per production rule in the tutor.

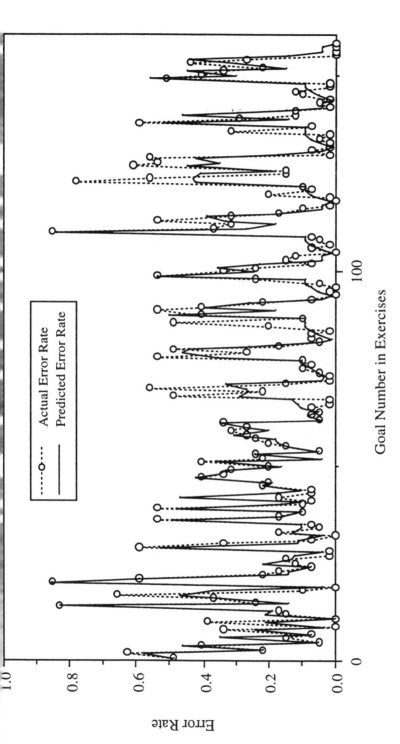

FIG. 2.1. Actual and predicted error rates across subjects at each goal in a set of required tutor exercises. From Corbett, Anderson, and O'Brien (1995). Reprinted by permission.

27

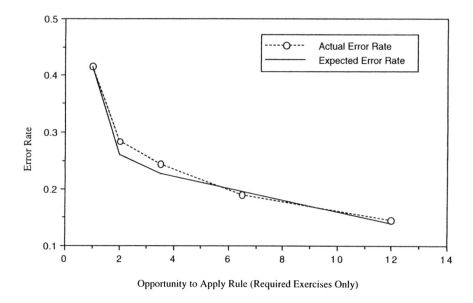

Opportunity to Apply Rule (Required Exercises Only)

FIG. 2.2.   Mean actual error rate and expected error rate for the ideal coding rules across successive rule applications. From Corbett and Anderson (1992). Reprinted by permission.

in the column nor what column was being processed. It would retrieve a different sum depending on what numbers were in the column. Thus, in contrast to stimulus-response bonds, which have specific actions, production rules can make their actions a function of the abstract structure of the information. As Table 2.2 shows later, this abstractness is achieved through the use of variables that make the rules specific not to certain elements (such as a specific number), but rather to the pattern of elements.

3. Goal Factoring.   In contrast to the generality achieved by abstraction, the goal factoring of productions allows productions to achieve restrictions on their range of application that were difficult to achieve in stimulus-response systems. Goal factoring refers to the fact that production rules are specific to particular goal types. For example, if the goal is to add, one set of production rules applies to a column of numbers, whereas if the goal is to subtract, a different set of production rules applies. Thus, the goal allows the system to respond differently to the same external state (i.e., a column of numbers), depending on the system's internal state (i.e., its goal).

4. Conditional Asymmetry.   On the other hand, production rules share a particular feature with stimulus-response bonds that serve to distinguish them as a computing medium from other cognitive formalisms, such as schema theories (Abelson, 1981; Bobrow & Winograd, 1976; Rumelhart & Ortony, 1976; Schank & Abelson, 1977), some pattern-completion neural systems (Rumelhart, Smolensky, McClelland & Hinton, 1986), and indeed, the general version of the prolog rule system (which allows forward and backward chaining). This is that there is a condition-action asymmetry. The flow of control goes from condition to action and does not progress in the other direction. Over the years, a substantial body of research has accumulated documenting the asymmetry that appears in knowledge when it achieves a procedural form (Anderson, Fincham, & Douglass, 1997; Kessler, 1988; McKendree & Anderson, 1987; Pennington, Nicolich, & Rahm, 1995). One example of this was the Rabinowitz and Goldberg experiment described in the preceding section. This is a significant contrast with knowledge in a declarative form. When knowledge has declarative form, it can be used in any direction. The knowledge that 4 * 3 = 12 can be used to go from 4 and 12 to 3 as well as from 4 and 3 to 12.[8] On the other hand, there is no way to generalize a set of production rules for doing long multiplication to doing long division. Essentially, to achieve efficiency in access, proceduralized knowledge has abandoned the flexibility of declarative knowledge.

Production Syntax

The formal syntax of ACT–R production rules is a bit complex and we begin this subsection describing the reason for this complexity. ACT–R is a precise theory of human cognition. Often to ease the burden of communication, we describe the theory informally. Often such informality has been seized on by critics to claim that ACT–R and theories like it are only "metaphors" or "computer metaphors." It is not a metaphor, and no more a computer metaphor than the theory of relativity is a mathematics metaphor. ACT–R comes with mechanisms for unambiguously delivering predictions given a set of initial conditions just as any scientific theory does. In ACT–R's case, that mechanism is a computer simulation, but this does not make ACT–R a computer metaphor any more than a computer simulation of the weather is a computer metaphor. The simulation is just a way to get unambiguous predictions from a set of assumptions that imply complex interactions.

The price of precision, particularly when there is a computer simulation, is formalism, and there is a formal syntax for specifying the symbolic atoms of ACT–R: the chunks and productions. We have already exposed the syntax of chunks, and it is fairly simple. The syntax of productions is more complex, but hopefully no more complex than is necessary to specify the

---

[8]Campbell (1997) presented data to suggest that sometimes (but only sometimes) we do actually access division facts through the multiplication table.

transformations that they compute. This subsection specifies this syntax, as it is key at certain places in the book. However, we have no love of formalism for formalism's sake, and to the extent that we can proceed with informal discussion, we do so.[9] In reading the production syntax, the reader should keep in mind that there is nothing implied beyond the goal transformations that these productions specify. It is easy to think that there is something more implied by the syntax. For instance, we have had people say to us, "Production rules have variables and neuroscientists have never found a variable in the brain." However, just as an integral sign in mathematics means nothing more than integrate and the *dx* means nothing more than the dimension being integrated over, so the ACT–R formalisms mean nothing more than the operations they help specify. In the case of variables, they just specify the transfer of information from goals to constrain retrievals in declarative memory and from results retrieved back to the goal structure. This transfer of information, which is specified by variables, most likely corresponds to neural pathways in the brain between goal areas and declarative areas (see Chapter 12).

Table 2.2 shows the formal production rules corresponding to the informal Table 1.1. As can be seen, both the condition and action sides of the productions correspond to a set of chunks. The condition of a production begins with a specification of a goal chunk (which defines the condition for applicability of the rule) and is followed by some other chunk pattern(s) that requires retrieval(s) from memory. The action involves creating and modifying goal chunks.

There are a few conventions that are important in reading these production rules. The production **Add-Numbers** is probably the best for expository purposes. Following the name of the production, there is the following goal chunk pattern:

```
=goal>
  isa ADD-COLUMN
  number1 =num1
  number2 =num2
  answer nil
```

Anything beginning with an equal sign denotes a variable. The variable =*goal* will be assigned to the current goal.[10] The > that follows =*goal* is a bit of syntax separating the chunk from its slots. The chunk pattern specifies

---

[9]In those cases where a running model is being described, the actual productions can always be reached by following the <u>Published ACT–R models</u> link from the ACT–R home page.

[10]The first chunk in a production describes the goal. By convention, we refer to this chunk as =*goal*, but this is not required.

TABLE 2.2
The Formal Specification of the Productions for Multi-Column Addition Example
(Compare to Table 1.1)

Start-Problem

=goal>
  isa ADDITION-PROBLEM
  column nil
==>
=newgoal>
  isa ADD-COLUMN
  column Ones
  note =carry
  carry Zero
=goal>
  column Tens
  carry =carry
!push! =newgoal

Read-Number1

=goal>
  isa ADD-COLUMN
  number1 nil
  column =col
=object>
  isa VISUAL-OBJECT
  value =num1
  row Top
  column =col
==>
=goal>
  number1 =num1

Read-Number2

=goal>
  isa ADD-COLUMN
  number2 nil
  column =col
=object>
  isa VISUAL-OBJECT
  value =num2
  column =col
  row Bottom
==>
=goal>
  number2 =num2

TABLE 2.2 (cont'd.)

Add-Numbers
 =goal>
  isa ADD-COLUMN
  number 1 =num1
  number 2 =num2
  answer nil
 =fact>
  isa ADDITION-FACT
  addend1 =num1
  addend2 =num2
  sum =sum
==>
 =goal>
  answer =sum

Extract-Answer
 =goal>
  isa ADD-COLUMN
  answer =sum
  note nil
  carry Zero
 =sum>
  isa NUMBER
  tens =num
  units =number1
==>
 =goal>
  answer =number1
  note =num

Process-Carry
 =goal>
  isa ADD-COLUMN
  answer =number
  carry One
 =fact>
  isa ADDITION-FACT
  addend2 One
  addend1 =number
  sum =new
==>
 =goal>
  answer =new
  carry Zero

TABLE 2.2 (cont'd.)

Write-Answer

=goal>
  isa ADD-COLUMN
  carry Zero
  answer =number
  column =col
=number>
  isa NUMBER
  value =value
  tens Zero
==>
!output! =value
!pop!

Last-Column-No-Carry

=goal>
  isa ADD-COLUMN
  number2 +
– carry One
==>
=goal>
  note Finished
!pop!

Last-Column-Carry

=goal>
  isa ADD-COLUMN
  number2 +
  carry One
  column =col
  carry =carrynum
=carrynum>
  isa NUMBER
  value =val
==>
!output! =value
=goal>
  note Finished
!pop!

TABLE 2.2 (cont'd.)

Next-Column
```
=goal>
  isa ADDITION-PROBLEM
  column =pos1
-carry Finished
  carry =carry
=next>
  isa NEXT-INFO
  before =pos1
  after =pos2
==>
  =newgoal>
  isa ADD-COLUMN
  column =pos1
  carry =carry
  note =newcarry
  =goal>
  column =pos2
  carry =newcarry
!push! =newgoal
```

Stop-Problem
```
  =goal>
  isa ADDITION-PROBLEM
  carry Finished
==>
  !pop!
```

in its isa slot that this goal be of type ADD-COLUMN. The slots number1 and number2 contain the two numbers read from the column to be added. The variables =*num1* and =*num2* take on the value of these numbers. (In production system terminology, we say a variable is *bound* to a value when it assumes that value.) Finally, there is a test that there is not yet a value in the answer slot by means of the nil specification. The second part of the condition of this production contains the pattern of the chunk to be retrieved:

```
=fact>
  isa ADDITION-FACT
  addend1 =num1
  addend2 =num2
  sum =sum
```

This is looking for some chunk (bound to =*fact*) that encodes an addition fact. The appearance of =*num1* and =*num2* (same as in the goal pattern) in the addend1 and addend2 slots tests that this addition fact relates the two numbers that the production is trying to add. The sum will be extracted from the sum slot of the retrieved chunk and bound to the =sum variable.

The action side of this production contains a simple modification of the goal:

```
=goal>
   answer =sum
```

which stores the sum in the answer slot of the goal. This also prevents this production rule from reapplying because the answer slot is no longer nil. It is worth emphasizing here again that the role of these variables is to specify retrievals.[11] The variables $=num1$ and $=num2$ are constraining what is being retrieved from the addition table to be a sum of the numbers in the goal, and the variable $=sum$ is specifying that the retrieved sum be returned to the goal.

The productions illustrate the full range of the goal transformations. Some productions like **Start-Problem** and **Next-Column** can create new goal chunks that are pushed on the goal stack. Most productions modify the state of the current goal chunk. Finally, productions like **Write-Answer** and **Stop-Problem** can pop goal chunks.

Restrictions on Production Rules

There have been a number of changes in going from ACT–R 2.0 to ACT–R 4.0 that have restricted the power of the production conditions. Reflecting the absence of list structures in the declarative representation, the powerful and obtuse pattern-matching facilities associated with list structures no longer apply in production rules. Also, the only negations allowed are of slot values. There are no longer unbounded negations of pattern structures, which enable modelers to implicitly embed complex searches in the matching of a production condition.

A major simplification of ACT–R 4.0 over ACT–R 2.0 is that the chunk retrieval does not participate in the initial selection of production rules. The test is made solely on the basis of the goal state. One motivation for this was to simplify and rationalize ACT–R's latency and conflict resolution calculations, as the next chapter discusses. Previously, a production rule would be considered in conflict resolution only if chunks could be retrieved to match all of its conditions. If there were multiple ways to match chunks to

---

[11]Variables appearing in the condition can also serve as tests. A variable in a goal slot tests that the slot is not empty (nil). This is used to distinguish **Next-Column** from **Start-Problem** in Table 2.2. Also, if the same variable appears in two goal slots, it serves to test whether these two slots have the same value. Finally, as discussed with respect to the subgoal return mechanism in the next section, variables can be used to specify the transfer of results from a subgoal to a goal.

the condition (each way called an *instantiation*) each instantiation was generated and ACT–R 2.0's conflict resolution had to choose among these instantitions. Now, conflict resolution chooses which production to try before any retrievals are done and then the retrievals are attempted in an effort to instantiate the production. If no instantiation of the chunk can be retrieved (e.g., we cannot recall what is 13 times 14), then the production rule fails and the system gets to try another production. Thus, retrievals for different productions are sequentially tried in ACT–R 4.0 rather than in parallel as in ACT–R 2.0.

Another major simplification is that only goal modifications can be performed on the right-hand side of a production.[12] Previously, it was possible to create and modify arbitrary declarative chunks. The current restriction comes from the desire to have a more principled theory of the origins of declarative chunks, as developed further in Chapters 4 and 5.

Another significant simplification is the drastic reduction in the size of production conditions. There is usually just one and never more than a few chunks being retrieved. For instance, in all of the production rules of Table 2.2, no more than one chunk is retrieved. These chunks usually serve as bridges between the goal specification in the condition and the goal transformations in the action. The chunks retrieved typically share certain elements with the slots of the goal. For instance, in **Add-Numbers** from Table 2.2 =*num1* and =*num2* are the shared elements. The retrieved chunks also usually share variables with the actions because the principal reason for retrieving them is to specify the action. In **Add-Numbers**, =*sum* is such a variable. In contrast, the production rules in ACT–R 2.0 typically involved many more retrievals with complex constraints between different retrievals, which were expressed by variables shared by multiple chunks in the condition.

In ACT–R 2.0, one could write a production rule that simplified a fraction, such as 24/56, in a single step:

Simplify-Fraction-In-One-Step
      IF   the goal is to simplify a fraction of the form numer1/denom1
             and numer1 = numer2 * factor
             and denom1 = denom2 * factor
             and there is no x greater than factor such that
                   numer1 = numer3 * x
                   and denom1 = denom3 * x
    THEN   the answer is numer2/denom2

---

[12]This restriction is not enforced in the simulation language ACT–R 4.0 for practical reasons. However, the theory has made this commitment.

This would report out 3/7 as the answer. Presumably, few people experience solving such a problem as a single mental step. Correspondingly, in ACT–R 4.0, the computation in this production would have to be broken up into a number of smaller rules. This reduced size has enabled the production rule to emerge as the procedural atom.

It is worth reviewing what this production rule does that no longer works in ACT–R 4.0. Note that the value of "factor" retrieved in "numer1 = numer2 * factor" is constrained to be the same as the value of "factor" as retrieved in "denom1 = denom2 * factor". For instance, suppose ACT–R 2.0 first matched 4 * 6 = 24 for the first chunk pattern, binding 6 to the factor role. Then, when it failed to find a multiplication fact of the form 56 = denom2 * 6 for the second chunk pattern, it would back up and try other values for "factor" in the first chunk pattern until one was found that worked. This backup is very implausible and is no longer possible in ACT–R 4.0. The negation at the end of the condition illustrates another feature no longer supported. To determine the truth of "there is no x greater than factor such that numer1 = numer3 * x and denom1 = denom3 * x," an exhaustive search of the multiplication facts yielding 24 and 56 would be necessary. Again, such an exhaustive search seems implausible in a simple step of cognition. In current ACT–R 4.0 the searches embedded in this one production would be distributed over multiple productions. One production would generate a candidate product like 3 * 8 = 24 and subsequent productions would test this product for the necessary features. A typical dimension of the transition from ACT–R 2.0 to 4.0, is this distribution of computation packed into a single ACT–R 2.0 production to computation over many ACT–R 4.0 productions. This has yielded production rules that lead to accurate performance predictions (Chapter 3) and rules that are capable of being learned (Chapter 4) at no cost in complexity or performance. It has supported the emergence of the production rule as an atomic component of thought.

Productions have very much the character of "directors" of declarative retrieval. That is, each production essentially does the next step of retrieval in elaborating a goal structure. Each production rule retrieves usually one, and at most, a few declarative chunks. These retrievals cannot make any branching decisions based on the contents of the chunks retrieved. Rather, retrieved information can be placed in goal chunks and decisions can be made in later cycles to fire one production versus others in response to the new retrieved contents of the goal. Thus, each cycle has the structure of: Decide on a production (on basis of goal context), retrieve (on specifications from the production), and modify the goal structure (using the information retrieved). The next chapter elaborates on how this works at the subsymbolic level.

The idea of one layer of retrieval per production cycle provides one definition of grain size of production rules. Another "operational" definition of the grain size of cognition is provided by the constraint that each discrete behavior (i.e., key press, eye movement, generation of an utterance) must be controlled by a separate production.[13] Thus, the maximum time per production is the time to perform one chunk retrieval, to perform one action, plus the 50-msec overhead associated with every production rule. Looking at latencies for such retrievals and actions leads to the conclusion that the temporal grain size of production rules in ACT–R 4.0 must be less than a second, perhaps sometimes less than 100 msec. The exact times per production vary with the information retrieved and action performed. In any case, the production rules in ACT–R 4.0 are about a factor of 10 finer in grain size than were the productions in ACT–R 2.0. Qualitatively, this is the most significant difference in the conception of cognition between the two theories.

Production rules in ACT–R 4.0 are simpler and more constrained than in ACT–R 2.0 and yet they can do the same work. The motivation for simplification is more than just economy of assumptions. The constrained rules lead to better predictions, as illustrated throughout the book. There is often the suspicion, however, that we have made modeling complex cognition more difficult. The analogy is that perhaps we have replaced programming in a high-level language with programming in machine code. However, this is not our experience, and perhaps this is the strongest evidence for the new constrained representation. The end of this chapter describes an ACT–R model for the Tower of Hanoi task. Anderson, Kushmerick, and Lebiere (1993) described a model for the Tower of Hanoi task that took full "advantage" of the greater flexibility of ACT–R 2.0. The current model is no more complex in number of lines of specification, is easier to read, and leads to much more detailed and accurate predictions. However, before describing the Tower of Hanoi model, it is necessary to discuss further ACT–R's goal structures and their relationship to production rule form.

GOAL STRUCTURES AND PRODUCTION RULES

Goal Structures in ACT–R

The original production systems of Newell and the original ACTE (Anderson, 1976) did not provide any special status for goal structures. Rather, they

---

[13]This constraint of one action per production is a style constraint and not enforced by ACT–R 4.0.

just responded to whatever patterns were in working memory. However, starting with ACT* (Anderson, 1983) goal structures became an increasingly frequent part of production system architectures and are part of each of the current four production systems (ACT–R, Soar, EPIC, 3CAPS). They reflect a lesson learned, which is that to properly model human cognition, it is necessary to represent its current purpose and organize behavior in response to that purpose. Efforts have failed to achieve organized cognition without the architectural primitive of a goal structure.

The existence of a goal structure creates a natural seriality to cognition, defined by changes in the goal structure. Each time the goal structure changes, there is a new goal state. At one level, cognition can be viewed as a sequence of these goal states. However, this does not necessarily mean only sequential firing of production rules. In EPIC, Soar, and 3CAPS, multiple production rules can fire in a cycle in response to the current goal state, which may only change after several rounds of parallel production rule firing. Only ACT–R has the constraint that in each cycle, just one production rule fires (which almost always produces some change in the goal state). However, ACT–R is not a serial system either. Much of what these other systems achieve with parallelism at the production-rule level, ACT–R achieves with parallelism at the subsymbolic level, as the next chapter discusses. Indeed, all systems are serial at whatever level they achieve transformation of the goal state and all systems are parallel at a finer grain level.

In ACT–R, there is always a stack of goals with production rules responding to the top goal on the stack—usually modifying it, popping it, or pushing another goal on the stack. ACT–R models are almost always of subjects doing some laboratory task such as solving an equation. The goal stack at the current point in time in such a task might be something like:

1. Add 3 and 4.
2. Solve $x - 4 = 3$.
3. Solve equations on screen.

with the subject responding to the top goal. Realistically, the goal on the bottom of the simulated stack, which represents the goal of performing the laboratory task, does not represent the ultimate goal of the subject. If we could peer below this goal, we might see something like:

4. Get experimental credit.
5. Pass introductory psychology.
6. Get college degree.

However, we, like most of cognitive psychology, have not bothered to peer beyond the goals we get subjects to adopt in our experiments.

This conception of the goal structure frequently raises a number of questions that we address here. The first question is how can there be any interrupt-driven cognition. If subjects were to hear "fire" in the middle of this experiment, presumably, they would not blissfully continue to solve equations but would focus on new goals. It is possible to model such switches in goal structure in ACT–R because one can have high-priority production rules that respond to such situations. These would be rules like:

> IF   the goal is to do any task
>   and one hears "fire"
> THEN   change the goal to escape the fire

This production illustrates that there can be rules in ACT–R that respond to all goals.[14] Cognitive psychology has tended not to be in the business of creating such emergency interrupts and studying the cognition that results. Therefore, we cannot say that ACT–R's mechanism is the right mechanism for modeling such interrupt handling because there is no data with which to assess it. All we can say is that there is no inherent contradiction between such interrupt handling and ACT–R goal structures.

A second question concerns how ACT–R can model people's ability to pursue multiple goals in parallel in an architecture that has only one current goal. Such tasks are modeled in ACT–R by setting a single goal to do the multiple-goal task and either switching serially among multiple subgoals or having rules specific for performing the multiple-goal task. This has been a successful maneuver as illustrated in Chapter 6, which models dual-task experiments.

A third question concerns the perfect-memory assumptions behind such a goal stack. In ACT–R, all of the goals on the stack are retained perfectly in order. If the current goal is popped, the next one is always there ready to take over. We have to confess to not being particularly sanguine about this feature. This assumption has not been stressed much because most cognitive tasks tend to have rather shallow goal structures (perhaps an indication that deep goal structures are problematical). One of the cognitive tasks that has the deepest goal structure is the Tower of Hanoi task—at least under certain strategies. As a later subsection displays, ACT–R has considerable success in modeling the available data from this task. Perhaps future research in this domain will expose problems with ACT–R's assumption of perfect goal memory.

---

[14]ACT–R 4.0 allows for type hierarchies in which different goal types can be specializations of a general goal type.

Thus, in ACT–R, the goal stack organizes the sequential structure of production-rule firing. However, we emphasize again that this does not imply that everything in the human mind is serial. ACT–R has a highly parallel subsymbolic structure. Also, as discussed in Chapter 6, there is the potential for parallelism between the production rule firing, perception, and motor action.

Types of Production Rules

There is a very close relationship between goals and productions in ACT–R. Every production rule responds to a goal state and potentially transforms it into a new goal state. Basically, production rules are means for choosing and specifying goal transformations. Usually, the transformations involve retrieval of information from declarative memory. Thus, the prototypical production involves a sequence of: goal match, declarative retrieval, and goal transformation. The production rules possible in ACT–R can all be classified in terms of what sorts of goal transformations they produce. There are essentially three things a production can do with respect to the goal stack: pop, push, or nothing. Orthogonal to this, the production can modify the current goal or not.[15] Although it is syntactically possible to have various combinations of one or more pushes, one or more pops, or other goal modifications, it is conceptually clearer to think of there being basically 6 (3 x 2) production types:

1. No Change (No Stack Change, No Goal Modification). It is possible to have a production rule that does no goal transformation. Such a production, to have a point, must take some external action. To prevent this production from firing forever, it must have some test for a state change produced by that action. An example of such a production rule is:

Hammer
  =goal>
  isa HAMMER-NAIL
  object =nail
  =state>
  isa NAIL-STATE
  object =nail
  state Protruding
  ==>
  execute strike of hammer

---

[15]In terms of the ACT–R simulation, if the production rule changes the type of the current goal, a focus-on command is required. If it just changes the slots, this is not required.

This production will keep hammering the nail as long as it is protruding. It might actually be better conceived of as a production that sets a subgoal to hammer once where this subgoal is discharged by motor routines. In this case, the production would really be an instance of Type 3.

2. Goal Elaboration (No Stack Change, Goal Modification).

There are production rules that take the current goal and refine it in some way, but leave the current goal as the focus. An example from multicolumn addition is:

Read-Number1
```
  =goal>
  isa ADD-COLUMN
  number1 nil
  column =col
  =object>
  isa VISUAL-OBJECT
  value =num1
  row top
  column =col
==>
  =goal>
  number1 =num1
```

This production records the first number to be added in the number1 slot of the goal.

3. Side Effect (Push on Stack, No Goal Modification).

There are productions that push a goal without modifying the current goal. Because they do not modify the current goal, the subgoal is being pushed for some side effect it will produce in the external world in or the mind of the subject. For instance:

Ask-Teacher
```
  =goal>
  isa SOLVE-EQUATION
  equation =equation
  =equation>
  isa EQUATION
  - left X
  - right X
==>
  =newgoal>
  isa ASK-FOR-HELP
  object =equation
  resource Teacher
  !push! =newgoal
```

This production responds to the fact that X is not isolated on the left or the right of the equation. It sets the subgoal of asking a teacher for help. Hopefully, this is not the only rule at the student's disposal.

4. Return Result (Push on Stack, Goal Modification). There are production rules that push a new goal, but also refine the current goal so that when they return to the goal, it is different and the same production rule does not repeat. An example from multicolumn addition is:

Start-Problem
  =goal>
  isa ADDITION-PROBLEM
  column nil
==>
  =newgoal>
  isa ADD-COLUMN
  column Ones
  note =carry
  carry Zero
  =goal>
  column Tens
  carry =carry
  !push! =newgoal

This production rule sets a subgoal to add the ones column and records in the column slot of =*goal* that it should next work on the tens column. The appearance of the variable =*carry* in the note slot of =*newgoal* and the carry slot of =*goal* is a means of returning a result from the subgoal to the goal. When =*newgoal* is pushed, the value of =*carry* is not yet known, but when =*newgoal* is achieved and popped, there is a value in its note slot and this value is passed back to carry slot of =*goal*. This mechanism for passing results from a subgoal to a parent goal is called the *subgoal return mechanism.* In this case, the subgoal is being called to output a result and to return the carry, but sometimes a subgoal is like a function call in programming and is only being called to find a result.

5. Pop Unchanged (Pop Stack, No Goal Modification). There are production rules that pop when a termination condition is met. These termination production rules may or may not modify the goal before they pop the goal. An example of a production that does not modify the goal is:

```
Write-Answer
  =goal>
  isa ADD-COLUMN
  carry Zero
  answer =number
  column =col
  =number>
  isa NUMBER
  value =value
  tens Zero
==>
  !output! =value
  !pop!
```

This production outputs the answer for the column and pops the goal of adding in that column.

6. Pop Changed (Pop Stack, Goal Modification).   The final possibility is to modify the goal before popping it. For instance, there is **Stop-Count** from the simulation of addition as repeated counting (see Table 4.1 in Chapter 4):

Stop-Count
```
  =goal>
  isa FIND-SUM
  arg1 =num1
  arg2 =num2
  count =num2
  current =ans
==>
  =goal>
  sum =ans
  !pop!
```

This production stops the count process when the count has reached the value of the second addition argument (e.g., 6 + 3 would yield the count: 6, 7, 8, 9 and then **stop-count** would fire). This production stores the final number as the sum. A popped goal serves as a new declarative chunk, so modifying its slot before popping can affect subsequent behavior.[16] Thus, the goal popped in the production above serves as a memory for the sum that can be directly retrieved without going through repeated counting.

These six rule types determine the behavior we see from subjects. In the preceding material, we have represented them in their ACT–R form, but

---

[16]Also, this value may be returned to the supergoal by the subgoal return mechanism.

more typically we give them in their English form, leaving the exact rules accessible over the Web.

Tower of Hanoi Example

There are certain tasks where the important factors determining performance reside at the symbolic level. These tend to be tasks that have an algorithmic character so that there is always only one next thing to do (and so, conflict resolution is not relevant) and where all the declarative information necessary is supported in the environment (and so, chunk retrieval is not problematic). In such cases, there is little error or variation in behavior and the relevant issues come to be the times to perform the productions in the production sequence, which in turn, are largely a function of the physical actions that have to be performed. Many human–computer interaction tasks have this character. It is interesting that GOMS (Card, Moran, & Newell, 1983), EPIC, and Soar, all of which do not have a subsymbolic level, have had some of their most successful applications to such tasks.

This subsection is concerned with such a task—subjects solving the Tower of Hanoi problem who know a subgoaling strategy. The Tower of Hanoi problem is a useful illustration of the symbolic level also because it makes heavy use of ACT–R's goal structure. Figure 2.3 shows a typical five-disk Tower of Hanoi problem. The subject's task is to move the five disks from Peg A to Peg C. The constraints on the movement of disks are that only one disk can be moved at a time and that a larger disk cannot be placed on a smaller disk. A number of other researchers (e.g., Egan & Greeno, 1974; Karat, 1982) have found that subjects use hierarchical goal structures to solve the Tower of Hanoi problem. With appropriate instructions, one can more or less guarantee that subjects will use hierarchical goal structures to solve the Tower of Hanoi problem. For instance, Ruiz (1987) taught subjects a strategy that involves the following two principles:

1. The overall goal of solving an n-disk pyramid problem can be accomplished by the subgoals of getting the nth (bottom) disk to the destination

FIG. 2.3.   The Tower of Hanoi problem. There are three pegs, A, B, and C, and five disks of different sizes, 1, 2, 3, 4, and 5, with holes in their centers so that they can be stacked on the pegs. Initially, the disks are all on Peg A, stacked in a pyramid. The goal is to move all the disks to Peg C. Only the top disk on a peg can be moved, and it can never be placed on top of a smaller disk.

peg and then getting the $(n-1)$-disk pyramid into the destination peg.

2. To get the nth disk to a peg, one tries to get the largest disk that is blocking its move out of the way. This second rule can recurse in that to move this blocking disk requires moving yet other disks.

Applied to a simpler goal of moving a four-disk tower (rather than a five-disk tower, to reduce size of trace) configuration, it generates a goal trace like the following:

To get the 4-pyramid to C, get the 4-disk to C and then the 3-pyramid to C
  To get the 4-disk to C, get the 3-disk out of the way to B
    To get the 3-disk to B, get the 2-disk out of the way to C
      To get the 2-disk to C, get the 1-disk out of the way to B
        The 1-disk can be moved to B
        The 2-disk can be moved to C
      To get the 3-disk to B, move the 1-disk out of the way to C
        The 1-disk can be moved to C
      The 3-disk can be moved to B
  To get the 4-disk to C, get the 2-disk out of the way to B
    To get the 2-disk to B, get the 1-disk out of the way to A
      The 1-disk can be moved to A
      The 2-disk can be moved to B
  To get the 4-disk to C, get the 1-disk out of the way to B
    The 1-disk can be moved to B
  The 4-disk can be moved to C
To get the 3-pyramid to C, get the 3-disk to C and then the 2-pyramid to C
  To get the 3-disk to C, get the 2-disk out of the way to A
    To get the 2-disk to A, get the 1-disk out of the way to C
      The 1-disk can be moved to C
      The 2-disk can be moved to A
  To get the 3-disk to C, get the 1-disk out of the way to A
    The 1-disk can be moved to A
  The 3-disk can be moved to C
To get the 2-pyramid to C, get the 2-disk to C and then the 1-disk to C
  To get the 2-disk to C, get the 1-disk out of the way to B
    The 1-disk can be moved to B
  The 2-disk can be moved to C
The 1-disk can be moved to C

Figure 2.4 illustrates the goal structure involved.

To implement this strategy, one needs to be able to stack a good number of goals. Specifically, in the preceding case, one needs to hold a plan like "move 1 to B in order to move 2 to C in order to move 3 to B in order to move 4 to C." Simon (1975) discussed a number of other ways of solving the problem. The one taught by Ruiz is sort of a blend of Simon's goal-recursive strategy, which involves subgoaling, and his sophisticated perceptual strategy, which involves choosing to move disks by size.

Ruiz (1987) forced subjects to implement this subgoaling strategy by requiring them to post each subgoal in a computer interface. Subjects did this by hitting two keys—one to designate the disk and the other to designate the destination peg. They had to hit another key whenever they thought they could make a subgoaled move and the computer would make the move. Table 2.3 shows the four production rules needed to implement this strategy in ACT–R. The production **Start-Tower** transforms a pyramid goal into the subgoal of moving the largest disk and modifies the pyramid goal to move a smaller pyramid (i.e., implements Step 1). **Final-Move** is just a special-case rule that applies when the pyramid has been reduced into a degenerate pyramid of a single disk. **Subgoal-Blocker** sets a subgoal to move the largest blocking disk out of the way (i.e., implements Step 2 in Ruiz's algorithm). The **Move** production moves a disk when there are no blocking disks.

Ruiz used a five-disk tower problem and there are 31 moves involved in solving this problem. Figure 2.5 compares the time for each move generated by the model with the latency profile of Ruiz's subjects. The model assumed

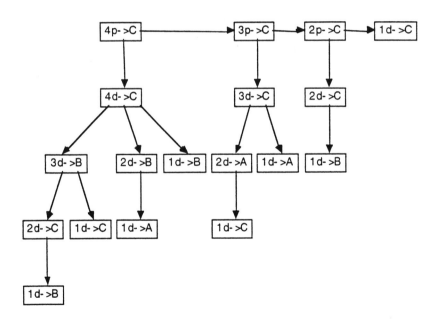

FIG.2.4   An illustration of the goal structure underlying the Ruiz's (1987) goal strategy for a four-disk tower problem. The letter p designates a pyramid and d a disk. Thus, 4p ->C denotes the goal of moving a four-disk pyramid to Peg C, while 2d -> A denotes the goal of moving the second largest disk to Peg A.

the default latency of .05 sec, for the **Start-Tower** production, 1.12 sec for the two move productions, and .69 sec for the **Subgoal-Blocker** production. Subjects were required to hit two keys in the computer interface to set each subgoal. Thus, the **Subgoal-Blocker** time of .69 sec is reasonable. Subjects had to hit a key to move the disk. The 1.12 sec for the move productions is also reasonable as it reflects the time to hit this key and then reencode the screen, which would change at that point. The R^2 between theory and data is .79, which is pretty good for 2 free parameters and 31 data points. This model is available on the Web for the reader to run, inspect the detailed trace, and play with the parameters.

There are a number of aspects about the Ruiz experiment that make it less than ideal. The interface he used perhaps structured subjects' behavior too much by forcing them to explicitly post each goal. His subjects were new to the interface and perhaps got a little faster over the problem as they became familiar with the interface. Correspondingly, the model tends to underpredict early points and overpredict late points. Pure pyramid problems he used are also quite simple and subjects quickly transition to a rote solution. This means one cannot use later trials where subjects are familiar with the interface.

TABLE 2.3
Implementation of the Subgoaling Strategy for the Restricted Case of Tower-to-Tower Problems (Model for Ruiz, 1987)

Start-Tower

IF	the goal is to move a pyramid of size n to peg x
	and size n is greater than 1
THEN	set a subgoal to move disk n to peg x
	and change the goal to move a pyramid of size n-1 to peg x

Final-Move

IF	the goal is to move a pyramid of size 1 to peg x
THEN	move disk 1 to peg x and pop the goal

Subgoal-Blocker

IF	the goal is to move disk of size n to peg x
	and y is the other peg
	and m is the largest blocking disk
THEN	post the goal of moving disk n to x in the interface
	and set a subgoal to move disk m to y

Move

IF	the goal is move disk of size n to peg x
	and there are no blocking disks
THEN	move disk n to peg x and pop the goal

To get a more demanding test of subject behavior, we applied the ACT–R model to some data we collected (Anderson, Kushmerick, & Lebiere, 1993). This data comes from subjects solving the four-disk problems in Fig. 2.6. These problems are cases where one has to move from one arbitrary configuration to another, so there is no possibility for subjects memorizing the sequence of moves. The interface was one in which subjects simply picked up a disk with a mouse and moved it to another peg. Unlike the Ruiz experiment, subjects were not monitored for using the subgoaling strategy. Nonetheless, they were strongly encouraged to in the instructions and the evidence is that they did. We restrict our analysis to those move sequences where they perfectly executed the minimal 15-move sequence required to solve these problems. All problems involve setting the same numbers of subgoals before a particular numbered move in the sequence.

Because the configurations are arbitrary, subjects cannot solve the task without first carefully encoding the position of each disk in both the start state and the goal state. We also assumed they had to reencode the goal after getting each major disk to its location because they had not been attending

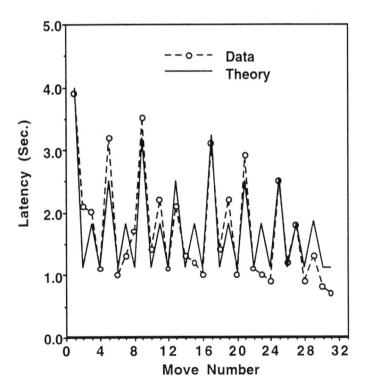

FIG. 2.5.   Data from Ruiz (1987) and the ACT–R simulation.

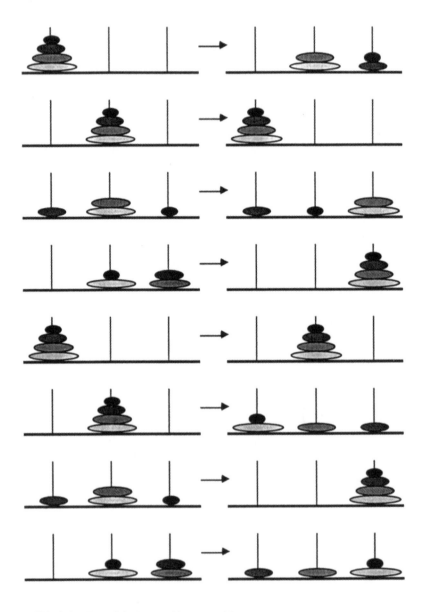

FIG. 2.6.   Four-disk Tower of Hanoi problems.

50

to the goal configuration during the interval and they might have forgotten it.[17] Table 2.4 shows the productions used to solve this task. The first four productions (**Encode-Current-Configuration, Encode-Target-Configuration, Find-Disk,** and **Done-Finding**) are responsible for encoding the screen prior to trying to place a disk. As in the Ruiz model of Table 2.3, **Start-Tower** subgoals placing the next largest disk and **Final-Move** places that disk. However, because disks are not in standard positions, one must note the location of the disk in the current state and the target state. Productions **Note-Current-Peg** and **Note-Target-Peg** do this. Then **Spare-Peg** can assign the remaining peg (not the one the disk is currently on, nor the one it is on in the goal configuration) as the spare peg. Another encoding production, **Note-Checkee**, has to note the peg on which the smaller disk to be checked is located. Then, the productions **Subgoal-Blocker** and **Move** can apply as before (except that **Subgoal-Blocker** does not have to post the subgoal). Again, this model is available over the Web.

This production system does not require a special action time for **Subgoal-Blocker** because subjects did not have to type their subgoals in. However, all the encoding productions (**Find-Disk, Done-Finding, Note-Current-Disk, Note-Goal-Disk, Note-Checkee**) required an encoding time, which was estimated. Also, a special action time was estimated for the move productions as in the previous model. Thus, the two estimated parameters were encoding time = 0.56 sec and move time = 2.15 sec. The move time is longer than the Ruiz estimate and reflects the complex mouse action required in this system. Figure 2.7 compares the predictions of the model with the data.[18] The correspondence is very good with $R^2 = .99$. As can be confirmed by running the model over the Web, the bumps in the figure are produced by the large encoding times.

Compare the productions in Table 2.4 with the productions in Table 2.5 that formed an ACT–R 2.0 model proposed for the same task (Anderson, Kushmerick, & Lebiere, 1993). There are only three productions and they are of much larger grain size than the productions in Table 2.4. Although they are stated briefly in their English form in Table 2.5, the actual ACT–R code was complex and required resorting to LISP tests in the production rules. This exemplifies some of the transition between ACT–R 2.0 and ACT–R 4.0. It is worth commenting on some of the condition lines in production Subgoal-Disks from Table 2.5[19] that might look innocent enough but that hide a great deal of complex computation.

---

[17]Thus, even in this task there is subsymbolic processing (i.e., forgetting at work).

[18]The model predictions are the same for all problems in Fig. 2.6.

[19]The actual ACT–R 2.0 code can be found in Table 12.2 of Anderson (1993), where it occupied a full page per production

TABLE 2.4
Implementation of the Subgoaling Strategy for the General Case of Tower of
Hanoi Problems (Model for Anderson, Kushmerick, & Lebiere, 1993)

Encode-Current-Configuration

| | IF | the goal is to solve a tower task of size n |
| | THEN | set a subgoal to encode disks less than or equal to n in the current configuration |

Encode-Target-Configuration

| | IF | the goal is to solve a tower task of size n |
| | THEN | set a subgoal to encode disks less than or equal to n in the target configuration |

Find-Disk

| | IF | the goal is to encode disks less than or equal to n in a configuration |
| | THEN | encode disk n in the configuration and transform the goal to encoding disks less than or equal to n_1 |

Done-Finding

| | IF | the goal is to encode disks less than or equal to 1 in a configuration |
| | THEN | encode disk 1 in the configuration and pop the goal |

Start-Tower

| | IF | the goal is to solve a tower task of size n greater than 1 |
| | THEN | set a subgoal to move disk n checking disk n -1 and change the goal to solve a tower task of size n - 1 |

Final-Move

| | IF | the goal is to move a tower of size 1 to peg x |
| | THEN | move disk 1 to peg x and pop the goal |

Note-Source-Peg

| | IF | the goal is to move a disk of size n and the source peg is not encoded |
| | THEN | encode location of disk n in the current configuration as source |

Note-Target-Peg

| | IF | the goal is to move a disk of size n and the location of the target peg is not encoded |
| | THEN | encode disk n in the goal configuration as the target peg |

Spare-Peg

| | IF | the goal is to move a disk and there is source and target peg |
| | THEN | the remaining peg is the other peg |

Note-Checkee

          IF   the goal is to move a disk of size n checking smaller disk m
       THEN   encode the peg on which disk m is located in the current
                        configuration

Subgoal-Blocker

          IF   the goal is to move a disk of size n checking m
                       and y is the other peg
                       and m is not at y
       THEN   set a subgoal to move disk m to y checking m - 1
                       and change the goal to check m - 1

Blocker-On-Other-Peg

          IF   the goal is to move a disk of size n checking m
                       and y is the other peg
                       and m is at y
       THEN   change the goal to check m - 1

Move

          IF   the goal is move disk of size n to peg x
                       and all smaller disks have been checked
       THEN   move disk n to peg x
                       and pop the goal

1. "Disk D1 is on peg P1 but should go to peg P2 in the configuration": This reflects the combination of a test of the current and goal configuration. As developed more fully in Chapter 5, ACT–R 4.0 assumes one can only encode information from one spatial location at a time.

2. "D1 is the largest disk out of place": Implementing a test for "largest" is complex and no longer supported as a primitive in ACT–R 4.0. Rather, it is now necessary to go through the more complex logic in Table 2.4 that tests each of the disks with a separate production firing.

3. "One cannot move D1 by to P2": Again, this is a complex test that is no longer supported. In the current system, one checks that each smaller disk is out of the way.

As one symptom of the larger grain size in ACT–R 2.0, we did not aspire to account for actual latencies as in Fig. 2.7. Rather, we simply concerned ourselves with the sequence of moves made and were content to note that ordinal relationships among the latencies supported our postulated goal structure.

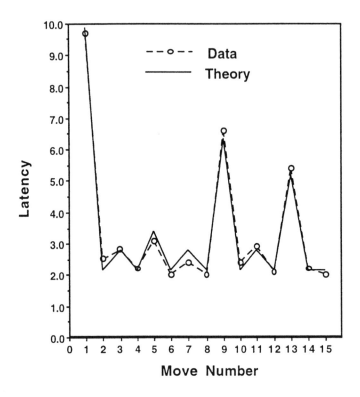

FIG. 2.7.   Data from Anderson, Kushmerick, and Lebiere (1993) and the ACT–R simulations.

The current model does not assign special latencies in the productions that push and pop subgoals.[20] These productions have the default latencies of 50 msec. Rather, the substantial latencies were required by experimental procedures for indicating subgoals (Ruiz's experiment), time to encode states (our experiment) in service of subgoaling, and time to make moves (both experiments). Still, subgoaling does a play critical role in organizing the behavior in the Tower on Hanoi task. This illustrates the point in the first chapter that goal structures provide the chemistry level in ACT–R, organizing the atomic level of production firings into coherent behavior.

---

[20]However, equally good fits could be obtained had we assumed somewhat longer times for pushes and pops.

TABLE 2.5
ACT–R 2.0 Productions from Anderson, Kushmerick and Lebiere (1993)

Subgoal-Disks

    IF   the goal is to achieve a particular configuration of disks
             and disk D1 is on peg P1 but should go to peg P2 in the configuration
             and D1 is the largest disk out of place and one cannot directly move
                  D1 to P2
             and disk D2 is one smaller than D1 and peg P3 is different than P1
                  or P2
  THEN   set a subgoal to move the D2 tower to P3 and D1 to P2

Move-Disk

    IF   the goal is to achieve a particular configuration of disks
             and disk D1 is on peg P1 but should go to peg P2
             and D1 is the largest disk out of place and one can directly
                  move D1 to P2
  THEN   move D1 to P2

Satisfied

    IF   the goal is to achieve a particular configuration of disks
             and it is achieved
  THEN   pop the goal

Conclusions

This chapter has specified ACT–R's representational assumptions with enough information about processing consequences to show how these representational assumptions resulted in performance at the symbolic level. For some members of the ACT–R community, this is the only level at which they use ACT–R, getting adequate models for the high-level tasks that they are interested in. The models of the Tower of Hanoi task illustrated how one could develop an accurate model at this level. However, for many other tasks, one needs to get down to the subsymbolic level, which is the topic of the next two chapters. However, even here, the representational assumptions serve a critical role as a framework for specifying these subsymbolic assumptions.

3

Performance

John R. Anderson
Christian Lebiere
Marsha Lovett
Carnegie Mellon University

OVERVIEW

ACT–R aspires to provide detailed and accurate models of the learning and performance of subjects across a wide range of experimental paradigms. In cognitive psychology, we typically measure the performance of subjects in two ways—what responses they choose to emit and how long it takes them to emit these responses. The former measure often is presented as "percent correct" or its complement "percent errors." One can be judgmental in this binary way in cases where there is a designated correct response. However, in other cases, there can be a richer category of potential responses and we simply calculate the percentage of responses that fill various categories. Usually, latency is measured as time to complete a task, but in some cases we can collect latency measures for intermediate responses (e.g., eye movements, mouse movements, key presses) on the way to task completion. As discussed in the first chapter, production systems address these two dependent measures of psychology more directly and more completely than any other modeling formalism. Current production systems are committed to the exact timing and identity of each response a subject emits.

The behavior of the ACT–R system and, in particular, its predictions about these two dependent measures are a function of the productions that fire. This chapter examines which productions ACT–R chooses to fire, how it instantiates these productions, and what determines the latencies of these production firings. This performance analysis assumes that we have a static system that is not changing as a function of experience. This is a typical assumption in much of the experimental research on human cognition. It is justified in cases where the behavior under study is at some relatively asymptotic level or the critical factors being investigated do not change over the range of experiences encountered in the experiment. The next chapter investigates learning issues—how an ACT–R model changes itself as a function of its experience. However, even in this chapter, much of the discussion is motivated by implicit assumptions about the learning problem, and at some points we are forced into an explicit discussion of learning issues. The separation of performance from learning is basically an expositional strategy. They are quite intertwined in the ACT–R theory.

The previous chapter already illustrated, in the case of the Tower of Hanoi task, how ACT–R could deliver predictions about response choice and latency. However, this was a model purely at the symbolic level. A production fired and incremented time by a set amount. There was no place for the latencies that vary continuously as a function of experimental manipulation, which occurs in many psychology experiments. The system always made the same choices. There was no room for the variability in human behavior. To model continuous functions and variability, we need to go to the subsymbolic level of ACT–R.

Figure 3.1 provides an overview of the various possible levels of analysis in ACT–R. The information in that figure is dense and we unpack its details as we go through the chapter. Figure 3.1 illustrates these levels in the abstract, but just to show that it corresponds to ACT–R reality, an example production system and a trace that realizes this abstraction are given in Appendix C and are available over the Web. Part (a) of Fig. 3.1 represents the symbolic level where there are goal states and productions transforming one goal state into another. Sometimes productions result in pushing to a subgoal or popping from a subgoal to return to a higher goal. This symbolic level of ACT–R was the topic of the previous chapter. As part of each production cycle, the system goes through a conflict resolution process in which it tries to determine which production to fire. This is the start of the subsymbolic level in ACT–R and it is illustrated in part (b) of Fig. 3.1 where productions are selected and tried serially until one is found whose condition can be matched. This conflict-resolution process is discussed in the next section. The process of retrieving chunks to match a production condition, illustrated in part (c) of Fig. 3.1, is the declarative part of the subsymbolic level and it is discussed in the following section. Throughout this chapter, we refer back to this figure and discuss the quantities that appear in it. Throughout this book, we refer to various subsymbolic quantities. Appendix D at the end of the chapter provides a definition of these terms and can be used for reference when reading this book.

CONFLICT RESOLUTION

On the basis of the information in the goal, ACT–R must commit to which production to attempt to fire. Because many productions may potentially fire, deciding which production to fire is referred to as conflict resolution.

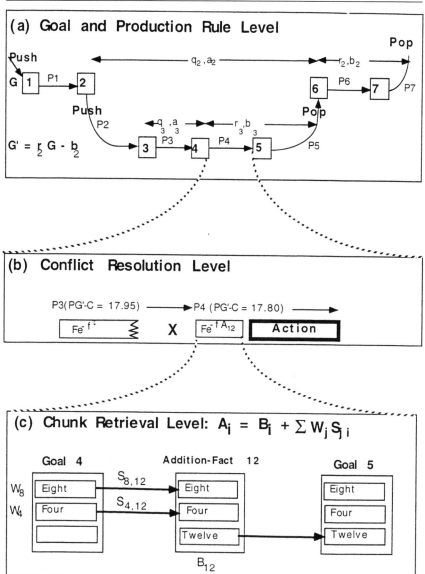

FIG. 3.1 Representation of the levels of assumptions in the ACT–R theory. This is discussed throughout the chapter.

Part (b) of Fig. 3.1 illustrates how this happens. The productions that satisfy the current goal are placed into the conflict set. It needs to be emphasized that the only test for getting into the conflict set is whether the goal matches. The retrievals required for the rest of the condition are only attempted if the production rule is selected from that conflict set. The productions in the conflict set are ordered in terms of their expected gain and ACT–R considers them according to that ordering. The expected gain of a production rule is defined as:

Expected Gain $= E = PG - C$ **Expected Gain Equation 3.1**

where P is the expected probability that the goal will be achieved if that production rule is chosen, G is the value of the goal, and C is the expected cost of achieving the goal if that production is chosen. The scale or "currency" for measuring cost in ACT–R is time. The quantity C is an estimation of the time to achieve the goal. The quantity G, the worth of the goal, can be thought of in terms of how much time ACT–R should be willing to spend on the goal.[1] PG is the expected gain if the production is taken, C is the expected cost, and the difference is the expected net utility of the production. Although this equation can be read as defining the rational estimate of a production's worth, it can also be read as a rule for trading off probability for cost according to the value of the goal. That is, because P and G multiply, one gives greater weight to probability as the goal becomes more valuable. This produces the speed-accuracy trade-off, which is an ubiquitous phenomenon in human information processing—people tend to expend more time to get improved accuracy when the stakes are high. Weighting accuracy more when the goal is more important is rational, and this rationality is embedded in the fundamental conflict–resolution equation.

Usually, the most highly valued production will fire and that will be that. However, part (b) of Fig. 3.1 illustrates the potential complication. In this case, P3 is first considered (because it has the highest $PG - C$ evaluation), but fails and then the lower valued P4 is tried and fires. P3 does not fire because there is a failure in retrieving the chunk to match its condition. The process of chunk matching is described in detail in the next section, but basically, when a production is selected, there is no guarantee that its nongoal chunks can be successfully matched.[2] If matching fails, ACT–R will try the next highest production in the conflict set and will keep trying lower-valued productions until one matches, as long as these productions

---

[1]An equivalent alternative would be to measure the goal in terms of some other subjective utility scale and then measure cost in terms of that scale.

[2]This scheme contrasts with ACT–R 2.0 where all productions were matched in parallel. We have since come to the conclusion that it was computationally too powerful an assumption to have these parallel matches. It required that the same chunk type be simultaneously accessed for an unbounded number of potentially contradictory matches.

have greater than zero expected utility. If no production can be found with positive expected utility, the goal is popped with failure.

There are two places where computation is highly parallel in ACT–R. One is at the conflict-resolution level where all productions are simultaneously matched against a single goal chunk and where the matching productions are ordered with respect to their highest expected gain. Although this ordering of productions is done in parallel, they are tried serially one after another. Because different productions require different chunk patterns to be matched against declarative memory, these retrievals need to be done serially. The other place for parallelism is in part (c) of Fig. 3.1 where all of the chunks are simultaneously accessed to retrieve the one that best matches the chunk pattern from a specific production. Thus, at both levels where ACT–R chooses the best (the highest valued production, the best matching chunk), the search for the best is carried out in parallel. As Chapter 12 discusses, this is the kind of parallelism that we think can be supported by the nervous system.

Should the $PG - C$ value for all applicable productions be negative, ACT–R will pop the current goal with failure and return to the higher goal that set it. This is the basic principle that underlies goal abandonment in the theory. In contrast to the automatic popping of a failed goal, popping a goal with success must be accomplished by a production firing. When a goal is popped with failure it can return a failure value to a slot of the parent goal. This failure value can be used to prevent the same subgoal from being pushed again. More generally, this failure value allows the higher goal level to detect and deal with the subgoal failure.

One agenda in elaborating the conflict-resolution principles in ACT–R is to specify how the quantities P, G, and C are calculated. A second agenda is to specify the stochasticity in the calculation of the expected gain. A third agenda is to discuss the behavioral evidence for this conception of conflict resolution. These issues are pursued in the next three subsections.

Role of *P, G,* and *C* in Conflict Resolution

Assigning probabilities or costs to production rules poses a serious difficulty because each production rule is just one component of a complex computation. How does one estimate the probability of success of that computation or its cost from the myopic perspective of an individual production? ACT–R solves this problem by separating the probability and cost for which the production is responsible from the probability and cost for which later productions are responsible. This is a relatively simple solution but one that has worked well. With respect to the probability P, there are two subprobabilities: q, the probability of the production working successfully, and r, the probability of achieving the goal if the production works successfully. The aggregate probability P is estimated as the product of these two:

$$P = qr$$ **Probability of Goal Equation 3.2**

This equation reflects the view that success in achieving the goal depends on the joint probability of the production rule being successful and subsequent rules eventually reaching the goal.[3] A number of factors will cause q to be less than 1. First, if a retrieval is attempted and fails, the production will fail. Thus, to the extent that the production fails to successfully retrieve, q will be less than 1. Also, if the production sets a subgoal and that subgoal fails, the production will fail. The next chapter discusses how q and r are learned from experience.

As in the treatment of P, the cost C consists of two subcosts:

$$C = a + b$$ **Cost of Goal Equation 3.3**

The cost a is the amount of effort in time that this production will take. The cost b is an estimate of the amount of time from when the production completes until the goal is achieved. The cost a is a sum of the match time and right-hand-side costs for the production. The next section of this chapter discusses the match time. The default value for the right-hand-side cost is 0.05 sec, but can be larger if subgoals are set, because achieving these subgoals is counted as part of the action. The cost of the production can also be longer when the production calls for executing an external action because one must include the time for the action (e.g., for a finger to strike a key). Both of these costs, a and b, are estimated on the basis of experience, as are q and r. The next chapter also discusses how these cost parameters are learned.

Part (a) of Fig. 3.1 illustrates the scopes of these parameters for two productions, P2 and P3. The parameters q and a refer to the production and any subgoals it might set. Thus, those quantities associated with production P2 in Fig. 3.1 (q_2 and a_2) have a scope that spans the subgoal that P2 sets (Cycles 2 to 5). In contrast, those quantities associated with production P3 (q_3 and a_3) only span a single production (Cycle 3) because that production sets no subgoals. The a quantities refer to the amount of time spanned and q quantities reflect the probability of success over that span. Thus, in the case of P2, a_2 refers to the cost of matching the production and achieving

---

[3]Anderson (1990, 1993) provided a more complex formula for combining q and r of which Equation 2 is only a special case. The simpler formula has been adapted for parsimony and to eliminate an extra parameter.

the subgoal, while q_2 refers to the probability of achieving that. In contrast, a_3 only refers to the matching time and action time for P_3 while q_3 only refers to the matching probability. In both cases, the downstream quantities r and b refer to the period until the production goal is popped (i.e., r_2 and b_2 cover cycles 6 and 7 while r_3 and b_3 cover cycles 4 and 5) The parameter r is the probability of achieving that goal and b is the amount of downstream time. We emphasize that a, b, q, and r, are estimates of the costs and probabilities. They may or may not be accurate estimates for the current situation.

The setting of the initial value G for a task goal is a topic about which ACT–R has little to say. When an experimenter tells a subject something is worth a dollar versus a penny, how does this convert to an internal value of G (which is thought of as being measured in time units)? How valuable is solving a puzzle, versus passing a course, versus saving one's life? ACT–R takes the agnostic economist's position of simply assuming these maps onto some internal values without deeply inquiring why. In practice, the parameter G may need to be estimated in fitting the data. Frequently, its exact value is irrelevant to the model's predictions.

However, once the value of a goal is set, ACT–R does have something to say. In particular, it has something to say about the values of subgoals set in pursuit of that goal. One might think that a subgoal should inherit the value of its supergoal. However, this ignores the fact that even if the subgoal is achieved there remains uncertainty about whether the supergoal will be achieved and there remains some potential cost. One has to subtract this from the expected value of the goal to calculate the expected value for the subgoal. As is illustrated in part (a) of Fig. 3.1, the expected value of the subgoal set by P2 is $G' = r_2 G - b_2$.[4] This value G' is *discounted from* G to reflect uncertainty (r) and cost (b) in achieving the goal even after the subgoal is achieved. Thus, G' reflects the maximum amount that should be expended in achieving the subgoal and this is the value attributed to this subgoal. Thus, the value assigned to a subgoal depends on the context in which it occurs. In the Table 3.1 instantiation of Fig. 3.1, $G = 20$, $r_2 = 1$, and $b_2 = 1$ and so $G' = 1 \cdot 20 - 1 = 19$.

Let us work through another hypothetical example of how these goal value computations might work. ACT–R might be trying to solve an equation. Suppose this goal is worth 20 sec. As a subgoal, ACT–R might try to collapse multiple occurrences of the variable x into a single occurrence [e.g., transform $3(x-2) = x - 7$ into $2x = -1$]. ACT–R may be confident of solving the equation if this can be achieved ($r = 1$), but expect another 2 sec of further work ($b = 2$). Therefore, the value of the collapse subgoal will be $G' = r \cdot G - b = 1 \cdot 20 - 2 = 18$. As a part of this subgoal, ACT–R may set

---

[4]This is different for ACT–R 2.0 where the value of the subgoal was set as $PG - C$. Thus was too severe a discounting.

a subgoal to perform a distribution [e.g., convert $3(x - 2)$ into $3x - 6$]. The expected probability of achieving the goal of collapsing x, even if distribution is successful, might only be $2/3$, and the further expected cost might be 3 sec. Thus, the value of the distribute subgoal would be $2/3 \bullet 18 - 3 = 9$. Note that this means that ACT–R will value a goal less the more deeply it is embedded in uncertain subgoals. As a consequence, ACT–R will more likely abandon deeply embedded subgoals. On an intuitive level, this seems right. For instance, in trying to prove a theorem, one is willing to spend less effort in trying to prove a subconjecture on the way to the theorem than one is willing to spend proving the theorem itself.

It is worth reviewing why conflict resolution requires keeping separate the four quantities a, b, q, and r. Separating the probability parameters (q,r) from the cost parameters (a,b) allows the system to be differentially sensitive to probability and cost as a function of the value of the goal (as implied by the $PG - C$ formula—see the earlier speed-accuracy discussion). Separating quantities associated with the current production rule (a,q) from the quantities associated with future rules (b,r) allows ACT–R to appropriately discount the value of the subgoal (to the value $rG - b$). Being able to assign appropriate values to subgoals is critical to ACT–R's use of the subgoal structure.

Stochasticity in Conflict Resolution

The actual conflict resolution behavior implied by the previous description is totally deterministic—there will be a highest valued rule in each situation and the subject will always choose that rule first. However, in the ACT–R simulation, some noise is added to these evaluation values. This noise is approximately normally distributed and serves to introduce some stochasticity into the behavior of the system. Thus, if two productions are competing in conflict resolution, a production is only chosen with a certain probability that reflects the difference between the two productions' evaluations relative to the noise in the evaluation process.

The noise added to each production's evaluation comes from a logistic distribution.[5] The logistic distribution closely approximates a normal distri-

---

[5]The logistic density is defined $p(\varepsilon) = \dfrac{e^{-\varepsilon/s}}{s(1+e^{-\varepsilon/s})^2}$ and has a cumulative

$P(\varepsilon) = \dfrac{1}{1+e^{-\varepsilon/s}}$. This produces noise ε for each expected value E_i with mean 0 and

variance $\sigma^2 = \dfrac{\pi^2 s^2}{3}$. In the ACT–R simulation, it is customary to set the noise by setting the s parameter.

bution but is computationally simpler. It is for this computational reason that we have used the logistic distribution within ACT–R.

It would be useful to have some analytic description of what the probability of selecting a production is. One could find out the probability by running Monte Carlo simulations, but closed-form descriptions are useful. Appendix A to this chapter discusses the properties of a distribution that approximates a normal distribution or a logistic distribution and has a number of analytic conveniences. In particular, it allows us to go from production evaluations to probabilities of being selected in conflict resolution. If E_i is the evaluation of alternative i, the probability of choosing that ith production among n applicable productions with evaluations E_j will be

$$\text{Probability of } i = \frac{e^{E_i / t}}{\sum_j e^{E_j / t}} \quad \textbf{Conflict Resolution Equation 3.4}$$

where the summation is over the n alternatives. The parameter t in the preceding distribution is related to the standard deviation, σ, of the noise by the formula $t = \sqrt{6}\sigma / \pi$.[6] Equation 3.4 is the same as the Boltzmann equation used in Boltzmann machines (Ackley, Hinton, & Sejnowsky, 1985; Hinton & Sejnowsky, 1986). In this context t is called the temperature. Equation 3.4 is sometimes referred to as a "soft-max" rule because it tends to select the maximum item but not always. The smaller that t is (and the less noise), the stronger the tendency to select the maximum item. Note that Equation 3.4 is an approximate closed-form characterization of ACT–R's conflict-resolution behavior. The actual predictions of the ACT–R theory depend on Monte Carlo simulations.

The connection of t to temperature in Boltzmann machines points to an interesting perspective on this noise parameter. The temperature parameter in Boltzmann machines plays an important role in enabling them to avoid local optima (or minima in their terminology) in finding globally optimal solutions. Similarly, as developed in detail in Chapter 8 on choice, noise in production selection allows ACT–R to identify better productions and to identify when the relative payoffs of different productions change.

Evidence: "Probability Matching" Experiments

This theory of conflict resolution plays a critical role in ACT–R's ability to

---

[6]And $t^2 = 2s^2$—see previous footnote.

account for many phenomena, particularly when it is added to ACT–R's theory of learning the a, b, q, and r parameters. We return to the theory throughout this book and particularly in Chapter 8 on choice. However, as a token of the power of this theory, this subsection considers its application to the simplest choice situation imaginable.

The simplest possible choice situation is one where a subject has to make a single choice between two options, each of which has a particular probability of success. Many such experiments have been performed in what is called the *probability-learning paradigm* where the subject chooses one of two alternatives, receives feedback as to whether that was the correct choice, and then repeats this over and over again. For instance, a subject might try to predict over and over again whether a possibly biased coin will come up heads or tails. Subjects' behavior in such experiments is often characterized as "probability matching." That is, if an option is correct on a proportion p of the trials, subjects choose that option with probability p. This behavior has often been judged irrational. It is argued that, if one alternative occurs

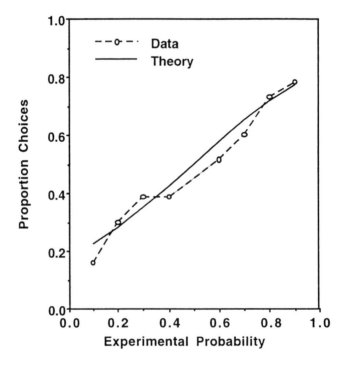

FIG. 3.2 Proportion of choices for experimental alternatives as a function of the probability. From Friedman et al. (1964).

with probability greater than .5, the subjects should choose that alternative with probability 1 to maximize their correct choices. We do not address the issue of the rationality of their behavior until the next chapter where we address learning issues, and further in Chapter 8 on choice. In this section, we are content with showing that behavior is not as simple as implied by the probability-matching characterization and that ACT–R can predict subjects' asymptotic behavior in these choice experiments.

Figure 3.2 shows some data from Friedman et al.(1964) that presents the proportion of times that their subjects chose one of two buttons as a function of the probability of it being reinforced. The data is from the last 24 trials of 48-trial blocks where probabilities of choice have appeared to have stabilized. As can be seen, subjects do not exactly probability match in this experiment. The best fitting linear equation giving probability of choice as a function of experimental probability (P) is:

$$\text{Choice probability} = .124 + .722P$$

The fact that this equation is not a simple identity (i.e., choice probability = P) points to the fact that subjects were not probability matching. In this experiment they were undermatching (i.e., not responding as extremely as the experienced probabilities). This undermatching is reflected in the slope .722, which is less than 1.

There is a simple ACT–R model for this task. Essentially, there were two productions in competition:

Choose-Button-1
      IF   the goal is to make a choice in the experiment
   THEN   press button 1
                and pop the goal

Choose-Button-2
      IF   the goal is to make a choice in the experiment
   THEN   press button 2
                and pop the goal

These productions have identical conditions and the one selected in conflict resolution will be the one with the momentarily higher value. Figure 3.2 also shows the predictions of the ACT simulation involving these two productions. We assumed that ACT had estimated P to be the true probability (an assumption elaborated on in the next chapter on learning and Chapter 8 on choice). More precisely, each production was given the following parameters:

$q =$ 1 since the rule always fires if selected

$r =$ true probability of that button

$a =$ .05 default action cost

$b =$ 0 since goal is popped and there are no more actions.

Thus, $P = qr =$ true probability and $C = a + b = .05$.

There is an analytical characterization of ACT–R's predictions in this experiment based on the Conflict Resolution Equation 3.4: If P_1 is the probability of choice 1 then the expected value for choice 1 will be $P_1G -$ .05 and for choice 2 will be $(1 - P_1)G - .05$. Then the probability of choosing alternative 1 is:

$$\text{Prob}(1) = \frac{e^{(P_1G-.05)/t}}{e^{(P_1G-.05)/t} + e^{[(1-P_1)G-.05]/t}}$$

It can be shown that:

$$\text{Prob}(1) = \frac{1}{1 + e^{(1-2P_1)G/t}}$$

The predictions of this equation depend on the ratio G/t and to simplify the analysis, we will set $t = 1$ (or $\sigma^2 = 1.64$) and just estimate G. The best fitting value of G is 1.54. Figure 3.2 shows that ACT–R can predict choice behavior assuming some noise in the conflict-resolution process. It might seem remarkable that the noise would be of just such a value so as to produce probability matching. However, as we see, exact probability matching is not the usual result, despite the popular supposition to the contrary. Rather, although choice probability does vary monotonically with experienced probability, there is only approximate probability matching.

One thing that should influence the response probability is the value of G. If a constant noise is added to $PG - C$, the larger the value of G, the greater the effect of P. Thus, more extreme response probabilities should occur when G is increased. Myers, Fort, Katz, and Suydam (1963) performed an experiment in which subjects were either not paid or given 10 cents for each correct response. Presumably, this should influence probability of choice. Figure 3.3 shows their results for conditions where the probabilities were .6, .7, or .8 for one alternative. As can be seen, subjects choose the

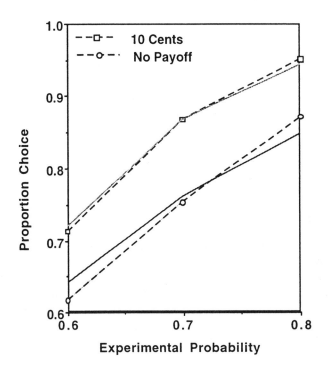

FIG. 3.3 Proportion choices for experimental alternatives as a function of payoff and probability. The dotted lines are data and the filled lines are theory. Data from Myers, Fort, Katz, and Suydam (1963).

more probable alternative considerably more frequently when there is a payoff for doing so.

To fit the model, a value for G of 2.86 was estimated in the zero payoff condition and a value of 4.66 in the 10 cents condition, continuing the assumption of $t = 1$. Figure 3.3 illustrates that this model provides a good fit to the data from the experiment.

This is just one example of how the ACT–R conflict-resolution mechanism can be used to predict choice behavior. Anderson (1990) used a precursor of ACT–R's conflict resolution to predict a variety of choice behavior in problem-solving search. Anderson, Kushmerick and Lebiere (1993) used it to account for detailed data about choices subjects made in an artificial navigation task. More recently, Lovett and Anderson (1995, 1996) pursued its application even more deeply, and Chapter 8 extends the theory to explain behavior in problem solving, choice experiments, and animal learning experiments.

RETRIEVAL

As part (c) of Fig. 3.1 illustrates, when a production rule is selected, it commits the system to try to perform the retrieval of the chunks specified in its condition. Much of the performance of the production system will turn on how these retrievals fare. Speed of performance is often a direct function of the speed of these retrievals. Depending on what is retrieved, the subject may wind up doing one thing or another. Errors of processing often reflect errors of different sorts in the retrieval process. This retrieval process is the connection between declarative and procedural memory, and it is controlled by the level of activation of the declarative chunks.

Activation-Based Retrieval

ACT–R makes chunks active to the degree that past experiences indicate that they will be useful at the particular moment. Using a common formula in activation theories, the activation of a chunk is a sum of a base-level activation, reflecting its general usefulness in the past, and an associative activation, reflecting its relevance to the current context. The activation of a chunk i is defined as:

$$A_i = B_i + \sum_j W_j S_{ji} \qquad \textbf{Activation Equation 3.5}$$

where B_i is the base-level activation of the chunk i, the W_j terms reflect the attentional weighting of the elements j, which are slot values of the current goal (in Fig. 3.1c Eight and Four are the goal slots that serve as sources), and the S_{ji} terms are the strengths of association from the elements j to chunk i. Figure 3.4 displays the chunk encoding that $8 + 4 = 12$ and its various quantities (with W_j terms for Four and Eight, assuming that they are sources). Activations in ACT–R can often be negative, but there is no particular significance to negative activations. As Chapter 7 discusses further, activation in ACT–R is an interval scale (Stevens, 1946) where differences are meaningful, but where there is not a natural zero.

Each of the components in Equation 3.5 requires comment:

Base-Level Activation B_i. The base-level activation of a chunk represents how recently and frequently it is accessed. The next subsection discusses how base-level activation changes with time and how there can be random fluctuations in base-level activation. The next chapter on learning discusses how these base-level activations are learned to reflect the past log odds that the chunks will be used.

Source Activations W_j. The source activations reflect the amount of attention given to elements of the goal. ACT–R assumes that there is a fixed capacity for source activation and that each element of the goal has an equal amount. As a scale assumption this capacity is set at 1 and if there are n elements in the slots of the goal each source element gets $1/n$ source activation. Thus, there are important consequences to what goal slots are filled—whatever slots are filled become sources of activation, and if extra slots are filled, they take source activation away from others. Lovett, Reder, and Lebiere (in press) speculated that there may be differences in total source activation which correspond to differences in cognitive capacity among individuals. Anderson and Reder (in press) speculated that subjects may be able to strategically alter the W_j values associated with various slots (subject to the constraint that the sum reflects the overall capacity).

Strengths of Association S_{ji}. The strength of association is a measure of how often the chunk i was needed when j was an element of the goal. The next chapter discusses how these associative strengths are learned. They are given a default setting at the start of any ACT–R simulation. As discussed in Anderson (1993), the S_{ji} terms can be thought of as estimations of the likelihood of j being a source present if chunk i is retrieved. More formally, S_{ji} is an estimate of $\ln[P(i|j)/P(i)]$ where $P(i|j)$ is the probability i will be needed, given j is a source and $P(i)$ is the base probability. ACT–R has developed a formula for setting initial values for these probabilities (given as Prior Strength Equation 4.2 in Chapter 4) in the case when i is

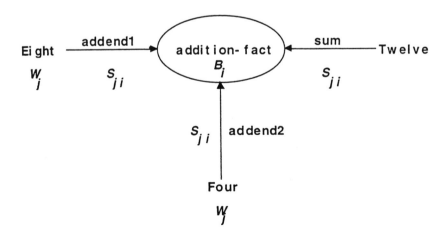

FIG. 3.4 Network representation of an ACT–R chunk.

connected to j (i.e., j is a slot of i or vice versa).[7] The initial estimate of $P(i|j)$ is $1/n$ where n is the number of chunks connected to j. The prior estimate of $P(i)$ is $1/m$ where m is the number of chunks in the declarative database. Thus, S_{ji} is estimated initially to be $\ln(m) - \ln(n)$. As the number of facts is often not known, we sometimes set S_{ji} to be $S - \ln(n)$ where S is an estimated constant. In any case, these formulas imply that S_{ji} values will decrease as the logarithm of the number of chunks attached to j. As a later section shows, this produces fan effects and interference effects in memory.

Changes in Base-Level Activation

If the Activation Equation 3.5 described everything determining activation, ACT–R would be a rigid system that displayed none of the fluctuations typical of human memory. This subsection describes how the base-level component of activation fluctuates and decays with time. It discusses what happens to the base-level activation from the moment when a new declarative chunk is created, assuming it never gets strengthened. The next chapter discusses how the base-level activation of a chunk grows with repeated use. When a new chunk is created it receives an amount of base-level activation whose value is taken from an approximately normal distribution with mean ß and variance σ_1^2. This initial base-level activation decays as a logarithmic function of time. Moreover, the activation of a chunk fluctuates from moment to moment with another variance σ_2^2. Thus, the base-level activation of a chunk at time t after its creation (assuming no intervening practice) is:

$$B(t) = ß - d \ln(t) + \varepsilon_i + \varepsilon_2 \qquad \textbf{Base-Level Equation 3.6}$$

Each part of the right-hand side of the equation deserves comment:

1. The initial expected value of the base-level activation is ß (at $t = 1$). Often ß is set to 0, as it is absorbed in other parameter estimates.

2. The factor $- d \ln(t)$ reflects decay with time. The parameter d is the decay rate and it is normally set at 0.5 in ACT–R simulations. Thus, as in ACT–R 2.0, the activation level decays as a logarithmic function of time. As we discuss later, this yields the empirically observed retention functions. Also, as shown by Anderson and Schooler (1991), the log odds of something appearing in the environment approximates such a function. Thus, activation serves its intended role of encoding log odds in the environment and yields adaptive behavior functions.

---

[7]If they are unconnected, $S_{ji} = 0$ initially.

3. The term ε_1 reflects some random noise in the initial base-level activation. It could reflect stochasticity in the nervous system but it could also reflect stochasticity in our knowledge of the true history of that chunk.[8] It reflects a one-shot randomness that stays with the chunk. Thus, some chunks start out lower than others and tend to stay lower, whereas other chunks start out higher and tend to stay higher.

4. The term ε_2 reflects moment-to-moment noise in the activation levels of the system. Again, it could reflect true stochasticity in the nervous system or just lack of knowledge on our part of the factors determining activation at a particular point in time.[9]

Both the permanent noise, ε_1, and the transient noise, ε_2, are generated in ACT–R according to logistic distributions, which approximate a normal distribution (the same distribution chosen for expected gain noise, again for computational reasons). These noise distributions have means zero and variances σ_1^2 and σ_2^2.[10] In ACT–R 2.0 the only noise was this second, moment-to-moment fluctuation. It led to unacceptable behavior in certain simulations. To get an adequate amount of nondeterminism in ACT–R 2.0, we had to set σ_2^2 sufficiently high to that the system radically switched from moment to moment in the knowledge to which it had access. Thus, for instance, to get 50% recall of a list σ_2^2 would have to be set so that a random half of the items fell below threshold. However, because the noise was random, there would be no relationship between the 50% that fell below threshold from one recall effort to the next. Although people do show some moment-to-moment variation in access to knowledge, they do not show as much as was displayed in ACT–R 2.0. ACT–R 4.0 can provide the right mix of transient noise and permanent noise. If our modeling is not sensitive to the distinction between moment-to-moment and permanent variation then we can treat $\sigma_1^2 + \sigma_2^2$ as a single variance, σ^2.[11]

Besides producing the right behavior, the base-level activation equation makes the system fundamentally more adaptive. We have already noted that the decay component allows ACT–R to adapt to changing needs with time. Also, the randomness in activations allows ACT–R to discover the true worth of different facts. Chapter 9 on cognitive arithmetic discusses this in more detail.

---

[8]For instance, we often do not know if a subject attends to a stimulus presentation or whether there are covert rehearsals.

[9]For instance, our estimate of sources of activation and strengths of association might have some error.

[10]Within the simulation these variances are set by setting the s parameter–see Footnote 5.

[11]In actual practice, when we want to set an aggregate variance in the ACT–R 4.0 simulation, we set one of σ_1^2 or σ_2^2 to a single σ^2 and the other to zero.

Relationship to Response Probability

When chunks in ACT–R fall below a threshold of activation τ, they can no longer be retrieved. Because of the stochastic volatility in activation levels, memory elements fall below this threshold for retrieval with a certain probability. Although in Monte Carlo simulations the activations either do or do not fall below threshold on a particular cycle, it is useful to have an equation that describes this probability. Given the assumption that the noise distribution is a logistic distribution, then the probability of a successful retrieval is:

$$\text{Probability} = \frac{1}{1 + e^{-(A-\tau)/s}} \qquad \textbf{Retrieval Probability Equation 3.7}$$

where τ is the threshold and $s = \sqrt{3}\sigma / \pi$ where σ^2 is the combined temporary and permanent variance in the activation levels. This equation

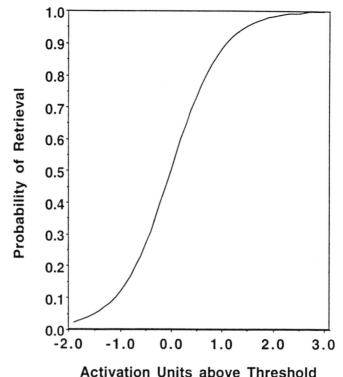

FIG. 3.5 Mapping of activation into probability of retrieval. This is based on the Retrieval Probability Equation 3.7 with $s = 0.5$.

implies a particularly simple formula for the odds of recall where odds = probability/(1 − probability): Odds = $e^{(A-\tau)/s}$. Thus, recall is an exponential function of the distance between activation level and the threshold. Figure 3.5 plots Equation 3.7 as a function of $(A - \tau)$ assuming a value of $s = .5$, which is a common value. It shows a sigmoidal function with probability being .5 when $A - \tau = 0$.

The Base-Level Equation 3.6 and the Retrieval-Probability Equation 3.3 can be combined to get predictions about retention functions. The A in Equation 3.7 is $\beta - d \ln t$ from Equation 3.6. Equations 3.6 and 3.7 can be transformed to express odds of recall as a power function of delay:

$$Odds = Ct^{-c}$$

where $C = e^{(\beta - \tau)/s}$ and $c = d/s$. Thus, ACT–R predicts that odds of recall

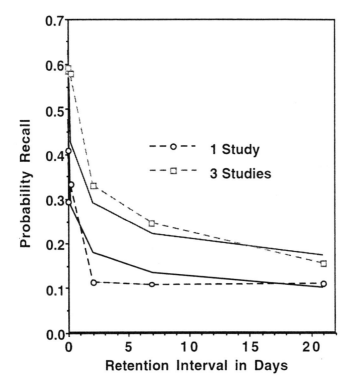

FIG. 3.6 Data from Runquist (1983) on the probability of recalling well-learned paired associates as a function of delay and number of studies. The straight lines are the predictions of ACT–R.

decrease as a power function of time. Rubin and Wenzel (1996) documented that the power function is one of a class of mathematical functions that describe retention functions over a wide range of domains.

As an illustration, we tried fitting an ACT–R model embodying this equation to the data of Runquist (1983), who looked at the probability of recalling paired associates at delays from 20 min to 21 days. The paired associates had either been studied one time or three times. The results are shown in Fig. 3.6. To fit this data, we estimated just the two parameters τ and s in the preceding equations, with the decay rate d fixed at .5 and $\beta = 0$.[12] Figure 3.6 displays the fit of ACT–R with parameter estimates $\tau = -3.37$ and $s = 1.75$. The overall correlation is .93 and ACT–R is capturing the basic forgetting functions.[13] The data itself appear a little noisy with some random nonmonotonicities in the retention curves.

Partial Matching

Items that fall below the retrieval threshold result in errors of omission. ACT–R can also produce errors of commission when it retrieves a chunk that only partially matches a production. In many domains, there are no exact matches and a system has to be prepared to accept the best matching memory—for instance, people's faces change and we need to still be able to recognize them; an object is often not quite where we saw it last but we still need to recognize it as what we are looking for, and so on. In order to give preference to perfect matches but not to totally disqualify partial matches, ACT–R subtracts from the activation level of an item an amount that reflects its degree of mismatch. ACT–R restricts the chunks it can partially match to those of the same type as specified in the production condition. Among the chunks of the specified type, all compete for a match to the production condition.

To explain partial matching, we need to complicate the analysis of how activation determines whether a chunk matches the condition of a production. The exposition to this point has assumed that this activation does not depend on the production. However, because of partial matching, the quantity that controls chunk retrieval is production-specific. This quantity is called the match score. It will differ from the general activation, A_i, to reflect the degree of mismatch, D_{ip}, between the chunk and the production condition. The match score for the match of chunk i to production p is:

---

[12]Different values of d and β would have just resulted in different values estimated values for τ and s.

[13]The effect of the extra study is to increase base-level activation, as is discussed in the next chapter.

$$M_{ip} = A_i - D_{ip} \qquad \textbf{Match Equation 3.8}$$

It is really this M_{ip} that should be used for the A in the Retrieval Probability Equation 3.7. In the case of a perfect match, $D_{ip} = 0$ and the match score is just the activation. Using this match score in Equation 3.7 creates the possibility that a chunk will be retrieved that only partially matches the pattern in the production condition.

The mismatch score D_{ip} is determined by the number of slots in which the chunk i mismatches the chunk pattern. ACT–R measures the difference between the values for each slot and then adds the differences together. Thus, it implements a city-block metric in judging the distance between a pattern and a potentially matching chunk.

Again, in actual simulations what ACT–R retrieves is determined by adding logistic noise to the activation and seeing what happens on a trial-to-trial basis. Still, it is useful to have closed-form solutions that describe the probability of a chunk being recalled. Using the approximation in Appendix A, the following equation describes (approximately) the probability of retrieving chunk i as a match to production p:

$$\text{Probability of retrieving } i \text{ for } p = \frac{e^{M_{ip}/t}}{\sum_j e^{M_{ip}/t}} \quad \textbf{Chunk Choice Equation 3.9}$$

where $t = \sqrt{6}\sigma / \pi = \sqrt{2}s$. This is basically the same as the Conflict Resolution Equation 3.4. As in that case, this is the Boltzmann "soft-max" rule, which tends to select the chunk with the highest match score, but which will sometimes select a lower-rated chunk because of noise. This is how partially matching chunks intrude and produce errors of comission.

Siegler and Shrager (1984) described an experiment where we can illustrate these partial-matching ideas at work. They asked 4-year-olds to retrieve the sums to various addition problems that had addends from 1 to 5. Partial matching involves misretrieval of chunks, and it is unclear whether all of these children had chunks for problem with addends greater than 3. Therefore, we only focus on the problems from $1 + 1$ to $3 + 3$. Table 3.1 reproduces the data for problems with addends from 1 to 3. The distribution of answers is given for each problem.

We simulated these data assuming that students had all the problems from $0 + 0$ to $5 + 5$ as possible answers to retrieve.[14] The critical production to be matched was:

---

[14]Because 5 + 5 is relatively distant for our largest problem 3 + 3, including it in the set or not has relatively little impact on the predictions.

IF the goal is to say what the sum of N_1 plus N_2 is
and $N_1 + N_2 = N_3$
THEN say N_3

This production could match any of the addition facts but there would be different match scores for different addition facts. Combining Equations 3.5 and 3.8 the match score was calculated as:

$$M = B + .5S_1 + .5S_2 - D$$

where B is the base-level activation, S_1 was the strength of association from the first addend and S_2 was the strength of association from the second addend. The mismatch, D, was calculated as:

$$D = \text{Penalty} * [\,|p_1 - f_1| + |p_2 - f_2|\,]$$

TABLE 3.1
Data from Siegler & Shrager (1984) and ACT-R's Predictions

Problem	*Data*									*Other Including Retrieval Failure*
	Answer									
	0	1	2	3	4	5	6	7	8	
1 + 1	—	.05	.86	—	.02	—	.02	—	—	.06
1 + 2	—	.04	.07	.75	.04	—	.02	—	—	.09
1 + 3	—	.02	—	.10	.75	.05	.01	.03	—	.06
2 + 2	.02	—	.04	.05	.80	.04	—	.05	—	—
2 + 3	—	—	.07	.09	.25	.45	.08	.01	.01	.06
3 + 3	.04	—	—	.05	.21	.09	.48	—	.02	.11
Predictions										
1 + 1	—	.16	.81	.03	—	—	—	—	—	.00
1 + 2	—	.01	.23	.69	.04	.01	—	—	—	.02
1 + 3	—	—	.01	.15	.77	.04	—	—	—	.02
2 + 2	—	—	.09	.14	.72	.02	—	—	—	.02
2 + 3	—	—	.01	.09	.18	.54	.08	.01	—	.09
3 + 3	—	—	—	.05	.08	.08	.66	.02	—	.11

where p_1 was the first addend in the problem, p_2 the second addend, f_1 the first addend in the fact, and f_2 the second. Thus, the sum of the absolute differences in the addends is multiplied by penalty, which is a parameter to be estimated.

To reflect the greater degree of practice and strength of facts with low addends, we set base-level activation (B) to be 1 for chunks that had a 1 or 0 addend, to be 0 for chunks with a 2 addend (and no lower addend), and to be −1 for chunks with only larger addends.[15] Chapter 9 on cognitive arithmetic shows that these are crude approximations to the base-level activations that ACT–R would learn, given the differential frequencies of these facts. The strengths of association were set to 1 in the case that the addend in the problem was part of the fact and 0 otherwise. We also set the activation threshold, τ, to 0. Thus, there were just two parameters estimated: s (the noise parameter) at .56 and penalty (the mismatch factor) at 1.30. As an example of the computations, consider the choice between chunks $1 + 1 = 2$ and $1 + 2 = 3$ as matches to a problem of $1 + 2 = ?$. The $1 + 1 = 2$ chunk would have a base-level activation of 1, the strength of association from "1" to the fact would be 2 because "1" appears twice in the fact, the strength from the "2" would be 1 because "2" appears as the answer, and the mismatch would be 1.30 because of the 1 unit mismatch between 1 and 2. Thus, its match score would be $1 + .5 * 2 + .5 * 1 - 1.30 = 1.20$. In contrast, consider the match to $1 + 2 = 3$. The base level would be 1, the strengths of associations for each addend would be 1 and there would be no mismatch penalty. Therefore, its match score would be $1 + 0.5 * 1 + 0.5 * 1 - 0 = 2.0$. The probability of retrieving $1 + 1 = 2$ rather than $1 + 2 = 3$ is determined by these match scores and the noise, which is controlled by the value of s of 0.56 in Equation 3.9. Thus, the probability of confusion between these two facts would be:

$$\frac{e^{1.20/0.56}}{e^{1.20/0.56} + e^{2.0/0.56}} = .19$$

In fitting the data, we had to consider the probability that each fact would be selected. Thus, the sum in the denominator involved 36 terms for the 36 facts from $0 + 0$ to $5 + 5$ rather than just the 2 terms given earlier. This reduces the .19 in the above equation to .16. The total probability of a spurious 2 response was .23, summing over all ways of retrieving 2 ($1 + 1 = 2$, $0 + 2 = 2$, $2 + 0 = 2$). Table 3.1 reproduces the predictions of the model. The predictions of the model correlate at .969 with the data,

---

[15]The exact difference among these strengths is irrelevant, as it can be compensated for by different estimates of the noise parameter s.

indicating that the model is picking up the major trends in the data with just estimating two parameters. This analysis is just an illustration of the potential of ACT–R to model a complex pattern of error data using the ideas of activation threshold and partial matching. Chapter 9 on cognitive arithmetic will elaborate on these ideas at great length.

Relationship to Latency

The activation (and more directly the match score) of a chunk also plays a critical role in determining the other basic dependent variable in cognitive research—latency of response. The chunks in a production rule are re-trieved one after another; and the total retrieval time is just the sum of the individual retrievals. Thus, the retrieval time for production p is:

$$\text{Retrieval time}_p = \sum_i \text{Time}_{ip}$$

where the summation is over the times, Time_{ip}, to retrieve the individual chunks i that have to be retrieved for production p. In point of practice, usually only a single chunk needs to be retrieved in a production and thus, the retrieval time is just the time for that chunk.

The following equation that describes the time to retrieve a chunk as a function of its match score M_{ip} and the strength, S_p, of the matching production:

$$\text{Time}_{ip} = Fe^{-f(Mi_p + S_p)} \qquad \textbf{Retrieval Time Equation 3.10}$$

where F is the latency scale factor and f is a factor scaling the match score and production strength. The time is thus an exponential function of the sum of the match score (and less directly the activation) of the chunk and the production strength.[16] We often work with the simplification that the production strength is 0 and only deal with the match score. As Appendix B discusses, there is reason to suppose that the parameter f is 1, in which case the critical expression simply is Fe^{-M}. F is a latency scale parameter

---

[16]In Appendix B to this chapter, we discuss some mechanistic realizations of this exponential function. As we develop in Appendix A, because of the distribution in the underlying activations, there is a distribution in times. The mean time bears an exponential relationship to mean activation level, but it is larger than predicted by the preceding equation by a constant multiplication factor. The parameter F that we estimate, assuming no variation in the activation levels, will be larger than the true F by this multiplication factor. However, it does not change any of our predictions.

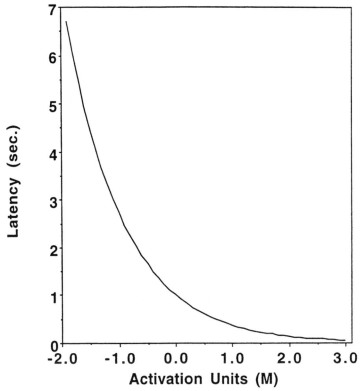

FIG. 3.7 Mapping of match scores into latency of retrieval. This is based on Retrieval Time Equation 3.10 with latency factor $F = 1$ sec, latency exponent $f = 1$, and production strength $S_p = 0$.

representing the time to retrieve a chunk when M is zero. If M is less than 0 (and negative activations are certainly possible in ACT–R) the latency will be greater than F, and if M is more than zero, it will be less than F. Because the equation is an exponential function, time will decrease ever more slowly as M becomes more positive and it will increase ever more rapidly as M becomes more negative. Figure 3.7 illustrates this function in the case that the latency scale F is 1 sec and the latency exponent, f, is the default 1. The existence of a retrieval threshold prevents retrieval times from becoming unboundedly long because low M values just result in retrieval failure. If τ is the activation threshold, the time for a retrieval failure will be $Fe^{-f(\tau+S_p)}$. For instance, if τ and S_p are 0, then the time for retrieval failure would be 1 sec in the case of Figure 3.7.

TABLE 3.2
Examples of Experimental Material in the Fan Experiment of Anderson (1974)

Material Studied	Target Probes	Foil Probes
A hippie is in the park.	3-3. A hippie is in the park.	3-1. A hippie is in the cave.
A hippie is in the church.	1-1. A lawyer is in the cave.	1-3. A lawyer is in the park.
A hippie is in the bank.	1-2. A debutante is in the bank.	1-1. A debutante is in the cave.
A captain is in the park.	—	2-2. A captain is in the bank.
A captain is in the church.	—	—
A debutante is in the bank	—	—
A fireman is in the park		—
A lawyer is in the cave.		
—		
—		
—		

The Fan Experiment

These assumptions about latency can be illustrated with respect to the research on the "fan effect" (Anderson, 1974, 1983). This research has played an important role in the development of the ACT theories, and it is important to show that ACT–R 4.0 can account for the phenomena involved in the fan effect. See Anderson and Reder (in press) for a thorough discussion of the application of the ACT–R model to fan data. This subsection reviews just enough to describe the effect and establish how the effect falls directly out of basic ACT–R assumptions.

Let us consider the first fan study by Anderson (1974) in which subjects studied facts such as "A hippie is in the park." The structure of the facts is illustrated in Table 3.2. As can be seen, the experiment manipulated the number of facts studied about the person and the location. "Fan" refers to the number of facts studied about a concept and the fan was varied from 1 to 3 orthogonally for both person and location. Subjects were drilled on the material to the point where they knew the material quite well, and the interesting results concerned the speed with which they could perform a recognition task based on the material that they had memorized. The results of the experiment in terms of latency to recognize the targets and to reject foils (which were recombinations of persons and locations) are displayed in Table 3.3. There are three main effects in this experiment. The first two are that latency increases with number of facts studied about person and

TABLE 3.3

Observed Times (in Seconds) to Accept Targets and Reject Foils
Data from Anderson (1974), with Predictions of ACT-R in Brackets

Facts About Location	Targets, Facts About Person			
	1	2	3	Mean
1	1.11	1.17	1.22	1.17
	[1.08]	[1.14]	[1.18]	[1.13]
2	1.17	1.20	1.22	1.20
	[1.14]	[1.22]	[1.27]	[1.21]
3	1.15	1.23	1.36	1.25
	[1.18]	[1.27]	[1.33]	[1.26]
Mean	1.14	1.20	1.27	1.20
	[1.13]	[1.21]	[1.26]	[1.20]
Facts About Location	Foils, Facts About Person			
	1	2	3	Mean
1	1.20	1.22	1.26	1.23
	[1.22]	[1.27]	[1.31]	[1.27]
2	1.25	1.36	1.29	1.30
	[1.27]	[1.32]	[1.36]	[1.32]
3	1.26	1.47	1.47	1.40
	[1.31]	[1.36]	[1.39]	[1.35]
Mean	1.24	1.35	1.34	1.31
	[1.27]	[1.32]	[1.35]	[1.31]

number of facts studied about location. The third is that subjects are generally slower to reject foils. The fan effect refers to the fact that latency increases with number of facts studied about a concept in a probe. In ACT theories, this has always been attributed to the decrease in associative strength with fan. This is also the mechanism by which ACT–R 4.0 accounts for the fan effect.

In the ACT–R 4.0 model the sentences were encoded as chunks with slots pointing to person, location, and the relation "in" (see Fig. 3.8). The strength of association to the chunk from a concept like *park* will decrease with the number of associations emanating from *park*. The actual ACT–R model for this task also includes production rules for performing such subtasks as encoding of the sentence and generation of a response. However,

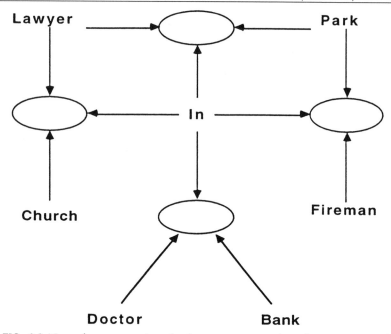

FIG. 3.8 Network representations for four sentences used in the experiment of Anderson (1974). The sentences are *The doctor is in the bank; The fireman is in the park; The lawyer is in the church;* and *The lawyer is in the park.* Ovals represent facts encoding these sentences, and the words represent concepts that are potential sources of activation.

these things are constant across all of the conditions of the experiment. The latency differences result from the retrieval of the proposition to match the probe. The critical productions for implementing this retrieval are the following ones:

Retrieve-by-Person
       IF   the goal is to retrieve a sentence involving a person and
                   a location
              and there is a proposition about that person in some location
       THEN   consider that person and location as the retrieved pair

Retrieve-by-Location
       IF   the goal is to retrieve a sentence involving a person and
                   a location
              and there is a proposition about some person in that location
       THEN   consider that person and location as the retrieved pair

Mismatch-Person
       IF   the retrieved person mismatches the probe
       THEN   say no

Mismatch-Location
    IF   the retrieved location mismatches the probe
  THEN   say no

Match-Both
    IF   the retrieved person and location both match the probe
  THEN   say yes

The basic scheme is to either retrieve a proposition involving the person (**Retrieve-by-Person**) or a proposition involving the location (**Retrieve-by-Location**). If the other term mismatches (detected by either **Mismatch-Person** or **Mismatch-Location**) then one rejects the probe; if it matches (**Match-Both**) one accepts the probe. This might seem a vulnerable scheme because one might retrieve (in the case of fan being greater than 1) some other proposition involving the term and then falsely reject the probe. However, if there is a target, it will be more active because it receives activation from both terms (person and location) and therefore will be retrieved in preference to a mismatching proposition.[17]

An alternative and simpler production system might seem to be the following:

Retrieve
    IF   the goal is to retrieve a sentence involving a person and
             location
            and there is a proposition involving both that person and
             location
  THEN   say yes

Fail
    IF   the goal is to retrieve a sentence involving a person and
             location
  THEN   say no

with **Fail** production given a lower value in the conflict resolution so that it only fires after the **Retrieve** production times out and so fails. This is a poorer solution because one would have to wait a long time for the **Retrieve** production to time out and so foils can only be rejected slowly. The first scheme can reject foils faster because it does not have to wait until retrieval failure. Thus, it is the preferred solution in paradigms like the fan effect where subjects are trying to maximize response speed.

---

[17]This is a variation of a logic suggested in the fan simulation on the disk that accompanied Anderson (1993).

In deriving predictions for this experiment, we ignore production strength (equivalent to assuming production strengths of 0)[18] and assume only correct matches are retrieved. In this case, we can predict latencies as a function of chunk activations and ignore the match scores. Let us first consider the activation predictions in the case of targets. The time to perform this retrieval will depend critically on the activation received from the person and location. Let S_{person} be the strength of association from the person and $S_{location}$ the strength of association from the location. The expected activation will be:

$$A_{target} = B + \frac{1}{3}S_{person} + \frac{1}{3}S_{location}$$

where B is the base-level activation. The $^1/_3$ values are in the equation because the person and the location will both receive a third of the source activation. The other third of the activation goes to the preposition *in*, and we assume it has such a high fan that its contribution is negligible. The activation in the case of foils will be either:

$$A_{foil} = B + \frac{1}{3}S_{person} \quad \text{if } \textbf{Retrieve-by-Person} \text{ applies}$$

or

$$A_{foil} = B + \frac{1}{3}S_{location} \quad \text{if } \textbf{Retrieve-by-Location} \text{ applies}$$

The response latency will be:

$$I + Fe^{-A}$$

where I reflects the time for all of the nonretrieval productions plus the action latency for the retrieval production. This assumes a latency exponent, f, of 1.

The critical quantities in accounting for the fan effect are the associative strengths, S_{person} and $S_{location}$. Using the Prior Strength Equation 4.2 (see discussion of strengths of association there), we set these to be $S - \ln(fan)$ where fan is the fan of that concept and S is an estimated constant. As noted earlier, this reflects the fact that the probability of a chunk, given a cue, decreases as that cue is associated with more chunks. Thus, the fan effect falls directly out of the statistical character of activation and strengths in the ACT–R theory.

We estimated three parameters in fitting this model. The intercept parameter I was estimated at .85 seconds, the time-scale parameter F at 0.61 seconds, and S at 1.45. We did not estimate a separate base-level activation,

---

[18]The predictions for this experiment do not depend on this simplifying assumption or the others that we introduce.

B, because its estimate is confounded with the estimate of the time scale F. Thus, we arbitrarily set the base-level activation B to be 0.

Table 3.3 gives the resulting predictions. The model does a good job of capturing the size of the fan effects and the relationship between targets and foils. The fan effect results because less activation spreads to the chunk from the high-fan source, and the target-foil difference results because two sources activate targets and only one source activates foils. The model fits the relative size of the fan effect compared to the target-foil effect. Note also that the size of the fan effect is predicted to be relatively similar for targets and for foils. Equal-sized fan effects have been difficult to accommodate in other models because the natural assumption was that responding negatively required an exhaustive search, which would be particularly slowed by fan. The current model avoids the need for exhaustive search in order to respond negatively. Also, the current model is the first theory that accounts for the differences between targets and foils without estimating an additional parameter. Foils are slower in the current model because a mismatch involves retrieving a less active fact, which only overlaps on one concept with the probe.

Retrieval Failure

A production can be selected requesting a retrieval, but that retrieval can fail resulting in a failure of the production. As noted earlier, the time to register a failure would be determined by the threshold, τ, for activation:

$$\text{Time for retrieval failure} = Fe^{-f(\tau + S_p)}$$

As illustrated in Fig. 3.1b, this retrieval failure time would be added to the total time to fire a production in that cycle. Such situations are relatively rare because productions that tend to lead to failed retrieval are biased against in conflict resolution because of their low probability of success (q, because the production failed to match) and high cost (a, because there was this wait for retrieval failure). Just as in the fan experiments, people frequently retrieve a basis for lack of knowledge. Thus, rather than wait for retrieval failure when asked what the capital of Zambia is, a person might retrieve the fact that they do not know much about African countries and so, just respond "don't know." The one occasion where subjects are likely to try retrieval is when asked a question about a domain for which they feel they should know the answer. Reder (1988) reported that subjects are slowest to say "don't know" to questions about domains with which they are most familiar, even though they are fastest to answer the questions they can about these domains.

Frequently, when subjects fail to retrieve something they do not give up but rather they have some backup strategy for finding the answer. The relationship between direct retrieval and backup computation has been studied at some length in the area of cognitive arithmetic, which has contrasted subjects' tendency to retrieve versus compute answers to arithmetic problems. Presented with a particular addition or multiplication fact, a subject has the option of retrieving it or calculating it. Reder (1987), Reder and Ritter (1992), Schunn, Reder, Nhouyvanisvong, Richards, and Stroffolino, (1997) and Siegler (1988) have argued that subjects make adaptive decisions in choosing to retrieve in those cases where retrieval is most likely to succeed and that they base their retrieval decision on the level of activation of the elements. Reder has argued that the decision to retrieve can be influenced by the past history of success with retrieval and that if more things have been retrieved one is more likely to choose retrieval. Siegler has argued that subjects are more likely to choose retrieval in the context of problem features where there has been a greater history of retrieval success.

SUMMARY

ACT–R 4.0 delivers on the promise of production systems to provide detailed and direct accounts of the performance structure of human cognition. Behavior takes place as a sequence of production firings. In each production firing, it is possible to identify three discrete stages:

1. Conflict Resolution: A production is selected that matches the goal and that has the highest evaluation relative to other productions that match the goal. The variability and distribution of choices made can be described by a single equation (Conflict Resolution Equation 3.4).
2. Declarative Retrieval: The transformations produced by the productions are determined by the chunks retrieved. The speed of these retrievals (Retrieval Time Equation 3.10) is determined by the activations of the chunks (Activation Equation 3.5) and their degree of match (Match Equation 3.8). The choice between alternative chunks is described by an equation similar to that used in the conflict-resolution stage (Chunk Choice Equation 3.9).
3. Production Execution: The production cycle concludes with the execution of the production. The time for this is determined largely by the amount of motor involvement. Chapter 5 and particularly Chapter 6 will discuss motor processes at great length.

Each of these stages is determined by a number of continuous-valued quantities stored with the chunks and production rules. The function of the next chapter, in part, is to describe how these subsymbolic quantities are learned through experience.

APPENDIX A

In many situations we are interested is in the maximum of a number of noisy distributions. The maximum of a set of such distributions (normal, logistic or many others that range from $-\infty$ to $+\infty$) converges to what is sometimes called the Gumbel distribution (Johnson, Kotz, & Balakrishhnan, 1995).

$$f(x) = \frac{e^{-(x-m)/s}e^{-e^{-(x-m)/s}}}{s}$$

Where m is the mode of the distribution and the mean is

$$\mu = m + \gamma s$$

where γ is Euler's constant and is approximately 0.577. The variance is

$$\sigma^2 = \frac{\pi^2}{6}s^2$$

Figure 3.9 displays some distributions for various values of m and s. As can be seen, these distributions are bell shaped but somewhat skewed to the right of their mode. The parameter m determines their location and the parameter s determines their width.

The extrema of many distributions that go from $-\infty$ to $+\infty$ converge on such a distribution. In the case of the normal-like logistic distribution,

$$f(x) = \frac{e^{-x/s}}{s(1+e^{-x/s})^2}$$

The extreme of v random variables from such a distribution converges to the distribution just given with the s parameters the same and $m = s \ln(v)$.

There are a number of attractive properties of these distributions. For instance, suppose we are interested in the maximum of n such distributions with location parameters m_1, m_2, ..., m_n but all with the same shape parameter s. The location parameter of this distribution will be:

$$m = s \cdot \ln(e^{m_1/s} + e^{m_2/s} + \ldots + e^{m_n/s})$$

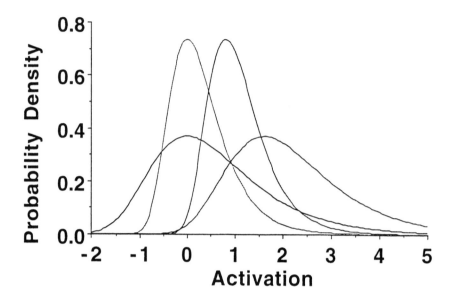

FIG. 3.9. Examples of Gumbel noise distributions assumed. The wide distributions have $s = 1$ and the narrow distributions have $s = 0.5$. For the narrow distributions, the left has $m = 0.0$ and the right $m = 0.8$. For the wide distribution, the left has $m = 0.0$ and the right has $m = 1.6$.

with shape parameter still s. Thus, the distribution of the maximum is just shifted to the right. If we are interested in the probability that the ith will be the highest, this probability is given by:

$$P(i) = \frac{e^{m_i/s}}{\sum_j e^{m_j/s}}$$

which, as the main chapter noted, is the same as the Boltzmann equation specifying the probability of being in state i with energy m_i, given temperature s. Although the equation is the same, the situation it describes is different. The Boltzmann equation describes the probability of being in one of a number of mutually exclusive states, whereas this describes the probability of one of many current alternatives being maximum. There is no conception of an extremum distribution in the Boltzmann situation.

This distribution can be converted into a Weibull distribution under the transformation:

$$t = Fe^{-fx}$$

which is the relationship proposed in the Retrieval Time Equation 3.10 between latency (t) and activation (x). The Weibull distribution has been proposed as a distribution of reaction times and especially the fastest of a set of processes that are racing against each other (Logan, 1988).

The Weibull density is:

$$g(t) = \tfrac{v}{\beta} t^{v-1} e^{-t^v/\beta}$$

It is related to the Gumbel density by the following transformation of parameters:

$$v = 1/fs$$

$$\beta = \frac{F^{1/fs}}{e^{m/s}}$$

Thus, ACT–R's assumption about noise in activation can be seen as supporting a Weibull distribution of resulting latencies. The mean and variance of the Weibull distribution are:

$$\mu = \beta^{1/v} \Gamma(1 + \tfrac{1}{v})$$
$$\sigma^2 = \beta^{2/v} [\Gamma(1 + \tfrac{2}{v}) - \Gamma^2(1 + \tfrac{1}{v})]$$

where Γ is the gamma function. Note that in terms of f and F (which characterize the latency transformation) and m and s (which characterize the activation distribution),

$$\mu = Fe^{-fm} \, \Gamma(1 + fs)$$

which is to say the expected latency is a multiplicative factor $\Gamma(1 + fs)$ larger than if there was not a distribution of activation.

If the product of f and s is 1, the Weibull density simplifies to an exponential density:

$$g(t) = \beta e^{-t/\beta}$$

where

$$ß = Fe^{-m}$$

Such a distribution has numerous analytical advantages. Although overall reaction times do not satisfy an exponential distribution, they are the sums of many events of which the exponentially distributed retrieval is only one. Such a sum of randomly distributed times might well look like the observed latency distributions, which are more normal in appearance.

We tend to favor $f = 1$, and $s < 1$, in which case the product of f and s is less than 1 and the v parameter of the Weibull is greater than 1. In this case, the individual retrievals tend to have a distribution more like behavioral latencies, as noted by Logan (1988).

Appendix B

The latency function in ACT–R is:

$$\text{Time} = Fe^{-fA} \qquad \textbf{Retrieval Time Equation 3.10}$$

There are two ways to conceive of the mechanism behind the latency function.

Rational Analysis Model

The origin of this latency function is the rational analysis of memory (Anderson, 1990; Anderson & Schooler, 1991). This analysis assumed memories were serially searched in the order of their likelihood of being needed. The latency of retrieval was determined by how many memories with likelihood greater than the target memory would have to be considered first. That analysis still could apply in ACT–R if we consider it to be searching through chunks in order of activation levels (which can be thought of as log likelihoods). To understand how this would work in ACT–R, it is necessary to make a distinction between the activation level, A_i, of a chunk i before it is considered for a match to a chunk and its match score, M_i, after any mismatch penalty is subtracted.[19] Suppose chunks are considered in order of their A_i looking for one of the largest M_i. Thus, it is quite possible that a number of chunks of higher A_i are be considered before the chunk with the largest M_i is accepted. The basic algorithm is described as follow:

1. Select chunk of next highest A_i.
2. Calculate its M_i.
3. If M_i is largest so far make it the target chunk.
4. If there is no chunk with A_i greater than the target's M_i select the target. Otherwise go back to step 1.

In the case where the target chunk is a perfect matching chunk, this algorithm will progress through all the partial-matching chunks with greater activation and stop at the target chunk. Thus, the critical factor determining latency factor is the number of partial matching chunks with activation greater than that of the target. In the case where the target chunk is a partial-matching chunk, this algorithm will also progress through any

---

[19]Because all the chunks matching to a production share the same strength production, we can ignore the contribution of production strength to match score.

chunks with greater A_i (but lesser M_j) than the target M_i before stopping.

The critical question concerns the distribution of A_i and the number that are greater than the target M_i. Anderson and Schooler assumed that the odds of memories would be distributed according to *Zipf's law*, which is a distribution of the frequency of items as a function of their values. Simon and Ijiri (1977) suggested that Zipf's law takes the form:

$$f(x) = ax^{-m}$$

However, the current situation is concerned with distribution of activations that are like log-odds, rather than the odds distribution just mentioned. Transforming this distribution by the function $x = e^y$ yields the following distribution:

$$g(y) = ae^{-fy}$$

where $f = m - 1$. This is an exponential distribution with a possible nonzero minimum. The expected proportion of chunks with activation greater than M_i is:

$$\int_{M_i}^{\infty} ae^{-fx}dx = \frac{a}{f}e^{-fM_i}$$

If there are C potential chunks and each takes t seconds to inspect, then the expected time is:

$$Fe^{-fM_i}$$

where $F = aCt/f$. The preceding expression is the Retrieval Time Equation 3.10.

Ijiri and Simon noted that m is frequently 2 and this implies that f is 1. We typically adopt this convention to reduce the number of parameters and, as illustrated in Table 3.3, the quality of the fits is quite good, even with this constraint.

Neural Model

The model just described gives a serial characterization of the search process. Another way to conceive of it, more in keeping with ACT–RN (Lebiere & Anderson, 1993; see Chapter 12, this volume), would be as a process in which the activation of the target chunk grew until it completely dominated all of the competing chunks. A reasonable model of this growth process is as a rich-gets-richer process in which the rate of change of the activation was a function of its match score M_i. One plausible growth function would be to make the activation grow as an exponential function of the current activation:

$$A'(t) = ge^{fA(t)}$$

The reason for this, rather than the simpler proportional growth function $A'(t) = gA(t)$ is to assure that activation always increases whether it starts out negative or positive. The solution of this differential equation is:

$$A(t) = -\frac{1}{f}\log(e^{-fM_i} - fgt)$$

where M_i is the initial activation as specified by the Match Equation 3.8. According to this equation, the activation completely dominates (i.e., becomes infinity) when:

$$t = \frac{e^{-fM_i}}{fg}$$

which is again the Retrieval Time Equation 3.10 with $F = 1/fg$. More generally, the time for activation to reach any level L is:

$$t = Fe^{-fM_i} - Fe^{-fL}$$

Thus, Fe^{-fL} is a constant for threshold L that is subtracted from all retrieval times independent of initial level and could be absorbed into the production action latency.

Appendix C: Productions and Trace that Instantiate the Abstract Analysis in Fig. 3.1

Productions

P1 Reverse-Args

    IF   the goal is to multiply num1 and num2 and the answer is not known

            and num1 is smaller than num2

    THEN   change the goal to multiply num2 and num1

P2 Subgoal-Addition

    IF   the goal is to multiply num1 and num2 and the answer is not known

            and num1 is not smaller than num2

    THEN   set a subgoal to add num1 to num1 num2 times starting

P3 Add-Once

    IF   the goal is to add num1 to num2 x times and this has been done y times

            and the sum of num1 and num2 is num3

    THEN   change the goal to add num1 to num3

            and increment y by 1

P4 Add-Once-Reverse (non-default a = .2)

    IF   the goal is to add num1 to num2 x times and this has been done y times

            and the sum of num2 and num1 is num3

    THEN   change the goal to add num1 to num3

            and increment y by 1

P5 Pop-Addition

    IF   the goal is to add num1 to num2 x times and this has been done x times

    THEN   pop the goal with the answer num2

P6 Retrieve-Output

    IF   the goal is to multiply num1 and num2 and the answer is known

            but the output form has not been retrieved

            and the answer has output form x

    THEN   set the answer to x

P7 Multiplication-Solved
> IF   the goal is to multiply num1 and num2 and the answer is known
> and the output form x has been retrieved
>
> THEN   output the answer x

Trace

Matching production REVERSE-ARGS.
1 productions out of 1 considered; expected gain of chosen is: 18.950
Cycle 0 Time 0.000: REVERSE-ARGS
Matching latency: 0.000
Action latency: 0.050

Matching production SUBGOAL-ADDITION.
1 productions out of 1 considered; expected gain of chosen is: 18.950
Cycle 1 Time 0.050: SUBGOAL-ADDITION
Matching latency: 0.447
Action latency: 0.050
> Matching production ADD-ONCE.
> 1 productions out of 2 considered; expected gain of chosen is: 17.950
> Cycle 2 Time 0.547: ADD-ONCE
> Matching latency: 0.250
> Action latency: 0.050
> Matching production ADD-ONCE.
> Matching production ADD-ONCE-REVERSE
> 2 productions out of 2 considered; expected gain of chosen is: 17.800
> Cycle 3 Time 0.847: ADD-ONCE-REVERSE
> Matching latency: 1.387
> Action latency: 0.050
> Matching production POP-ADDITION.
> 1 productions out of 1 considered; expected gain of chosen is: 17.950
> Cycle 4 Time 2.285: POP-ADDITION
> Matching latency: 0.000
> Action latency: 0.050

Matching production RETRIEVE-OUTPUT.
1 productions out of 1 considered; expected gain of chosen is: 18.950
Cycle 5 Time 2.335: RETRIEVE-OUTPUT
Matching latency: 0.585
Action latency: 0.050

Matching production MULTIPLICATION-SOLVED.
1 productions out of 1 considered; expected gain of chosen is: 18.950
Cycle 6 Time 2.969: MULTIPLICATION-SOLVED
Matching latency: 0.000

Action latency: 0.050
The answer is 12

Top goal popped.
Run latency: 3.019
?

Appendix D: ACT–R's Variables and Parameters

α prior number of successes for Probability Learning Equation 4.5

A_i activation of chunk i; see Activation Equation 3.5

a expected cost of matching and firing a production, typically measured in seconds

assoc   weighting of prior strength in Posterior Strength Equation 3.1

β prior number of failures for Probability Learning Equation 4.5

B_i base-level activation of chunk i

b expected cost, measured in seconds, from the firing of a production to the resolution of the goal

C cost incurred with trying to achieve the goal if a particular production is selected, typically measured in seconds; see Cost of Goal Equation 3.3

d decay rate in Equations 4.1, 4.4, 4.7, and 4.8; given default value of 0.5

D_{ip} mismatch penalty for match of chunk i to production p.

ε_1 permanent noise in base-level activation

ε_2 temporary noise in base-level activation

E expected gain of a production; see Expected Gain Equation 3.1

f latency exponent in Retrieval Time Equation 3.11; given default value of 1.0

F latency scale factor in Retrieval Time Equation 3.11

G value of the goal

m total number of chunks in Prior Strength Equation 4.2

m number of experienced successes for Probability Learning Equation 4.5

M_{ip} match score for chunk i in production p

n number of associated chunks in Prior Strength Equation 4.2

n number of failures for Probability Learning Equation 4.5

P probability of the goal should the production be chosen; see Probability of Goal Equation 3.2

q probability of a production succeeding including matching of condition and achievement of subgoals

r probability of achieving the goal if the production succeeds

R_{ji} $e^{S_{ji}}$

S_{ji} strength of association between source j and chunk i

S_p production strength

s parameter controlling noise in ACT–R logistic noise distributions for utilities and activations; it is related to the variance of the noise distribution by the formula $\sigma^2 = \pi^2 s^2 / 3$

S estimated constant in setting S_{ji}—see discussion of strengths of association

t temperature used in Conflict Resolution Equation 3.4 and Chunk Choice Equation 3.9

τ retrieval threshold of activation in Retrieval Probability Equation 3.7

W_j attentional weighting of the source j in Activation Equation 3.5

z total prior cost for Cost Learning Equation 4.6

4

Learning

John R. Anderson
Christian Lebiere
Carnegie Mellon University

The previous chapter discussed how ACT–R can model human cognition, assuming that the person has a certain set of knowledge structures with a certain set of parameters. That chapter displayed some examples of the relatively high degree of precision in the predictions of ACT–R models. For purposes of expository simplification, the examples were rather small, but later chapters display more complex models. The success of ACT–R's performance models makes the topic of this chapter all the more compelling. How did that knowledge get in there in the first place? Performance models should be learnable.

Table 2.1 classified ACT–R's assumptions about learning into a 2 x 2 scheme that paralleled the 2 x 2 classification of the performance assumptions. One dimension is whether the assumptions are concerned with the acquisition of procedural knowledge or whether they are concerned with the acquisition of declarative knowledge. The other dimension is whether they are concerned with symbolic learning (the acquisition of the chunks and productions themselves) or whether they are concerned with subsymbolic learning (the acquisition of the parameters that govern the deployment of these knowledge elements). The four sections of this chapter address the topics defined by the four cells of this classification.

LEARNING OF CHUNKS

Classically, philosophers have proposed that there are two sources for knowledge—we can encode knowledge through our senses or create knowledge through our minds. Correspondingly, there are two sources for chunks in the ACT–R theory. First, they can be encoded directly from the environment. Chapters 5 and 6 describe ACT–R's perceptual component in more detail, but basically, when objects are attended to in the environment, ACT–R can synthesize representations of them in the form of chunks. The other way ACT–R can create chunks is in the action side of production rules. However, a significant restriction on ACT–R 4.0 over past theories is that the only chunks that productions can create are goal chunks.[1] These goal chunks essentially store the solutions to past problems. As discussed in Chapter 2, goal chunks become repositories for abstract knowledge, even as chunks from the environment become repositories for concrete knowledge.

ACT–R can recreate a chunk by moving attention again to the same object or by solving the same goal. However, ACT–R avoids creating of duplicate chunks. Rather, it merges the new chunk with the old. In the case of goal chunks, the decision to merge is made at the time the goal is popped. If the goal chunk is the same as an existing chunk when it is popped, it is merged with that chunk. The merged chunk is given a combined strength in accordance with the principles set forth in the third section of this chapter.

Addition-by-Counting Example

One of the classic and much-studied cases of knowledge growth is the acquisition of the addition table. Children at one point do not know their addition facts, but can solve addition problems by repeated counting because they know how to count. Repeated counting is one way to learn the addition facts, and it is believed that at least some children learn their addition tables by storing the results of repeated counting (Siegler, 1987; Zbrodoff, 1979). Chapter 9, on cognitive arithmetic, pursues modeling this transition in great detail, and this chapter describes a related problem in the third section. Here, we would like to describe it briefly as an example of learning goal chunks.

Table 4.1 provides English descriptions of the critical production rules that represent both the counting and the retrieval strategy. If the answer is stored, **Retrieve-Sum** will just retrieve the answer and say it. However, if it is not known, **Retrieve-Sum** will fail and **Subgoal-Counting** (which is lower valued in the conflict resolution because it has higher cost) will apply and set the goal to find the sum. The goal will be a chunk like:

```
Memory1
    isa FIND-SUM
    arg1 Three
    arg2 Two
    sum nil
```

---

[1] As in many cases, this is a restriction in theory rather than implementation. To facilitate user exploration in 4.0, we allow users to create any chunks they want in a production's right-hand side. The simulations corresponding to the models presented in this book tend to observe the restriction of creating only goal chunks. The chunk merging described in this chapter only applies to goal chunks and not to other chunks that might be created in the action of production.

TABLE 4.1

Productions to Implement an Addition by Counting

Retrieve-Sum
>   IF   the goal is to answer a question about the sum of n1
>   and n2 and n1 and n2 have been found to have a sum
>   THEN   make the goal to say the sum

Subgoal-Counting
>   IF   the goal is to answer a question about the sum of n1 and n2
>   THEN   set a subgoal to find the sum of n1 and n2
>   and make the goal to say the sum

Start-Count
>   IF   the goal is to find sum of n1 and n2
>   THEN   push a goal to increment n1 counting from zero to n2

Pop-Find-Sum
>   IF   the goal is to find the sum of n1
>   and n2 and it is found
>   THEN   pop the goal

Increment-Count
>   IF   the goal is to increment n1 counting from n3 to n2
>   and n4 is one more than n
>   and n5 is one more than n3
>   THEN   make the goal to increment n4 counting from n5 to n2

Stop-Count
>   IF   the goal is to increment n1 counting from n2 to n2
>   THEN   pop the goal with the answer n1

Say
>   IF   the goal is to say x
>   THEN   say x and pop the goal

---

where nil denotes that the sum has yet to be calculated. **Start-Count** will respond by setting up a process of counting up and **Increment-Count** counts up. Eventually, when **Stop-Count** pops the goal, it will store its result in the chunk that encoded the goal of finding the sum. That chunk will then be available to be retrieved next time. For example, the following is a run of this system faced with the goal of adding 3 + 2. It computes the answer by repeated counting:

Cycle 0: Subgoal-Counting
Cycle 1: Start-Count
Cycle 2: Increment-Count
Cycle 3: Increment-Count
Cycle 4: Stop-Count
Cycle 5: Pop-Find-Sum
Cycle 6: Say
  Five

The following is a second run and this time, it retrieves the answer:

Cycle 7: Retrieve-Sum
Cycle 8: Say
  Five

The following is the chunk that was created to represent the goal of finding the sum. The chunk then remained as a repository of the sum for the second episode:

Memory1
  isa FIND-SUM
  arg1 Three
  arg2 Two
  sum Five

where the sum has now been filled in with Five. This example is a little unrealistic in that it assumes a one-trial transition from computation to retrieval. The third section of this chapter and Chapter 9 on cognitive arithmetic go into greater detail about how gradual buildup of strength is essential for this chunk to be reliably retrieved.

Relationship to Other Learning Theories

The idea of storing goal chunks has strong relationships to a number of ideas already in the field. It has a clear relationship to chunking in Soar by which the results of computations are stored. In Soar, past computations are stored in terms of production rules, whereas in ACT–R, they are stored in terms of declarative chunks. However, as is discussed in Chapter 12, production rules in Soar do not really correspond to production rules in ACT–R, and often ACT–R's declarative chunks behave like Soar productions.

ACT–R can also be thought of as a production-system implementation of Logan's (1988) proposal of storing the results of computations. In Logan's theory, copies of the answer are kept and later problems can be answered by retrieving a copy fast enough to beat out computation. As more problems are encountered, more copies (in Logan's theory, not ACT–R) are stored. Assuming a variability in their speed of retrieval, the more copies there are, the more likely it is that the fastest retrieval will beat out computation. In ACT–R, just one chunk is created and that chunk is strengthened every time it is used or an attempt is made to create an identical chunk. However, in either system, the decision between computation and retrieval will be determined by whether the answer can be retrieved quickly enough.[2] It may take a number of practice trials before it is reliably retrieved in both systems. Later in this chapter, when we discuss subsymbolic learning, we describe an ACT–R simulation of this shift from computation to retrieval.

Both Reder (1988, 1996) and Siegler (1988, 1996) have theories where subjects decide between retrieving and computing answers. In Reder's theory, subjects assess the activation levels of declarative elements and decide to try to compute if the elements are not sufficiently active. However, the threshold for retrieval can be influenced by what she calls extrinsic factors. For instance, Reder has shown that subjects can respond to instructions or global base rates in deciding to retrieve. In Siegler's theory, subjects use both the past problem's history of retrieval success and general past success of the retrieval strategy in deciding whether to retrieve. Thus, in both models, subjects' decision to retrieve is influenced both by a particular item's strength and the general success of retrieval. ACT–R can reflect this mixture of efforts. Overall, history of retrieval success influences the relative utility of the compute production versus the retrieve production. Strength of the memory chunk determines the success of the retrieve production should it be tried first in the conflict resolution.

LEARNING OF PRODUCTIONS

Up to this point, we have always assumed models that start out with all of the production rules that they need. However, the rules used in these models had to be acquired somewhere in the subject's experience. One of the significant challenges for a production system has been to come up with an adequate theory of production rule learning. Only two production systems have floated serious proposals: ACT and Soar. Although Soar has stayed with its one chunking mechanism, ACT has had a history of various proposals for production-rule learning.

---

[2]This is true in ACT–R as long as the retrieval production is preferred in conflict resolution.

Past ACT Mechanisms for Learning Production Rules

A major dimension in the evolution from ACT* to ACT–R was a change in the process by which production rules were learned. In ACT* (Anderson, 1983), there were no less than four basic mechanisms for production-rule learning. These were:

1. Discrimination. If a rule successfully applied in one situation and did not in another situation, variants of the rule would be generated by adding condition elements that restricted the productions to the appropriate situations.
2. Generalization. If two rules were similar, a generalized production was produced by either deleting condition elements or replacing constants by variables.
3. Composition. If there was a sequence of rules that applied in a situation, a new single rule could be formed that performed all the actions of the sequence.
4. Proceduralization. If a rule retrieved some information from declarative memory and used this information to instantiate an action to be performed, a variant of the rule could be created that eliminated the retrieval and just performed the instantiated action.

The basic motivation for these learning procedures was the observation that people became more tuned in their application of knowledge (discrimination), generalized their knowledge (generalization), came to skip steps in procedures (composition), and eliminated retrieval of declarative knowledge (proceduralization). Although there are indisputably such behavioral trends, there were at the time no data to test whether these specific ACT* mechanisms captured the actual way these general functions were achieved. The ACT* learning mechanisms really constituted a research proposal, and we went out and did experiments trying to find detailed evidence of their existence. We found ample evidence for the production rule as the unit of skill acquisition (Anderson, 1987; Anderson, Conrad, & Corbett, 1989; Singley & Anderson, 1989), but we generally failed to find any evidence for these mechanisms of production formation. It would be too strong to say our research disconfirmed these learning mechanisms because their behavioral consequences were underspecified. It would be accurate to just say that we usually failed to find positive evidence for them.

The one exception to the lack of behavioral evidence came in our work on a model of category learning (Anderson, Kline, & Beasley, 1979). The ACT* model of categorization conceived of production rules as reflecting various categorization rules. For instance, production rules might be learned of the form:

> IF   the goal is categorize a stimulus
>   and it is a red circle
> THEN   it is in category 1

The process of category learning was modeled by ACT* discrimination and generalization mechanisms. For instance, the feature test for red could be eliminated (generalization) or a test for size could be added (discrimination). Although the ACT* production-rule model still gives good accounts of many categorization phenomena, it suffers from at least one fatal flaw. That is, it places this knowledge in procedural form, so the knowledge cannot be flexibly used. Thus, the rule just given would give no basis for going from the fact that a circle is in category 1 to a prediction of its color. In contrast, subjects trained to categorize have been shown to be capable of displaying their knowledge flexibly (Anderson & Fincham, 1996; Heit, 1992). This flexibility suggests that categorization behavior in ACT–R depends on declarative knowledge. This is an idea we have started to pursue in ACT–R 4.0 (Anderson & Betz, 1997). The history of this effort illustrates the moral that just because phenomena exist (generalization and discrimination), it does not follow that they should be embedded in production-learning mechanisms.

The lack of empirical evidence for the ACT* production-learning mechanisms is one of the reasons for our abandonment of them. A second reason was frequent problems with their computational misbehavior. Because they were automatic learning mechanisms, they would "kick in" many times and produce unwanted production rules. This phenomenon of excessive production-rule formation has also been a problem with the chunking mechanism in Soar, which is another automatic mechanism for creation of production rules.

The third reason for abandoning the ACT* production-rule learning mechanisms is that our studies of skill acquisition made salient a phenomenon that really had no explanation in ACT*. In our studies of how subjects acquired new procedures, we saw that they gave a lot of attention to how specific problems were solved and seemed to learn from examples (e.g., Anderson, Farrell, & Sauers, 1984; Pirolli & Anderson, 1985). For instance, Anderson (1993) described how a student learned to make LISP arithmetic function calls from observing that typing (+ 712 91) into LISP resulted in the sum 803 being printed. By analogy, the student induced the general rule that any arithmetic computation could be accomplished by typing left parenthesis, operator, operands, and right parenthesis. After observing how prevalent learning from examples was, ACT–R was given a general learning mechanism in which production rules were created in the process of problem solving by analogy to examples.

The experience with the analogy learning mechanism has been somewhat more successful than with the ACT* production-learning mechanisms. In particular, researchers have been able to get their ACT–R models to learn the production rules needed to perform complex problem-solving tasks (Blessing & Anderson, 1996; Taagten, 1997; Wallach, 1997). The analogy mechanism in ACT–R 2.0 involved the following steps:

1. At some point in time, a declarative knowledge structure (set of chunks) was created to represent the understanding of a step in a problem-solving task.
2. At another point in time, when a similar problem-solving state was reached, this declarative structure could be retrieved and used as a basis for analogy. Two searches are evoked at this point. The first was among past examples to serve as the source of the analogy. For each example considered, a second search was conducted among the different ways of making a correspondence between the past example and the current problem.
3. Analogy was an architectural primitive that created a production rule to represent ACT–R's understanding how the example applied to the current situation. This production rule was then available for later use if needed without re-analogy. However, it had to be strong enough to fire.
4. If a production rule was not strong enough to fire, it had to be re-analogized. It would be strengthened and eventually become available. Anderson and Fincham (1994; Anderson, Fincham, & Douglass, 1997) provided evidence for this gradual appearance of production rules.

Although ACT–R 2.0 analogy seemed a step forward, it was not without its problems. These problems were with respect to Steps 1 and 2 in its specification. With respect to Step 1, the mechanism was not able to create the full range of productions. Also, analogy created productions that were of the ACT–R 2.0 scale, and these were increasingly out of character with the smaller grain size ACT–R 4.0 productions.

With respect to Step 2, the analogy mechanism remained somewhat out of control—a problem that had haunted the earlier ACT* learning mechanisms. For one thing, it would occur when not needed and so still had the problem of promiscuously creating production rules. For another thing, many times it had problems finding the right example. Furthermore, it became harder to integrate this step in the serial ACT–R 4.0 conflict-resolution scheme than it was in the parallel ACT–R 2.0 scheme.

Production Compilation

To resolve the problems we had with controlling analogy, we finally decided to cut the Gordian knot and simply eliminated the troublesome Step 2. In Step 1 a specific goal (called a *dependency* goal) is created to understand a problem-solving step. Now, when this goal is popped, a production rule is automatically compiled from the dependency structure. This rule is available for later uses but, as before, it may take some recreations before it is strong enough to fire reliably.

This created a naming dilemma for us with respect to continuing to call this learning mechanism "analogy." As *analogy* is typically used in cognitive science, it refers to larger scale mappings like the ones done in ACT-R 2.0 productions and not the atomic mappings of ACT-R 4.0 productions. Second, as *analogy* is typically conceived, it involves making a correspondence between a past example and a current problem. By deleting Step 2, we had eliminated this correspondence phase. Thus, the term *analogy* seemed misleading at best, and we have now chosen to call the ACT-R 4.0 production-learning mechanism *production compilation*, which seems more appropriate. Chapter 10, on analogy to examples, discusses how this production-compilation mechanism fits in with what the cognitive science field studies under the label of *analogy*.

The current formulation of production compilation reflects the newest idea in ACT-R 4.0, finalized just as the theory is going to press. As such, it is necessarily the most tentative. However, the reports we have been getting from our users have been uniformly positive. They find it much more workable than the earlier analogy mechanisms.

The current formulation of production compilation permits a variant of our answer to a long-standing criticism of the ACT theories of procedural learning. Both in ACT* and ACT-R, new production rules ultimately derive from declarative knowledge. Conversion from declarative to procedural knowledge was achieved by the proceduralization mechanism in ACT*, by the analogy mechanism in ACT-R 2.0, and now by the production-compilation mechanism in ACT-R 4.0. This general transition from declarative to procedural knowledge has been called *knowledge compilation* in the ACT theories. There is a line of research that is often viewed as challenging this ACT assumption that procedural knowledge originally comes from declarative knowledge. This is research that has shown that people can acquire procedural knowledge, but are unable to acquire the corresponding declarative knowledge for various reasons including amnesia (e.g., Cohen, Eichenbaum, Deacade, & Corkin 1985), drug administration (e.g., Nissen, Knopman, & Schacter, 1987), or because the structure of the task is obscure (e.g., Broadbent, Fitzgerald, & Broadbent, 1986).

There is nothing inherently contradictory to ACT–R in the fact that a subject can use production rules to perform a skill without being able to report the declarative origins of these rules.[3] This is because the declarative origins may be forgotten by the time of the report. For instance, amnesiacs can rehearse declarative instructions and examples for short periods of time. Indeed, Phelps (1989) argued that for amnesiacs to learn many tasks, they need to be given special support in retaining such information for the short term.

However, in ACT–R 2.0, this general response was somewhat weakened because there was this Step 2 where a past example had to be retrieved. Similarly, in ACT*, the proceduralized knowledge had to be initially part of long-term memory. Thus, the argument became that the declarative knowledge was temporally retained but subsequently forgotten. In contrast, in ACT–R 4.0 production compilation, the production rule is created immediately upon popping the dependency goal—hence, at zero delay. So, the need is eliminated to maintain the declarative information even over a minimal delay.

To describe ACT–R 4.0 production compilation in detail, it is necessary to describe the special declarative structure from which productions are compiled. These are chunks of type DEPENDENCY and represent a person's understanding of a particular step in a problem-solving episode. A *dependency* is created when a person sets a goal to understand a bit of an example or instruction. When this dependency goal is popped, a production rule is induced from the dependency and added to the production system. The process of creating a production rule has some subtleties. The next two subsections go through the details of the dependency structure and the subtleties in production rule creation. A final subsection demonstrates how production compilation can model behavior in an experimental task.

Inducing Productions From Dependency Structures

In Chapter 2, the fourth section outlined the six basic kinds of production rules in ACT–R that were defined in terms of the goal transformations they produced. ACT–R can create these six possible types of production rules by understanding steps of problem solution that represent these different kinds of goal transformations. It creates a goal to represent the dependencies in a particular problem-solving step. That is, it chooses, as a goal, to reflect on the problem solution. If this goal is successfully achieved and popped, a production will be compiled (in addition to the dependency which remains

---

[3]However we want to withhold judgment about what is the best ACT–R model for each of these demonstrations.

as a declarative structure). For example, Table 4.2 gives a DEPENDENCY chunk, Example, encoding a student's understanding of a step in a multi-column addition problem. This is the step where the two numbers are added. The student has filled in its goal slot with Goal1, which is the state of the ADD-COLUMN goal before the sum is retrieved, its modified slot with

TABLE 4.2

Dependency, Chunks, and Resulting Production for Multicolumn Addition
from Table 2.2

Example
  isa DEPENDENCY
  goal Goal1
  modified Goal2
  constraints Fact34

Goal1
  isa ADD-COLUMN
  number1 Three
  number2 Four
  answer nil

Goal2
  isa ADD-COLUMN
  number1 Three
  number2 Four
  sum Seven

Fact34
  isa ADDITION-FACT
  arg1 Three
  arg2 Four
  sum Seven

Add-Numbers
  =goal>
    isa ADD-COLUMN
    number1 =number1
    number2 =number2
    sum nil
  =addition-fact>
    isa ADDITION-FACT
    arg1 =number1
    arg2 =number2
    sum =sum
  ==>
  =goal>
    sum=sum

Goal2, which is the state of the goal after the retrieval, and the constraints slot with the critical addition fact, Fact34. On popping this dependency subgoal, ACT–R not only stores this dependency chunk, but also creates the production rule, **Add-Numbers**, at the bottom of the table.

The production rule learned in Table 4.2 is quite a bit more general than the example and will add any two numbers. It achieves this abstraction by the introduction of variables. Thus, the production rule is more than a simple restatement of the dependency. ACT–R will variabilize any chunk that occurs in two or more slots anywhere in the condition or in the action. The assumption is that these co-occurrences are not accidental but indicate a general rule. Thus, it transforms the Three, Four, and Seven in the examples into =number1, =number2, and =sum in the production. It also variabilizes items that are names of chunks specified in the production. Thus, Fact34 becomes =addition-fact in the production rule in Table 4.2. Although there are no examples of this in Table 4.2, any terms that just appear once as a slot value in a single chunk are left as constants. The assumption here is that the rule must be specific to these terms.

The ability to go from a specific example to a general rule reflects an inductive leap on the part of ACT–R. It is worth analyzing the assumptions by which ACT–R chooses to variabilize an example. Although the basic principle is just to variablize repeating terms, one can discriminate three subcases of repeating terms:

1. The first case is when the variable (like =sum in the example) appears both in the condition and the action of the production rule. This case of variabilization goes back to the PUPS theory of analogy (Anderson & Thompson, 1989) and was given a rational analysis in Anderson (1990). Lewis (1988) reported an empirical investigation of this variabilization rule and it appears to be the default behavior of people in many situations. For instance, if to achieve the goal of deleting the word *dog* from a text one types *e dog*, the natural inference is that typing *e x* will delete any word *x*. That is, one assumes both that the first element must be *e* and that the second element can be variabilized. In ACT–R terms:

```
=goal>
  isa DELETE
  word =word
==>
=subgoal >
  isa TYPE
  first e
  second =word
```

This is because *dog* appears both in the condition and the action, but *e* only appears in the action. The underlying logic is that the slot role of the item in the action (not its identity) is what achieves its slot role in the goal. That is, the appearance of =*word* in the second slot of =*subgoal* is what achieves its role in the word slot of =*goal*. This logic does not apply to elements that only appear once, like *e*.

2. The second case is when the variable (like =*number1* and =*number2* in the example in Table 4.2) appears in multiple condition chunks (usually the goal and some retrieval chunk). As in the earlier example, they usually serve as part of the bridge between the goal and the action (in the case in Table 4.2, the bridge goes from =*goal* to =*number1* and =*number2* through =*fact* and then to =*sum*, which also appears in the action). Thus, this case is really just an extension of the configural assumption that underlies Case 1. Note that the chunk head =*addition-fact* is variabilized too, so that it can participate in this bridging pattern.

3. The third case, not illustrated in Table 4.2, but illustrated later in Table 4.3, is that the variable appears in multiple goal chunks in the action. The assumption here is that this is a mechanism for passing results from the first goal called to the next through the subgoal return mechanism.

The basic principle that unifies these three subprinciples for variabilization is that the terms being variabilized appear in multiple chunks.[4] This notion of variabilizing the connecting elements is similar to the variabilization principle used in Soar. It is impressive how often these default variabilization rules work. This success suggests that ACT–R's default variabilization rules have captured an inductive primitive of the mind. However, as with any inductive principle, there will be occasions where they will produce the wrong rule, and the next subsection, includes a discussion of how to deal with these occasions.

Special Slots of the Dependency Structure

An important function of a dependency structure is to encode what goal manipulations are involved in the example. Four slots specify various aspects of the goal transformation. As the dependency structure in Table 4.2 illustrates, the goal slot holds what the goal was like before the problem-solving step. The constraints slot holds chunks that serve as the bridges from condition to action and become retrieval patterns in the compiled rule. The modified slot holds what the changed goal looks like (if there has been a

---

[4] It is also the case that a variable will be introduced if the same term appears in multiple slots of the same chunk. In this case, it serves as a test for identity of the slots.

TABLE 4.3
Dependency, Chunks, and the Resulting Subgoal-Count
Production from Table 4.1

Example1
  isa DEPENDENCY
  goal Goal3
  modified Goal4
  stack Goal5

Goal3
  isa ANSWER-QUERY
  arg1 Two
  arg2 Four
  relation Sum

Goal4
  isa SAY
  arg Six

Goal5
  isa FIND-SUM
  arg1 Two
  arg2 Four
  sum Six
  count Zero

Subgoal-Counting
  =goal>
    isa ANSWER-QUERY
    arg1 =arg1
    arg2 =arg2
    relation Sum
    answer nil
==>
  =subgoal>
    isa FIND-SUM
    arg1 =arg1
    arg2 =arg2
    sum =sum
    count Zero
  =subgoal1>
    isa SAY
    arg =sum
  !focus-on! =subgoal1
  !push! =subgoal

TABLE 4.4
Dependency, Chunks, and the Resulting Pop-Find-Sum Production
From Table 4.1

Example2
  isa DEPENDENCY
  goal Goal6
  modified Goal6
  stack Success

Goal6
  isa FIND-SUM
  arg1 Two
  arg2 Four
  sum Six

Pop-Find-Sum
  =goal>
    isa FIND-SUM
    arg1 =arg1
    arg2 =arg2
    sum =sum
  ==>
    !pop!

---

change). The stack (not illustrated in Table 4.2) slot indicates any changes to the goal stack in terms of pushes and pops: If the value of the stack slot is a goal chunk, then that goal is pushed as a subgoal, if the value is Success, the current goal is popped with success; if the value is Failure, the current goal is popped with failure. The dependency structure in Table 4.3, which results in the creation of the production **Subgoal-Counting** (from Table 4.1), illustrates the simultaneous use of the modified slot and the stack slot. Table 4.4, which results in the creation of the production **Pop-Find-Sum** (also from Table 4.1), illustrates the use of Success in the stack slot.[5] Note that a !pop! appears in the resulting production.

ACT–R can learn all and only the six sensible production possibilities that were identified in the fourth section of Chapter 2. These six basic productions were classified in a 2 x 3 scheme, according to whether they modified the goal or not and whether they involved no change to the stack, a push, or a pop. The modified slot of the dependency structure specifies the first dimension, whereas the stack slot specifies the second dimension.

---

[5] Note all the slots in the goal of **Pop-Find-Sum** are variabilized. This is because they appear implicitly in the action as slot values of the unchanged goal.

TABLE 4.5
Dependency, Chunks, and the Resulting Multiply-Zero Production

---

Example3
  isa DEPENDENCY
  goal Goal7
  modified Goal8
  specifics Zero

Goal7
  isa CALCULATE-PRODUCT
  arg1 Five
  arg2 Zero
  product nil

Goal8
  isa CALCULATE-PRODUCT
  arg1 Five
  arg2 Zero
  product Zero

Multiply-Zero
  =goal>
    isa CALCULATE-Product
    arg1 =arg1
    arg2 Zero
    product nil
  ==>
  =goal>
    product Zero

Four other slots, generals, specifics, don't-cares, and differents, are needed because sometimes the default rules for variabilization are not appropriate. As an example of the issue of variabilization consider a student learning the mathematical rule that $X * 0 = 0$. Table 4.5 gives an example where it is necessary to use the specifics slot. (Note that the example asserts that 0 is specific and so prevents it from being variabilized.) Without this information, the following incorrect production rule would be learned because Zero and Five appear both in Goal7 and Goal8:

Multiply-Zero
  =goal>
    isa CALCULATE-PRODUCT
    arg1 =arg1
    arg2 =arg2
    product nil
  ==>
  =goal>
    product =arg2

in which the Zero has been variabilized (as $=arg2$) because it occurs in both Goal7 and Goal8. To assure that Zero remains a constant in the resulting rule, the dependency lists the Zero in its specifics slot. Note, however, that the Five is appropriately variabilized as $=arg1$ (because it appears unchanged as a slot in both Goal7 and Goal8 and does not appear in the specifics slot).

The generals and dont-cares slots achieve the opposite function of the specifics slot. If something appears just once in the condition, it would normally have been left as a constant in the resulting production. However, if it appears in the generals slot, it will be variabilized, whereas if it appears in the dont-cares slot, it will be omitted. The difference between variabilization and omission is that the empty slot value nil cannot match to a variable. Therefore, omitting the test altogether (dont-cares) makes the condition even more general.

The final slot is the differents slot. It allows ACT–R to encode that it is critical that one item be different from another item. Table 4.6 illustrates a dependency structure with the constraint that six not be one.[6] The learned production retrieves a factorization of a number subject to the constraint that the first term of the factor not be one.

The constraints, specifics, generals, dont-cares, and differents slots reflect facilities for directing production compilation in a way that was not possible in ACT–R 2.0. They reflect places where the instruction that accompanies examples can direct what is learned. They also reflect where people's knowledge of the semantics of the domain (e.g., what it means to multiply by zero) can influence what is learned. We would expect that, in the absence of instruction or background knowledge, people would induce the default form of the ACT–R rules.

An Example of Production Compilation

Reflecting the looser sense of modeling in earlier versions of ACT–R, there have not been detailed models of how ACT–R 2.0 analogy was involved in the moment-by-moment execution of experiments. One of the lessons we have learned is the need to compare proposed mechanisms closely with data. This production compilation mechanism, being new and still somewhat tentative, does not have an abundance of correspondences to data. However, researchers are starting to develop models that involve production compilation in the detailed accounting of empirical results. Chapter 10, on

---

[6] Note that there is a list here. DEPENDENCY chunks are the only case in ACT-R where lists are processed as arguments. Although not illustrated in Tables 4.2–4.6, one can have lists in the stack, specifics, generals, dont-cares, differents, and constraints slots, in which case all the elements are processed.

Example4,
  isa DEPENDENCY
  goal Goal9
  modified Goal10
  constraints Six*four
  difference (Six One)

Goal9
  isa FACTOR
  arg Twenty-Four
  prod1 nil
   prod2 nil

Goal10
  isa FACTOR
  arg Twenty-Four
  prod1 Six
  prod2 Four

Six*four
  isa MULTIPLICATION-FACT
  arg1 Six
  arg2 Four
  product Twenty-Four

Non-Trivial-Factor
  =goal>
    isa FACTOR
    arg =arg
    prod1 nil
    prod2 nil
  =multiplication-fact>
    isa MULTIPLICATION-FACT
    arg1 =arg1
    arg1 One
    arg2 =arg2
    product =arg
==>
  =goal>
    prod1 =arg1
    prod2 =arg2

learning by analogy to examples, contains a fairly elaborate application. This subsection describes a simpler application by Niels Taatgen (see Taatgen, 1997, for an earlier model) to a classic experimental paradigm in psychology, which is the contrast between reversal-shift and extradimensional-shift problems (Kendler & Kendler, 1959).

In these experiments, subjects have to classify stimuli that vary on two dimensions such as size (large or small) and color (red or green). Initially, one dimension is relevant—for instance, all red objects might be positive and all green objects might be negative. After the subject has reached the criterion of 10 consecutive correct classifications, the reinforcement scheme changes. In the reversal-shift condition, the values switch on the same dimension—for instance, green will now be positive and red negative. In the extradimensional shift, the other dimension now becomes relevant—for instance, large objects might be positive and small objects negative. Young children typically find extradimensional shifts easier and older children and adults find reversal shifts easier.

Table 4.7 shows some results from Kendler and Kendler illustrating the classic pattern with children (58 to 72 months in age) classified according to their learning rate. The slower learners find reversal shifts harder, whereas the faster learners find the extradimensional shifts harder. The table also shows the results from Taatgen's ACT–R simulation. In the case of the slow-learning simulation, ACT–R created separate production rules for each of the four stimuli (large-red, small-red, large-green, small-green). In the reversal-shift condition, it had to learn four new rules to reverse the answer to all stimuli because the classification for all four changes. On the other hand, in the extradimensional shift condition it only had to learn two new rules because only two stimuli change. Thus, for the slow-child model the reversal-shift condition is easier because it involves learning only two rules. The exact process by which these new rules came to dominate the old rules depended on conflict-resolution learning, which we describe in the fourth section of this chapter. For now, we are more interested in the process by which the rules are created.

TABLE 4.7
Results and Taatgen's Simulation (in parentheses) of Kendler and Kendler (1959): Mean Number of Trials to Criterion of 10 Correct Classifications

	Type of Shift	
	Reversal	Extradimensional
Fast child	6 (6.4)	15.8 (18.2)
Slow child	24.4 (23.2)	9.0 (11.3)

TABLE 4.8
Critical Knowledge Elements in Simulating the Slow Child in the
Kendler and Kendler (1959) Experiment

(a) Critical Rule
Build-Dependency
  =goal>
    isa DEPENDENCY
    modified =end-goal
  =end-goal>
    isa GEN-GOAL
    prop1 =p1
    prop2 =p2
    answer =answer
  ==>
  =start-goal>
    isa GEN-GOAL
    prop1 =p1
    prop2 =p2
  =goal>
    goal =start-goal
    specifics (=p1 =p2)
  !pop!
(b) Declarative Structures
  Dependency1
    isa DEPENDENCY
    goal Start-goal1
    modified Cat-goal1
    specifics (Small Green)
  Cat-goal1
    isa GEN-GOAL
    prop1 Small
    prop2 Green
    answer No
  Start-goal1
    isa GEN-GOAL
    prop1 Small
    prop2 Green
    answer nil
(c) Resulting Production
Gen-Goal1
  =goal>
    isa GEN-GOAL
    prop1 Small
    prop2 Green
    answer nil
  ==>
  =goal>
    answer No

Table 4.8 shows the critical elements of this process in the case of a model for the slow child. When the simulation makes an error, it pushes a goal to learn a new production to represent the correct mapping. This goal is of type DEPENDENCY and it is passed in its modified slot the goal with the study stimulus correctly classified. Production **Build-Dependency**, given in Part (a) of Table 4.8, represents a rule for completing the dependency. The production creates =*start-goal*, which represents the goal before the answer was filled in, places this in the goal slot of the dependency, and notes that the resulting rule has to be specific to the values in the property slots. Part (b) of Table 4.8 shows an example of the completed dependency, Dependency1, with the modified goal, Cat-goal1, and the original goal, Start-goal1, which the production created. Part (c) of Table 4.8 shows the production, Gen-Goal1, that results when this dependency is popped. It is a rule for classifying a small green stimulus.

The production rules that are learned for the fast-child model focus on a single dimension. This focus enables the model to learn faster, initially because it only has to learn two rules—one for each value of the critical dimension. Successful practice in using one dimension inclines the system to use that same dimension to learn new rules when the old rules no longer apply after the subject is transferred from the original condition. This gives the reversal-shift condition the advantage. This tendency to stick with the same dimension depends again on conflict–resolution learning. However, for current purposes, the important observation is that the model again learns new productions by this process of creating and completing a dependency. It is just that the fast-child model has a different procedure for completing the dependency than the slow-child model. The slow-child model thinks rules should be specific to particular examples, whereas the fast-child model thinks rules should be specific to dimensions.[7] This difference illustrates the idea that dependencies reflect understanding of a problem-solving step and different subjects can have different understandings. Others (e.g., Chi, Bassok, Lewis, Reimann, & Glaser, 1989) have proposed that the difference between good and poor learners can be explained in terms of how they understand examples.

LEARNING OF DECLARATIVE PARAMETERS

To this point, we have discussed how new symbolic structures are learned. However, as the previous chapter discussed, the actual behavioral realization of these structures depends very much on the subsymbolic parameters associated with them. This section discusses the learning of declarative

---

[7]The exact pattern of simulated predictions in Table 4.7 depends on the conflict resolution process and in particular on the estimated noise in this process. For a more detailed understanding of this, the reader is encouraged to inspect the running model on the Web.

parameters, and the next section discusses the learning of procedural parameters. These subsymbolic parameters in ACT–R are estimates of probabilities of events and costs of actions. ACT–R's learning of these parameters is really a statistical estimation of the probabilities and costs. Therefore, ACT–R's subsymbolic learning is sometimes called *statistical learning*.

The declarative parameters associated with chunks determine their level of activation. There are two declarative parameters that the system learns: the base-level activations of chunks and the strengths of associations among chunks. In both cases, "learning" really comes down to using past experience to estimate the quantities that these parameters are supposed to reflect. The activation of a chunk is taken to reflect the log posterior odds that the chunk will be needed (*needed* means "match to a production in the next cycle"), given the current context (where the current context is defined by the elements of the goal). In Bayesian terms, if H_i is the hypothesis that chunk i is needed and E are the elements in the current context, then the posterior odds of needing chunk i in the current context is:

$$\frac{P(H_i|E)}{P(\overline{H}_i|E)} = \frac{P(H_i)}{P(\overline{H}_i)} \prod_{j \in E} \frac{P(j|H_i)}{P(j|\overline{H}_i)}$$

where the multiplication reflects the assumption that the conditional probabilities are independent. The quantity $P(H_i|E)/P(\overline{H}_i|E)$ is the posterior odds, the quantity $P(H_i)/P(\overline{H}_i)$ is the prior odds, and the quantities $P(j|H_i)/P(j|\overline{H}_i)$ are the likelihood ratios.

The odds formula just shown is given in multiplicative terms. However, it is natural to think of activations as adding. Because the logarithmic transformation converts multiplication into addition, we think of activation as reflecting log odds. More precisely, the activation A_i of a chunk is an estimate of the log posterior odds $\ln[P(H_i|E)/P(\overline{H}_i|E)]$, the base-level activation B_i is an estimate of the log prior odds $\ln[P(H_i)/P(\overline{H}_i)]$, and the strength of association S_{ji} is an estimate of the log likelihood ratio $\ln[P(j|H_i)/P(j|\overline{H}_i)]$. This yields the equation given earlier:

$$A_i = B_i + \sum_j W_j S_{ji} \qquad \textbf{Activation Equation 3.5}$$

where W_j is the attention that can be given to source j.[8] The next subsec-

---

[8] The term W_j can be thought of as reflecting the validity of cue j. Lovett, Reder, and Lebiere (in press) have also suggested that it reflects the capacity of an individual to attend to a cue. In any case it is not subject to learning as are the quantities B_i and S_{ji}.

tions discuss the learning of the two quantities, B_i and S_{ji}, and the general evidence for this conception of their learning.

Before discussing these, it is worthwhile to be precise about what H_i is. This is the hypothesis that the chunk i will be used in the next production cycle. A successful use is counted as occurring whenever a chunk is retrieved by a production that actually fires. A successful use is also counted as occurring each time an identical copy of the chunk is created. As noted in the first section of this chapter, ACT–R does not maintain multiple copies, but rather reflects repetition by increasing the strength of a single chunk.

Learning of Base-Level Activations

Each chunk has a base-level activation, B_i, which reflects some context-independent estimate of how likely that chunk is to match to a production. This depends on the frequency and recency with which that chunk has been used. Precisely, it is an estimate of the log odds that an item will be used. Anderson and Schooler (1991), in a series of environmental studies, showed

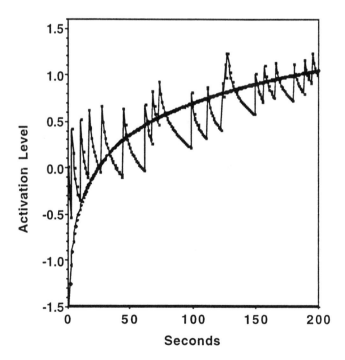

FIG. 4.1 Growth in strength when 20 presentations are randomly presented over 200 sec. The smooth curve is the prediction of the approximation formula.

that the odds that an item will be needed are related to its history of past exposure by the formula:

$$\text{Odds} = a \sum_{j=1}^{n} t_j^{-d}$$

where a is a scaling constant and the item has been encountered n times in the past at lags $t_1, t_2, \ldots, t_n$ from the present. This means that the formula for base-level activation should be:

$$B_i = \ln(\sum_{j=1}^{n} t_j^{-d}) + \beta \qquad \textbf{Base-Level Learning Equation 4.1}$$

where $\beta = \ln(a)$ and typically gets absorbed in the estimates of other parameters. Figure 4.1 shows the growth of B_i, assuming 20 encounters randomly scattered over the first 200 sec. In this function, $\beta = 0$ and $d = 0.5$, which are the default values in ACT–R. As can be seen, the function slowly grows, although it shows some decay from presentation to presentation.

The Base-Level Learning Equation has a number of interesting consequences. First, if there has been a single presentation t time units ago, then base-level activation will simply be $\beta - d \ln(t)$, which is the earlier Base-Level Equation 3.6. As discussed in Chapter 3, this combined with the response functions implies that odds of recall and latency of recall should be power functions of delay, which is the common empirical result known as the Power Law of Forgetting (Rubin & Wenzel, 1996). Second, it is less obvious, but the Base-Level Learning Equation also predicts the Power Law of Learning (Newell & Rosenbloom, 1981). If the n presentations in that equation are spaced approximately evenly, the quantity Σt_j^{-d} is closely approximated by $nT^{-d}/(1 - d)$ where T is the total life of the unit (i.e., the time since its creation at time $T = t_1$). This means the activation is closely approximated as $\ln[n/(1 - d)] - d \ln T$. The smooth line on Fig. 4.1 shows the prediction of this function given the default $d = 0.5$ and $n = 0.1T$, which is the average number of presentations by time T if 20 are spread out uniformly over the 200 sec. Combined with ACT–R's response assumptions, this predicts the Power Law of Learning for the dependent measures of latency and odds of recall.

An issue concerns specification of the lags of encounter, the t_j terms in the Base-Level Learning Equation 4.1. There were two ways a chunk could be encountered, and each way has its own definition of t_j:

1. It can be created or merged. If it is encoded from the environment, it is created at the moment when attention moves to the object that this chunk encodes. It can be recreated and merged into the original chunk if attention moves to that object again. The lag t_j for this is measured from when attention moves to the object. If it is a goal chunk, the first t_1 is measured from when the goal was created. If a subsequent goal chunk is merged with it, the t_j is measured from the time of the merging.

2. It is matched to the condition of a production that fires. In this case, the t_j is measured from the time at the start of the cycle when the pattern matching began.

An Example of Base-Level Learning

The preceding subsection described how declarative chunks can gradually accrue base-level activation with practice. Thus, as facts are practiced, they can come to be more and more reliably retrieved. The consequences of this gradual accrual of base-level activation are nicely illustrated in a recent experiment by Zbrodoff (1995). The first section of this chapter discussed a simple addition model that would either retrieve an addition fact (e.g., 3 + 4 = 7) or compute an addition fact by counting. It is difficult to study such variation in adult subjects because they tend to know their addition tables. Therefore, Zbrodoff used an alphabet arithmetic task developed by Logan and Klapp (1991) where people do addition on the alphabet—for example, C + 4 = G, because G is 4 past C in the alphabet sequence. Her task involved subjects judging the validity of such alphabet arithmetic problems. She manipulated whether the addend was 2, 3, or 4 and whether the problem was true or false. She had 2 problems of each of the 6 (3 x 2) kinds for 12 problems. She also manipulated the frequency with which problems were studied in sets of 24 trials. In the control condition, each of 12 problems occurred twice per set of 24 problems. In the standard condition, the +2 problems occurred three times, the +3 problems twice, and the +4 problems once.[9] In the reverse condition, the +2 problems occurred once, the +3 problems twice, and the +4 problems three times. Each block of her experiment involved eight repetitions of these sets of 24 problems. There were three blocks for 576 problems in all.

Figure 4.2 presents the data from her experiment as a function of the addend separately for each block (curves within panels) and for each condition (across panels). As can be seen in the control condition, subjects take longer to solve the larger addend problems, times decrease with

---

[9] This is called the standard condition because it appears in the real world that small-addend problems are more frequent than large-addend problems (Hamann & Ashcraft, 1986; Thorndike, 1922).

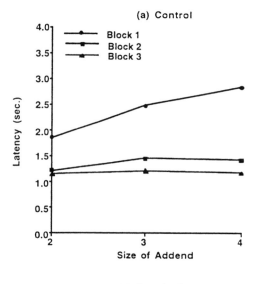

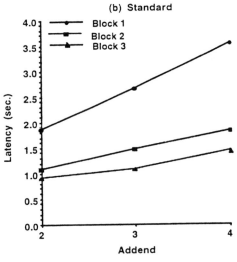

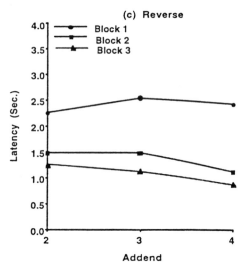

FIG. 4.2 Data from Zbrodoff (1995) showing the effect of addend and practice on judgment time: (a) control condition (b) standard condition, and (c) reverse condition.

126

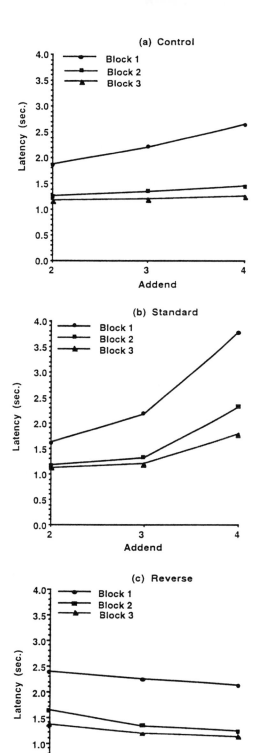

FIG. 4.3 Simulation of data from Zbrodoff (1995) showing the effect of addend and practice on judgment time: (a) control condition (b) standard condition, and (c) reverse condition. Compare with Fig. 4.2.

127

practice, and the addend effect diminishes with practice. In the standard condition, the addend effect is magnified compared to the control condition. In the reverse condition, the effect is diminished and even reversed with enough practice. Zbrodoff explained this data by assuming that subjects initially solve these problems by a counting algorithm that produces the addend effect. With enough practice, they come to store the answer and the critical variable becomes how much practice that answer has had.

We simulated these data assuming the computation-versus-retrieval model described earlier (in the first section of this chapter). Basically, the model used the same production set as in Table 4.1, except that when counting or retrieval was done, the answer was compared with the problem and a "yes" or "no" answer was given. Thus, if the activation of the target fact was above threshold, subjects would respond by retrieval. Otherwise, they would count. In this model, practice has two effects on response time. First, it increases the probability of retrieval thus, bypassing computation. Second, it decreases the time to perform the retrieval.

We fitted the model to the 27 data points in Fig. 4.2. Our intuition was that the result largely depends on computation switching to retrieval. Therefore, we set all the timing parameters at a default of 1 sec (these timing parameters were time to count up by one, intercept, and retrieval scale factor F). We just tried to find values of the threshold parameter τ and activation noise parameter, s, that yield the best transition from computation to retrieval (see Retrieval Probability Equation 3.7). These values were $\tau = 2.27$ and $s = 0.66$. The value of s is consistent with other estimates.[10] The overall R^2 was .90, which is good considering that just two parameters were estimated. Figure 4.3 presents the predictions of the theory from running 500 simulated subjects in each condition. It produces the same basic trends as are seen in the data (Fig. 4.2).

This experiment nicely illustrates the potent effects of practice on retrieval. Subjects switched in this experiment from exclusive reliance on computation to nearly exclusive reliance on retrieval. Although it was this switch that produced the largest effect on latency, practice also had a large effect on the relative retrieval times. Comparing extremes, the mean time with which subjects performed the retrieval decreased from about 100 msec in first block of the low-frequency conditions (once per problem set for 8 presentations by block's end) to about 10 msec in the third block of the

---

[10] The value of τ is a bit hard to interpret unless one gets into the details of base-level activation and associative strengths for this experiment (see the end of Chapter 7 for a detailed discussion of the relationship between the threshold and activation levels), but it can basically be thought of as defining the best fitting 50th percentile between computation and retrieval given all the other parameters.

high-frequency conditions (three times per problem set for 72 presentations by block's end).

More generally, Chapter 7, on list memory, reports how these assumptions about base-level learning lead to accurate predictions about human memory. The rises and falls on base-level activation, illustrated in Fig. 4.1, serve to capture much of the volatility of human memory. Chapter 9 presents a much more extensive application of ACT–R to the phenomena involved in cognitive arithmetic. That model involves not just base-level learning, which was used in this Zbrodoff simulation, but also associative learning, described in the next subsection.

Learning of Associative Strengths

The strength of association from a cue j to a chunk i adjusts the base-level activation of the chunk to reflect how probable the chunk is in the context of the cue. The associative strengths, S_{ji}, are supposed to estimate a log likelihood ratio measure of how much the presence of j in a goal slot increases the probability that i is needed. For example, the $4 + 8 = 12$ fact (see Figs. 3.1 and 3.4) becomes much more likely when 4 is in the goal. To specify how ACT–R estimates S_{ji} requires introducing some new notation. Let C_j represent the event that j is in a goal slot and N_i represent the event that i is needed. Then, for the Activation Equation 3.5 to calculate log posterior odds, S_{ji} should be an estimate of the log conditional probability ratio $\log(P(C_j|N_i)/P(C_j|\overline{N}_i)$ where $P(C_j|N_i)$ is the probability that j is present in the goal, given that chunk i is needed and $P(C_j|\overline{N}_i)$ is the probability that j is present, given that i is not needed. ACT–R approximates this ratio by $R_{ji} = P(C_j|N_i)/P(C_j) = P(N_i|C_j)/P(N_i)$ which is a measure of how more or less probable i is in the context of j than its base probability. This approximation can be justified by the observation that conditionalizing the presence of j on the absence of needing just one chunk i will change $P(C_j|\overline{N}_i)$ little from $P(C_j)$ because there are so many chunks. Adopting this approximation for analytic convenience, this subsection discusses how to calculate S_{ji}. For expository convenience, we discuss how to calculate the quantity before the logarithmic transformation. That is, we discuss how to calculate R_{ji} where $S_{ji} = \ln(R_{ji})$.

On the creation of a new chunk, i, the R_{ji} are set to default prior strengths R_{ji}^* that reflect guesses as to what the strengths of association should be. The value of R_{ji}^* will depend on whether j is connected to i in declarative memory. It is considered to be connected if j appears as a slot value element in chunk i. Thus, for example, 4 is connected to the chunk encoding that $4 + 8 =$

12. Otherwise, they are considered unconnected. If they are unconnected, $R_{ji}^* = 1$ (or equivalently $S_{ji} = 0$), which reflects the assumption that i is no more or no less likely in the presence of j than its base probability. If they are connected, the strength depends on the ratio between n, the number of chunks connected to j, and m, the number of chunks in declarative memory. As a default, it is assumed that $P(N_i|C_j) = 1/n$ (i.e., all chunks connected to j are equally likely when j is present) and $P(N_i) = 1/m$ (i.e., all facts in declarative memory are equally likely). Thus,

$$R_{ji}^* = (1/n)/(1/m) = m/n$$

$$S_{ji}^* = \ln(m/n) = \ln(m) - \ln(n) \qquad \textbf{Prior Strength Equation 4.2}$$

With experience, one gathers evidence about what the true probabilities are. The empirical proportions are $P_e(N_i|C_j)$ and $P_e(N_i)$ and are estimated from frequency counts F. $P_e(N_i|C_j)$ is defined as $F(N_i \& C_j)/F(C_j)$ where $F(N_i \& C_j)$ is the number of times i has been needed when j is present in a goal slot and $F(C_j)$ is the number of times j has been present in a goal slot. Similarly, $P_e(N_i)$ is empirically defined as $F(N_i)/F(i)$ where $F(N_i)$ is the number of times i is needed and $F(i)$ is the number of production firings since i was created. R_{ji} is a weighted combination of the prior estimate, R_{ji}^*, and the empirical ratio, $E_{ji} = P_e(N_i|C_j)/P_e(N_i)$. A typical Bayesian solution to such estimation problems is to take a weighted average of the prior (weighted by some constant assoc) and the empirical value (weighted by the number of observations $F(C_j)$):

$$R_{ji} = \frac{\text{assoc}*R_{ji}^* + F(C_j)E_{ji}}{\text{assoc} + F(C_j)} \qquad \textbf{Posterior Strength Equation 4.3}$$
$$S_{ji} = \ln(R_{ji})$$

This is the same equation that was used in ACT–R 2.0.

Equation 4.3 implies the fan effect, which has played a major role in other ACT theories and was discussed in the previous chapter. The fan effect refers to the fact that the time to retrieve trace i given a component j increases as the number of memories associated to j increases. A typical fan experiment might manipulate the number of facts (i terms) a subject studies about a fictitious person (j) and observe an impact on speed in recognizing any fact. The number of facts studied will increase n in the Prior Strength Equation 4.2 and so lower R_{ji}^*. Similarly, as more facts are studied about a person, any one will be less probable when the person appears. This lowers $P_e(N_i|C_j)$ and so E_{ji}.

Research on the fan effect has shown that with practice, the critical variable in determining latencies becomes the probability ratio, E_{ji}, and not fan, R_{ji}^* (Anderson, 1976, p. 287; Anderson & Reder, in press). For instance, suppose that two facts are learned about the *hippie* and one of them is "The hippie is in the park" and four facts are learned about *lawyer* and one of them is "The lawyer is in the bank." Initially, subjects are faster to retrieve the two-fan *hippie* fact than the four-fan *lawyer* fact because there is only one interfering fact. This follows from the Prior Strength Equation 4.2 where n is the differential fan. However, suppose only one third of the time when a fact about *hippie* is tested it is the "hippie in park" fact and the other two thirds of the time the other *hippie* fact is tested. In contrast, suppose half the time when a *lawyer* fact is tested, it is "lawyer in bank." Then, the *lawyer* fact comes to be retrieved more rapidly. According to the Posterior Strength Equation 4.3, this is because the particular *lawyer* fact has a greater E_{ji} than the particular *hippie* fact.

In addition to predicting the fan effect, it turns out that Posterior Strength Equation 4.3 implies priming effects, whereby associatively related primes speed up access to target information. Indeed, as reviewed in Anderson and Milson (1989), there is a wide range of memory phenomena that are predicted by the rational analysis of memory underlying the equations we have reviewed. ACT–R, embodying that rational analysis, inherits these predictive successes.

LEARNING OF PROCEDURAL PARAMETERS

The previous section described declarative learning, where the critical questions were selecting what, if any, chunks to retrieve and how fast to retrieve these chunks. This section describes procedural learning, where the critical questions are determining which, if any, productions to fire (conflict resolution) and how fast these productions will fire. A number of parameters associated with a production rule determine its firing. The strength parameter S_P determines the time for the retrieval aspects of a production rule firing. With respect to conflict resolution, there are two probability parameters, q (probability that a production is successful) and r (probability of achieving the goal), and two cost parameters, a (cost of executing the production) and b (future costs after the production has fired until the goal is achieved). In each case, the learning processes produce statistical estimates of the appropriate quantities that these parameters are supposed to reflect.

Production Strength

Production strength, S_P, is an estimate of the log odds that a production will fire in the next cycle. It increases according to the same computation as does the growth of chunk strength (See Base-Level Learning Equation 4.1):

$$S_P = \ln\left(\sum_{j=1}^{n} t_j^{-d}\right) + \beta$$ **Production Strength Equation 4.4**

where the summation is over the various time lags t_j that have passed since the uses of the production.[11] As in the case of chunk strength, ß is typically absorbed in other parameter estimates.

As in the case of chunks, the lags t_j have two definitions. One involves the situation where the production rule is created (or recreated and merged with the existing rule). In this case, the t_j corresponds to the time since the moment of creation. The other case is where an existing production rule is fired. In this case, t_j corresponds to the time since the start of the cycle when it fired.

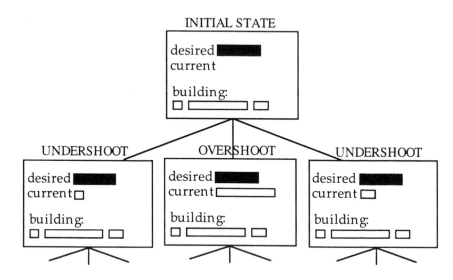

FIG. 4.4 Initial and successor states in the building sticks task. From Lovett (1994). Reprinted by permission.

---

[11] The d in this equation need not be identical to the d in Equation 4.1, although both default to 0.5.

Note that production strength influences speed of a production if it is selected by conflict resolution, but it does not determine whether the production is selected. In the previous ACT*, speed and conflict resolution were both determined by a single strength measure at the cost of considerable confusion. ACT–R achieves greater clarity by separating the measure of production-rule success from frequency of use. In ACT–R, it is possible to learn that a production rule is less successful and so ACT–R will choose it less often, but still increase its strength on its occasional use and so, come to execute it more quickly.

Basically, ACT–R's production-strength mechanism is the equivalent of Thorndike's Law of Exercise, whereas its rules for learning probability and cost become the equivalent of Thorndike's Law of Effect (Thorndike, 1913). The research of Lovett (Lovett & Anderson, 1996) nicely illustrates the separation of these two factors. She explored the effect of practice with problem-solving operators that yield differential success. Figure 4.4 shows her task, which she called the *building-sticks task*. It is an isomorph of Luchins' waterjug problem (Luchins, 1942; Luchins & Luchins, 1959). The goal in this task is to construct a stick of a particular desired length, given three stick lengths from which to build (there is an unlimited supply of sticks of each length). There are basically two strategies to use in trying to solve this problem. The undershoot strategy is to take smaller sticks and build up to the target stick. The overshoot strategy is to take the stick longer than the goal and cut off pieces equal in length to the smaller stick until one reaches the target length. Lovett arranged it so that only one strategy would work for a particular problem and gave subjects problems where one of the two strategies worked on a majority of the problems (and she counterbalanced over subjects which strategy was the more successful).

A later subsection describes an ACT–R model for her choice data (for more details, see Lovett & Anderson, 1996, and Chapter 8). However, for the current purpose, the interesting qualitative results concerned the subjects' choice among the two strategies and their speed of choice. Showing sensitivity to the differential success rate, they came to prefer the more successful strategy. However, they also sped up on both strategies. They did not speed up as much on the less successful strategy, but this was because they chose it less frequently.

It is adaptive both to speed up on the less successful operator and to choose it less frequently. One strategy is more successful, and subjects are justified in having a bias toward that strategy. On the other hand, both strategies are increasing in their base frequency above what they had been before the experiment. Thus, subjects are justified in allocating more of their mental resources into making both strategies run rapidly.

134

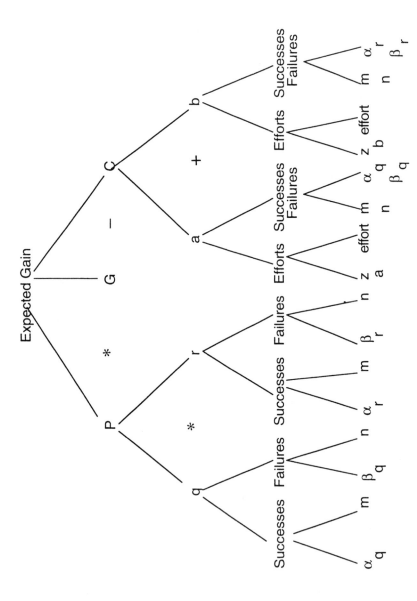

FIG. 4.5 Representation of the quantities relating conflict resolution decision to learning of production parameters.

Production Rule Success and Cost

Which production is chosen is often more important than how rapidly it is executed. The production selected is the one with the highest expected gain. Figure 4.5 displays the quantities that underlie the calculation of expected gain. As Chapter 3 discussed, the expected gain of a production is calculated as $PG - C$, where P is the estimated probability of achieving the goal if that production is taken, G is the value of the goal, and C is the estimated cost of achieving the goal if that production is taken. P is defined as the product of the underlying parameters q and r. The parameter q is the probability of successful execution of the production, which includes successfully performing any retrievals and achieving any subgoals. It is estimated as:

$$q = \frac{\text{Successes}}{\text{Successes } + \text{ Failures}}$$ **Probability Learning Equation 4.5**

The parameters Successes and Failures in this equation refer both to events before the beginning of the simulation and to outcomes after the beginning of the simulation. Anderson (1993) used α to refer to the number of prior successes, β to refer to the number of prior failures, m to refer to number of experienced successes, and n to refer to number of experienced failures. Then, the equation becomes:

$$q = (\alpha + m)/(\alpha + \beta + m + n)$$

This formula can be viewed as giving a weighted average of the prior probability, $\alpha/(\alpha + \beta)$ and the empirical proportion, $m/(m + n)$. As the number of experiences, $m + n$, increases, the estimate of q becomes dominated by the empirical proportion. A similar function describes the estimation of r, which is the probability that the goal will be achieved should the rule successfully fire.[12]

ACT–R also uses statistical learning to estimate its cost parameters a and b whose sum determines C. The parameter a describes the expected effort spent executing the production rule. This effort includes both the rule's retrieval time and its action time, which may be significant if that action includes the fulfilling of a subgoal. It is estimated as:

$$a = \frac{\text{Efforts}}{\text{Successes } + \text{ Failures}}$$ **Cost Learning Equation 4.6**

---

[12]The default values for both q and r are $\alpha = 1$ and $\beta = 0$, which can be viewed as being optimistic about the prospects of a new production

where *Efforts* is the total amount of time taken over all past uses of the production rule, successful or failed. In Anderson (1993), as in the case of the probability estimates, these quantities were divided into prior costs before the simulation and experiment costs after the simulation. The parameter z refers to total prior effort. Then the equation becomes:

$$a = (z + \sum_{i}^{m} \text{effort}_i) / (\alpha + \beta + m + n)$$

This formula gives a weighted average of a prior estimate $z/(\alpha + \beta)$ and empirical average of past efforts $\Sigma \text{effort}_i/(m+n)$. A similar formula describes the estimation of b except that the efforts going into Σeffort_i are further costs after the production executes until the goal succeeds or fails.[13]

An important issue in learning r and learning b concerns the scope over which these probabilities and costs are defined. As the previous chapter discussed, r and b for a production refer to all productions that fire after it that are concerned with achieving its goal. When the goal is popped, it is popped with either success or failure. The r parameter for each production that fired in the sequence that led to the goal being popped will be credited for the eventual success or failure. The b cost assigned to a production will be the time from which it fired until the popping of the goal.

A frequent question asked about ACT–R is, "how does one really know which productions were responsible for a success or failure?" The goal structure enables ACT–R to implicitly reason about this problem and restrict its credit assignments to rules that were logically involved in trying to achieve the current goal. Productions involved in achieving subgoals of the current goal receive blame or credit (for its b and r parameters) according to whether the subgoal failed or succeeded. Only the production that set the subgoal will receive blame or credit (for its a and q parameters) according to whether the suboal failed or succeeded. It certainly is possible for an innocent production rule to be blamed for the mistake of another one in achieving the goal. However, it will get credit in successful sequences, whereas the buggy rule will only receive discredit. It is also possible for a mistaken production to be on a line of productions that lead to success because other productions compensated for its mistake. However, it will, therefore, be on a relatively costly path and productions that more directly lead to the solution would come to be preferred.[14]

---

[13]The default value of z is 0.05 for a and 1 for b. Because $\alpha + \beta = 1$ for both, a starts out at $0.05/1 = 0.05$ and b at $1/1 = 1$.

[14] Dietterich (1997) intoduced a similar hierarchial scheme to help guide reinforcement learning.

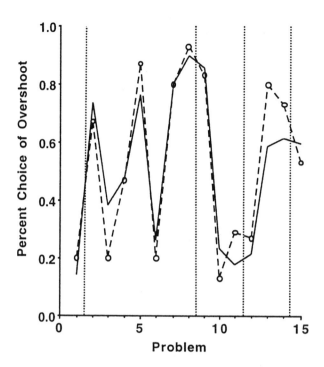

FIG. 4.6 Mean percent choice of overshoot in the first experiment of Lovett and Anderson (1996). A dotted line connects the data points and the solid line expresses the theory.

Application to an Experiment About Learning Conflict-Resolution Parameters

These ideas can be illustrated in a simulation of an experiment by Lovett and Anderson (1996). We have already introduced Lovett's building-sticks task earlier in this chapter with respect to Fig. 4.4. This is an isomorph of Luchins' waterjug problem, and one of Lovett's early experiments was based very closely on one of Luchins' experiments. Subjects received a sequence of 15 problems:

Problem 1. This could be solved by either the overshoot or undershoot method.
Problems 2–8. These could be solved only by the overshoot method.
Problems 9–11. These could be solved only by the undershoot method.
Problems 12–14. These could solved only by the overshoot method.

TABLE 4.9
Production Rules for the Building Sticks Task

Encode

    IF   the goal is to solve the BST task
    THEN   calculate the undershoot difference between the goal and the second largest
           stick
           and calculate the overshoot difference between the largest stick and the goal

Decide-Under

    IF   the goal is to solve the BST task
           and the undershoot difference is less than the overshoot difference
    THEN   choose undershoot

Decide-Over

    IF   the goal is to solve the BST task
           and the overshoot difference is less than the undershoot difference
    THEN   choose overshoot

Force-Under

    IF   the goal is to solve the BST task
    THEN   choose undershoot

Force-Over

    IF   the goal is to solve the BST task
    THEN   choose overshoot

Problem 15. This could be solved by either method and indeed was identical to problem 1, although no subject reported being aware of this.

Figure 4.6 shows the results from this experiment. Two basic factors determine the data in the figure. First, the appearance of specific problems has a large effect and is responsible for some of the ups and downs. For instance, 80% of the subjects choose to use undershoot on the first problem. It is a problem where the undershoot option gets one closer to the goal. The goal stick is 125 pixels in length, the undershoot stick is 55 pixels and the overshoot stick is 250 pixels. Thus, the undershoot stick gets one to a distance of 70 pixels from the target, whereas the overshoot stick gets one to 125 pixels. Second, the history of success also has a large effect. Across the seven problems (2–8) that are solved by overshoot, there is an increasing tendency to choose overshoot. This drops off as undershoot begins to be successful (Problems 9–11) and picks up again as overshoot resumes its success (Problems 12–14). On the last problem, which is identical to Problem 1, subjects now choose overshoot 53% of the time (rather than the prior 20%), reflecting their greater history of success with that operator.

To simulate subject behavior, we used the production rules in Table 4.9. Other production rules were responsible for executing the strategies and backing up if blocked, but the ones in Table 4.9 represent the critical decision-making productions. The full set of production rules is available over the Web. Basically, there were two productions to choose overshoot and two productions to choose undershoot. The **Decide-Under** and **Decide-Over** productions decide on the basis of the differences between the sticks and the goal (i.e., which got closest to the goal), whereas the **Force-Under** and **Force-Over** productions decide arbitrarily.

Figure 4.6 illustrates the predictions of the ACT–R model for this task. There were three parameters involved in fitting the data. The first modeled the potential for misperceiving the problem. If d_u was the undershoot difference and d_o was the overshoot difference, we assumed that there was some normally distributed noise in these perceptions and that the probability of perceiving overshoot as closer was (using a logistic approximation):

$$\frac{1}{1 + e^{(d_o - d_u)/s}}$$

We estimated s to be 18.2, which implies a standard deviation of 33.0 pixels ($\sigma = \pi s / \sqrt{3}$) in the perception of the differences d_o and d_u.

Depending on which way the problem was classified, three of the four productions described above could be chosen (one of the decide productions not being applicable). Then, the choice among the productions would be determined by their r probabilities of success.[15] We set the α and β terms of Equation 4.5 to 0.5 except for the α for the two decide productions, which was a free parameter to be estimated. This reflected the idea that the subject had some prior experience favoring hillclimbing. This value of α was estimated as 14.61, which means it was worth about 15 trials of success. The applicable productions were chosen according to the probability formula given in the previous chapter (Conflict Resolution Equation 3.4). Every time a production led to a success, it had its successes counter increased and every time it experienced a failure, it had its failures counter increased.

The final parameter involved the noise in the expected gain. This controlled mapping of expected gain into probability of choosing a production rule (Conflict Resolution Equation 3.4). Assuming a value of G of 20, the s parameter for the logistic distribution was .717, which implied a standard deviation of 1.30.

---

[15] There is also some cost learning going on in this experiment, but these effects are minor.

Thus, the three estimated parameters were the noise in perception of 33.0 pixels standard deviation, the noise in evaluation of 1.30 standard deviation, and α for decide productions of 14.61. The overall fit is quite good, yielding an R^2 of .866. The actual performance plotted in Fig. 4.6 is the average of many runs and the behavior varies from run to run.

On average, by the end of the experiment the probability of success associated with **Decide-Over** had switched from 0.97 to 0.95, **Decide-Under** from 0.97 to 0.78, **Force-Over** from 0.50 to 0.83, and **Force-Under** from 0.50 to 0.72. These probabilities plus the noise determine choice on the last problem. Note that these changes do not involve a dramatic depression of the productions that choose undershoot: The success for **Decide-Under** has gone from 0.97 to 0.78, whereas the success for **Force-Under** has actually gone up to 0.72. However, given the expected-gain noise, there is enough of a difference between these undershoot productions and the overshoot productions to produce the change in behavior observed in the subjects. On problems where overshoot appears closer, **Decide-Over** will usually apply. On problems where undershoot appears closer, **Force-Over** has a slight edge over the two undershoot productions and will more often apply.

Optimality of Choice Behavior

We promised in the previous chapter that we would return to the issue of the optimality of choice behavior. Chapter 8, on choice, discusses this further, but we can provide a preliminary discussion here in the context of how the choice parameters are learned. People have been characterized as *probability matching* in their choice behavior, which means that they choose alternatives with the probabilities that these alternatives prove successful rather than exclusively choosing the most successful alternative. As the previous chapter noted, describing subjects as probability matching is somewhat simplistic. Nonetheless, subjects typically do not absorb into a behavior pattern where they only choose the most successful behavior. As shown, the experiment just simulated in Fig. 4.6, this is produced in ACT–R because of noise in the choice evaluation.

There are a number of views of this noise in the evaluation process. One is that it just reflects inherent noise in the system and the subject is behaving as optimally as would be allowed by their noisy systems. However, this noise can also reflect our own ignorance as to the controlling factors rather than problems within the subject. Thus, we saw in Fig. 4.6 that what might appear to be highly erratic choice behavior is, in fact, subjects' responding reasonably to problem characteristics. Indeed, even in simple two-alternative choice situations some of the subjects' behavior is in response to apparently predictive patterns in the data (Feldman, 1963; Jarvik, 1951). The subjects' reliance on problem appearance in the building-sticks task is not unreasonable. It turns out that the experimental design frustrates this reliance, and subjects learn to rely less on it. In other research, Lovett and Schunn (1997) found that subjects can learn to completely disregard a feature like distance from the goal with enough negative experience. However, attention to potentially predictive features can appear as simple nonoptimality in the eyes of an experimenter who fails to see the problem from the perspective of the subject.

Deviation from just selecting the most successful alternative has an adaptive function because it allows the system to learn about its environment. If things change, then one is not going to know this unless one occasionally tries an alternative that has been less successful in the past. A very simple form of this is the *two-armed bandit problem,* studied in statistics (Berry & Frisedt, 1985), where one has to choose between two alternatives, each of which has a constant but unknown probability of payoff. Even in such a simple constant situation it is optimal to sometimes choose the alternative that has displayed the lower payoff because one might learn with more data that it really has the better payoff. In an environment where things can change, it makes even more sense to sample the alternative with the poorer track record (Goldberg, 1990).

In this regard, we should note that our description of the ACT–R theory of conflict-resolution learning has ignored a complication. To this point, all the past successes are equally weighted in coming up with a current estimate. However, as is reviewed in Chapter 8, there is evidence that subjects discount their past experiences, such that the most recent experiences are weighted the most. In fact, the ACT–R simulation allows one to discount experiences according to the same summation rule that is used for the Base-Level Learning Equation 4.1 and the Strength Learning Equation 4.4. In this case the Successes and Failures appearing in the Probability Learning Equation 4.5 are calculated:

$$\text{Successes or Failures} = \sum_{j=1}^{m,n} t_j^{-d} \quad \textbf{Event Discounting Equation 4.7}$$

and the Efforts appearing in the Cost Learning Equation 4.6 are calculated:

$$\text{Efforts} = \sum_{j=1}^{m,n} t_j^{-d} \, \text{Effort}_j \qquad \textbf{Effort Discounting Equation 4.8}$$

Our discussion in this chapter describes what happens when $d = 0$ and there is no decay. Chapter 8, on choice, describes an ACT–R theory that uses this decay for successfully modeling a variety of choice phenomena.

The extreme version of a decay theory yields pure probability matching. If only the last event is weighted significantly (because of rapid decay), this system will simply choose what worked last. Thus, it tends to choose alternatives in proportion to their frequencies of success. Such a theory predicts that subjects always repeat the last success. This prediction is too strong, but there is a tendency for such short-term effects to hold. There is also some tendency for subjects (human and other organisms) to learn how stable their environment is and to adjust more rapidly in a less stable environment. As Chapter 8 reviews, many species in many situations are sensitive to the timing of their successes and failures.

Thus, characterizations of probability-matching behavior as nonrational are simplistic. First, people and other organisms often deviate empirically from pure probability matching. Sometimes, they settle down into just selecting the more successful alternative, but more often, they do not. However, to characterize the failure to select just the more profitable alternative as nonrational is a classic example of *experimenter error*. It assumes that the subject's representation of the situation should be the same as the experimenter's. The subject's behavior is shaped by an evolutionary history where the goal was to succeed in the world at large and not in a particular experiment. In that world at large, it makes sense to pay attention to potential predictors of success besides past success and it makes sense to be sensitive to the potential for the world to change. ACT–R provides a more robust approach, given the true complexity of the world.

5

The Visual Interface

John R. Anderson
Michael Matessa
Christian Lebiere
Carnegie Mellon University

Theories of higher-level cognition typically ignore lower-level processes such as visual attention and perception. They simply assume that lower-level processes deliver some relatively abstract description of the stimulus situation on which the higher-level processes operate. This certainly is an accurate characterization of our past work on the ACT–R theory (e.g., Anderson, 1993). The typical task that ACT–R has been applied to is one in which the subject must process some visual array. The array may contain a sentence to be recognized, a puzzle to be solved, or a computer program being written. We had always assumed that some processed representation of this visual array is placed into declarative memory in some highly encoded form, and we modeled processing given that representation.

The strategy of focusing on higher-level processes might seem eminently reasonable for a theory of higher-level cognition. However, the strategy creates two stresses for the plausibility of the resulting models. One stress is that the theorists are granting themselves unanalyzed degrees of freedom by assuming a processed representation of the input. They can choose ad hoc representations to make their theories fit the data. It is not always clear whether the success of the model depends on the theory of the higher-level processes or on the choice of the processed representation. The other stress is that the theorist may be ignoring significant problems in access to that information, which may be contributing to dependent variables such as accuracy and latency. For instance, the visual input may contain more information than can be held in a single attentional fixation, and shifts of attention (with or without accompanying eye movements) may become a significant but ignored part of the processing. To avoid these stresses we decided to join the growing number of efforts (e.g., Kieras & Meyer, 1994; Wiesmeyer, 1992) to embed a theory of visual processing within a higher-level theory of cognition.

The choice to focus on vision was largely strategic, reflecting the fact that most of the tasks modeled in ACT–R have involved input only from the visual modality. To be more precise, most tasks have involved processing input from a computer screen. Therefore, we developed a theory of the processing of a computer screen. However, although we started with a theory of the visual interface, we have recently become concerned with a more general theory of the coordination of perception, action, and cognition. This more general system is described in the next chapter on ACT–R/PM. This chapter describes ACT–R's visual interface and the evidence for its connection to the cognitive system. The visual interface is the most developed part of ACT–R/PM and major parts of it are incorporated into ACT–R/PM.

The visual interface in this chapter and ACT–R/PM in the next chapter reflect a general effort to close the gap between the external world and ACT–R. This gap reflects one of the few remnants of the era of informal theorizing in psychology that can be found in computer simulation models. Computer simulation models typically specify precisely the internal operations that are taking place in processing information but leave it largely up to informal judgment to decide on exactly what corresponds to the input and output of the theory. We want to create a theory of these connections with as much precision as the internal simulations. Such a theory should remove anything implicit about how an ACT–R model relates to the behavior obtained from subjects. To accomplish this we are moving to having ACT–R simulations interact with the same software that presents the experiment to the subject. The ACT–R Visual Interface was the first effort to do this and contained a number of primitive actions to supplement the ACT–R cognitive system. Basically, the visual interface allows an ACT–R simulation to operate the computer application just as a subject can. The simulation has access to the same computer screens that the subject sees, must scan these screens like a subject must, and must enter keystrokes and mouse motions.[1] The data from the simulation are collected by the same software that collects the human's data and are subject to the same analyses. The one difference between an ACT–R simulation and a human is that ACT–R's whole world is the computer screen, the mouse, and the keyboard, whereas this is only a small part of the subject's world. Many of the simulations in this book can interact with the same software the subjects used. With the exception that there is not a human body in front of the terminal, we would want to claim that the behavior of these ACT–R simulations would be indistinguishable from those of human subjects.[2]

---

[1] To be more precise, we pass an iconic representation of the screen to ACT–R and enter events into the event stream that correspond to keystrokes and mouse movements.

[2] These simulations can be accessed at our Web site. They are implemented in the more general ACT–R/PM system—see Chapter 6.

One of the early dividends of this effort to develop a serious theory of the processing of the external world has been progress on the long-standing issue within the ACT–R theory concerning the origins of knowledge. As outlined at the beginning of the previous chapter, ACT–R now has a theory of the origins of declarative knowledge. This theory claims that all declarative chunks are either past goals or encodings of objects from the environment. Thus, ACT–R's visual interface provides it with a sensory basis for knowledge.

ACT–R's visual interface consists of a theory of visual perception and attention as well as their relationship to higher-level cognition. It is important to define our approach to visual attention and perception from the outset: We require a theory of visual attention and perception that is psychologically plausible, but it is not our intention to propose a new theory of visual attention and perception. Therefore, we have embedded within ACT–R a theory that might be seen as a synthesis of the attentional spotlight theory of Posner (1980), the feature-synthesis theory of Treisman (Treisman & Sato, 1990), and the attentional theory of Wolfe (1994). The resulting ACT–R theory of visual attention provides a set of motivated constraints on ACT–R models of higher-level cognition.

Figure 5.1 provides a basic overview of the system. There are three entities to be related: the ACT–R theory of higher-level cognition, the environment with which the system is interacting, (in ACT–R's case, this is the computer application), and an iconic memory, which is a feature

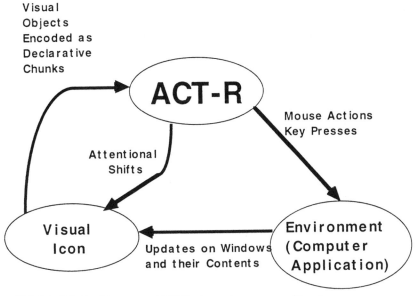

FIG. 5.1: Relationship among ACT–R, the environment, and iconic memory.

representation of the information on the screen. As can be seen, there is a limited number of actions that ACT–R can take—it can issue keystrokes and mouse presses to the computer, and it can move its attention around the iconic memory. Wherever it moves its attention it can synthesize the features there into declarative chunks, which can then be processed by the ACT–R system. The computer program that it is interacting with can issue updates to the screen (and thence to the visual icon) either spontaneously or in response to actions of ACT–R.

The subsequent sections of this chapter flesh out this basic description. The next section focuses on the theory of visual attention, which determines what ACT–R encodes from the screen. The section after that focuses on the theory of pattern recognition that underlies the synthesis of chunks that ACT–R can recognize. The final section considers an application of this system to a typical problem from the HCI literature.

VISUAL ATTENTION

The ACT–R visual interface implements a feature theory of perception. The information in the visual icon consists of features, but ACT–R cannot process features directly. It can only process chunks that represent the objects that these features compose. In the ACT–R visual interface, there is a variable-sized spotlight of attention that can be moved across the visual field. When the spotlight fixates on an object, its features can be recognized as a pattern. Once recognized, the objects are then available as chunks in ACT–R's declarative memory and can receive higher-level processing. The following is a potential chunk encoding of the letter H:

Object
    isa VISUAL-OBJECT
    screen-position (125 100)
    value H

That is, it is represented as a visual object with a particular value and screen position (125 100), which gives the x–y coordinates of the object's center. We do not mean to imply that actual lists of integers are part of the chunk representation. This is just a way of denoting the stored locations. The next chapter, ACT–R/PM, describes a different system where locations are encoded as chunks.

In the ACT–R visual interface, on appearance of an object in the visual field, the features composing the object (e.g., the vertical and horizontal bars composing an H) are available but the object itself is not recognized. The system can respond to the appearance of a feature anywhere in the visual field, but only when it has moved its attention to that location can it recognize the conjunction of features that correspond to the object. For instance, it can respond immediately to a vertical bar but can recognize an H only after moving attention to that object. Thus, in order for the ACT–R theory of higher-level processing to "know" what is in its environment, it must move its attentional focus over the visual field. In ACT–R the calls for shift of attention are controlled by explicit firings of production rules. It will take time for ACT–R to encode visual information, and ACT–R is forced to honor the limited capacity of visual attention.

What information can ACT–R use to guide where it looks on a screen? There are three types of information it can use to guide where attention goes. One is that it can look in particular locations and directions. The second is that it can look for particular features. The third is that it can look for objects that have not yet been attended. It can conjoin these in scanning requests, asking for things like "Find the next unattended pink vertical bar to the left of the current location."

This kind of search deserves a number of comments. First, note that this request searches for a conjunction of visual features (pink and vertical). It had at one time been argued that attention could only be drawn by single features (e.g., Treisman & Gelade, 1980). However, a more current view is that attention can be guided by conjunctions of features but that such conjunction searches are more noisy (Wolfe, 1994). Second, ACT–R can specifically restrict itself to unattended objects. There is evidence that people have difficulty returning attention to attended objects even if they want to (Klein, 1988; Tipper, Driver, & Weaver, 1991). Although ACT–R can restrict itself to unattended objects, it is not more difficult for ACT–R to attend to previously attended objects than to previously unattended objects. Thus, this "inhibition of return" is not modeled in ACT–R, nor are details such as the noise in attentional component. At some point in time, ACT–R's attentional module might be extended to incorporate these details. Right now it should be viewed as a system that is consistent at a general level with what is known about visual attention but that does not model the microstructure of these attentional processes. As stated earlier, our goal is to focus on how the cognitive system uses visual attention.

A final general comment is that ACT–R can select the scale of the features it looks for and the size of the object it is recognizing. Thus, as shown later, ACT–R can recognize either letters or words as objects. Also, depending on how it sets its feature scale, it would recognize either the H in Fig. 5.2 or the Xs that compose it.

The best way to understand how this theory works is to study its application to various tasks that involve visual perception. The next subsections describe ACT–R's theory of visual attention applied to the Sperling task, the subitizing task, and the visual search task.

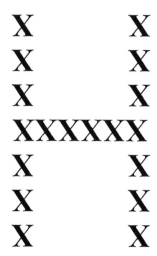

FIG. 5.2: ACT–R can either see the Xs or the H, depending on how it sets its attention scale.

The Sperling Task

Sperling (1960) reported a classic study of visual attention. Figure 5.3 illustrates the material he used in one of his experiments. In the whole-report condition he presented subjects with brief exposures (50-msec, followed by a mask) of visual arrays of letters (three rows and four columns) and found that on average they could report back 4.4 letters. In the partial-report condition he gave subjects an auditory cue to identify which row they would have to report. Then he found that they were able to report 3.3 letters in that row. As he delayed the presentation of the auditory cue to 1 sec after the visual presentation he found that subjects' recall fell to about 1.5 letters. Figure 5.4 shows his results as a function of the delay in the tone. Subjects' recall at a second's delay fell to about a third of the whole report level because

X	M	R	J
C	N	K	P
V	F	L	B

FIG. 5.3: Example of the kind of display used in a visual-report experiment. This display is presented briefly to subjects, who are then asked to report the letters it contains.

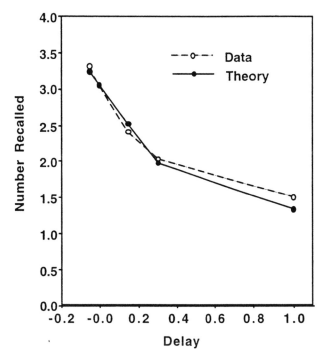

FIG. 5.4: Number of items reported for a row of four as a function of the delay on the cue identifying the row. Data from Sperling (1960).

they were only able to report as many items from the cued row as they happened to encode without the cue. This research has been interpreted as indicating that subjects have access to all the letters in a visual buffer but they have difficulty in reporting them before they decay away.

This experiment and other subsequent research have two dimensions of significance. One is information about the limited duration of visual sensory memory. The general importance of this limitation has been questioned (Haber, 1983) because people seldom have to process visual information given in 50-msec exposures. The other significance is that it indicates how fast visual attention can move over an array. This information is quite relevant to many domains, including many experimental tasks involving higher-level cognition. This is why it is important to show that the ACT–R theory of visual attention can model this result.

There is an ACT–R model of this task in which the letters in the visual array are encoded by the visual interface as sets of features grouped into unidentified objects. When a report row has not been identified the following production would apply:

Encode-Screen
          IF   one is encoding digits without a tone
                 and there is an unattended object on the screen
          THEN   move attention to that object

Once a row has been identified, different productions would fire depending on the tone. For instance, the following production is responsible for reporting the top row:

Encode-Top-Row
          IF   one is encoding digits and there is a high tone
                 and there is an unattended object in the top row
          THEN   move attention to that object

and there are similar productions for the middle and bottom rows.

These productions call for attention to be moved to unattended objects. When the production moves attention to the location of that object, the letter is recognized and a chunk created to encode it. If no tone is presented, **Encode-Screen** will encode any letter in the array; if a tone is present, productions like **Encode-Top-Row** will encode letters in the cued row. After the visual array disappears, the following production is responsible for the report:

Do-Report
          IF   the goal is to report the digits
                 and there is a chunk encoding an item
          THEN   report the item

This production will report only those letters that have been encoded, because only these have a chunk representation in declarative memory.

The number of letters encoded in the whole-report procedure is essentially equal to the number of **Encode-Screen** productions that can fire before the iconic memory of the letters disappears. Physically, the stimulus is only presented for 50 msec, but the critical issue is the duration of the stimulus or the "icon" in the visual system. We estimate that it must be 4.4 times the firing time per production because 4.4 items are recalled on average. In fitting the data in Fig. 5.4, three parameters were estimated. Two of these were the duration of the icon at 810 msec and the time for each production firing to move attention and encode another digit at 185 msec. Note that $4.4 \times 185 = 810$.

To understand the fit to the data in Fig. 5.4, it is necessary to think through how the advantage of the partial report works. First, consider the situation before the tone is encoded. Subjects have a 1/3 chance of guessing the right row, in which case they will be able to report the four letters. They have a 2/3 chance of guessing wrong, in which case they would only start encoding the row once they switched to that row.[3] There will be some delay in time for the tone to be perceived and for attention to switch to the correct row (note that in Fig. 5.4 subjects never report all four items and are doing better given a 0.05-sec head start on the tone than a simultaneous presentation). This is the third parameter, the switch-over delay, which is estimated to be 335 msec. This can be seen as 150 msec to register the signal (the time for auditory signal to get from the ear to being registered in the goal chunk) and 185 msec for an attention-changing production to fire (same time as all other attention-switching productions). Thus, the effective time spent encoding an array if the tone is presented t msec after the array will be $810 - (t + 335)$. Thus, the predicted number of digits reported is

$$(1/3) \times 4.0 + (2/3) \times [(810 - (t + 335))/185] = 3.04 - 0.0036t$$
$$\text{if } 810 - (t + 335) > 0 \text{ (or } t < 475)$$

or

$$(1/3) \times 4.0 = 1.33$$
$$\text{if } 810 - (t + 335) < 0 \text{ (or } t > 475)$$

Figure 5.4 presents the predictions of this model. As can be seen, it does a nice job of simulating the data. The ACT–R model of this task consists of the production rules given plus a rule to switch from attending to reporting. It actually predicts a two-legged function that decreases linearly until the threshold delay is reached (475 msec) and then is flat at the minimum of 1.33 items. The sharp bend in the function might well be rounded by random variations in the exact duration of iconic memory as well as by variability in the time for production firing.[4] However, the function gives the essence of the theory and that theory does a good job of accounting for the data. In part, it is implementing the standard understanding of the data but it makes clear both the control structure of the task (which is vague in the standard understanding) and the need to postulate the switching time (335 msec) to consistently account for the data. For purposes of comparison with later modeling efforts, the critical number is the 185 msec for switching attention. This number comes directly from the slope in Fig. 5.4. Every 185 msec the memory report is dropping by 2/3 of an item.

---

[3]This model assumes that once a subject starts reading a row, the subject will continue to read in the row—this is how ACT–R's visual interface operates, in that it has a bias to read left-to-right and top-down.

[4]In ACT–R/PM, there is the potential to introduce variability in the actions—see the next chapter.

The Subitizing Task

In the Sperling task, time is controlled by the duration of the iconic memory and the interest is in how many things can be attended to in that time. Another way to measure switching time for attention is to see how long it takes to attend to a number of objects on a screen. One way to get people to attend to all of the objects on a screen is to ask them to say how many objects there are. This is precisely what is done in a subitizing task (see the recent discussion by Simon, Cabrera, & Kliegl, 1994) in which a number of objects are presented to a subject and the subject must identify as quickly as possible how many objects are on the screen. Figure 5.5 illustrates the classic result obtained (Jensen, Reese, & Reese, 1950) in this task, which is that latency increases with the number of digits to be identified. There is an apparent discontinuity in the increase, with the slope being much shallower until three or four items and then getting much steeper. The slope is about 50 msec until three or four items and approximately 275 msec afterwards. Figure 5.5 also shows the results from the ACT–R simulation described later.

In the ACT–R subitizing model there are special productions to recognize one object, two objects (as lines), three objects (as triangles), and familiar configurations of larger number of objects (such as five on a die face), and there is a production that can count single objects. This is the basic model

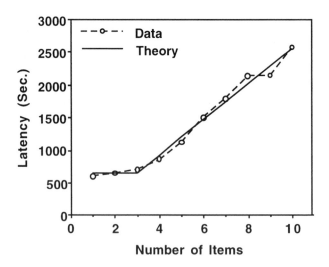

FIG. 5.5. Amount of time to name the number of objects in a presentation as a function of the number of objects. Data from Jensen, Reese, and Reese (1950).

of the subitizing task that has been proposed by researchers such as Mandler and Shebo (1982).[5] Again, what ACT–R adds to this standard model is an explicit theory of the control structure. Table 5.1 gives some of the productions used in modeling the task. Faced with an array of objects, **Start** will move attention to some part of the screen and the largest pattern will be recognized. This model has the capacity to see patterns of one, two, and three objects. Depending on which pattern is attended to, one of the productions **See-One**, **See-Two**, or **See-Three** will apply to initialize the count. After that point **Attend-Another** will move attention to other unattended objects and **Add-One** will add 1 to the count. When there are no more unattended objects, **Stop** will report the count.

There are a number of noteworthy aspects of this model. First, it makes clear that successful performance of subitizing depends on ACT–R's ability to tag items in the visual array as attended so that double counts are avoided. Second, beyond three items, subitizing depends on retrieval of counting facts. One could have an alternative model that aggregated additional items in units larger than one. Thus, six objects might be counted by twice attending to three objects and adding $3 + 3 = 6$. However, retrieval of such addition facts would be slower than retrieval of counting facts because additional facts are less well practiced. Also, the remaining objects after the first group has been segmented may not themselves form a group. The model in Table 5.1 predicts a flat function from 1 to 3 and an equal rise from 3 to 4 as from 4 to 5 and beyond—neither of which is quite true. This may reflect some probability of counting in the sub-three range and some probability of pattern matching for four elements. Although the model could be complicated to incorporate these ideas, it did not seem worth it to make the points we wanted to with this example. Moreover, the correlation between prediction and data is already .995.

The ACT–R model provides an accounting for the 275 msec slope that holds beyond four digits. There is a 185-msec time to switch attention to a new object as in the Sperling model. In addition, we estimated a 90-msec time to retrieve the counting fact in production **Add-One**—"x is one more than the count." Although this 90 msec depends on other parameters controlling declarative retrieval, it is consistent with ACT–R's model of cognitive arithmetic (see Chapter 9). Thus, the 275 msec represents 185 msec for attention switching and 90 msec for fact retrieval.

---

[5]Peterson, Morton, and Simon (1997) described an ACT–R model of how these configurations are learned. That model shows that there is nothing magical about three or four. It is just that the combinatorics are such that the number of possible configurations of more than three or four objects is too many to learn.

TABLE 5.1
Productions Involved in the Subitizing Task

Start		
	IF	the goal is to count the objects starting from a count of 0
	THEN	move attention to some object on the screen
See-One		
	IF	the goal is to count the objects starting from a count of 0 and a single object has been attended
	THEN	initialize the count to 1
See-Two		
	IF	the goal is to count the objects starting from a count of 0 and a line of two objects has been attended
	THEN	initialize the count to 2
See-Three		
	IF	the goal is to count the objects starting from a count of 0 and a triangle of three objects has been attended
	THEN	initialize the count to 3
Attend-Another		
	IF	the goal is to count the objects and the count is not 0 and there is another unattended object
	THEN	move attention to that object
Add-One		
	IF	the goal is to count the objects and the count is not 0 and another object has been attended and X is one more than count
	THEN	reset the count to X
Stop		
	IF	the goal is to count the objects and there are no more unattended objects
	THEN	respond with the count

A Visual Search Task

Another way to investigate the time to shift attention is to display an array of objects and ask subjects to search among them for a target object. If one can manipulate the number of objects that a subject must search through, one can manipulate search time. The slope of the function relating search time to number of objects attended gives an estimate of the time to move attention. This straightforward logic is complicated by the fact that subjects can select which objects to attend to on the basis of their features. Thus, for instance, in looking for a red object, subjects will not be affected by the number of green objects in the array.

An example of such a paradigm and its complexities is Shiffrin and Schneider's (1977) study of visual search. In their Experiment 2, subjects had to detect a target item (number or digit) when it was presented in a visual display of one to four items (frame size). The target letter was in a memory set of one to four items (memory set size). For instance, subjects might hold a memory set of B and K and be asked if either element occurred in a visual array that contained G, K, M, and F (in which case they would respond yes). Subjects were either in what was called the varied-mapping or the consistent-mapping condition. In the varied-mapping condition both distractors and the memory set items were letters (drawn from the same pool on each trial), and in the consistent-mapping condition the memory set was composed of numbers and the distractors were letters (therefore, they were always drawn from different pools).

Figure 5.6a shows their results. Judgment times increase with memory set size and frame size, but the effects are much stronger for the varied-mapping condition. The frame-size effects show that subjects pay a cost for the number of objects they must attend to. The size of the memory set and the consistent-varied manipulation both modulate the cost of the number of items in a frame.

We developed an ACT–R model in which this per-item cost reflects both

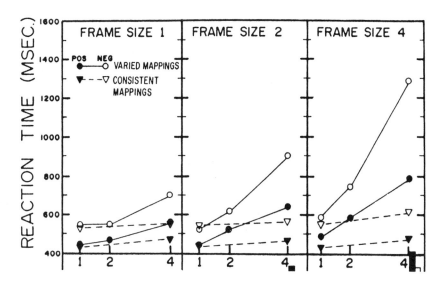

FIG. 5.6a. Results of the simulation from Shiffrin and Schneider (1977).

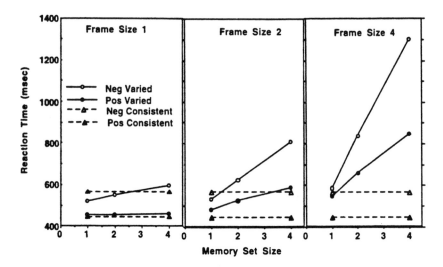

FIG. 5.6b. Result of the ACT–R simulation.

the fraction of the items they must attend to on the screen and the time to judge those items that they do attend to. It involved the following stages:

1. *Preparation*: Upon receipt of the memory the model found a feature that was common to all members of the memory set. If there was more than one such feature, then the feature was selected that was least frequent among the distractors.[6] (There was always a "null" feature that all items had in common.) This defined the target feature. The features used were those proposed by McClelland and Rumelhart (1981; we describe them in more detail in the next section) plus one global feature to encode whether the character was left-facing, right-facing, or symmetric. This global feature often proved to be most discriminative. Also, because Schneider and Shiffrin claim that their subjects developed an ability to automatically discriminate letters from numbers, we added a special discriminating feature for numbers.

2. *Search*: ACT–R directed attention to a location on the basis of the target feature. On presentation of the display, the system examined all positions that had the target feature. If no position had the target feature, it randomly selected one position to look at.[7] It would look at

---

[6]In the ACT–R simulation, we effect this selection through base-level activation values.

[7]We assumed that subjects could not inhibit looking at one position on the screen.

more only if more than one position had a target feature. This search was self-terminating in the case of positive trials, but all positions with the target feature had to be examined in the case of negative trials. The first production that applies to start the scanning is:

Encode-Object
IF   the goal is to search for an object with feature F
        and an unattended object with feature F occurs in location L
THEN   move attention to that object

3. *Judgment*: For each position examined, the model decided whether that item was in the memory set. In the case of the consistent-mapping condition this could be done by simply judging whether the item was a number, and this judgment could be done by a direct retrieval of a category label. In the case of the varied-mapping condition it was necessary to determine if the item was in the memory set. This did not require a sequential search but was done by a production pattern-match test whose time increased with the size of the set. This is analogous to existing ACT models for fan experiments and the Sternberg task (see Chapters 4 and 7). The basic productions for the two conditions are:

Judge-Consistent-Positive
IF   the goal is to search for an object with feature F
        and object attended is a number
THEN   pop the goal and respond yes

Judge-Consistent-Negative
IF   the goal is to search for an object with feature F
        and object attended is a letter
THEN   move attention to another object with feature F

Judge-Varied-Positive
IF   the goal is to search for an object with feature F
        and object attended is in the memory set
THEN   pop the goal and respond yes

Judge-Varied-Negative
IF   the goal is to search for an object with feature F
        and object attended is not in the memory set
THEN   move attention to another object with feature F

Terminate-No

    IF   the goal is to search for an object with feature F
           and there are no unattended objects with feature F
    THEN   respond no

According to this model, the consistent condition enjoys two advantages over the varied condition. First, only one position will have to be examined because numbers have acquired a unique feature through the extensive training. In contrast, in the extreme condition for the varied condition (frame size 4, set size 4, negative trial), an average of 2.83 item positions had to be examined. Second, one can judge whether an object is the target simply by recognizing that it is a digit. In contrast, the target set had to be examined during judgment in the varied condition and this condition suffered a "fan" effect (see Chapter 3) such that time was greater the more letters in the target set.

The ACT–R model for this task was fit using the 185 msec parameter estimate for the time to switch visual attention. In addition, the time to make a response was estimated at 209 msec and the latency factor F was estimated at 139 msec (which affected the varied condition only). Finally, to account for the longer negative times in the consistent condition, we estimated a nondefault latency of 172 msec for **Judge-Consistent-Negative**. Figure 5.6b displays the predictions of the model. The R^2 between the data and the predictions is .948 and the average mean deviation in prediction is 39 msec. The parameter values are also quite reasonable. The actual model is not very different from the original Shiffrin and Schneider's model. This reflects a reoccurring theme in ACT–R modeling efforts, which is that ACT–R often serves to implement theories already out in the literature. ACT–R serves as a means of integrating these models. For instance, the ACT–R model fit the Schneider and Shiffrin data using the same 185 msec attentional shift estimate that was used for other models in this section. It also used the same memory search mechanism as used for the Sternberg task in Chapter 7.

Conclusions

This section has shown that the ACT–R theory is consistent with some of the classic results from the literature on visual attention. In each of three tasks the ACT–R model fit the data assuming a time of about 185 msec to switch attention. In the Sperling task, attention-switching is the only activity. In the subitizing task, additional time is also required to set up and increment a count. In the Shiffrin and Schneider task, judgment time plays a significant role. In more cognitively loaded tasks, other processes play still more significant roles. However, every time visual attention switches, approximately another 185 msec is added to the processing time.

PATTERN RECOGNITION

Visual attention gets the system to process an object. The pattern recognition module converts this object into a chunk, which ACT–R can then process. We have used the rational analysis of categorization (Anderson & Matessa, 1992) to provide a theory of how objects are assigned to patterns. This section briefly reviews that theory and its application to pattern recognition.

The Rational Theory of Categorization

The fundamental equation of the rational theory of categorization specifies the calculation of the posterior probability that an instance with features F comes from category k. The *Pattern Recognition Equation* states that the posterior probability will be proportional to the product of the prior probability and the conditional probabilities:

$$P(k|F) \sim P(k) \prod_{f \in F} P(f|k) \qquad \textbf{Pattern Recognition Equation 5.1}$$

where $P(k)$ is the prior probability of being in category k and $P(f|k)$ is the conditional probability of displaying feature f given that the object comes from category k. This quantity can basically be thought of as a match to a category based on feature overlap. This equation is used in the visual interface to determine the identity of an object. Thus, if attention moved to the letter D the following chunk would be created:

```
Obj 74
   isa VISUAL-OBJECT
   value "D"
   screen-pos (75 100)
```

where the value slot encodes the category (in this case the letter). The categories for recognizing visual objects (in this example D) and their features are not things that the visual interface dictates. They can be specified by the user, although the visual interface does come with a default set of features for letters and numbers. Also, like the rational theory for categorization, this theory of object recognition is not intended as a process model of recognition. Rather, it is just a specification of what chunk gets created to encode the environmental object.

The theory of categorization is concerned with predicting what categories subjects will assign objects to, but in most of the ACT–R applications there is very little uncertainty about what category an object should be assigned to. In typical experiments the stimuli are familiar letters and words, and they are exposed sufficiently long such that there is no confusion about what was seen. Therefore, in most ACT–R applications this aspect of the model is totally unproblematic. Thus, in solving equations, for instance, subjects do not have any question about what the numbers and letters are.

Nonetheless, one can get action out of the model by degrading the stimuli or making them ambiguous or by introducing novel stimuli. In these situations the underlying theory of pattern recognition comes to the fore-front.[8] The theory does apply to the recognition of degraded familiar patterns, as when subjects are asked to recognize brief and often masked presentations of letters and words. The next subsection discusses one such phenomenon from this literature.

The Word Superiority Effect

The word superiority effect has become a litmus test for theories of percep-tion. The effect refers to the fact that it is easier to recognize a letter when it occurs in a word context than it is to recognize a letter alone. Thus, presented with a brief exposure of *WORD* (usually followed by a mask), subjects are better at making a forced choice between whether the last letter was *D* or *K* (both of which make a word) than they are given a brief visual presentation of a *D* and making a forced choice between a *D* or *K*.

In a test of whether ACT–R's pattern recognition component could model this effect, we used the corpus of four-letter words compiled by McClelland and Rumelhart (1981) and used the same features to define letters that they used. When presented with a single letter, ACT–R would try to recognize a letter pattern. When presented with a four-letter string, it would try to recognize a word pattern. It chose the word or letter that was most probable according to Pattern-Recognition Equation 5.1. This equation requires hav-ing a prior probability $P(k)$ of each word or letter, which was set to a quantity proportional to the square root of the item's frequency (based on the work of Anderson & Schooler, 1991, investigating the relationship between frequency in the environment and memory). Equation 5.1 also requires the

---

[8]Basically, in the ACT–R visual interface module, either one can set a flag so that the pattern recognition process is enabled or one can set the flag so that the letters and words are directly represented in the visual icon rather than the component features.

conditional probabilities $P(f|k)$ of the features given the pattern. We set $P(f|k) = .94$ if f is a feature that should be present for the pattern and $P(f|k) = .04$ if f is a feature that should be absent. These values are rather arbitrary, but they represent the assumption that it is more likely, in a sloppy encoding, that a feature would not be encoded than that a feature would be mistakenly encoded. Although this seems like a plausible assumption, the simulation results do not depend on it. Moreover, ACT–R's prediction of a word superiority effect does not depend on the values assigned to $P(f|k)$ or $P(k)$, although the actual level of the recognition rates does.

When single letters were presented, the model recognized letter patterns, and when words were presented, it recognized word patterns. This was done by changing the size of the attentional spotlight as discussed earlier. This meant that for four-letter words, the model was dealing with four times as many features as for pattern recognition. It based its response on either the letter that it recognized in the letter condition or the word it recognized in the word condition (from which it extracted the letter). In the forced-choice procedure, it chose the letter if it was one of the alternatives or guessed randomly if not. Noise was introduced by having a 25% probability of a feature being switched (i.e., added the feature if it was not part of the letter and removed it if it was).[9] The model's error rate in the letter condition was 37% and in the word condition 26%. These are similar to the typical error rates and the typical differences in studies of the word-superiority effect.

The word-superiority effect occurs in this model because the word context provides more information (four times as many features) for decision making and the signal is consequently more reliable in the presence of noise. For instance, if the subject only perceived the top half of the D it would be ambiguous among many letters. However, there is no ambiguity in the context of a word beginning WOR_ as to the letter given this partial feature information. This model assumes that subjects perceive an object and do not have access to the basis of their perception. Thus, given the top half of the D, a subject might perceive R. Thinking they perceived R and given a choice between D and K they have no option but to guess; they do not have access to the features that gave rise to the R perception and that would allow them to choose between D and K. This is consistent with the basic premise in the visual interface that ACT–R only has access to the chunks encoding objects and not to the perceptual features that define these objects.

APPLICATION TO MENU
SELECTION DATA

As part of writing a recent report on ACT–R for the journal *Human*

---

[9]Loss of features could be due to the brief presentation, whereas erroneous features could be due to the mask.

Computer Interaction (Anderson, Matessa, & Lebiere, 1997), we were motivated to think about how ACT–R's visual interface would deal with the task of menu selection. That article described a fit of ACT–R to some menu selection data reported by Nilsen (1991) that had been addressed in the same issue by the EPIC theory of Kieras and Meyer. This is the first case of a model where the visual interface is serving a significant role in a real ACT–R application. The previous results reviewed in this chapter served just to illustrate how the visual interface realizes standard models of visual information processing and to extract 185 msec as an estimate of the time to switch attention. The menu search task is not necessarily more complex than these earlier experiments but does reflect a domain of application for which ACT–R was intended. Many experiments modeled in ACT–R do involve menu selection as a subtask (e.g., see Chapter 11).

Fit to the Nilsen Data

Nilsen's task involved selecting a digit from a menu of the digits 1-9 randomly ordered vertically. The data to be modeled is the time for subjects to move a mouse from the home position above the menu to the target item. Figure 5.7 shows the time for this action as a function of the serial position of the item in the menu. The best-fitting linear function to these data has a slope of 103 msec per position.

These results depend on the fact that the items in the menu are ordered

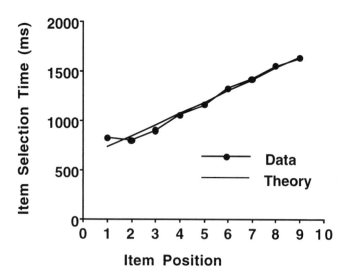

FIG. 5.7: Observed and predicted menu selection times. Observed data are from Nilsen (1991).

randomly. Because the subject does not know where the target item is, a critical component to latency has to be a serial search of the list looking for the target item. Subjects tend to move the mouse down as they scan for the target (we have mouse movement and eye scanning data confirming simultaneous movement). Thus, once they identify the target, the distance to move the mouse tends not to vary much with serial position. Thus, when the target position is unknown, time is dominated by visual search. In contrast, if the position of the item was known (as in a fixed-order menu), the critical latency component might be a Fitts Law (Fitts, 1954) description of the motion. In this case, time would be a logarithmic function of distance, and Nilsen has data from such a condition that confirm this relationship.

ACT–R's model for this task is essentially the same model as proposed for the Shiffrin and Schneider data (Fig. 5.6). We assume that, given a target, subjects selected one of its features and scanned down the menu for the first item with that feature. If this was the target they stopped. If not, they scanned for the next item that contained the target feature.

The two critical productions are

Hunt-Feature
    IF   the goal is to find a target that has feature F
                and there is an unattended object below the current location
                    with feature F
   THEN   move attention to closest such object

Found-Target
    IF   the goal is to find a target
                and the target is at location L
   THEN   move the mouse to L and click

The first production, **Hunt-Feature**, moves attention down looking at objects that have a feature in common with the target. The movement of attention to an object will cause its identity to be encoded. If it is the target letter, **Found-Target** can apply. The production **Found-Target** will retrieve the location of the target and move the mouse to that location.

The time to reach a target will be a function of the number of digits that precede it and have the selected feature. Given the McClelland-Rumelhart feature set, there is a .53 probability that a randomly selected feature of one number will overlap with the feature set of another number.[10] Using the now standard estimate of 185 msec for a shift of attention, ACT–R predicts 185 $\times$ .53 = 98 msec per menu item, which is close to the slope, 103 msec, in the Nilsen data. The fit of the ACT–R model to the data is illustrated in

---

[10]Unlike the Shiffrin and Schneider consistent mapping condition, we did not assume that subjects had enough practice or time to create a special feature that discriminated numbers from letters.

Fig. 5.7. This is a striking demonstration of how the ACT–R theory can be used to predict new data sets using old parameters.

The Kieras and Meyer EPIC model is able to do an equally good job assuming a model in which there are eye movements every 103 msec. This seems an improbable speed of eye movement, which is conventionally set at about 200 msec (and in fact subjects do not fixate each item). Kieras and Meyer suggest an alternative model in which as many as three items are processed in each gaze. Either of these models would predict no effect of distractor similarity on search time. The next subsection examines this prediction.

Effect of Distractor Set

A critical difference between ACT–R and EPIC is the fact that ACT–R predicts an effect of distractor similarity on time to search a menu. To test this prediction, we performed a menu search task in which subjects had to select either a capital letter or digit in a background of letters or digits. There is a 53% probability overlap of the number-on-number condition, 39% in the number-on-letter condition, 42% in the letter-on-number condition, and 43% in the letter-on-letter condition. Thus, these overlap scores predict that there will be less ability to use features to guide search in the number-on-number condition.

Table 5.2 presents the results from subjects for menus of size 9 as in the Nilsen experiment. As predicted by ACT–R, subjects are significantly ($F_{1,20}$ = 104.77; $p < .01$) faster when the distractors are from a different category than the target. This is a confirmation of ACT–R's conception of visual attention and a token of its potential for modeling human-computer interaction (HCI) tasks. Although the interaction is predicted, there is one unexpected result in the data. This is the significant effect of background, with subjects slower (41 msec) in the presence of a letter background ($F_{1,20}$ = 29.96; $p < .001$). We have no explanation for this effect.

The strongest prediction of the ACT–R theory is that there should be a significant interaction between serial position, target, and background.

TABLE 5.2
Time to Select a Target in Different Backgrounds

Target	Background	
	Number	Letter
Number	1324 msec	1293 msec
Letter	1253 msec	1366 msec

Because there is a greater feature overlap in the number-on-number condition than in any other, ACT–R predicts a steeper slope because it will have to consider, on average, more distractors before the target. In fact, there are significant interactions between target and position ($F_{8,160} = 6.49$; $p < .001$), background and position ($F_{8,160} = 4.30$; $p < .001$), and target, background, and position ($F_{8,168} = 2.18$; $p < .05$). There are significant differences among slopes, with 103 msec in the number-on-number condition, 84 msec in the number-on-letter condition, 80 msec in the letter-on-number condition, and 82 msec in the letter-on-letter condition. Thus, the basic effect is a steeper slope in the number-on-number condition, as predicted.

Figure 5.8 plots the predictions of the ACT–R theory for number and letter targets holding constant the background as numbers (because of the main effect of background in the analysis of variance). ACT–R is already committed as to the slopes in these cases. For number targets it is $185 \times .53 = 98$ msec (actual slope is 103 msec) and for letter targets it is $185 \times .42 = 78$ msec (actual slope is 80 msec). The only degree of freedom in estimating this is the "intercept" when the serial position is 1. This was

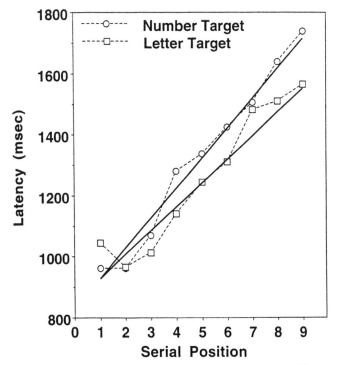

FIG. 5.8: Observed and predicted menu selection times for number and letter targets against a number background.

estimated as 927 msec. This is a striking confirmation of the ACT–R analysis of menu scanning in comparison to the EPIC model, which fails to predict these effects of target-background interaction.

CONCLUSIONS

This chapter has mainly looked at phenomena that are concerned only with visual attention to establish the general correctness of this theory. However, the issues of visual attention are important to ACT–R because they are involved in almost every task that ACT–R performs. Visual attention plays a central role in a number of the following chapters that are concerned with specific content areas. Much of our experimental research with ACT–R is on skill acquisition, which involves the evolution of more efficient scanning strategies. For instance, Anderson, Matessa and Douglass (1995) and Anderson and Douglas (submitted) showed that as subjects repeatedly solve a fixed set of equations they come to know where to look for critical information. Haider and Frensch (in press) also showed that improved scanning strategies are an important part of skill development.

One of the important contributions of this chapter has been to place visual attention squarely within the domain of higher level cognition. Most existing research on visual attention has looked at low-level peripheral effects, ignoring that there is a mind guiding the eye. The ACT–R model shows how a cognitive system can control where the visual system is attending to achieve its information-processing goals. In terms of ACT–R principles, there is no difference between a production that shifts attention to a location on a screen and a production that retrieves an addition fact from memory.

6

Perception and Action

Michael D. Byrne
John R. Anderson
Carnegie Mellon University

Experimental psychology has traditionally been partitioned into separate subdisciplines, with surprisingly little communication across the boundaries. Cognition has traditionally occupied one subdiscipline, with perception and action occupying another subdiscipline. As a result, theories of cognition have typically neglected the perception and action side of our everyday experience. However, it is possible—even likely—that cognition is constrained by human perceptual-motor capabilities. Furthermore, it is likely that perception and action are constrained by cognition. If such constraints exist, then by ignoring them, cognition researchers have been negligent in their pursuit of a complete picture of human cognition.

The goal of this chapter is to pave the way for investigations into a more complete theory of cognition that pays more than marginal attention to perception and action. This theory is called ACT–R/PM (for ACT–R Perceptual Motor) and consists of a set of modules for perception and action that are integrated with the cognitive facilities of ACT–R. We believe this theory is the most complete theory of cognition, perception, and action to date. We demonstrate some of the potential of this new architecture by modeling a task with both perceptual-motor and cognitive demands.

PREVIOUS APPROACHES TO PERCEPTION AND ACTION

Despite the traditional barriers between cognition and perception and action, some limited work in integrating the two subfields has gone on before. Much of this work is motivated by real-world situations where perception, action, and cognition routinely interact, such as piloting an airplane. One of the better summaries of these efforts can be found in Card, Moran, and Newell's (1983) *Psychology of Human-Computer Interaction*, which presents a synthesis of work in this areas and a framework for predicting cognitive/perceptual/motor performance, the Model Human Processor (or MHP). The MHP has been used to analyze and predict performance on several complex tasks involving the interleaving of cognition, perception, and action, such as transcription typing (John, 1996) and call handling by telephone operators (Gray, John, & Atwood, 1993). Some attempts have also been made by the Soar community (Newell, 1990) to incorporate perceptual/motor constraints with a theory of cognition. An excellent sample of other work in this area can be found in Elkind, Card, Hochberg, and Huey (1990).

Before describing the current approach to integrating cognition with perceptual-motor capabilities, it is instructive to review in more detail the foundation upon which it is based. The current system is based on the Visual Interface for ACT–R, which was described in the previous chapter, and EPIC (for Executive Process Interactive Control), a brainchild of Meyer and Kieras (e.g., 1997). The Visual Interface was our first foray into dealing with perceptual-motor issues. While we think it has a number of insights, we also recognize that it is incomplete in many ways. EPIC, on the other hand, is a system designed primarily to model perceptual-motor constraints, with cognition taking a somewhat peripheral role. In some ways, the two systems have taken steps toward one another, and ACT–R/PM is their synthesis.

The ACT–R Visual Interface

Work on ACT–R and perception/action has already been presented in this volume (Chapter 5) in the form of the ACT–R Visual Interface. The Visual Interface gives ACT–R the ability to interact with simple computer displays via a visual attention system and extensions for mouse and keyboard manipulation. The Visual Interface is capable of handling the relatively simple perceptual-motor requirements typical of psychology experiments, and has provided good fits to a number of such experiments. This is an important step toward removing the homunculus from the input/output aspect of ACT–R. On the other hand, the Visual Interface is not well suited for modeling tasks that have richer or more demanding perceptual-motor components, which may be more typical of tasks outside the laboratory. The Visual Interface needs to be expanded on three key dimensions in order to more adequately model human cognition:

1. *Parallelism.* The Visual Interface enforces a strictly serial model of cognition, perception, and action. However, there is a significant amount of parallelism possible, as, for instance, when people move both the mouse and their eyes at the same time. Also it is possible to overlap cognition with perception and action, as when one thinks about a problem while navigating (walking, driving) to a destination. Although we think cognition is basically serial, as it is in ACT–R, one can clearly perform a number of perceptual and motor operations in

parallel with it. The seriality in the visual interface is not a significant limitation when one is modeling tasks such as those in the previous chapters where the logical structure of the task eliminates opportunity for overlap. However, many real-world tasks have this potential, and people certainly take advantage of it. Many of these tasks are of interest to researchers in the psychological community.

2. *Wider Range of Actions.* The Visual Interface supports only three basic motor operations: mouse moves, mouse clicks, and keystrokes. Although this is a useful set, it is limited in scope. Furthermore, each motor operation in the Visual Interface has a single execution time associated with it; for example, every mouse movement in a particular model may be set to take 1.1 sec, regardless of the actual distance to be moved. Such approximations provide a useful starting point, but a great deal more is known about human motor performance and this knowledge could and should be incorporated.

3. *Dynamic Displays.* The Visual Interface presented in Chapter 5 allows ACT–R to "see" a computer display, and represents an important step in integrating ACT–R and perception. The Visual Interface is a feature-based theory of perception that has several important capabilities, such as categorization-based object recognition and the ability to interact with the same experimental software with which human subjects interact. However, this interaction is limited in important ways. The Visual Interface assumes that displays are essentially static. Thus, if a screen object moves or only a portion of the screen changes, the Visual Interface is unable to correctly represent these new states of the screen. For static environments in which the task consists of viewing and reacting to a display that does not change after it appears, this is perfectly adequate. For even simple dynamic tasks, however, this is considerably less than optimal.

Thus, although the Visual Interface is a good "first pass" at integrating ACT–R with perception and action, it is still incomplete in several areas. An immediate and obvious question, then, is whether integrating a strong and more complete set of perceptual–motor mechanisms with a production system such as ACT–R is feasible. The answer is a resounding "yes," as such a system, called EPIC, has recently emerged (Meyer & Kieras, 1997).

EPIC

EPIC consists of a series of individual "processors," each of which handles one aspect of the total perceptual-motor-cognitive system. Most processors handle a single aspect of one input or output modality; for example, the Ocular Motor Processor handles only the "output" of eye movement commands. Figure 6.1 presents the system diagram, showing all of EPIC's processors.

In EPIC, each processor works in parallel with the other processors. Thus, EPIC can be outputting mouse movements (handled by the Manual Motor Processor) while simultaneously perceiving a new object on the screen (handled by the Visual Processor) and computing a stimulus-response mapping (Cognitive Processor).

EPIC is both exceptional and ordinary. It is exceptional in that the designers of EPIC have gone to great lengths to ensure that the various subcomponents of EPIC reflect the most current knowledge, synthesized from the human performance literature, about the timing information appropriate to the input or output modality which they control (Kieras & Meyer, 1996). There is a notable exception, though, and this is where EPIC is ordinary: the Cognitive Processor. EPIC's Cognitive Processor is based on a simple production system interpreter called the Parsimonious Production System, or just PPS (Covrigaru & Kieras, 1987). PPS, as the name suggests, is a minimalist production system in several ways. There is no conflict resolution mechanism, so all productions that match on a given cycle fire in parallel. Production matching is simple: All chunks in memory can be

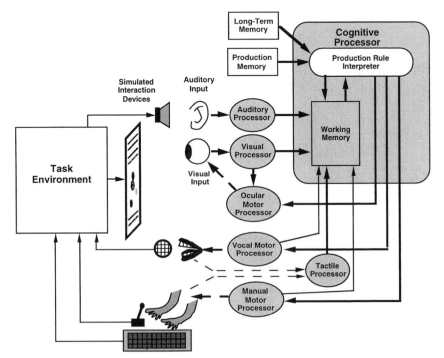

FIG. 6.1 Overview of EPIC architecture.

matched instantly by all productions, meaning that declarative memory is not "graded" in any way—all chunks are either instantly available or not at all available to productions. Nor does PPS contain any kind of learning mechanism. This simplified model of thought has been useful for modeling certain classes of cognition, most notably transfer of routine cognitive skills (Bovair, Kieras, & Polson, 1990; Kieras & Polson, 1985).

In EPIC's relatively short lifetime, it has been applied to a number of tasks with great success: psychological refractory period (PRP) experiments (Meyer & Kieras, 1997), various tasks from the human-computer interaction and human factors literature, including some manual tracking tasks (Kieras & Meyer, 1997), telephone operator interaction (Kieras, Wood, & Meyer, 1997), menu selection (Hornof & Kieras, 1997), and others. These successes provide convincing evidence that the effort put into the specification of EPIC's individual perceptual-motor processors has resulted in faithful mirroring of the human perceptual-motor system, at least at the level of movement specification and timing (the details of how the motor system executes, e.g., a mouse movement are not part of EPIC).

On the other hand, the tasks to which EPIC has been applied have a particular flavor to them: They all have very simple cognitive requirements. They all require only the cognition necessary for "routine skill" (Card et al., 1983) behaviors; that is, they do not involve problem solving or even retrieval from long-term declarative memory. Either the tasks are so cognitively simple that these kinds of thinking are not required, or the subjects are so skilled in the tasks that the demanding cognitive components have been routinized, which is typical of tasks from the human performance literature.

However, this is quite atypical of the tasks to which ACT–R has been applied. Most of the tasks that have been modeled with ACT–R have strong cognitive demands for problem solving, learning, memory retrieval, or some combination of those abilities. This is not to say that the class of tasks covered by EPIC is trivial or uninteresting; however, ACT–R's theory of cognition is both more plausible and more complete. We point out two examples of the problems that result from EPIC's minimalist approach to modeling cognition:

1. EPIC does not remember anything not currently in view unless productions are written to explicitly construct long-term representations of the objects; that is, EPIC predicts that subjects should be able to remember nothing about a previously seen display if they were not warned in advance that they would be asked to remember the contents of the display. And if they were asked, their memory for the display should be perfect, also hardly a tenable prediction.

2. Because productions can fire in parallel, EPIC is left making predictions such as that a person can simultaneously solve a mental arithmetic problem and a mental multiplication problem. Later in this chapter, we report a PRP experiment that exposes EPIC's problems in this regard.

Thus, for the tasks EPIC was designed to model, it contains an adequate approximation to human cognition, but for more sophisticated tasks, such as those that have been approached by ACT–R, EPIC's model of cognition is inadequate. The strengths of EPIC's perceptual-motor system, however, are hard to dismiss. A more complete approach, then, could be to incorporate an EPIC-like perceptual-motor system with ACT–R's model of cognition. The next section describes just such an approach.

A THEORY OF COGNITION, PERCEPTION, AND ACTION: ACT–R/PM

ACT–R/PM has been designed and built to provide a more complete psychological theory of human performance, including serious consideration of both the cognitive side and the perceptual-motor side of behavior. The perceptual-motor system is conceptualized as a layer between cognition (which consists of ACT–R's procedural and declarative memories and mechanisms) and the external environment. That is, the environment does not directly provide inputs to cognition, nor can cognition directly influence the environment. Communication between cognition and the outside world is mediated by the perceptual-motor capabilities of the system. The goal of this effort is to retain the positive aspects of the ACT–R Visual Interface while incorporating many of the advances in perception and action found in EPIC.

In building ACT–R/PM, we integrated ACT–R with much of EPIC's perceptual-motor system. From ACT–R, we took the theory of cognition and the Visual Interface (see Chapter 5). From EPIC, we borrowed ideas and components that ACT–R lacked: a richer system for manual motor control, parallel operation of system components, and timing parameters for speech and audition. The resulting synthesis eliminates many of the weaknesses found in ACT–R and EPIC. For example, ACT–R had been unable to model tasks involving overlapping of perceptual-motor and cognitive operations (e.g., the telephone operators in Gray et al., 1993) and had a simplistic theory of motor movement. These problems are addressed with EPIC's parallelism and Manual Motor Processor. On the other side of the coin, EPIC's cognitive parallelism and limited scope are replaced by ACT–R's serial but richer production system. Hopefully, this should yield a system capable of modeling both dynamic, high-performance perceptual-motor tasks and sophisticated cognition.

Like EPIC, ACT–R/PM contains several modules that work in parallel with one another (see Fig. 6.2). Productions send commands to the modality-specific modules via right-hand-side actions. For example, to shift attention in the visual array, a production would send a MOVE-ATTENTION command to the Vision Module specifying the new location to be attended. Perceptual-motor modules output results in one of two ways. First, they can create or modify chunks in ACT–R's declarative memory. Following up on the previous example, once the Vision Module has executed the requested MOVE-ATTENTION, a chunk representing the visual object at that location will be placed in declarative memory. The second kind of output from the perceptual-motor modules is output to the environment, such as keystrokes, mouse clicks, or speech.

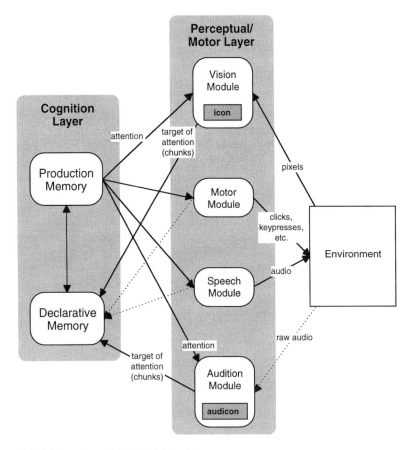

FIG. 6.2 Overview of ACT–R/PM architecture.

Each module has several commands it can receive from the cognition layer, as well as a connection to the environment. The environment can be a simulated one or, as with the Visual Interface, the same software with which human subjects interact. Timing of a given perceptual motor operator depends on the individual module associated with that operator, which in turn reflects a simple theory of the perceptual or motor domain built into the module. Because of the asynchronous nature of ACT–R/PM, different modules and the central production system can operate in parallel. Thus, for instance, other productions can fire when a movement command has been issued but not yet completed.

The perceptual-motor layer is made up of four modules: Vision, Speech, Motor (in particular, "manual" motor), and Audition. They vary somewhat in their complexity and completeness, with Vision and Motor being the most developed, and Speech and Audition little more than fragments of timing information. We describe these in the following subsections.

The Vision Module

The Vision Module in ACT–R/PM is based on the ACT–R Visual Interface described in Chapter 5, with some implementational enhancements. As described in the previous chapter, the Visual Interface is a synthesis of Posner's (1980) spotlight theory of attention, Triesman's (Triesman & Sato, 1990) theory of feature synthesis, Wolfe's (1994) attentional theory, and Anderson's (Anderson & Matessa, 1992) theory of rational categorization. Visual perception in the Visual Interface, and thus ACT–R/PM's Vision Manager, roughly works as follows: the visual scene (a computer display) is parsed into basic visual features, which are stored in an iconic memory, or icon. Attention can be directed to locations in the icon, where features are synthesized by the rational categorization algorithm into representations of visual objects in the form of declarative chunks. This differs from EPIC's visual perception system primarily in that it is feature based rather than object based (see the fourth section of Chapter 5 for an example of the ramifications of this difference).

The Vision Module is a reimplementation of the Visual Interface with several enhancements:

1. Besides encoding objects from the environment it also encodes locations. This gives ACT–R a location-based as well as an object-based representation of the environment. This makes it easier to reason about locations and direct attention to locations. For instance, it is possible to direct attention to a location and encode the fact that there is no object at that location.

2. The Vision Module allows productions to discriminate between the current state of the visual system and past states. Under the old Visual Interface, when a chunk was created to represent a visual object, it was often impossible to tell if that chunk was the currently attended chunk or a memory of a previously attended chunk.

3. The Vision Module can now handle movement and change. The Vision Module can be instructed to track moving objects, can adjust to very small movements of objects it is trying to attend to, and can correctly identify objects that it has already attended to on changed displays. All of these features help support cognition in dynamic environments.

These enhancements are primarily designed to make it possible to use the Vision Manager to model tasks with dynamic displays in which objects move and/or disappear and do not represent substantial changes to the underlying theory. Overall, the Vision Module can be thought of as a more comprehensive visual system than the Visual Interface, while building on the foundation laid by the older system.

The Motor Module

ACT–R/PM's Motor Module is based directly on the specifications described in Kieras and Meyer's (1996) description of EPIC's Manual Motor Processor. Taking advantage of the parallelism built into ACT–R/PM, ACT can now issue motor commands and then fire other productions while the Motor Module performs the requested action. Actions typically have several parameters, such as hand (left/right) and location. Performing an action is divided into two phases, preparation and execution. The Motor Module can only prepare one movement at a time; requests by the cognition layer to prepare another movement while one is in preparation are ignored.

The preparation phase of movement performance occurs when a command is received and the Motor Module is computing the parameters necessary to actually execute the movement. The duration of the preparation phase depends on the difference between the specification of the previous movement and the current movement. If the current movement is identical to the previous movement, no preparation is necessary. If there are differences, however, then the preparation time depends on the number of new features that need to be prepared. Some action types, such as PUNCH (the simple downstroke-upstroke of a finger at its present location on a keyboard), require three features to be prepared: the type of movement (PUNCH), the hand, and the finger to use. However, if the last action was also a PUNCH, then the movement type does not need to be prepared, cutting down preparation time. Similarly, if the last action was also a PUNCH and the last hand is the same as the currently specified hand, then only one feature (the finger) needs to be prepared. Other movement types, such as MOVE-CURSOR, use a similar hierarchical sequence to determine the number of features that require preparation. ACT–R/PM continues the EPIC convention that features are prepared at a rate of 50 msec per feature.

After movement preparation completes, movement execution begins. The time taken for movement execution depends on the characteristics of the movement to be executed. Simple down-up keystrokes take a fixed time, whereas movements that require positioning of a hand or finger to a new location take time according to Fitts's Law (e.g., Fitts, 1954; Card et al, 1983), given in the Fitts Equation:

$$\text{Movement time} = k \log_2(\frac{d}{w} + 0.5) \qquad \textbf{Fitts Equation 6.1}$$

where d is the distance to be moved, w is the width of the target, and k is a constant that depends on time scale and the specific type of movement to be performed (e.g., finger point vs. mouse move vs. joystick move). The value of k for a mouse move is typically 100 msec/bit. This model of hand movement as preparation of features followed by execution of movement governed by Fitts's Law is borrowed from EPIC (especially Kieras & Meyer, 1996), based on various summaries of work on motor movement (e.g., Rosenbaum, 1980).

The Audition and Speech Modules

The Audition and Speech Modules give ACT–R/PM rudimentary abilities to process sound and speech, but they are not yet fully developed. The Audition Module is designed to work similarly to the Vision Module. There is a store of features called the *audicon*, and these features can be transformed into ACT chunks by way of an attention operator. Features in the audicon are, of course, not things that have spatial extent like visual features, but instead have temporal extent—they are sound events. These events have onsets and offsets, take some time before they can be detected by the Audition Module (called the *content delay*), and take time to be encoded into chunks (the *recode time*). Basic kinds of simulated sounds currently supported are tones, digits, and simple strings. Finally, the audicon has a decay parameter, a time delay computed from sound offset after which the sound is no longer available to the Audition Module, and therefore to ACT–R.

The Speech Module gives ACT–R/PM a rudimentary ability to speak. This system is not designed to provide a sophisticated simulation of human speech production, but to allow ACT–R to speak words and short phrases for simulating verbal responses in experiments. The Speech Module understands only one command, SPEAK, to speak specified text. Speech output works in much the same way as motor output: Speech is first prepared and executed. Preparation is assumed in this case to be fixed at two movement features (as per EPIC) before detectable vocal output occurs, and execution time is determined by the length of the string.

Clearly, the Speech and Audition Modules will require considerable work before they are able to model complex listening/speaking experiments, but they do provide a system that allows hearing of simple stimuli and responding with simple short responses, which represents a considerable percentage of psychology experiments that use audio and speech, particularly those based on brief reaction times.

THE THEORY AT WORK:
PSYCHOLOGICAL REFRACTORY PERIOD

One of the original motivations for constructing ACT–R/PM as a parallel system was to enable ACT–R to model experiments in which subjects clearly overlapped processing. Probably the simplest experimental paradigm for which there is evidence for such overlapping is PRP experiments. EPIC has been extensively applied to PRP tasks, and therefore they offer an excellent domain for comparison with ACT–R. Before delving into the relationship between ACT–R/PM and PRP experiments, some familiarity with the PRP paradigm is required.

PRP Basics

PRP experiments are among the simplest dual-task experiments conceived by experimental psychologists and have a long and rich history (see Pashler, 1994, and Meyer & Kieras, 1997, for excellent reviews of the PRP literature). Interest in PRP experiments grew out of interest in more complex everyday dual-task behavior, such as carrying on a conversation while driving a car. Because such complex tasks are difficult to analyze in the laboratory, the essence of dual-task behavior was boiled down to the simplest dual-task situation, represented by PRP experiments. PRP tasks can be thought of as discrete, special cases of the more continuous real-world tasks. If limitations on dual-tasking ability appear in these simplest cases, then they should certainly appear in more complex situations.

PRP experiments require subjects to perform two tasks, usually called Task 1 (T1) and Task 2 (T2), which consist of simple responses to the presentation of simple stimuli. Typically T1 and T2 are choice reaction tasks (e.g., say the word "high" upon detection of a high-pitched tone or the word "low" for a low-pitched tone), and the stimulus modality, response modality, and task difficulty are often manipulated in PRP experiments. Subjects are explicitly instructed to complete Task 1 before completing Task 2. Finally, there is a delay between presentation of the T1 stimulus and the T2 stimulus, called the stimulus onset asynchrony (SOA). Response times of PRP experiments are typically plotted as a function of SOA, as in Fig. 6.3, which represents more or less typical results of many PRP experiments.

There are several things to note about the graph in Fig. 6.3. First, note that T1 is unaffected by SOA, a typical PRP finding. This makes sense in that subjects are instructed to give Task 1 priority over Task 2, and flat curves for T1 are taken to mean they have done just that. Second, notice the curve for T2 (called a PRP curve). The T2 reaction time is elevated at short SOAs and gradually falls until it is more or less flat as well. The elevation at short SOAs, called the PRP effect, indicates some kind of delay in responding to T2 and is the source of the term *psychological refractory period*. The PRP effect has been used to argue for a variety of limitations and properties of the human cognitive-perceptual-motor system, including bottlenecks of

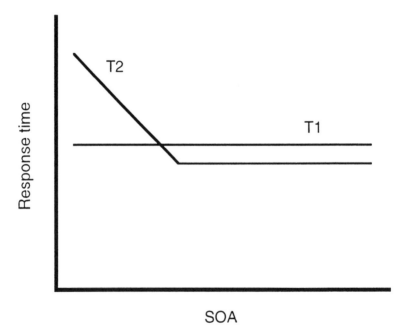

FIG. 6.3 Typical results of a PRP experiment.

various kinds (see the reviews for exhaustive discussions of this and numer-ous other debates PRP experiments have sparked).

The curves also suggest some kind of parallelism—as with most PRP experiments, the T2 reaction time at very small (or zero) SOA is typically measurably less than the sum of T1 and T2 reaction times at long SOAs. If the human system were completely serial, at SOA zero, the T2 response time should be the simple sum of the T1 and T2 base reaction times, but it is usually found to be less in PRP experiments. Thus, there must be some kind of overlapping of the Task 1 and Task 2 processing.

Another factor that has received a great deal of attention in PRP experiments is the difficulty of Task 2. If Task 2 difficulty is manipulated by simply increasing the demands of the cognitive component of the task, then different predictions emerge about what should happen to T2 response time. If ACT–R is correct about the serial nature of cognition, then the data would more or less correspond to the predictions of the "response selection bottleneck" model proposed by Pashler (e.g., 1994). This model proposes that the cognitive processing of Task 2 cannot overlap with the cognitive processing of Task 1, so making Task 2 more difficult will often have the effect of simply moving the T2 PRP curve up uniformly at all SOAs. An illustration of this logic appears in Fig. 6.4. The figure represents the sequences of Task 1 and an "easy" and "hard" version of Task 2, with Task 2 difficulty reflected in longer times for the cognition part of the task. Figure 6.4a shows what can happen at short SOAs. Although cognition for Task 1 and perception for Task 2 can be overlapped, the cognitive component of Task 2 must wait for the cognitive component of Task 1 to complete before it can begin. At longer SOAs, depicted in Fig. 6.4b, cognition for Task 2 can proceed as soon as Task 2 perception is complete. Notice that in both cases, the longer cognition time for the hard version of Task 2 is reflected in the response times.

In contrast, the parallel cognition module in EPIC predicts that, in certain cases, this is not what should be observed. Because the cognitive processing for Task 1 and Task 2 can be done in parallel in EPIC, EPIC predicts that there are many cases in which difficulty and SOA should interact. In particular, the EPIC–SRD model (Meyer & Kieras, 1997; SRD stands for strategic response deferment) predicts that the difficulty effect should disappear (or be greatly reduced) at short SOAs when Task 1's perception and response selection (cognition) completes later than Task 2's perception and response selection. Under these conditions, because Task 2 is proceeding during Task 1 processing, Task 2 is "waiting" for Task 1 to finish, and the difficulty effect is absorbed into the wait time. This logic is depicted in Fig. 6.5, which again represents two sequences of Task 1 with both an easy and hard Task 2. Figure 6.5a represents the situation at short

(a)

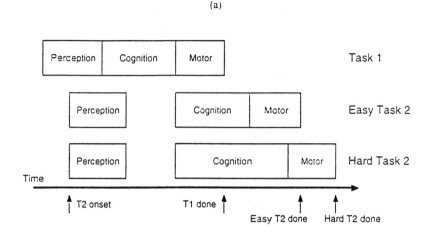

(b)

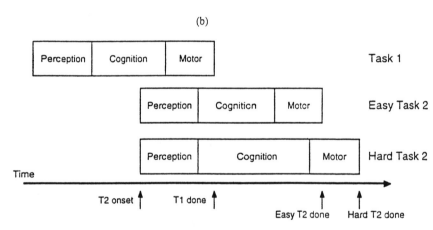

FIG. 6.4.   Schematic illustration of stages of processing in the central bottleneck
model of the PRP effect, at (a) short and (b) long SOAs.

SOAs when Task 1 perception and cognition takes longer than perception
and cognition for Task 2. Because cognition for Task 1 and Task 2 can be
done in parallel in EPIC, the Task 2 response time is unaffected by Task 2
difficulty—the difficulty effect is said to be "absorbed." At longer SOAs,
however, when Task 2 is not waiting for Task 1 to finish, the difficulty effect
reappears, as depicted in Fig. 6.5b.

(a)

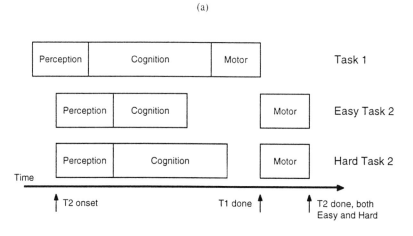

(b)

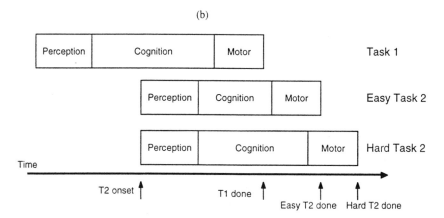

FIG. 6.5. Schematic illustration of stages of processing in the EPIC PRP model, at (a) short and (b) long SOAs.

Clearly, EPIC and ACT–R disagree about what should happen in case where Task 1 perception and cognition take longer than Task 2 perception and cognition. Thus, modeling a PRP experiment seems like a good initial testbed for ACT–R/PM, providing the opportunity to test its ability to overlap cognition with perceptual-motor activity and potentially testing one of the central claims of ACT–R, the serial nature of cognition.

A Simple PRP Model

We decided first to apply ACT–R/PM to a PRP experiment which lacked any significant cognitive component. This would illustrate how ACT–R/PM applies to such a task and how its noncognitive components are totally determined. For this purpose, we chose to first model data from Karlin and Kestenbaum's (1968) PRP study (Experiment 1, 2-2 condition). As the longest observed mean response time in this study is just over 500 msec—hardly enough time for much cognition—this should provide a good test of the low-level integration between cognition and perception/action in ACT–R/PM.

In this study,[1] the participants had extensive practice with two tasks, both of which were choice reaction time tasks. For Task 1, participants were briefly shown a digit on a display, with the digit being either a 1 or a 2. If the presented digit was a 1, participants were to respond by pressing a key with the little finger of their left hand, whereas for a 2 the key was pressed with the ring finger. Task 2 was also a two-choice reaction with button-press responses. Participants heard either a low tone (600 Hz) or a high tone (3000 Hz) and responded with a right-handed button press, either with the middle or index finger, respectively. Twelve different SOAs were used, ranging from 90 to 1150 msec. Results are presented in Fig. 6.6.

The results here are fairly typical in that the curve for Task 1 is essentially flat and the curve for Task 2 is elevated at short SOAs and flat at longer SOAs. Notice also that this exhibits dual-task savings. If the tasks were performed purely sequentially, the fastest expected Task 2 response time at the 90 msec SOA would be the Task 1 mean time, 383 msec, plus the fastest Task 2 time, 284 msec, minus the SOA of 90 msec, for a total of 577 msec ($383 + 284 - 90 = 577$). The observed mean, however, is 514 msec, meaning that there is approximately 60 msec of overlap to account for. This would have been impossible for older instantiations of the ACT theory, which serialized not just cognition but all activity.

The ACT–R/PM model handles the experiment with four productions (one for each stimulus in each task), which simply map results from perception onto motor commands. From the cognition standpoint, nothing happens until the digit is recognized. When it is, the appropriate production fires and sends the corresponding motor command and sets a marker in the goal enabling the Task 2 productions. These productions do essentially the same thing, one for the high tone and one for the low tone. However, the Task 2 productions do one other thing at short SOAs—they wait. They are

---

[1]There were several other conditions presented in the original Karlin and Kestenbaum (1968) paper. This condition was chosen as the most representative; other aspects of the original experiments have failed to replicate (Van Selst & Jolicoeur, 1997).

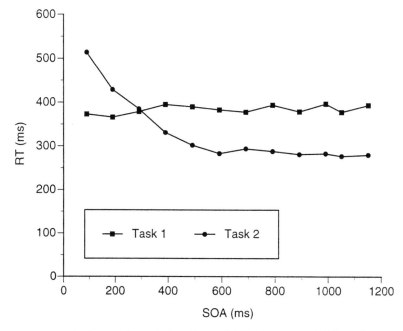

FIG. 6.6 Results from Karlin and Kestenbaum (1968) Experiment 1, 2-2 condition.

forced to wait because at short SOAs, the motor command for Task 1 is still being prepared by the Motor Module, which is only allowed to prepare one command at a time. Thus, the Task 2 command is not sent until the Task 1 movement has been initiated, which ensures that the Task 2 response does not precede the Task 1 response, as per the task instructions.

Table 6.1 shows the timing involved in performing the two tasks. There is an initial 135 msec to encode the digit,[2] 50 msec for the appropriate production to fire to request the keypress, 150 msec for the features of that action to be generated by the Motor Module (three features: punch, left hand, ring/little finger, each taking 50 msec), 50 msec to initiate the action, and 10 msec for the key close to register. In the case of the second task, there is 50 msec for the tone to be detected, 50 msec for the production, 100 msec to prepare movement features (two new features—right hand, index/middle finger—each 50 msec), 50 msec for initiation, and 10 msec for the key close to be detected. Except for the visual encoding time and

---

[2]Recall from Chapter 5 that we estimated 185 msec to switch attention and encode an object. This is decomposed into 50 msec to switch attention and 135 msec to encode. We assume that switch has already occurred.

TABLE 6.1
Sequencing of the Karlin and Kestenbaum Model

Task 1		Task 2	
	Present digit		
135 msec	Encode digit	SOA	Present tone
50 msec	Fire production	50 msec	Detect tone
150 msec	Generate movement features	|	
50 msec	Initiate movement	|	slack time
10 msec	Key closure	50 msec	Fire production
		100 msec	Generate movement features
		50 msec	Initiate movement
		10 msec	Key closure

the 50 msec production time, all of these latencies are taken from EPIC. The productions for the second task wait until the initiation of the first action. Thus, as illustrated in Table 6.1, the overlap between the two tasks is the 50 msec to detect the tone in Task 2 and the 10 msec to register the key closure in Task 1.

Figure 6.7 presents the fit of the model to the data. Overall, the fit is a good one, although the model slightly underpredicts the Task 2 response time, particularly at intermediate SOAs where the curve is flattening out. However, the fit is impressive in light of the fact that it is essentially a zero-parameter fit. That is, no parameters were estimated to fit the model to the data; the default values for all timing parameters were used without adjustment.

The lesson to take from this example is how the specification of the task dictates the degree of parallelism and degree of seriality. The perceptual modules, the motor module, and cognitive system can all run in parallel. However, when multiple demands are made on one of these systems we get seriality. In this case, multiple demands are being made of the motor system for manual action, and one must be postponed until the other is ready. EPIC has this sort of seriality built into it in terms of its use of perceptual and motor modules. However, it does assume unlimited parallelism in terms of its use of the cognitive production system. This turns out not to be an issue in the Karlin and Kestenbaum experiment because there is no overlap between the two single productions that fire. In the next experiment we look at a situation where there is the possibility of cognitive overlap and hence we can discriminate between the two theories.

A Cognitive PRP Experiment

The Karlin and Kestenbaum experiment is typical of PRP experiments, making use of simple tasks such as choice reaction time (but see Carrier & Pashler, 1995, for an exception). Such cognitively lean experiments do not map closely onto what has been the main goal of ACT–R, which is the modeling of higher-level human cognition. In order to make PRP experiments more cognitive, we have selected two relatively simple tasks that also include an important cognitive component: memory retrieval. ACT–R has a strong theory of memory retrieval based on the activations of declarative units and spreading activation from the goal. Thus, including a retrieval component augments the simple perceptual-motor requirements of the typical PRP task to provide a true perception-cognition-action experiment. One of the most developed theories of retrieval with ACT–R is in the domain of arithmetic (Chapter 9, this volume); therefore, we chose single-digit multiplication and addition as the two tasks for our experiment. This allowed us to manipulate the difficulty of Task 2 by varying the size of the operands involved in the problem. Finally, we wanted to test the EPIC–SRD prediction of a reduced difficulty effect at short SOAs.

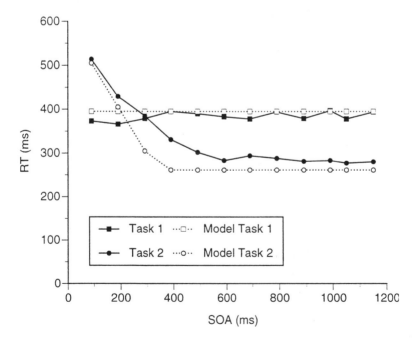

FIG. 6.7 ACT–R/PM model fit of the Karlin and Kestenbaum data.

Methods

Participants.   Participants were 29 Carnegie Mellon undergraduates who participated for credit in a psychology course.

Stimuli and Procedures.   Participants were presented with two tasks: multiplication as Task 1, and addition as Task 2. The multiplication task consisted of the audio presentation of two one-digit numbers, to which participants were to respond verbally with the product of the two numbers. Each number was digitized audio of a person's voice, and the audio clips were normalized for volume and length, which was fixed at 400 msec. There was a 500-msec pause between the completion of the first audio clip and the onset of the second clip.

Multiplication problems were randomly generated and used the numbers from one to nine. Problems never used the same number for both multiplicands, the number one was never the first digit presented, and participants never received the identical problem on consecutive trials. Response time for the multiplication task was measured from the onset of the second digit to the detection of the spoken response.

The addition problems were single-digit addition verification problems, presented visually. Each problem consisted of an addend, the plus sign, the second addend, the equals sign, and a result, such as $6 + 3 = 10$. If the result was the correct answer to the addition problem, participants were to respond by pressing the 6 key on the numeric keypad section of the keyboard. If the result was incorrect, participants were to respond by pressing the 4 key on the numeric keypad section of the keyboard. Participants were instructed to use two different fingers (to prevent hand movements) of their right hand for the two keys.

Again, addends were randomly selected digits with the constraint that digits were not repeated within a problem. For foils, the result was off from the correct answer by 2, 1, −1, or −2, and the amount of deviation was randomly selected.

As is standard for PRP experiments, participants were instructed to respond to the first task (multiplication) first. The experiment software rejected addition responses that occurred prior to multiplication responses to further enforce this constraint.

Participants first completed 120 practice trials consisting of 40 multiplication-only trials, then 40 addition-only trials, and then 40 dual-task trials. After practice, participants received three blocks of trials. Each block was divided into five sets of 40 trials: one multiplication-only set, one addition-only set, and three dual-task sets. Ordering of sets within a block was random.

Design. For multiplication-only trials, there was a single within-subjects factor, block, with three levels. For addition-only trials, there was the same block factor and an additional two-level difficulty factor; trials were either "easy" or "hard." For easy problems, each addend was between one and four, inclusive; for hard problems, each addend was between six and nine, inclusive. The numbers used in each problem were randomly generated (according to the problem constraints) on a trial-by-trial basis.

Dual-task trials had factors of block (three levels), difficulty of addition problem (two levels), and 10 levels of stimulus onset asynchrony (SOA). SOA was defined as the amount of time elapsed between the onset of the second digit in the multiplication problem (audio) and the presentation of the addition problem. The SOAs used were 0, 100, 200, 400, 500, 600, 800, 1200, 1800, and 2400 msec.

Materials. An Apple Power Macintosh 8500/120 with a standard Apple PlainTalk microphone was used to present all stimuli and record all data. Audio stimuli were presented using the computer's built-in speaker. Visual stimuli were presented in 18-point sans serif (Helvetica) text on an Apple 17-in color monitor.

Results. An alpha level of .01 was used for all tests. Some of the degrees of freedom reported contain decimal values, which is a result of applying the Greenhouse-Geiser correction for nonsphericity in within-subjects tests. Error rates were low for all subjects (approximately 5%), and error rates were not a function of any independent variables, so error rates are not considered in the discussion of the results.

Single Task. Single-task results are summarized in Fig. 6.8. For the multiplication, there were no reliable effects of block. For addition, there were reliable effects of both block, $F(2, 56) = 30.52$, $p < .001$, indicating some speedup over time, and of difficulty, $F(1, 28) = 35.80$, $p < .001$, indicating that "hard" problems were indeed slower. There was also an interaction $F(2, 56) = 11.12$, $p < .001$, with a slightly larger difference between easy and hard problems on block 2. Further, multiplication did indeed take longer than addition verification, as was expected.

Dual Task (PRP). Figure 6.9 presents the standard PRP curve, showing both multiplication and addition performance as a function of SOA, aggregating across blocks. Note that PRP effects are substantial, with participants slowing by approximately a full second from SOA 2400 to SOA

0. Again, as expected, the addition problems are faster than the multiplication problems at long SOAs.

Ideally, participants should be responding to Task 1 first and without regard to Task 2, and thus there should be no effect of SOA on Task 1 RT. In this experiment, that was the case. There was also no effect of block, so there is no evidence for learning in multiplication performance (mirroring the single-task data).

The more critical measure is reaction time for Task 2, which in this case is the addition. There was, as expected, a large effect of SOA, $F(9, 252) = 193.14, p < .001$, and a large effect of difficulty, $F(1, 28) = 39.34, p < .001$. Participants also sped up somewhat over time (mirroring the single-task data), resulting in a main effect of block, $F(2, 56) = 7.85, p = .001$. Note also that there is evidence for overlapping of processing; the base (single-task) reaction time means for the combination of Task 1 and Task 2 should be 2216 and 2426 msec for easy and hard addition problems, whereas the SOA 0 reaction times in the dual-task experiment are faster than these values (2073 and 2247 msec, respectively).

Most critical for the evaluation of the EPIC–SRD model is the interaction of difficulty and SOA; the EPIC–SRD model predicts that such an interaction should occur because there should be a greatly attenuated difficulty effect at short SOAs. We did find a difficulty-SOA interaction, $F(4.42,$

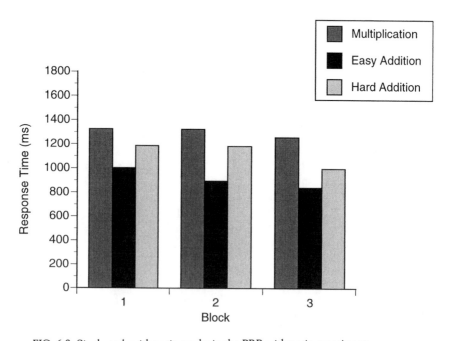

FIG. 6.8 Single-task arithmetic results in the PRP arithmetic experiment.

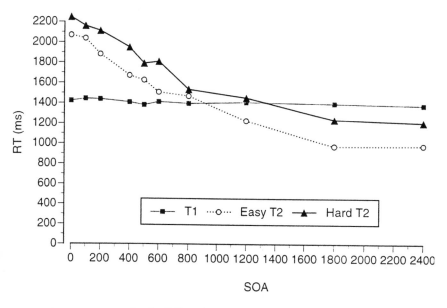

FIG. 6.9 PRP curve for the PRP arithmetic experiment.

123.68) = 3.86, p = .004. However, this interaction is not driven by a monotonically nondecreasing difficulty effect of SOA, as the EPIC–SRD model predicts—it is driven primarily by fluctuating difficulty effects across most SOAs. Figure 6.10 presents the difficulty effect as a function of SOA, which hardly appears to indicate absorption of the difficulty effects at short SOAs. Trend analysis on the means differences reveals no reliable trend in the size of the difficulty effect, and fitting a linear function through the means produces a line with a near-zero slope (0.025) and an r^2 of only .07. Thus, there does not appear to be any systematicity in the size of the difficulty effect, which does not support the predictions of the EPIC–SRD model.

Single- Versus Dual-Task Performance.   A second key prediction of the EPIC–SRD model is that there should be no increase in response time as a function of being in the dual-task situation for Task 1. This should also be true for Task 2 at long SOAs. This is not what was observed—Fig. 6.11 presents the single-task versus dual-task response times for multiplication and addition. For addition problems, only the long SOAs of 1800 and 2400 are included in this analysis, though both hard and easy problems are included.

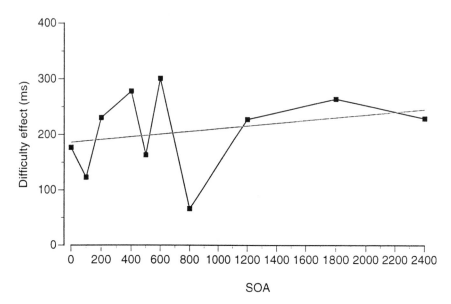

FIG. 6.10 Difficulty effect as a function of SOA for the PRP arithmetic experiment.

The overall effect of the dual task was about 100 msec in both multiplication and addition, and this difference is reliable (for multiplication, $F(1, 28) = 37.46$, $p < .001$, and for addition, $F(1, 28) = 8.34$, $p = .007$). The dual-task effect did not interact with block or with difficulty of addition. Clearly, something caused the reaction times to elevate when the participants entered the dual-task situation, although it is not entirely clear what that was, nor is it predicted by the EPIC–SRD model. The typicality of this result is difficult to assess, because the PRP literature has generally not presented single-task versus dual-task comparisons (but see Pashler & Johnston, 1989, for another example of dual-task slowing).

Discussion

Overall, the results of this experiment are consistent with typical PRP findings. PRP effects were observed at short SOAs, and the total time for the dual task suggests overlapping of processing. Further, there was no systematic increase of the difficulty effect as SOA increased, and there was an effect of being in the dual-task condition on response time for both multiplication and addition. Overall, these results are problematic for EPIC in several ways:

1. The difficulty effect is based on different content of facts in long-term declarative memory, which EPIC has in only very primitive form.
2. The difficulty effect does not systematically shrink as SOA approaches zero, which EPIC–SRD predicts should happen when Task 2 response selection can complete before Task 1 response selection.
3. There is a penalty for Task 1, and Task 2 at long SOAs, associated with being in a dual-task condition.

On the other hand, these results are equally problematic for ACT–R using the Visual Interface, because that instantiation of ACT–R cannot possibly reproduce the total time savings in the dual-task condition. However, as we show later, ACT–R/PM predicts all of these effects.

An ACT–R/PM Model of the PRP Experiment

The suggestion of overlapping of processing in PRP experiments is one of the key considerations that ACT–R/PM was designed to address. The question remains, however, of whether this potential for overlap is realized in quantitatively realistic way. In order to assess this, a model of the arithmetic-based PRP experiment was constructed. The basic approach taken was to fit model parameters to the single-task version of each task and use those parameters to predict performance in the dual-task situation.

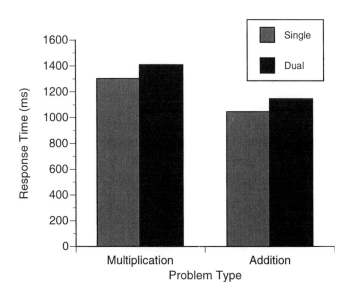

FIG. 6.11 Dual-task effects on multiplication and addition.

TABLE 6.2
Sequencing in the PRP Arithmetic Model

Task 1		Task 2	
Present second digit auditorily			
(first digit already presented and encoded)			
200 msec	Detect digit	SOA	Present problem visually
350 msec	Recognize (recode) digit	|	
~92 msec	Production to encode digit	|	slack time
Variable	Production to retrieve fact	|	
~92 msec	Production to generate answer and attend Task 2 stimulus location	|	
100 msec	Speech feature generation	135 msec	Encode visual
50 msec	Speech initiation	~92 msec	Production to encode 1st argument
100 msec	Audio detection	~92 msec	Production to encode 2nd argument
		~92 msec	Production to encode 3rd argument
		Variable	Production to retrieve fact
		50 msec	Production to compare answers
		150 msec	Motor feature generation
		50 msec	Movement initiation
		10 msec	Key closure

Table 6.2 describes the models for the two tasks and their relationship. We describe these models individually and their fit to single-task performance. Then we describe their combination in the dual-task model.

Single-Task Performance. For both multiplication and addition, the model goes through four steps: (1) perceive, (2) encode, (3) retrieve, and (4) respond. For multiplication, the basic perception process consists of applying a LISTEN-FOR operator until a chunk representing the sound is produced. Encoding consists of retrieving from memory a chunk that maps the raw chunk produced by the listen operator (e.g., the sound "3") to a semantic chunk representing the number (e.g., 3). Once both numbers have been encoded and stored in the goal, retrieval begins. The two operands serve as retrieval cues from which activation spreads. A fact is retrieved that corresponds to the multiplication fact involving those two numbers. Responding in the multiplication task involves retrieving a chunk that maps the semantic representation of the result (e.g., 27) to the verbal code for the number (e.g., the audio string "twenty-seven"), and then issuing a SPEAK command to speak the string.

For addition, the process is similar. The model begins by moving attention to the equation on the screen, which it takes in as a single phrase. The two operands are extracted from the representation of the phrase and then encoded into semantic units as was done for multiplication. Here the model has a choice: It can either retrieve the answer from declarative memory via production **Addition-Retrieve**, or encode the answer on the screen via production **Addition-Encode-Answer**.

Addition-Retrieve
IF   the goal is to do the addition task
            and the two operands have been encoded
            and there is an addition fact with those operands
THEN   place the result of the addition fact in the goal

Addition-Encode-Answer
IF   the goal is to do the addition task
            and the two operands have been encoded
            and there is a semantic code for the answer on the screen
THEN   encode the answer in the goal

Both **Addition-Retrieve** and **Addition-Encode-Answer** have to fire to verify the addition fact on the screen, and there is no necessary ordering of their firing. If **Addition-Retrieve** fires first, then the two operands and the operator serve as activation sources in the retrieval of the addition fact. However, if **Addition-Encode-Answer** fires first, then the operands, the operator,[3] and the answer all serve as activation sources for retrieval. This involves a trade-off: Retrieval of the answer from memory with four sources (two arguments, operator, answer) versus only three is faster when the answer on the screen is correct, but slower when the answer on the screen is incorrect. Thus, given no clearly superior strategy because the trials were half correct and half incorrect, the model randomly picks between the two productions with equal probability of each firing first. Finally, once all three numbers have been encoded and an answer retrieved, the model compares

---

[3]Actually, as we discuss later, the operator was only specified in the dual task. However, the same analysis applies when the operator is not specified in the single task.

the two answers, the retrieved one and the one encoded from the screen.[4] If they match, a production fires to punch the ring finger, and if there is a mismatch, another production fires to punch the index finger.

The latency for the model to complete a given trial is dependent on several factors. First, there are various parameter values that affect the time to completion, such as digit delay and recoding times, ACT–R's latency scale (F), activation noise(s), and the base-level activations of the chunks used for digit encoding. Parameter values used to fit this model are given in Table 6.3. Because activation noise is used in this model, results tend to vary from trial to trial. Also, the type of problem and the numbers that appear in each problem both affect response latency. Thus, the retrieval latencies are listed as variable in Table 6.2. These also vary because of the different base levels and associative strengths used for the arithmetic facts. The values were taken from Lebiere and Anderson's work (Chapter 9 of this volume) on mental arithmetic. In general, facts involving smaller numbers are retrieved faster than facts involving larger numbers, and addition facts are generally faster than multiplication facts. Because operands are randomly generated for each problem, this adds variability to the model. Finally, the choice of strategy for the addition problem combined with the correctness of the addition problem also affects latency. For these reasons, all model predictions are based on the mean of 100 Monte Carlo runs of the model.

Fit of the model to the single-task data is shown in Fig. 6.12. Overall, the fit of the model to the data is good. The fact that multiplication is slower than addition is a direct result of the different chunk base levels and S_{ji} values used; multiplication chunks generally have lower base levels than addition chunks and have lower S_{ji} values with their operands than addition chunks. This advantage for addition occurs despite the fact that the perception and encoding take longer for addition (as the visual system has to deal with three numbers and the auditory system only two, and on multiplication trials one of the numbers is handled before the trial actually begins—multiplication trials begin at the onset of the second operand). The difficulty

TABLE 6.3
Parameters Used in the PRP Arithmetic Model

Parameter	Value
Noise(s)	0.27
Latency factor (F)	0.85
Digit recode time	350 msec
Digit detection delay	200 msec
Base level activation for encoding chunks	3.00

---

[4]This is similar to the model for the fan effect described in Chapter 3.

effect found in the addition problems is also a result of the base levels and activations used—larger operands are seen less often and thus have lower base levels, so they are retrieved more slowly. This effect is fairly large; hard problems impose a roughly 200 msec increase in response time for a task that, in its easy form, takes around 900 msec. This is a more than 20% slowdown that the model is able to reproduce. Of course, fitting the single-task situation is only part of the story.

Dual-Task Performance.   Dual-task performance is somewhat more complex than the simple union of the two tasks. There are two related issues to address when considering the dual-task situation: (1) How will goal management/task switching be handled, and (2) where and when should cognitive, motor, and perceptual processing be overlapped? When considering goal management and task switching, there are several approaches one could take, and the approach taken impacts the model's ability to produce the dual-task effect observed (this is the increased response time associated with being in the dual-task condition). Probably the most obvious approach to goal management is to have a dual-task goal that does the multiplication and addition tasks as subgoals. That is, the model would begin the task with

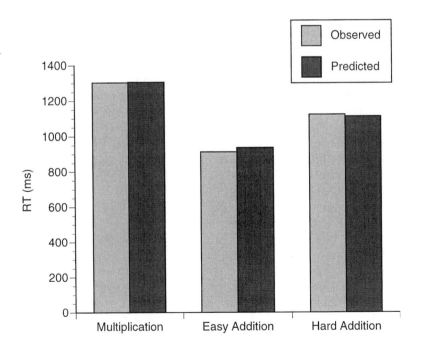

FIG. 6.12 Model and data for single-task versions of multiplication and addition.

a "do dual-task" goal on the stack, push and then pop a "do multiplication" subgoal, then push and pop a "do addition" subgoal. This approach has two drawbacks. First, it is difficult to manage overlap in processing between subgoals, because the subgoals are in a sense "unaware" of the overall dual-task situation. Second, in this scheme, the dual-task effect ought to come from the additional pushing and popping of subgoals. Although these additional pushes and pops would occur, they do not produce the kind of dual-task effects seen in the data. In fact, for multiplication, the additional push produces no dual-task effect at all. The time for the extra push gets "absorbed" into the time the model spends waiting for the second multiplication operand to be presented. For much the same reason, this kind of model generates no dual-task effect for the Task 2 addition at long SOAs either, because the extra pop and push get absorbed into the time the model spends waiting for the Task 2 stimulus to appear.

An alternative approach, and the one we took, involves using a single goal throughout the entirety of each dual-task trial. This allows for better control over interleaving but does raise another issue, that of task control: How does the model keep track of whether it is doing multiplication or addition? We handled this by adding a slot to the goal to represent the operator, either multiply or add. The presence of this additional operator in the goal means that the operands receive less source activation because source activation must be divided evenly among more slots. This single-goal approach reduces basic task-switching overhead, but predicts that retrieval times may be slower due to the divided source activation. In this model, this dividing of the source activation among the two operands and the operator does indeed slow down retrieval of the arithmetic facts. Although it is true that the operator also becomes a source and does spread some activation to help retrieve the arithmetic facts, the fan is so high from the operator that this has little impact. The net effect of this single-goal-with-operator strategy is to minimize task switching time, but in such a way as to cause a resulting slowdown in arithmetic fact retrieval. This produces a dual-task effect, but one based on increased retrieval time, not on goal management cost.

There is also the question of overlapping cognitive and perceptual-motor operations. Although it is theoretically possible to overlap in a wide variety of places (e.g., Task 2 perception with Task 1 perception/encoding/retrieval), the overall savings in time seen in the data, although clearly present, are not great enough to indicate more than a small amount of overlap. In fact, the amount of saving (around 200 msec at an SOA of 0 msec) suggests that the savings might come from simply overlapping the Speech Module's processing of the response in Task 1 with the Visual Module's perception of the Task 2 stimulus. This is the approach that was taken in constructing the dual-task model.[5] Thus, the same production that initiates the speech processing also initiates the attention shift:

T1-Respond
IF   the goal is to do the dual-task and there is an answer for T1
          and there is a verbal code for the answer
          and there is a visual location to attend
THEN   speak the verbal code
          and move attention to that location

It is after this last Task 1 production has fired that the cognitive system is now free to devote its production firing to Task 2. Thus, by postponing movement of visual attention until this point, the model guarantees that no Task 2 productions will intrude to delay Task 1 productions.

The critical question is whether, given these structural commitments (i.e., the goal strategy producing the dual-task effect and the relatively conservative approach to overlap), one can get the parameters estimated from the single-task model to produce behavior in the dual-task model that is quantitatively close to that observed in the laboratory. Figure 6.13 presents the fit of the model to the data. Note that the model generates a PRP effect that is much like the effect observed in the data. In the model, this is a result of postponing any processing of Task 2 (the addition) until the response for Task 1 has been selected. There is, however, a total savings in time when the two tasks are done together; that is, the sum of the two single-task times is greater than the T2 response time at SOA0. This savings comes from the parallelism built into ACT–R/PM. This parallelism comes into play immediately after the **T1-Respond** production fires. At that point, three things are going on in the model in parallel: (1) The cognition layer is executing a production that switches the operator in the goal and clears out the other slots in the goal, (2) the Speech Module is preparing and executing the vocal response, and (3) the Vision Module is shifting attention and recognizing to the equation on the screen. Without this parallelism, ACT–R would actually predict that the dual-task version should take longer than the sum of the single-task parts because of the dual-task cost. The model exhibits a dual-task cost similar to the one observed in the data. As described earlier, this is a result of the operator being stored in the goal. Because of this extra slot, there is less source activation supplied to the operators, and thus retrieval of the appropriate arithmetic facts is slower.

Note also that the model predicts that the difficulty effect should be roughly constant across SOAs. This is not quite what was observed, as the

---

[5]Many of our subjects reported that they did not look at the addition problem until they had solved the multiplication problem.

difficulty effect fluctuates up and down some in the data. In general, the data are simply noisier than the model. The lack of variability in the model is also likely responsible for the poor fit at 1200 msec SOA. Because the model almost always completes Task 1 response selection in less than 1200 msec, Task 2 is usually not forced to wait. Thus, the model produces very little PRP effect at 1200 msec. However, there were a number of subjects who had mean multiplication times much higher than the model who still showed evidence of a PRP effect at 1200 msec, which drives up the overall mean. Other work on ACT–R and individual differences (Lovett, Reder, & Lebiere, in press) suggest that it is possible to produce such individual differences, although that was not the focus of the current model.

Overall, though, the model fits the data quite well. Figure 6.14 presents the observed means as a function of the predicted means, an R^2 of .97. The quality of the fit of the ACT–R/PM model is impressive given that all the parameters were estimated for the single-task condition. ACT–R with the Visual Interface did not have the perceptual-motor capabilities to simulate any overlap in processing, and could not have generated such a fit. EPIC,

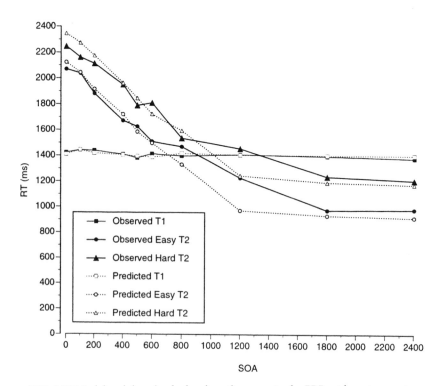

FIG. 6.13 Model and data for dual-task performance in the PRP arithmetic experiment.

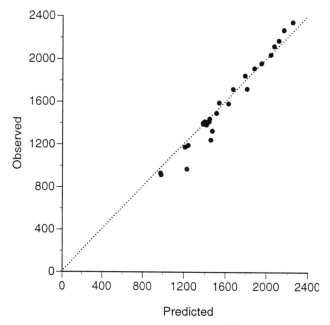

FIG. 6.14 Observed versus predicted means for the PRP arithmetic experiment and the ACT–R/PM model.

on the other hand, lacks the cognitive capability to simulate even fairly simple retrievals, and thus cannot handle the difficulty effect or the dual-task effect found here. Moreover, even if EPIC could produce the difficulty effect, it would seem to be committed to predicting that the effect should vanish at short SOAs because processing on Task 1 and Task 2 would be overlapped. Overall, by combining features of the two theories, a better model of performance on this task emerges.

SUMMARY

The world we live in is richer than one in which pure cognition or pure perception and action would suffice, but rather requires a mix of the two. ACT–R/PM represents an important step in integrating a serious theory of cognition, ACT–R, with a serious set of perceptual-motor constraints, borrowed largely from EPIC. The cognitive capabilities of ACT–R are well-documented (e.g., this volume), but until now the perceptual-motor properties of ACT have been somewhat impoverished. ACT–R/PM is another step beyond the Visual Interface in solving this problem, by incor-porating a system of asynchronous peripheral modules to handle the perception/action side of behavior. The individual modules themselves are generally patterned after those found in EPIC, with the exception of the Vision Module, which is patterned largely after the ACT–R Visual Interface.

A good starting challenge for a more complete system is a task that is dominated by neither cognitive nor perceptual-motor requirements, but rather a mixture of both. Traditionally, PRP tasks have been a good demonstration of our ability to overlap different kinds of processing, but have had relatively weak cognitive demands. In order to better test ACT–R/PM, we created a new PRP task that has a clear declarative memory retrieval component, an arithmetic PRP task. The results of this experiment are difficult to handle with a system that handles exclusively cognition or exclusively perception and action well, but not both.

Therefore, the experiment was amenable to modeling with ACT–R/PM. The combination of a strong theory of cognition with serious perceptual-motor constraints has yielded a system that is capable of handling the challenge of this PRP experiment. Of course, although PRP experiments are illustrative of dual-task situations, this is still a limited demonstration of ACT–R/PM's abilities. A fully integrated theory of cognition, perception, and action could potentially have a wide range of application that goes far beyond this simple laboratory task and into areas such as mental workload, manual tracking, perceptual-motor errors, typewriting, divided attention, high-performance human-machine interaction, and so on. This simple dual task modeled here merely scratches the surface. Just as HAM evolved from models of simple memory experiments into its current form (ACT–R) and expanded its range of application to domains such as choice and scientific discovery, ACT–R/PM applied to these simple PRP experiments will hopefully begin a widening of the ACT theory into integrated cognitive-perceptual-motor tasks. There are certainly many challenges for ACT–R/PM to face, but sound models of PRP experiments represent a promising start on which to build more sophisticated models.

7

List Memory

John R. Anderson
Daniel Bothell
Christian Lebiere
Michael Matessa
Carnegie Mellon University

From our vantage point on psychology it seems that more experiments have been run using the list memory paradigm than any other experimental paradigm (for recent reviews see Healy & McNamara, 1996; Raajimakers & Shiffrin, 1992). This is a paradigm in which subjects are presented with a list of words and then are tested for their memory of the words. The test may involve an attempt to recall the words in their presented order, in which case it is called serial memory; an attempt to recall the words in any order, in which case it is called free recall; an attempt to recognize the words, in which case it is called recognition memory; or an attempt to do something involving the words (like stem completion) but not requiring that the subject consciously retrieve these words, in which case it is called implicit memory.

The list memory paradigm was the paradigm that Ebbinghaus used in the first experiments on human memory (although he used nonsense syllables). It continued to be used in a great many studies in the subsequent decades. Ebbinghaus and other early researchers usually used serial memory tests. With the rise of cognitive psychology, research on human memory grew in importance and the list memory paradigm seemed to rise with it. The free-recall paradigm was initially of great importance in showing the effects of organizational factors on memory. More recently, recognition memory has become important in discriminating among major theories of memory. The implicit memory research is almost exclusively a phenomenon of the last two decades but has risen to perhaps the hottest area of research in cognitive psychology. The serial memory version of this paradigm has not been forgotten and is currently prominent in the form of tests of immediate or working memory.

Numerous theories have been proposed to account for phenomena in one or more of these subdomains of list memory, but there does not seem to be an integrated account that spans all of the domains. Different subdomains involve different aspects of cognition—memory for serial order, free recall strategies, structure of lexical memory, and so forth. Therefore, it is natural that detailed accounts of specific subdomains should focus on different aspects of the cognitive system. Still the similarity of the learning experience (study a list of words) creates the expectation that there should be some way of integrating these accounts. This chapter tries to do this by applying ACT–R to the list memory experiments in the order of serial memory, recognition memory, free recall, and implicit memory.

SERIAL MEMORY

The area of serial memory has had the longest history of research in psychology. It started with Ebbinghaus's interest in relatively permanent memory, evolved into an interest in transfer among lists, and most recently has focused on theories of memory span. It has seen a fair amount of theory in the last third of this century (e.g., Baddeley, 1986; Burgess & Hitch, 1992; Conrad, 1964; Ebbinghaus, 1885; Estes, 1973; Lewandowsky & Murdock, 1989; Murdock, 1993; Richman, Staszewski, & Simon, 1995; Shiffrin & Cook, 1978; Wickelgren, 1965a; Young, 1968). Although the ACT–R theory is applicable to all types of serial recall paradigms, this chapter describes an application of ACT–R to the relatively immediate recall of relatively short lists, as this is where most of the recent interest has been. Much of the recent theory has been dominated by Baddeley's theory of the phonological loop. His theory assumes that the amount that can be maintained in a memory span is the number of words that can be rehearsed in approximately 2 sec. The strong evidence for this proposal comes from research showing that people can maintain fewer words that take longer to articulate—either because the words have more syllables or have syllables that are longer to articulate. In one very influential study Baddeley, Thompson, and Buchanan (1975) looked at the number of words (out of five) that could be repeated back as a function of syllable length of the words. Varying syllable length from one to five, they found that the amount recalled was approximately equal to the number of words that could be said in 2 sec.

Anderson and Matessa (1997) published an application of ACT–R 2.0 to serial memory tasks. The models reported there were mathematical approximations to the ACT–R theory, whereas this chapter reports the results from actual running simulations (reflecting the more efficient implementation of ACT–R 4.0). This allows us to deal more adequately with the effects of rehearsal strategy and partial matching. We could not always capture their effects in the Anderson and Matessa article with closed-form equations.

The ACT–R theory shares with Baddeley's theory an emphasis on time-based decay (based on Base-Level Equation 3.6 or Base-Level Learning Equation 4.1). However, it also emphasizes important roles for associative interference (based on Prior Strength Equation 4.2[1]) and for confusions among items in a list (based on Match Equation 3.8). In fact, there is good evidence for all of these factors as reviewed by Anderson and Matessa. Holding retention time constant, subjects are worse when they must remember more items, indicating associative interference. Confusions among items that are similar sounding (acoustic confusions) or are in similar positions (positional confusions) are a major fact of memory span performance. It is a major challenge to be able to integrate these factors together. This section shows that ACT–R can do this. Rather than reporting applications of ACT–R to past experiments as in Anderson and Matessa, ACT–R is applied here to some new data that were collected expressly to provide a powerful test of the predictions of the ACT–R theory.

An ACT–R Model of Serial Recall

A key issue concerns the nature of the representation of the serial list. Our assumption is that a list is organized as a set of groups and each group is represented as a set of items. Most critically we assume that there is a chunk for each group encoding its position in the list and a chunk for each item encoding its position in the group. Positional coding, rather than associative chaining, has been advocated by a number of researchers (Burgess & Hitch, 1982; Conrad, 1965; Johnson, 1991; Shiffrin & Cook, 1978; Slamecka, 1967; Young, 1968). Figure 7.1 illustrates a possible representation for a list of 9 digits grouped as 329 714 856. There is substantial evidence for such a grouped representation (e.g., Bower & Winzenz, 1969; Johnson, 1970), and it is part of other models of serial memory (e.g., Estes, 1973). Each oval in Fig. 7.1 represents an ACT–R chunk. There is one chunk for each group and each element. A group chunk encodes the list the group is in, the size of the group, and its position in the list. Thus, the first group chunk encodes a group of size 3 in the first position of the list. This is indicated by pointers from *Group1*, *Size3*, and *List*. The elements are represented by chunks encoding the position of the element in the group, its group position in the list, the list it is in, and its content. Thus, for example, the first element 3 is encoded by a chunk with pointers to *1st*, *Group1*, *List*, and *Three*. Performance is going to depend critically on the retrieval of these chunks. Most critical is the link to the list context. There are so many links to the *List* context in Fig. 7.1 that we have had to merge them. However, in actual fact,

---

[1]In all the simulations in this chapter, associative strength learning is turned off. Therefore, the Posterior Strength Equation 4.3 is not applicable.

List is the least used index into each chunk.[2] Terms like *1st, Group1,* and *Three* will appear in thousands of contexts. Thus, fan (number of associations) out of *List* becomes critical.

Retrieval of chunks encoding list elements is orchestrated by the following production rule:

Get-Next
    IF   the goal is to retrieve the nth element of the mth group of
              the list
              and x is the element at position n in group m in the list
    THEN set a subgoal to process x
              and update the goal to retrieve the n+1st element

Each element is then produced by the following production:

Type-Item
    IF   the goal is to process an item
              and the item is associated with a key
    THEN type the key.

This production rule is specific to typing as the output mode because this is the output modality in the experiment to be reported. Similar productions could produce the response by means of written or verbal report.

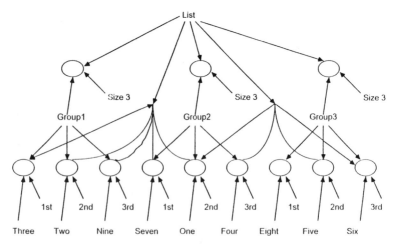

FIG. 7.1. Network representation of the chunk structure encoding a nine-element list.

---

[2]The assumption here is that each list will have its own token. Perhaps to avoid ambiguity, we should have called this something like *List-7136*.

In addition to retrieving the elements of a group, it is also necessary to first retrieve the groups themselves:

Retrieve-Group
      IF   the goal is to retrieve the mth group of the list
              and x is a group of size s in position m of the list
    THEN   set as a subgoal to retrieve the s elements of the group x
              starting in position 1
              and update the goal to retrieve the m + 1st element

This also retrieves the size, s, of the group. The group size is important because it allows the system to know when to terminate recall of the group.

Note that it is a feature of both **Get-Next** and **Retrieve-Group** that they recall in the forward direction. This forward bias to serial recall played an important role in Anderson and Matessa (1997) and is a critical feature in the experiment reported here.

According to the ACT–R theory, the critical factor determining speed and accuracy of retrieval will be the activation of the chunks that encode the group and item information. According to Activation Equation 3.5, this activation will be a sum of base-level activation and associative activation. The base-level activation will in turn be determined by the amount of practice (through rehearsal) that these chunks received and how long ago those rehearsals were. As lists get longer the delays will tend to increase, thereby decreasing base-level activations (Base-Level Learning Equation 4.1). The associative activation will come from the list element. As the list is longer, there will be more associations from the list element and less associative activation to any member of the list. This is basically a fan effect (see Chapter 3). Therefore, performance will go down with list length memory because of both increased delay impacting base-level activation and increased fan impacting associative activation.

Although this chapter presents the results of Monte Carlo runs of ACT–R simulations, it is useful to have an equation that gives the approximate activation values that determine performance. The approximate equation that characterizes activation levels in serial memory experiments is:

$$A = B + \ln n - d \ln T - W \ln L$$

where B reflects the constant factors, n is the number of presentations and rehearsals, T is time since presentation, L is the length of the list, d is the decay rate, and W is the attentional weighting of the list context. The decay parameter is 0.5, which is the value used throughout this book. The value of the W in this simulation is 1 because the list is the only useful source of activation.[3] Thus, the effective equation for serial recall becomes the Serial Memory Equation:

$$\text{Activation} = \ln n - 0.5 \ln T - \ln L \quad \textbf{Serial Memory Equation 7.1}$$

ignoring the constant. This equation is only approximate, and the predictions presented come from the running ACT–R simulation.

There is one additional important aspect to the ACT–R model of serial recall. This is partial matching of chunks, which can produce positional confusions. Partial matching of the group slot will cause ACT–R to retrieve an element from a corresponding position in another group. Partial matching of the position slot will cause ACT–R to retrieve an element from another position in the current group. The degree of mismatch (D_{ip} in Match Equation 3.8) between elements is proportional to their distance apart. Thus, for instance, the mismatch between *First* and *Second*, *Second* and *Third*, or *Group1* and *Group2* is $1 \times D$, whereas the degree of mismatch between *First* and *Third* or *Group2* and *Group4* is $2 \times D$. D is referred to as the scale factor for mismatches. This similarity-based confusion produces many more positional confusions between adjacent elements than distant items. The existence of positional confusions within and between groups is well documented (e.g., Aaronson, 1968; Bjork & Healy, 1974; Lee & Estes, 1981; Nairne, 1992). We do not deal with acoustic confusions because the study to be reported involves digits, which are not particularly confusable acoustically. Acoustic confusions were handled in Anderson and Matessa, again by the mechanism of partial matching.

To review, the key assumptions in the ACT–R model of serial recall are the hierarchical representation of the list, the activation-driven recall, and the potential for positional confusions through partial matching. A later subsection describes in more detail the ACT–R model of serial recall and its consequences for base-level activation and associative activation. However, first, the next subsection describes the experiment that is the target of the modeling efforts.

A Study of Backward and Forward Recall

Like the Baddeley theory, the ACT–R theory claims that timing of the recall is important to memory performance and that with the passage of time

---

[3]In the standard ACT–R 4.0 simulation, source activation (W) is divided equally among all goal slots. Because positional information is in the goal slots, this means the source activation for the list would be less than 1. However, Anderson and Reder (in press) have speculated that subjects can dynamically reallocate source activation to more useful sources. We modified the simulations in this chapter to enable this focused source activation.

memory chunks can decay to the point where they are no longer available for recall. However, in addition it claims that the activations of the memory chunks have a strong influence on the timing of recall (Retrieval Time Equation 3.10). Thus, there is a feedback loop between timing and activations, with higher activations yielding shorter retrieval times and shorter times yielding higher activations. Because there has not been research that has delved into this interaction between timing and recall, Anderson, Bothell, Lebiere, and Matessa (in press) performed an experiment that focused on this issue. They looked at memory span for digits, presented at the typical rate of 1 per second. They varied list lengths from 3 to 12 digits to get a good range of performance and measured both the timing and the accuracy of recall. They also looked at both forward and backward recall to manipulate the delay between presentation and recall. In forward recall the digits presented first are recalled first, whereas in backward recall the digits presented last are recalled first. This creates very different delays for the recall of digits that are studied in the same serial position. Anderson et al. also controlled the grouping of the digits by presenting them visually segregated into units. All the groups were of length 3 except for the last, which varied from 2 to 4 to accommodate various list lengths.

A series of boxes would appear on the screen—one box for each group. The number of items that would appear in each box was made obvious by the number of spaces in the box. Thus, the subject knew immediately the number of and structure of the items to be studied. However, while subjects were studying the items they did not know whether they would be tested in the forward or the backward condition. This was done to test the same memory structure in different orders. The items were presented one at a time in the appropriate spaces within the appropriate boxes. When one digit appeared, the other disappeared, so only one digit was visible at a time. As soon as the last digit disappeared a signal appeared telling subjects the direction in which to recall the digits. The cursor would either move to the first slot in the first box (for forward recall) or the last slot in the last box (for backward recall). As each digit was typed the cursor moved to the next slot (or previous slot in the case of backward recall). The subject could skip over positions by typing a space or terminate the recall by hitting the return key. However, the subject could not back up and change recall of a digit.

Figure 7.2 shows the serial position curves for the various list lengths. Both Figs. 7.2a and 7.2b plot the probability of correctly recalling a digit in position as a function of serial position in input. For forward recall (Fig. 7.2a) output order is the same as the input order, but for backward recall (Fig. 7.2b) output order is the reverse of the plotted input order. The forward recall curves are quite typical, showing decreased accuracy with serial position. There is an upturn for the last item, indicating a weak recency

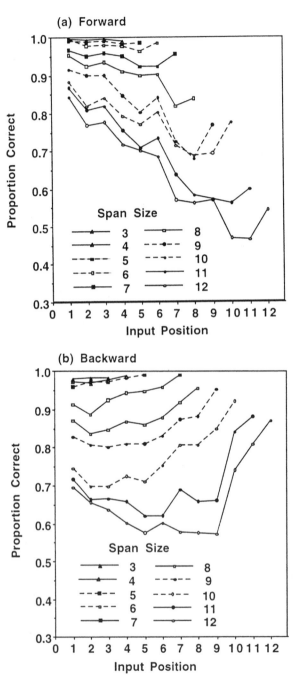

FIG. 7.2. Probability of correct positional recall for items recalled in (a) the forward direction and (b) the backward direction.

208

effect. Henson, Norris, Page, and Baddeley (1996) have argued that this one-item recency effect is due to decreased positional confusion regarding the last item. The backward curves largely show a weak primacy effect and a stronger recency effect spanning many items. Because input and output are reversed, this indicates better recall for the first items recalled just as in the forward recall. Such contrasting serial position curves for backward and forward recall is typical (e.g., Hinrichs 1968; Li & Lewandowsky, 1995; Metcalfe & Sharpe, 1985). These curves also show some effect of the group structure. There are steep drops in the forward recall curves at positions 3 and 6, which are chunk boundaries. Thus, subjects show significant drops in recall from group 1 to group 2 and from group 2 to group 3. The group structure is less apparent in backward recall, but there are precipitous rises from positions 9 to 10 in the lists of length 11 and 12, which correspond to the boundary defining the first group recalled.

Figure 7.3 shows the times to type the digits as a function of input positions. These are the means of the mean correct recall times for each subject. Here the group structure shows through very clearly. Large spikes occur in the latency curves whenever subjects must begin recall of another group. In the case of forward recall the latency associated with recalling the first group is much longer than the other latencies, whereas in backward recall all group boundaries have comparable latencies. This suggests that in backward recall subjects start all over again from the start of the list with each group, whereas in forward recall they maintain some positional information within the list from group to group. Also, in both forward and backward recall, the size of these spikes is very much a function of list length with longer lists resulting in larger spikes. In contrast, there is relatively little difference in within-chunk latency as a function of list length. This suggests that subjects are doing all of their recall for a group before typing any of the items. Other research (e.g., Cowan, 1992; Sternberg, Monsell, Knoll, & Wright, 1978) has found increased latency for all list items as a function of list length, but this research has not tried to control group structure. The increased latency for all items may reflect the fact that different subjects used different structures and the data were averaged over different structures.

This one experiment has brought together many of the powerful effects documented in the memory span literature. The study indicates a rich pattern of data reflecting factors such as direction of recall, list length, and grouping. The data in Figs. 7.2 and 7.3 should serve as a substantial challenge to any theory including the ACT–R theory.

The ACT–R Simulation

We developed an ACT–R simulation of this task. Table 7.1 gives a trace of the simulation studying and recalling the nine-element list whose repre-

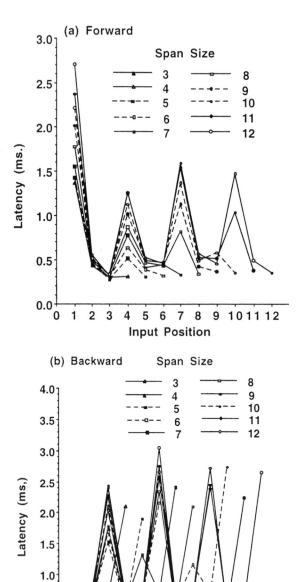

FIG. 7.3. Time to recall digits as a function of serial position and list length for (a) forward recall and (b) backward recall.

sentation is in Fig. 7.1. Part (a) illustrates the study process, part (b) illustrates the forward recall, and part (c) the backward recall. During study, ACT–R is interleaving study and rehearsal. The productions **Attend-Start** and **Attend** are responsible for encoding the digits as they appear on the screen. The first production, **Attend-Start**, encodes a digit at the beginning of a group, creating a chunk for both the group and the item. The second production, **Attend**, deals with the digits within a group.

The rehearsal strategy illustrated in part (a) of Table 7.1 is one where the system starts at the beginning of a list and keeps rehearsing until it comes to the end of the list. As the list keeps growing, the model takes longer to complete a rehearsal loop, and usually it does not get to the end of the list in the last loop. Along with this linear rehearsal it interleaves rehearsal of the current item. **Rehearse-Start** initiates recall at the beginning of the list, and **Rehearse-Reset** reinitiates recall at the beginning of the list when the current end of the list has been reached. The production **Rehearse-Item** is responsible for stepping through the items in serial order, whereas **Rehearse-Current** is responsible for rehearsing the current item. These two productions compete, and either is equally likely to fire next. This is a rehearsal strategy that is biased to rehearse the beginning of the list but has some probability of rehearsing all the members of the list. **Rehearse-Abort** stops rehearsal when a new item appears so that this new item can be encoded. **Rehearse-Next-Group**, which first appears on cycle 17, fires when one group has been rehearsed and switches rehearsal to the next group.

In forward recall (part (b) of Table 7.1), productions **Retrieve-Group** and **Start-Group** (a variant of **Retrieve-Group** for the first group) retrieve the group chunks. A production **Dispatch-Three-Groups** sets subgoals to retrieve the groups in the order encoded. For each group, the productions **Get-Next** and **Get-Next-Start** (a variant of **Get-Next**) retrieve the individual item chunks, and **Dispatch-Three-Items** sets subgoals to type each in the order encoded. Then the production **Type-Item** types the individual digits. Note that this scheme retrieves all the items in a group before typing any. This corresponds to the data indicating that the subjects tended to do just that.

For backward recall (part (c) of Table 7.1), the rehearsal and encoding processes have identical structure because the subjects do not know how they will be tested. The structure of the recall is the same except with respect to the productions that dispatch the subgoals. The production **Dispatch-Three-Items-Backward** is like **Dispatch-Three-Items** except that it sets the subgoals to type the items in opposite order. On the other hand, the productions for dispatching groups in backward order only subgoal one group at a time. In contrast, the forward productions subgoaled all the groups. Therefore, when the group is completed in backward recall, the

TABLE 7.1
Study and Recall of "329 714 856"

(a) Study		
Cycle 0 Time 0.000: attend-start	Study	3
Cycle 1 Time 0.200: rehearse-start		
Cycle 2 Time 0.334: rehearse-item	Rehearse	3
Cycle 3 Time 0.879: rehearse-reset		
Cycle 4 Time 0.929: rehearse-item	Rehearse	3
Cycle 5 Time 1.462: rehearse-abort		
Cycle 6 Time 1.512: attend	Study	2
Cycle 7 Time 1.712: rehearse-current	Rehearse	2
Cycle 8 Time 2.246: rehearse-abort		
Cycle 9 Time 2.296: attend	Study	9
Cycle 10 Time 2.496: rehearse-current	Rehearse	9
Cycle 11 Time 3.105: rehearse-abort		
Cycle 12 Time 3.155: attend-start	Study	7
Cycle 13 Time 3.355: rehearse-item	Rehearse	2
Cycle 14 Time 3.891: rehearse-item	Rehearse	9
Cycle 15 Time 4.518: rehearse-abort		
Cycle 16 Time 4.568: attend	Study	1
Cycle 17 Time 4.768: rehearse-next-group		
Cycle 18 Time 4.942: rehearse-item	Rehearse	7
Cycle 19 Time 5.573: rehearse-abort		
Cycle 20 Time 5.623: attend	Study	4
Cycle 21 Time 5.823: rehearse-item	Rehearse	1
Cycle 22 Time 6.455: rehearse-abort		
Cycle 23 Time 6.505: attend-start	Study	8
Cycle 24 Time 6.705: rehearse-current	Rehearse	8
Cycle 25 Time 7.212: rehearse-abort		
Cycle 26 Time 7.262: attend	Study	5
Cycle 27 Time 7.462: rehearse-current	Rehearse	5
Cycle 28 Time 8.019: rehearse-abort		
Cycle 29 Time 8.069: attend	Study	6
Cycle 30 Time 8.269: rehearse-item	Rehearse	4

TABLE 7.1
(cont'd)

Cycle 31 Time 8.872: rehearse-next-group		
Cycle 32 Time 9.052: rehearse-abort-last	Rehearse	6

(b) Forward Recall

Cycle 1 Time 9.000: start-group		
Cycle 2 Time 9.782: retrieve-group		
Cycle 3 Time 9.905: retrieve-group		
Cycle 4 Time 9.992: dispatch-three-groups		
Cycle 5 Time 10.042: get-next-start		
Cycle 6 Tim e 10.244: get-next		
Cycle 7 Time 10.383: get-next		
Cycle 8 Time 10.644: dispatch-three-items		
Cycle 9 Time 10.694: type-item	Recall	3
Cycle 10 Time 11.198: type-item	Recall	2
Cycle 11 Time 11.701: type-item	Recall	9
Cycle 12 Time 12.208: get-next-start		
Cycle 13 Time 12.357: get-next		
Cycle 14 Time 12.656: get-next		
Cycle 15 Time 12.808: dispatch-three-items		
Cycle 16 Time 12.858: type-item	Recall	8
Cycle 17 Time 13.359: type-item	Recall	7
Cycle 18 Time 13.866: type-item	Recall	4
Cycle 19 Time 14.369: get-next-start-skip		
Cycle 20 Time 14.701: get-next		
Cycle 21 Time 14.986: get-next		
Cycle 22 Time 15.220: dispatch-three-items		
Cycle 23 Time 15.270: skip-item	skip	
Cycle 24 Time 15.770: type-item	Recall	5
Cycle 25 Time 16.276: type-item	Recall	6

(c) Backward Recall

Cycle 1 Time 9.000: start-group		
Cycle 2 Time 9.604: retrieve-group		
Cycle 3 Time 9.920: retrieve-group		
Cycle 4 Time 10.237: dispatch-three-group-backward		
Cycle 5 Time 10.287: get-next-start		
Cycle 6 Time 10.458: get-next-skip		
Cycle 7 Time 10.620: get-next		
Cycle 8 Time 10.837: dispatch-three-items-backward		

TABLE 7.1
(cont'd)

Cycle 9 Time 10.887: type-item	Recall	6
Cycle 10 Time 11.392: skip-item	skip	
Cycle 11 Time 11.896: type-item	Recall	8
Cycle 12 Time 12.401: start-group		
Cycle 13 Time 12.942: retrieve-group		
Cycle 14 Time 13.165: dispatch-two-group-backward		
Cycle 15 Time 13.215: get-next-start		
Cycle 16 Time 13.442: get-next		
Cycle 17 Time 13.634: get-next		
Cycle 18 Time 13.755: dispatch-three-items-backward		
Cycle 19 Time 13.805: type-item	Recall	4
Cycle 20 Time 14.306: type-item	Recall	1
Cycle 21 Time 14.809: type-item	Recall	9
Cycle 22 Time 15.315: start-group		
Cycle 23 Time 15.842: dispatch-one-group-backward		
Cycle 24 Time 15.892: get-next-start		
Cycle 25 Time 15.988: get-next		
Cycle 26 Time 16.241: get-next-skip		
Cycle 27 Time 16.493: dispatch-three-items-backward		
Cycle 28 Time 16.543: type-item	skip	
Cycle 29 Time 17.047: type-item	Recall	3
Cycle 30 Time 17.553: type-item	Recall	2

simulation must scan through all the groups in the list up to the to-be-re-called group. Thus, the structure for backward recall of the list in Fig. 7.2 is: recall group1, recall group2, recall group3, retrieve members of group3, recall group1, recall group2, retrieve members of group2, recall group1, and retrieve members of group1. This restarting contributes to recall latencies at the beginning of subsequent groups that are as long as the latency at the beginning of the first group. The other factor is that the later groups being unpacked have not been practiced for a while. The backward protocol in Table 7.1 also illustrates failure to retrieve a couple of items. These are cases where the activation of the critical items randomly fell below threshold.[4] The system is able to skip over the missing items and resume recall in place by means of the **Skip-Item** production. It can use the visual structure of the

---

[4]It is also possible for the activation of the group chunk to randomly fall below threshold, in which case the whole chunk will be skipped.

recall display to know where to begin the next group.

In both forward and backward recall it is the forward-moving **Retrieve-Group** and **Get-Item** productions that are responsible for retrieving the items. Forward or reverse recall is achieved by subgoaling the group to be recalled in either forward or reverse order by different Dispatch productions.

The protocol in Table 7.1 illustrates another feature of ACT–R's recall that results from the partial matching. In the forward recall, part (b), note that the 8 from the first position of the third group is recalled as the first member of the second group. In addition, the 7 that is the first member of the second group is recalled in the second position of the second group. Finally, because the 8 is "used up" nothing is recalled in the first position of the third group.[5] In the backward recall, note that the 3 and the 2 of the first group (recalled last) are reversed. These kinds of positional confusions are typical of serial recall and are produced by partial matching of the positional information.

The exact timings of the item recalls and their probabilities of success depend on random fluctuations in the activation levels. We ran 620 trials per condition, which corresponded to the number of observations from the experiment. This yielded fairly stable predictions. These predictions depend on four estimated parameters:

1. The activation noise level, s, estimated to be 0.300 (corresponding to a variance of 0.296)—see Retrieval Probability Equation 3.7.
2. The activation threshold, τ, estimated to be -0.35—see Retrieval Probability Equation 3.7.
3. The time scale parameter, F, for retrievals, estimated to be 220 msec—see Retrieval Time Equation 3.10.
4. The scale factor, D, for mismatches, estimated to be 2.5.

In addition a number of productions were given non-default action times (the default is 50 msec). These times were just set to plausible ballpark values:

5. The time to encode an item, which was 200 msec. This is the ballpark time established from the simulations of visual attention (see Chapter 5).
6. The response time to type an item, which was set to 500 msec.
7. The time to rehearse an item, which was set to 500 msec to reflect speech time.
8. The intercept time to start recall, for the **Start-Group** production, which was set to 500 msec.

---

[5]This is achieved by explicitly marking the chunk encoding the item as recalled.

The last four parameters are constant across all the simulations reported in this chapter, whereas the first four parameters, s, τ, F, and D, were estimated to produce a good fit to this experiment. However, our search for these four parameters was informal and there is no guarantee that we found the ones that produce optimal fits. The D parameter, reflecting positional similarity, is unique to this experiment but the other three, s, τ, and F, are potentially estimated anew for each experiment. Table 7.2 tracks all of the parameter estimates. At the end of the chapter we discuss the issue of variations in the s, τ, and F parameters across experiments.

Figures 7.4 and 7.5 show the resulting simulated recall behavior. The latency profiles in Fig. 7.5 capture the general structure of the profiles in Fig. 7.3. The overall R^2 between the two sets of latencies is .946. The accuracy profiles in Fig. 7.4 do not match as well, producing an overall R^2 of .906. Nonetheless, the correspondences between the profiles are quite compelling. This indicates some of the power of ACT–R to account for a complex data pattern. The model is predicting 300 numbers, estimating only four parameters and without carefully optimizing the fit.

To summarize what lies behind the ACT–R account of the data: The latency data speak to a very systematic group-by-group recall procedure that subjects are using to pace their recall. This strategy is implemented by the basic production rules that execute the task. Within this relatively fixed procedure there is considerable variation in latencies at chunk boundaries as a function of list length. This is produced by increasing interference in associative activation from the list context.

With respect to the accuracy data, recall of items varied considerably as a function of both list length and input position. ACT–R does not change the fundamental algorithm to predict these variations. These variations reflect the changes in activations of the elements being retrieved. These activations increase with rehearsal (base-level activation), decrease with time (base-level activation), and decrease with memory list length (associative activation). These are all basic processes in the ACT–R theory, and they combine to form the behavioral profiles in Figs. 7.4 and 7.5. Both time-based decay and associative interference are required to account for the span limitations. The very different recall profiles for forward and backward recall reflect differences in the time at which the same items are recalled. On the other hand, in the backward data one can look at recall of items that have the same delay between study and test. For instance, the last item is always cued immediately after the offset in its presentation. However, as Fig. 7.2b illustrates, recall for this item systematically drops, reflecting the contribution of associative interference from the other items. In addition to associative activation, which produces the differences among lists, and base-level decay, which produces the recency effect, the rehearsal strategy assumed by ACT–R

TABLE 7.2

Parameter Estimates of Various Experiments

	Serial Recall	Burrows* & Okada (1975)	Raeburn* (1974)	Ratcliff, Clark, & Shiffrin (1990)	Murdock (1962)	Glenberg et al. (1980)	Roberts (1972)	Johnston, Dark, & Jacoby (1985)	Hayman & Tulving (1989)	Toth, Reingold, & Jacoby (1993)
s (noise)	0.3			0.55	0.7	0.6	0.85	0.65	0.3	0.45
τ (threshold)	-0.35			1.8	3.2	1.4	2.9	0.9	-0.45	0.1
F (latency scale sec)	0.22	4.15	2.29	2	2	2	2	1.3	0.5	0.5
D (partial match serial position)	2.5		2.5							
P (partial match list context)				1.5				1.5	1.5	
Respond (sec)	0.5			0.5	0.5	0.5	0.5	0.5	0.5	0.5
Encoding (sec)	0.2		0.2	0.2	0.2	0.2	0.2	0.2	0.2	0.2
								0.5		
								0.7		
Rehearse (sec)	0.5	0.5	0.5	0.5	0.5	0.5	0.5	0.5	0.5	
Intercept (sec)	0.5	0.5	0.6							
Time (R^2)	0.946	0.957	0.886					0.910		
Accuracy (R^2)	0.906			0.970	0.923	0.860	0.990	0.921	0.962	0.979
Base activation	0.24	2.19	1.1	0.35	0.35	-1.51	0.52	-1.47	-1.07	-1.22
Associative activation	0.61	1.64	1.9	2.5	0.6	0.35	0.6	4.51	1.4	0.91
Average activation	0.85	3.83	3.0	2.85	0.95	-1.27	1.12	3.04	0.33	-0.31

* Because accuracy data are not modeled there was no need to estimate the s or τ parameters for these experiments. There was also no study process modeled in the Burrows and Okada experiment.

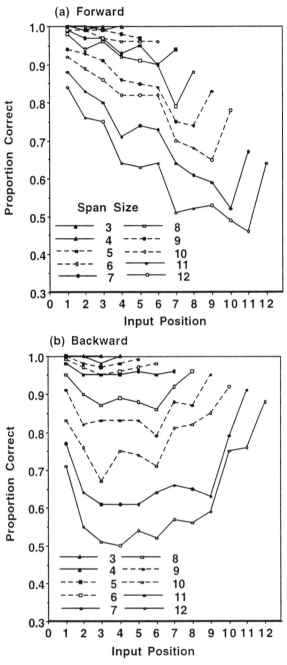

FIG. 7.4. Results of simulation: Predicted probability of correct positional recall (a) for items recalled in the forward direction and (b) for times recalled in the backward direction. Compare with Fig. 7.2.

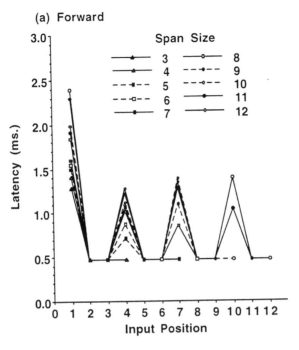

(a) Forward

Span Size

3		8	
4		9	
5		10	
6		11	
7		12	

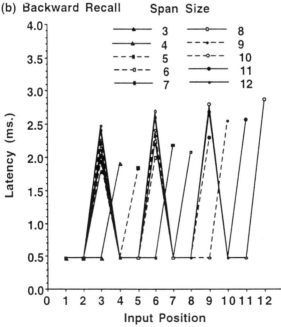

(b) Backward Recall   Span Size

3		8	
4		9	
5		10	
6		11	
7		12	

FIG. 7.5. Results of simulation: Time to recall digits as a function of serial position and list length for (a) forward recall and (b) backward recall. Compare with Fig. 7.3.

is critical. The tendency for the earlier items to receive greater rehearsal is what is producing the primacy effect.

RECOGNITION MEMORY

A very different way of testing memory involves simply showing subjects the words in the list and asking them whether they recognize the items. To keep the subjects honest these target words are mixed in with distractors (or foils) that they have not seen. The ACT–R model for this task is basically the one that Anderson and Bower (1972, 1974) developed 25 years ago, where it is assumed that a memory trace is set up that encodes that an item occurred in a particular list. Thus, ACT–R records that words occurred in the list by means of chunks like the one illustrated in Fig. 7.6, which encodes that the word *imply* occurred in *List3*. This is the same representation used in serial memory.[6]

Recognition of a word is achieved by productions like

Recognize-a-Word
> IF   the goal is to judge whether the word occurred in a context
>   and there is a trace of seeing the word in that context
> THEN   respond yes

This is a very straightforward model, which views recognition memory as a simple process. The memory trace just consists of two items—the word and the list context. In recognizing a word, a subject has access to both sources of association (in contrast to free recall, where the subject has only access to the list context). Thus, the activation of a memory trace can be written:

$$A = B + W_w S_w + W_L S_L$$

where W_w is the attentional weight given to the word, S_w is the strength of association from the word to the trace, W_L is the weight of the list context, and S_L is the strength of association from the list context to the trace. Although the word becomes an important additional source of activation, the $W_w S_w$ term remains constant across conditions. As in the case of the Serial Memory Equation 7.1, base-level activation can be expanded to show the effect of rehearsal time, decay, and list length:

---

[6]In Fig. 7.6 we do not show encoding of position. As discussed later, we continue use of positional information for the short Sternberg lists but not for the longer lists.

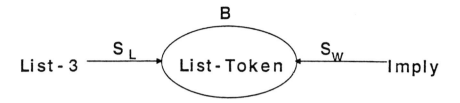

FIG. 7.6. A chunk encoding that the word *imply* has occurred in *List-3*.

$$A = B' + \ln n - d \ln T - W_L \ln L$$

where B' reflects constant effects including $W_w \, S_w$. Thus, just as in serial recall, the critical variables remain the amount of rehearsal n, delay time T, and the list length L.

Ignoring the constant, using the standard setting of the decay parameter d to 0.5, and assuming an equal division of source activation between word and list context so that $W_L = 0.5$, the equation becomes the Recognition Memory Equation:

$$\text{Activation} = \ln n - 0.5 \ln T - 0.5 \ln L$$

Recognition Memory Equation 7.2

This is the critical activation equation for this section. This is identical to the Serial Memory Equation 7.1, except that the list length is weighted by 0.5 reflecting the division of source activation (the Ws) between the list and the word. Again, this only gives an approximation to the results of the simulation, and the predictions come from simulation runs.

An additional relevant factor in recognition memory involves partial matching to either the word or the list context. Partial matching to the word will produce false alarming to similar words. There are ample experiments showing effects of distractor similarity on recognition memory (e.g., Anisfeld & Knapp, 1968; Underwood & Freund, 1968). Similarly, subjects are likely to false alarm to a word if it occurred in a similar list (e. g., Anderson & Bower, 1974).

This section focuses on three results that have proven important in the last 25 years of research and theory on recognition memory. These are latencies to recognize items, particularly in the Sternberg paradigm, the relationship between list length and list strength, and the effects of context in recognition memory. One subsection is devoted to each topic.

The Sternberg Paradigm

The Sternberg paradigm is one in which subjects see a relatively small list of items and then are presented with a single item and have to judge whether that item is from the list. As the result was originally described and is still described in many textbooks, the claim is that there is a linear relationship between the number of items in the memory set and time to make this judgment. In fact, the relationship is more typically curvilinear and extends out to lists as long as 20 items (Briggs, 1974). Figure 7.7 shows some data from Burrows and Okada (1975) illustrating this relationship and a fit of the ACT–R model, described next.

Because Burrows and Okada do not report the details of presentation timing or practice, we simulated in ACT–R only the recognition judgment task and not the study. For this recognition judgment task we used a model similar to the model of sentence recognition in studies of the fan effect (discussed in Chapter 3). This kind of model seems appropriate for time-pressured recognition judgments. On presentation of a probe, the subject retrieves the most active item from the list:

Retrieve-a-Candidate
      IF   the goal is to recognize whether a word is in the list
             and X is some word in the list
     THEN   consider X as the retrieved word

If the probe is a word in the list, that candidate word will be most active because it receives activation from the probe. Thus, it is only necessary for the preceding production to retrieve one item. The subject then checks whether the retrieved item matches the probe and responds "yes" if it does:

Match-Word
      IF   the goal is to recognize whether a probe word is in the list
             and the probe word matches the retrieved word
     THEN   say yes

In the case of a foil, some list member will be retrieved (because no condition is placed on which word to retrieve) only to be rejected as mismatching the probe by **Mismatch-Word**:

Mismatch-Word
      IF   the goal is to recognize whether a probe word is in the list
             and the probe word does not match the retrieved word
     THEN   say no.

For its success, this scheme relies on the fact that if the word was studied, the chunk encoding its occurrence in the list will be more active than chunks encoding the occurrence of other items. This will be the case because this chunk will receive activation from the probe word.

Because Burrows and Okada do not describe the study process, we just modeled the test phase of their experiment, assuming that chunks had an activation that depended only on list length and ignoring the effect of the number of rehearsals, n, and delay, T. Thus, the recognition equation simply becomes:

$$\text{Activation} = 3.76 - 0.5 \ln L$$

where L is the length of the list and 3.76 is the activation of an element in a list of length 1 in the ACT–R simulation.[7] This activation value and the latency scale F parameter (see Retrieval Time Equation 3.11) trade off such that there is only one degree of freedom in fitting the data. Thus, we left

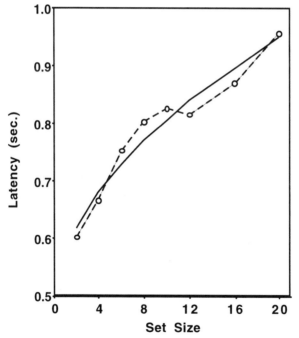

FIG. 7.7. Observed (dotted lines) and predicted (solid lines) latencies for recognizing probes as a function of set size.

---

[7]The value 3.76 is just the value delivered by ACT–R simulation for relatively arbitrary reasons—see the discussion later in this chapter.

the activation value at its default and estimated F at 4.15 sec. Then using Retrieval Time Equation 3.11, ACT–R's prediction for latency is

$$\text{Time} = I + Fe^{-A} = 0.5 + 4.15e^{-3.76}L^{0.5} = 0.5 + .097L^{0.5}$$

where 0.5 is the fixed intercept I (which is the same as the intercept parameter used in the serial recall model), F is the latency factor estimated at 4.15, and $0.097 = 4.15e^{-3.76}$.[8] The fit of this one-parameter model is basically identical to that of a logarithmic equation given by Burrows and Okada (which has two parameters) and is slightly worse than their bilinear model (which has four parameters). Although this does involve the estimation of one parameter, it does make the parameter-free prediction that latency should increase as a function of the square-root of list length. The data do correspond closely to this predicted form with an R^2 of .957 for the square-root function as compared to .908 for a linear function.

To have better tests of ACT–R it would be useful to have data with better specification of the presentation timing and information about the effect of serial position on latency. Raeburn (1974) reported such an experiment, in which items were presented at the rate of 1.5 sec per item and tested at a delay of 1.2 sec. Figure 7.8 presents his data as a function of serial position of the targets plus the mean performance for foils.

We developed a running ACT–R simulation of these data. In modeling the study of the items we wanted to carry over as much of the representations and processes as possible from the model in the previous section for serial memory. This seemed desirable because the lists were of similar length and the presentation timings were similar. The same productions were used for encoding and rehearsal. The recognition judgment at test was made by productions used for the Burrows and Okada simulation. As in the case of the Burrows and Okada data, we estimated the parameter, F, in fitting the data. This was estimated at 2.29 sec. However, in this experiment only we also needed to estimate a nondefault intercept parameter of 0.6 sec.[9]

The quality of the fit is quite good, with a mean error of prediction of 19 msec and an R^2 of .886 with just two parameters estimated. The data and the model both reflect strong effects of target versus foil, set size, and serial position. It is worth reviewing what produces these effects in the ACT–R model. The effect of target versus foil is due to the lower activation of the chunk retrieved by **Retrieve-a-Candidate** in the case of a foil because the probe is not a source of activation. The effect of serial position reflects the

---

[8]Although we estimated F at 4.15, it would have been mathematically equivalent to use the equation just given and estimate 0.097 as our free parameter.

[9]As can be seen comparing Figs. 7.7 and 7.8, the minimum times in Raeburn's data are longer than the averages for comparable list lengths in the Burrows and Okada data.

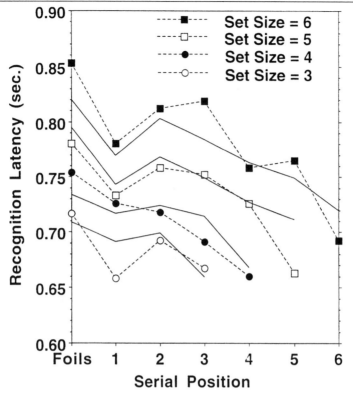

FIG. 7.8. Data (in dotted lines) from Raeburn (1974): time to recognize an item for lists of various lengths as a function of serial position. The predictions of the ACT–R model are in solid lines.

effects of extra rehearsal of the beginning of the list and shorter recency of the end of the list. These are the same factors operating in the memory span except that time to recall in memory span is also affected by order of output in span tests. Finally, the effect of set size is due to the combined effects of decreased associative activation and increased decay of base-level activation, because on average the delay is longer between presentation and test.

Recognition Memory and Signal Detectability Analysis

The Sternberg task is one where lists tend to be short, accuracy is nearly perfect, and interest is focused on latency. As lists become longer, interest shifts to recognition accuracy. In ACT–R, errors on targets (false negatives) will occur because of low activation levels, which result in failed retrieval of the target chunk. Errors on foils (false alarms) will occur because ACT–R retrieves similar contexts to the target contexts and accepts the partial match.

The ACT–R model of recognition with longer lists involves a number of changes from the simulation we used for the Sternberg recognition memory task. First, given the long length of the lists and given that this was not a serial memory test, ACT–R no longer represented the serial order of the list and just stored the fact that the word occurred in the list (see Fig. 7.6).[10] As a consequence, ACT–R could not use serial position as a basis for rehearsing items but rather just rehearsed each item that came to mind (i.e., the item that is momentarily most active) a maximum number of times, which we set to two. Thus, the critical rehearsal rule was

Rehearse
    IF   the goal is to study the words in a list
           and there is a trace of a word which has occurred in the list
           and has not been rehearsed 2 times
    THEN   rehearse it one more time

The following two rules accepted targets and rejected foils:

Accept
    IF   the goal is to recognize if a probe word occurred in the list
           and there is a trace of that word in the list
    THEN   accept it

Reject
    IF   the goal is to recognize if a probe word occurred in the list
    THEN   reject it

where the rejection rule was rated lower in ACT–R's conflict resolution (which means it will only fire if the acceptance rule fails). Thus, the **Reject** rule has to wait for the **Accept** rule to time out before it fires. We used this rather than the reject rule in the previous simulation that retrieved some trace because (1) latency was not critical, making the longer time-out latency for **Reject** acceptable, and (2) sometimes no chunk (after mismatch penalty) was above threshold because of the longer list structure. False alarms occur when the **Accept** rule partially matches to a memory of the word in another context. False negatives occur when no trace involving the word, including memory of it in the list, is above threshold and the **Reject** rule applies.

---

[10]Also as a consequence, the D parameter for positional confusions is no longer relevant.

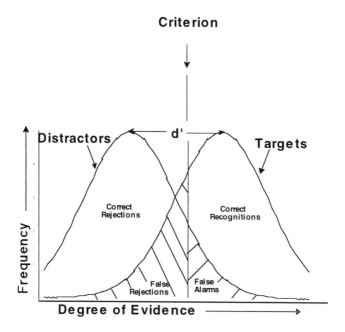

FIG. 7.9. Distribution of evidence for targets and distractors (foils) in a recognition memory experiment.

The focus on accuracy with longer lists and the occurrence of both false negatives and false alarms raise the issue of how one is going to measure the accuracy of recognition memory. Subjects could guarantee they would recognize all targets if they just accepted all words. This would be at the expense of false alarms to all foils. A frequent measure of recognition memory is called d'. The fundamental logic of this measure is illustrated in Fig. 7.9. It is assumed that the targets and foils have some distribution of evidence for list membership and that subjects set up some criterion for acceptance such that anything above the threshold is accepted. The proportion of correct acceptances of targets is the proportion of the target distribution above the criterion. Similarly, the proportion of false alarms is the proportion of the foil distribution above the criterion. Assuming normal distributions with equal variance, one can use these two proportions to estimate the distance the two distributions are apart in terms of standard deviations. This measure is called d'. ACT–R produces d' measures in essentially the same way. Targets and foils define two distributions of activation (or, more precisely, match scores), and by setting a threshold, τ, ACT–R is setting a criterion for separating targets and foils.

Sometimes experiments are performed in which subjects are not simply asked whether they recognize the words or not but rather are asked to rate their confidence on an n-point scale (e.g., 1–9) that the word was in the list. In terms of Fig. 7.9, this can be conceived of subjects setting up $n-1$ criterion points to separate the scale into n regions for the n confidence values. Often data from such experiments are used to plot what are called z-ROC functions. The probability that subjects will rate targets and foils with confidence $i+1$ or greater is used to define an ith "hit" rate and an ith "false alarm" rate. With an n-point scale, $n-1$ different hit and false alarm rates are obtained, and these are transformed into z scores from the standard normal distribution. The z scores for the hit rates are plotted as a function of the z scores for the false alarm rates. Figure 7.10 shows an example of such a z-ROC function in the case of a nine-point scale (which yields 8 pairs of z scores).[11] The curve is typically linear, which is taken as evidence that the underlying target and noise distributions are normal. It is also the case that the slope of the plot is less than 1, which is taken as evidence that the distribution is broader for targets than for foils.

Strictly speaking, ACT–R 4.0 is unable to produce such z-ROC curves. The obvious quantity within the theory that would allow such curves to be generated is the match score. One might think about mapping different match scores onto different levels of confidence or varying the threshold such that different match scores were required to recognize a word. However, ACT–R does not have access to its match scores, nor does it have direct control over its criterion. The lack of access to activation or match scores turns out be a feature that distinguishes ACT–R from Reder's SAC theory (Reder & Schunn, 1996). We would not want to argue, however, that it is a fundamental feature. Here we would like to display what would happen if we used differential match scores to map out a z-ROC function.

The curve in Fig. 7.10 comes from an ACT–R model for recognition of longer lists and was obtained by varying the threshold, τ, from 1 to 3 in 0.25 intervals. It reproduces the character of the empirical z-ROC curves including the slope of less than 1. The slope is shallow because targets get differing amounts of practice and some targets do not get encoded at all. This variability of encoding results in a distribution of match scores for targets that is wider than the distribution for foils. The actual slope in Fig. 7.10 is 0.75, which is close to the slope that is obtained in actual experiments (e.g., Ratcliff, McKoon, & Tindall, 1994). However, we could have manipulated the study procedure to produce greater or lesser variability in the encoding process. So we would not want to imply that ACT–R makes a firm prediction about the slope—only that it should be definitely less than 1. This same

---

[11]Another way to obtain such curves is to ask subjects in different conditions to accept words with stricter or weaker criteria (sometimes encouraged by introducing different payoffs for hits and penalties for false alarms). The numbers of hits and false alarms systematically increase as subjects adopt laxer criteria, thus producing a series of points for a z-ROC curve.

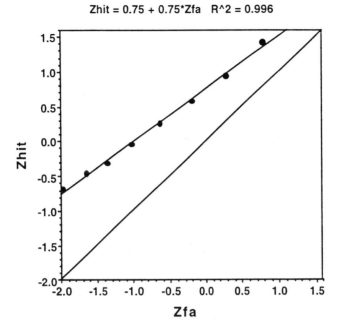

FIG. 7.10. ACT–R's prediction about the z-ROC curve.

prediction was part of the Anderson and Bower (1972) model and for the same reason.

List Strength and List Length Effects

Recently, a considerable stir has been caused by what are called the list strength and list length effects on recognition memory (e.g., Ratcliff, Clark, & Shiffrin, 1990). Recognition memory for individual items deteriorates as the list has more items (the list length effect). It also gets better as items are studied more (the list strength effect). The interesting question is what happens when some items of the list are studied more often or longer and others are not. By analogy to the list length effect, one might imagine that if some items are studied more (this is analogous to making the list longer) the remaining items in a list would suffer greater interference. Just these effects occur with mixed lists in free recall where extra study for some items makes other items less available. However, in recognition memory there is no effect of amount of study of other items. Ratcliff et al. (1990) proclaimed that no extant theory of memory could accommodate these results. Since that time a number of theories (e.g., McClelland & Chappel, 1994; Shiffrin

& Steyvers, 1997) have been modified or proposed to accommodate the result. It turns out that ACT–R is in this list of theories, although we have to say this result was far from our mind when we proposed the ACT–R theory in 1993, and we have only recently realized that it explained these effects.

A representative experiment that captures these results is Experiment 4 reported by Ratcliff et al. (1990). In five conditions they had subjects either study 10 items four times (the 10PS condition for "pure strong"), 16 items four times (the 16PS condition), 16 items with half presented four times and half presented one time (the mixed condition, which contains 8 strong items, designated 16MS, and 8 weak items, designated 16MW), 16 items each presented once (the 16PW condition for "pure weak"), or 40 items each presented once (the 40PW condition). Figure 7.11 displays the results measured in terms of d'. For otherwise comparable lists there is a length effect—worse performance for longer lists. It can also be seen within the 16 item lists that there is a strength effect—performance is worse for words that are only presented once (W words are worse than S words). However, there is effectively no difference between items that come from mixed or pure lists. That is, holding list length and the strength of the target items constant, there is no effect of the strength of the other items in the list.

Figure 7.11 also presents the results from an ACT–R simulation of this experiment using the production set described in the previous section. In addition to the parameters that are held constant in all the simulations, the latency factor F was set to be 2.00 sec, which is comparable to its value in the Raeburn experiment.[12] Each word was associated with three nonlist contexts, which could serve as sources of false alarms. Three parameters were estimated:

1. The activation threshold τ, which was estimated to be 1.8.
2. The parameter s, which controls the noise in the activation values. This was estimated to be 0.55.
3. A P parameter for the partial matching penalty between list contexts (see Match Equation 3.8). This was estimated to be 1.5.

The correspondence between the model and the data is quite good. The Recognition Memory Equation 7.2 directly implies that list strength and list length will have an effect on recall. More study results in increased practice producing greater base-level activation. Longer lists result in greater fan, producing less associative activation. In addition to these two major factors, there are two minor factors. First, longer lists also result in longer delays.

---

[12]In experiments where latency is not a dependent-measure prediction, our predictions are only weakly dependent on the setting of F. Therefore, in these experiments we satisfied ourselves with ballpark setting and did not search for a good fitting parameter.

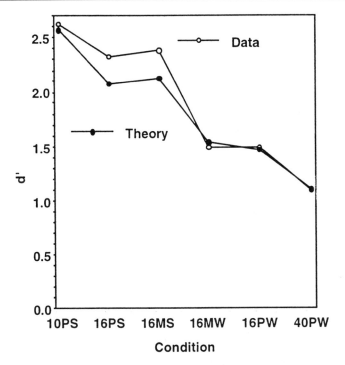

FIG. 7.11. Effects of list length and list strength from Ratcliff, Clark, and Shiffrin (1990). Data are the dotted lines and model the solid lines.

Second, there is rehearsal borrowing in the mixed list conditions such that weak words get rehearsed at the expense of strong words. Rehearsal borrowing is weak in the simulation: There are on average 2.00 rehearsals for 16PS words, 1.99 rehearsals for 16MS words, 1.96 rehearsals for 16MW words, and 1.61 rehearsals for 16PW words. Thus, weak words enjoy a rehearsal advantage in the mixed condition over the pure condition, but these differences in number of rehearsals are weak compared to the one versus four difference in number of presentations. ACT–R explains the differences among the conditions as follows:

10PS versus 16PS: The 10 PS condition is at an advantage because of lower associative interference and shorter lag to test.

16PS versus 16MS: These two conditions are equivalent on the important factors of list length (associative interference) and number of presentations (differential practice). The 16MS condition does suffer a very little from rehearsal borrowing but has a somewhat shorter delay until test.

16MS versus 16MW: The 16MS condition has advantages of number of presentations, differential rehearsal, and slightly shorter delays until test.

16MW versus 16PW: These two conditions are again equivalent on the important factors of associative interference and number of presentations. The 16MW condition has slightly more rehearsal but also slightly longer delay until test.

16PW versus 40PW: The 40PW items are at a disadvantage with respect to associative interference and delay until test.

The critical variables from Recognition Memory Equation 7.2 are n, which will be dominated by number of presentations and L, the list length. These factors are basically the same in the mixed conditions as in the corresponding pure conditions.

Context Effects in Recognition Memory

As noted earlier, the current theory of recognition memory is basically a descendant of the Anderson and Bower (1972, 1974) theory. That theory has been undergoing a bit of a revival lately, with Bower (1996) using it as part of his theory of implicit memory. There is a perception held by some in the field that the Anderson and Bower theory was discredited by Tulving's demonstrations of encoding specificity. Although these demonstrations did cause some difficulty for the HAM version of the theory proposed in 1972 and 1974, they do not extend to the current ACT–R version. It is worth reviewing here what these demonstrations were and why they do not extend to the current version of the theory. Anderson (1983) developed the basic explanation of these Tulving demonstrations in ACT*, and we update that explanation here for ACT–R 4.0.

The most direct demonstrations of the context dependency of recognition memory involved experiments such as those reported by Tulving and Thomson (1971). Subjects would study a pair of words like *train-black* with instructions that they would be tested for their memory for the second word in the pair, namely, *black*. Their ability to recognize *black* was much lower if they were later asked to recognize the item in the pair *white-black* than in the pair *train-black*. The HAM theory assumed that traces were formed with a certain probability of recall but, if formed, they would be recalled with certainty. Given this assumption, Tulving and Thomson's results were mysterious. If a trace for *black* had been formed it should be retrievable in all contexts and it should not matter whether it is tested in *train-black* or *white-black*. However, it is very easy to produce this sort of context dependency in the current theory, which assumes traces are always formed but these traces vary in their availability. The effect of the original study is to create an association between *train* and the trace encoding the fact that *black* occurred in the context. At test, *train* becomes a source of associative activation and makes the trace more retrievable.

An elaboration of this basic demonstration involved the demonstration that words that could be recalled could not be recognized. Again subjects studied pairs of words like *train-black* and were either tested on their recognition memory for the item *black* or on their ability to retrieve the word *black* primed with *train*. Table 7.3 shows a typical pattern of results obtained by Tulving and Wiseman (1975). There are at least two noteworthy results in this experiment. The first is that subjects were better able to recall the words than recognize them. This result was used to challenge the generate-recognize theory of free recall, which the next section discusses. The other result is that many words could be recalled but not recognized (also, some words could be recognized but not recalled). Words in the recall-but-not-recognize category (called *recognition failures*) were again a challenge to the direct-access assumption. A trace had been formed (as the words were being recalled), but subjects were unable to access this trace in a recognition memory test.

The explanation of this dissociation between recall and recognition is not very different from the explanation of the Tulving and Thomson context-specificity result. There are two test contexts. One involves presenting *black* and asking for its recognition, and the other involves presenting *train* and asking for its studied associate. However, both involve going back to the original *train–black* trace, whose availability will depend upon its activation. This will in turn depend on a base-level activation, an associative activation, and some temporary random noise (Activation Equation 3.5 and Base-Level Equation 3.6). The base-level activation component will produce some correlation between these two forms of test because it is the same base level in either test. However, the temporary random component and the associative components are not shared and they will cause the correlation to be far less than perfect. This poor correlation in activation results in recallable words that cannot be recognized and recognizable words that cannot be

TABLE 7.3
Proportion of Words in Various Conditions

	Recognized	Not Recognized	Totals
Recalled	.30	.30	.60
Not recalled	.10	.30	.40
Totals	.40	.60	1.00

recalled. As Hintzman (1992) noted, a wide range of correlations is obtained between recognition and recall.

Which is better, recognition or recall, depends on the strengths of the associations, S_{ji}, between *black* and the trace versus *train* and the trace. As noted by Rabinowitz, Mandler, and Barsalou (1977), there is a peculiarity in those studies that find recall better than recognition, which is that the stimuli are chosen so that *train* evokes *black* occasionally in free associate tests but not vice versa. They looked at the relationship between recognition of *black* and recall of *train* given *black* as a prompt. They found that recall is much poorer in the reverse direction (*black* as a prompt for *train*), confirming that target words (*black*) are poorer cues to memory than cue words (*train*). Moreover, recognition failure is much lower when one conditionalizes on recall in the reverse direction. That is, the probability is very high that one can recognize *black* in a recognition test conditional on being able to recall *train* given the cue of *black*. This is what one would expect because either in the recall or recognition test one is looking at the ability of *black* to evoke the trace and so is tapping the same S_{ji} (the j is *black* and the i is the trace). Thus, Tulving and his associates were able to get recall to be better than recognition because they created a situation where the recall test provided better cues for memory than did the recognition test.

A wide range of results has been obtained over the years concerning levels of recall, levels of recognition, and levels of recognition given recall. Attention has focused on a regularity called the Tulving-Wiseman Law (e.g., Flexser & Tulving, 1970; Nilsson & Gardiner, 1993; Tulving & Wiseman, 1975). This concerns the relationship between probability of recognition $p(Rn)$ and probability of recognition given recall $p(Rn|Rc)$:

$$p(Rn|Rc) = p(Rn) + 0.5[p(Rn) - p(Rn)^2]$$

This indicates a relatively weak relationship between the two. It turns out that ACT–R very closely predicts the Tulving-Wiseman function (for details see Anderson, Bothell, Lebiere, & Matessa, in press). The two measures—$p(Rn)$ and $P(Rn|Rc)$—are somewhat related because of the shared base-level activation between recall and test, but they are substantially unrelated because of the uncorrelated temporary noise and variability in the S_{ji} between the cues j and the chunks i.

FREE RECALL

Free recall is an experimental paradigm where the subject is allowed to recall the items of a list in any order. The removal of the constraint of recalling in serial order may seem to simplify the task from serial recall. However, in fact it complicates the task substantially because it frees the subject to choose among a wide variety of strategies for studying items and recalling them. Some subjects repeat groups of words over and over again, other subjects look for associative or categorical relationships among the words, and still other subjects make up stories involving these words. The more organizational structure that subjects try to impose on the material, the better memory they display (e.g., Mandler, 1967).

The generate-test model described in Anderson and Bower (1972) and realized in the FRAN simulation model (Anderson, 1972) was an attempt to extract the essence of these strategies. The assumptions of the FRAN model were:

1. The subjects maintain in a short-term memory a small set of about four items from the list, which they rehearse and among which they try to find relationships. When a new item is encountered it enters this buffer and an old item is removed. This is basically the buffer model of Atkinson and Shiffrin (1968), with the added assumption that subjects search for semantic relationships among the items in the buffer.
2. At time of recall subjects try to generate candidate items, using among other things the associative relationships that they have laid down.
3. Every time subjects generate a word they then try to recognize it. Thus, the recognition process discussed in the previous section is embedded as part of the recall process.

The SAM theory of Raaijmakers and Shiffrin (1981) was another attempt to achieve an abstract characterization of this process. In that theory items were generated according to strength of association to the context and to the last retrieved item. The subject then judged each item on the basis of its familiarity (rather than retrieval of contextual information as in the Anderson and Bower theory).

The ACT–R model for free-recall experiments in this section is simpler than either SAM or FRAN in that it omits an embedded recognition process. The model simply needs to be able to recall the elements. It has a buffer of four elements for rehearsal, and when a new element comes in, the simulation randomly replaces a member of the buffer. This buffer is implemented by storing the items in slots of the goal. After that the system randomly chooses items to rehearse from the buffer as time allows. At time of recall, ACT–R dumps the members of the buffer and then recalls items whose activation is above a threshold. Thus, if P_B is the probability the item is still in the buffer, the probability of recalling the item is approximately

$$\text{Probability of recall} = P_B + (1 - P_B)\, P(\text{activation} > \tau)$$

where τ is the threshold. The activation for an element would vary with the number of times it has been rehearsed, the length of time since those rehearsals, and the fan out of the list node (determined by list size). Although the predictions in this section come from actual simulations, it would be useful to have in hand an equation approximately giving the activation levels. In this case with a single source of activation (the list—the word is not presented), the operative equation is identical to the serial memory equation and is the Free Recall Equation:

$$\text{Activation} = \ln{(n)} - 0.5\ln(T) - \ln(L) \quad \textbf{Free Recall Equation 7.3}$$

where n is the number of encodings and rehearsals, T is the time since encoding, and L is the list length.

Serial Position Effects

One of the basic results about free recall is the serial-position curve, which is a function giving probability of recall as a function of position of the item in the input sequence. Figure 7.12a shows some data gathered by Murdock (1962) looking at recall of lists that varied in length from 10 to 40 words, presented at 1 or 2 sec for each word. These results show the classic recency effect, which is the high level of recall at the end of the list, and the primacy effect, which is the somewhat higher level of recall at the beginning of the list. The performance level is somewhat flat in intermediate positions with levels higher for shorter lists or for lists with more study time. Figure 7.12b shows the corresponding predictions of the ACT–R model. The latency-scale parameter F was preset to 2.0 sec (same value as Ratcliff et al., 1990) for this experiment. The estimated parameters for this simulation were $\tau = 3.2$ and s (activation noise) $= 0.70$. The recency effect in ACT–R is produced by the probability that the item is still in the buffer, plus the short delay in recall while the primacy effect is produced by the extra rehearsals given to the target item. The overall correspondence is quite good, with an R^2 of .911 predicting 135 points with two estimated parameters.

Under this analysis the striking recency effect is due to the tendency to rehearse and recall first the last few items of the list. In experiments where interfering activity is given after the list to wipe out the buffer, the advantage of the last few items disappears and they often show poorer recall—the so-called negative recency effect (Craik, 1970; Gardiner, Thompson, & Maskarinec, 1974). In experiments where an effort is made to eliminate rehearsal the primacy effect largely goes away and so does the negative recency effect when tested after a delay (Baddeley, 1986). In such studies, where subjects are prevented from forming a rehearsal buffer and forced just

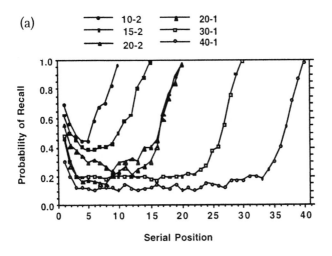

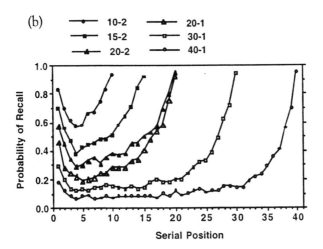

FIG. 7.12. Probability of recall of lists of various lengths and amount of study time as a function of serial position. (a) Data from Murdock (1962). (b) Predictions of the ACT–R model.

to process the item under study, one also sees a diminished positive recency effect. Performance tends to drop off continuously from the end of the list.

Figure 7.13 shows some data from an experiment by Glenberg et al. (1980) that tries to eliminate rehearsal. Subjects studied pairs of words for 2 sec. In one condition they studied 36 such pairs (for 72 items) each preceded by 4 sec of distracting activity, while in the other condition they studied 9 such pairs (for 18 items) each preceded by 22 sec of distracting activity. The experiment was designed so that subjects spent 216 sec studying the list. The effect of the distraction was to prevent any cumulative rehearsal and force subjects just to attend to the presented items. In both conditions there was 20 sec of intervening activity before recall. As can be seen, the recency effect is reduced (no longer are subjects recalling nearly 100% of the last item) and there is no primacy effect to speak of.

In the ACT–R simulation of these data, we took a very extreme interpretation of the intervening activity and assumed that it eliminated the buffer and all rehearsal. Thus, there was just a single study when the item was presented. Recall began 20 sec after the last presentation. Recall was determined by the activation of the chunks in declarative memory. Figure 7.13 presents the predictions of the ACT–R model with $s = 0.60$ and $\tau = 1.40$.[13] The fit is quite good, with an R^2 of .860.

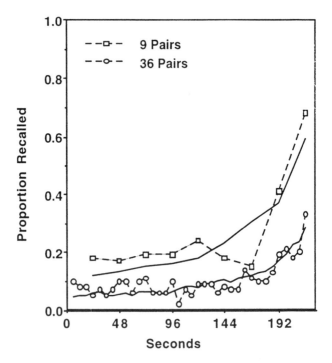

FIG. 7.13. Data from Glenberg et al. (1980) in which interspersed arithmetic was used to eliminate use of a rehearsal buffer. The dotted lines are the data and the solid lines are the predictions of the ACT–R model.

[13]The latency-scale parameter F was preset to 2.0 as in the other free-recall experiments.

Note that ACT–R predicts a recency effect for the Glenberg et al. data even in the absence of a buffer. This is because activation decreases as a logarithm of delay (Free Recall Equation 7.3). Glenberg, Bradley, Kraus, and Renzaglia (1983) proposed that recency varies roughly as a function of the logarithm of the ratio of the interitem presentation interval (IPI) to the retention interval (RI). In Fig. 7.13 note that the serial position curve is steeper for the 9 pairs condition where the IPI/RI ratio is 24/20 than the 36 pairs condition where it is 6/20. ACT–R predicts this regularity as a consequence of the logarithmic transformation of time in the Free Recall Equation. Consult Anderson, Bothell, Lebiere, and Matessa (in press) for details.

List Length and List Strength Effects

We have discussed list length and list strength effects in recognition. In free recall researchers have also examined how memory for list items increases with the length of the list or the amount of time per item. Figure 7.14a shows some data from Roberts (1972) displaying how number of words recalled increases as the list length increases from 10 to 40 items and as study time increases from 0.5 to 8 sec per item. As Fig. 7.14b shows, the ACT–R model (same simulation as in the Murdock experiment—see Fig. 7.12) does a good job in accounting for this pattern of data. The parameters in this model fit were $\tau = 2.9$ and $s = 0.85$. The correspondence is particularly good, and the overall R^2 is .990.

The ACT–R model's correspondence to the Roberts data is much more immediate than through the simulation. It is basically a direct consequence of the Free Recall Equation 7.3. In that equation, n, the amount of practice per item, is going to be proportional to the amount of study; L is the list length. As an approximation we can assume T is equal to total study time and therefore is equal to nL. Substituting $T = nL$ into the Free Recall Equation 7.3 we obtain:

$$\text{Activation} = 0.5 \ln n - 1.5 \ln L$$

where n is now study time per item. This equation does not include the constant factor, but it states how activation varies with study time and list length. ACT–R predicts that log odds of recall should be equal to this quantity divided by the noise parameter s plus some constant, that is,

$$\log \text{odds} = \text{constant} + \text{activation}/s$$

If we set s to 1, which it nearly is in the fit, this predicts:

$$\log \text{odds} = \text{constant} + 0.5 \ln n - 1.5 \ln L$$

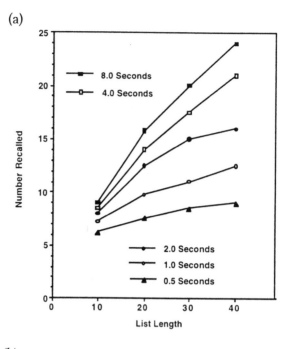

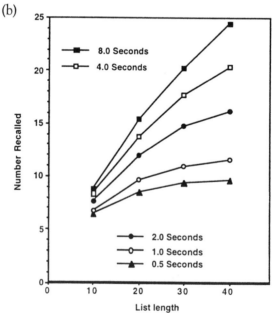

FIG. 7.14. (a) Data from Roberts (1972) showing how number of words recalled increases with depth lengths and study time. (b) Predictions from ACT–R.

Thus, ACT–R makes parameter-free predictions about the log-odds differences among the 20 Roberts conditions. Figure 7.15 displays this predicted relationship for the 20 conditions of Roberts experiment. The line in the graph reflects the prediction, with the constant estimated at 4.63. The correlation between log odds and this parameter-free activation estimate is .983.

IMPLICIT MEMORY

The most recent domain of interest in list-learning experiments has been implicit memory. Such experiments involve demonstrations that subjects are facilitated in their memory for words in ways that they do not realize. Many of these demonstrations involve perceptual facilitation. For instance, subjects may be able to read words faster that they have studied in a list, even though they may not be able to remember seeing these words (Feustel,

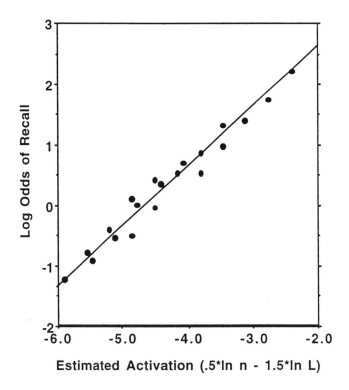

FIG. 7.15. Predicted relationship between study time (n) and list length (L) and observed odds of recall.

Shiffrin, & Salasoo, 1983; Johnston, Dark, & Jacoby, 1985; Johnston, Hawley, & Elliott, 1991; Watkins & Gibson, 1988). Other work (e.g., Hayman & Tulving, 1989; Jacoby, Toth, & Yonelinas, 1993) on implicit memory involves word fragment completion. For instance, subjects might study a word like HARE. Then, later they will be tested with a fragment like H_R_ and be asked to complete it as a word. They are more likely to complete it as HARE after seeing the word than as other possible completions like HIRE or HURT. Sometimes subjects will show this tendency even when they are explicitly instructed not to complete the fragment with the word they have studied. They make these "errors" because they do not explicitly remember seeing the word but their system has been implicitly affected by seeing the word. One of the reasons for excitement about this research is that some types of amnesic patients show normal levels of implicit memory but show almost no explicit memory for the word (Graf, Squire, & Mandler, 1984).

There have been a number of attempts to account for these results in terms of activation-based network theories of memory (Bower, 1996; Reder & Gordon, 1996; Reder et al., 1997; Reder & Schunn, 1996). The fundamental idea is that declarative network structures can be left in heightened states of activation as a result of processing. These heightened states, which can facilitate later processing, constitute an implicit memory for the words. In contrast, explicit memory requires adding new declarative network structures rather than just priming existing ones. This basic idea of other researchers can be easily incorporated into the ACT–R system, as this section describes. Although this idea could be extended to priming of conceptual information, this section focuses on priming of lexical information. Typical tasks involve reading a word, judging whether a word is correctly spelled, or completing a word fragment. In all cases the subject must get access to information about word spelling.

Relationship Between Word Naming and Word Recognition

Figure 7.16 shows the ACT–R representation for a word, its spelling, and its occurrence in a list. The letters are stored as part of a spelling chunk, and the word is stored as having occurred in the list as part of a context chunk.[14] Reading the word requires retrieving the word from the letter representation. The operative production is:

---

[14]To deal with conceptual priming we would have to elaborate this representation to include a distinction between words and concepts, but this is not done in the current figure for the sake of simplicity.

Read-Word
>   IF   the goal is to read a word consisting of the letters L1, L2, L3,
>   and L4
>   and L1, L2, L3, and L4 spell Word
>   THEN   say Word

Reading a word will strengthen the base-level activation of the chunk encoding the word's spelling. As a consequence, the next time that word is presented or a fragment of the word is presented, the subject will be faster and more likely to access that chunk.

An ACT–R model was developed for the first experiment of Johnston et al. (1991). Subjects in their experiment studied 96 four- or five-letter words at the rate of one word per 2 sec. The first and last 4 words were buffers but the middle 88 were critical. Subjects were then tested with 206 words that consisted of a buffer of 30 words followed by the 88 critical words mixed in with 88 foils. The words were presented for recognition camouflaged in dots that disappeared at either a slow rate or a fast rate. The subjects were to read the word as fast as they could. In the ACT–R simulation the reading of the word was governed by the **Read-Word** production just given. The actual timing consisted of three components. There was the time to encode the letters (estimated at the default of 200 msec during study, 750 msec during test in the fast uncovering condition, and 950 msec during test in the slow uncovering condition), the time to retrieve the word in the **Read-Word** production, and the time to say the word (given a standard estimate of 500 msec). After reading the word, ACT–R recognized the word

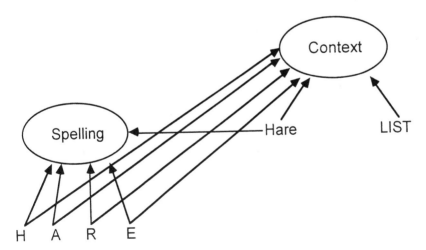

FIG. 7.16. A representation that encodes lexical information at this spelling chunk and list information at the context chunk.

using the same productions as used in this chapter's Recognition Memory Section to model the length-strength effect. ACT–R simulated 32 subjects, the same number as in the Johnston et al. experiment. The nondefault parameter settings were the encoding times (set longer than usual to reflect the difficult encoding conditions), the latency-scale parameter F set at 1.30 sec, the activation noise parameter s set at 0.65, and the activation threshold parameter τ set at 0.90.

Table 7.4 presents the data and the simulation results broken down according to whether the word was a target or a foil, whether the word was recognized or not, and whether the uncovering was fast or slow. The correspondence between data and model is good. The R^2 between simulation and data is .921 in the case of the percentages and .910 in the case of latencies. Two effects are apparent in the data and the simulation. First, ACT–R is faster at reading words it has seen before. Second, it is faster at recognizing words it thinks it has seen. Note that it is approximately as fast at reading a word that it has seen before but it thinks it has not seen (a false negative) as a word that it has not seen before and thinks it has (a false alarm). This dissociation between reading and recognition occurs because the spelling chunk supports the reading process, whereas the context chunk supports the recognition judgment. The context chunk can be low in

TABLE 7.4
Reading Time and Recognition Proportions for Words From the Simulation

		Fast Uncovering	
		Recognized	*Not Recognized*
Target		Hits	False negatives
		1313 msec (1324)	1521 msec (1446)
		73% (75%)	27% (25%)
Foil		False alarms	Correct rejections
		1455 msec (1531)	1670 msec (1724)
		39% (37%)	61% (63%)
		Slow Uncovering	
		Recognized	*Not Recognized*
Target		Hits	False negatives
		1481 msec (1531)	1737 msec (1658)
		72% (72%)	28% (28%)
Foil		False alarms	Correct rejections
		1789 msec (1718)	1876 msec (1918)
		35% (36%)	65% (64%)

Note: Data from Johnson, Hawley, and Elliott (1991), simulation in parentheses.

activation without the spelling chunk being low in activation.

Note that, holding constant whether the word is presented, ACT–R is slower to read words that it does not recognize. The overall ordering of conditions in terms of reading times is hits < false negatives, false alarms < correct rejections. It has been argued that this is evidence that subjects use perceptual fluency as a basis for performing word recognition—that is, that they tend to say that they recognize words which they can read more rapidly. This claim has come in for considerable dispute. For instance, Poldrack and Logan (1997) argued that, although there is a difference in the latencies for targets and foils, there is so much overlap in the latency distributions that subjects would be very poor in the recognition judgments if they used their reading times as a basis for making recognition judgments. Watkins and Gibson (1988) have argued that the correlation between identification time and recognition performance is due to item selection effects such that items that are more easily identified also tend to be more recognizable.

ACT–R's explanation for why the reading latencies are shorter for yes's than no's is a variation of the item selection argument. To understand what is happening in ACT–R, it is important to appreciate the contribution of associative strengths to the reading times and to recognition accuracy. Because the letters are part of the goal, associative activation from the letters influences both the reading times and the recognition judgment. Reading time will be determined by the S_{ji} terms from the letters to the word chunk, and the recognition judgment will be influenced by the S_{ji} terms from the letters to the context chunk.[15] Both of these associations involve the same sources (js) but different chunks (is—either word or context chunk). Because of the fan effect, some sources will have weaker associations than other sources. That is, some letters appear in relatively few words and so will have strong associations to both these words and the word contexts. This means that words that are read faster are also more likely to produce recall of contexts (resulting in hits if they occurred in the study context and false alarms if they occurred only in other contexts).

Fragment Completion

Hayman and Tulving (1989) reported a study on stem completion that shows some of the subtlety of implicit memory tests. Subjects studied lists of 160 words. These included 16 primacy fillers, 64 critical words, and 80 recency fillers. Subjects performed two fragment completion tests. The first test involved 32 words that the subject had studied plus 32 words not studied. The second test involved the other 32 studied words, 32 nonstudied

---

[15]In the case of recognition, the word and the list context will also be sources of activation.

words, plus whatever words the subjects had not successfully completed in the first test. These repeated words were either tested with the same fragment or a different fragment. For instance, if the original word was *aardvark* the two fragments were either *a—d—rk* or *-ar-va—*. Note the two are complementary. Table 7.5 displays the results and the ACT–R simulation of these results.

The simulation modeled the data, assuming subjects tried to retrieve the words by means of productions like:

Complete-Fragment-1-3

      IF   the goal is to complete a word consisting of the letters
                  L1 __ L3 __
                  and L1, L2, L3, and L4 spell Word
    THEN say Word

Probability of firing this production will depend on both the base-level activation of the word and the strength of association from L1 and L3 to the word. Because of the base-level factor, there will be a higher probability of completing the word if it had been studied. The latency-scale parameter F was set to 0.5 sec in fitting these data, and s was estimated at 0.3 and τ at –0.45. The other parameters were kept constant. The correspondence between model and data is quite good, with an overall R^2 of .962.

There are two results in the data. First, subjects and simulation are almost twice as good at completing words they have studied. This shows the base-level strengthening effect of that experience. Second, they are worse when retested in the same way with the same string on which they have failed. This is because one is conditionalizing on items that are likely to have low base-level activations and associative strengths. There is no deficit for

TABLE 7.5
Proportions of Fragments Solved and ACT–R Predictions (in Parentheses)

	Studied Words		Nonstudied Words	
	Test 1	Test 2[a]	Test 1	Test 2[a]
	Same fragments in Test 1 and Test 2			
Conditional	.32 (.36)	.17 (.20)	.20 (.20)	.09 (.13)
Control		.36 (.38)		.18 (.23)
	Different fragments in Test 1 and Test 2			
Conditional	.35 (.38)	.34 (.34)	.19 (.21)	.19 (.22)
Control		.37 (.36)		.17 (.22)

[a]Test 2 responses are conditional on failure in Test 1.

items tested with different fragments. The conditional performance on the different fragments reflects a plus–minus effect. As in the case of the same fragment condition, one is conditionalizing on lower base-level activations, which should result in lower recall. On the other hand, one is testing with new letters, which might have stronger associations. Indeed, because the two fragments are complementary only one will have the first letter, which is probably the best cue for the word. This was represented in the ACT–R model by setting the strengths of association from the first letter much higher than for the other letters (4.0 vs. 0.4). This setting of associative strengths was basically determined to produce equal recall of the different fragments in the conditional tests as control fragments, so the model does not really predict this effect (although it does predict better performance in the conditional test for different fragments than for same fragments).

Process Dissociation

Jacoby's process dissociation methodology has attracted a great deal of interest. It is a methodology for estimating the contribution of implicit and explicit memory to performance in a task. Table 7.6 gives some representative results that come from the first experiment of Toth, Reingold, and Jacoby (1994). Subjects studied a list of words. For half of these words they made semantic (pleasantness) judgments and for the other half they made nonsemantic (vowel) judgments. Then they were later given word stems and asked to complete the stems. In the indirect condition they were asked to complete the stem with the first word that came to mind. In the inclusion

TABLE 7.6
Proportion of Stems Completed with Critical Items and Estimates of Controlled and Automatic Influences of Memory in Toth, Reingold, and Jacoby's (1994) Experiment 1 (ACT–R Predictions in Parentheses)

| Performance Measure | Study Processing | | |
	Semantic	Nonsemantic	New
Test			
Indirect	.51 (.53)	.45 (.44)	.30 (.31)
Inclusion	.60 (.59)	.47 (.45)	.29 (.31)
Exclusion	.33 (.37)	.43 (.42)	.26 (.31)
Estimate			
Controlled	.27 (.22)	.03 (.03)	—
Automatic	.42 (.47)	.45 (.44)	—

condition they were asked to complete the stem with a word they studied if they could (but they were to try to complete the word with some word). In the exclusion condition they were told to complete the stem with a word they had not studied. All stems had multiple completions, only one of which was the target word that they might study. The data presented in Table 7.6 are the proportion of target words generated in each of these conditions. In addition, Table 7.6 shows the proportion of completions with the designated target to new words that had not been studied.

Toth et al. proposed that subjects' performance in this task can be conceived of as reflecting a probability C of retrieving the word in a controlled way and a probability A of retrieving it in an automatic way. The probability I of retrieving the word in the inclusion condition is the probability of retrieving it by controlled means and, if that fails, by automatic means:

$$I = C + A(1 - C)$$

whereas the probability in the exclusion condition is probability of retrieving it by automatic means but not being able to retrieve it by controlled means to exclude it:

$$E = A(1 - C)$$

Toth et al. noted that the probability of retrieving it by controlled means can be estimated:

$$C = I - E$$

With C estimated, the probability of retrieving it by automatic means can be estimated:

$$A = E/(1 - C)$$

The same ACT–R model as used for the Hayman and Tulving experiment was used to model this experiment. As in the previous simulation, a studied word would have a somewhat more active encoding of its spelling. This produced the advantage of either semantic or nonsemantic processing in the indirect condition where we simply had ACT–R report the first word that it retrieved. The effect of semantic processing was modeled by giving ACT–R two rehearsals of the item. This increased both the strength of the spelling representation and the strength of the encoding of the trace storing the fact that the word occurred in the list. Retrieval of this contextual trace was necessary in both the inclusion and exclusion conditions. In the inclusion condition, ACT–R output the first word that it retrieved if it recognized it as studied or if it could not generate any other completions that it recognized as studied. It rejected this first word only if it could not recognize it as coming from the list and could generate another word that it could so recognize. In the exclusion condition, ACT–R generated a word only if it could not recognize it as coming from the list. The recognition judgment was based on retrieval of a trace encoding the word in the list context, which was facilitated by the rehearsal in the semantic condition.

Table 7.6 also displays the predictions of the ACT–R model. Two parameters were estimated to fit these data. One was the threshold parameter τ, which was estimated at 0.1, and the other was the activation noise parameter s, which was estimated at 0.45. The ACT–R model closely reproduces the data, including Jacoby's estimates of controlled and automatic probabilities, A and C. It is worth reviewing the ACT–R account of the basic effects:

1. There are more target completions of studied words than new words because the target word has its spelling more active and is more likely to be retrieved.
2. Performance is better in the indirect condition for semantic processing than for nonsemantic processing because rehearsal further strengthens the word representation.
3. Recall is slightly higher in the inclusion condition than in the indirect condition because ACT–R has some probability of rejecting a first candidate if it was not studied.
4. Recall is lower in the exclusion condition than in the indirect condition because ACT–R is throwing out words it can recognize as studied.
5. Effects in 3 and 4 are greater in the semantic condition because ACT–R has a higher probability of retrieving the contextual trace on which recognition judgment depends.

One can derive estimates from the ACT–R simulation of an automatic and controlled components using the Jacoby equations. However, it does not follow that any quantities in the ACT–R simulation correspond exactly to the automatic and controlled components. Roughly speaking, there are three critical quantities in the ACT–R analysis: $P(\text{first})$, which is the probability of generating the target word first; $P(\text{all})$, the probability of generating the target word at all; and $P(\text{recognize})$, the probability of recognizing the word. Then, according to ACT–R, performance in the three conditions derives from these underlying quantities as follows:

$P(\text{indirect}) = P(\text{first})$

$P(\text{inclusion}) = P(\text{first}) + [P(\text{all}) - P(\text{first})] \, P \,(\text{recognize})$

$P(\text{exclusion}) = P(\text{first}) \, [1 - P(\text{recognize})]$

Both $P(\text{first})$ and $P(\text{all})$ will increase with manipulation that cause the subject to process the lexical item and so behave roughly like Jacoby's automatic components. Conversely, $P(\text{recognize})$ will vary with manipulations that produce explicit encoding of the contextual trace and so behave, roughly, like Jacoby's controlled component.

PARAMETER VARIATION

Table 7.2 was given earlier to track the parameters used in fitting the models to the experiments and the proportion of variance accounted for. Except for s, τ, and F, the parameters have been held constant across the experiments. The variations in s, the noise parameter, are rather small. One reason for variation in this parameter is that it will reflect hetero-geneity in the population of subjects and variability in items and how subjects attend to them. The more variable they are, the larger will be the estimate of this parameter, which controls variance in ACT–R activations. Better performance on some items will be modeled by higher ACT–R activations and worse performance by lower activations. Thus, the mixture of activations produced by s will tend to mirror the mixture of performances of subjects.

The other two parameters, τ and F, do appear to vary more dramatically from experiment to experiment. It turns out that these variations are related to the mean activation level of memory chunks. The bottom line in Table 7.2 shows these activations at the point at which study is completed and before testing begins. In the experiments with multiple conditions these averages are calculated over the conditions. The activations are sums of base-level activations and associative activations when the goal is set to retrieve these items. These base-level and associative activations are also shown. These mean activations fluctuate from experiment to experiment. The exact activation levels in ACT–R are somewhat arbitrary. The activa-tions reflect things like how many chunks are in the system, and in any simulation the number is going to be much less than the true number. The τ and F parameters serve to map activation levels onto performance. This is particularly apparent in the case of the τ parameter, where probability of recall is a function of the gap between τ and activation. Similarly, latency is a function of the gap between the logarithm of F and the activation level.

Retrieval time will be equal to the exponential of the difference between ln F and activation.[16]

Figure 7.17 plots τ and ln F as a function of average activation level. We have separately plotted t from the free-recall experiments (Murdock, Glenberg, Roberts—F does not vary across these experiments). Although the relationship is not perfect, there is an approximately linear relationship between τ and ln F and average activation over the experiments. Thus, a major reason for the fluctuation in τ and F is to compensate for the arbitrary differences in mean activation levels from experiment to experiment. Activation is an interval scale in ACT-R where absolute differences are meaningful but there is no meaningful zero.

It might seem strange that the curve for the free-recall τ is so far above other t curve in Fig. 7.17. The reason for this is that in the free-recall models a word can be recalled if, on any cycle before recall terminates, its noise brings it above threshold. Thus, there are many opportunities to recall a

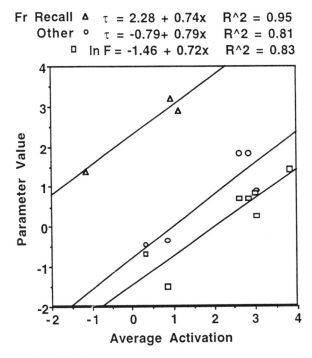

FIG. 7.17. Relationship between average activation in an experiment and the threshold parameter τ and the logarithm of the latency factor.

---

[16]According to Retrieval Time Equation 3.10, Time $= Fe^{-M}{}_i = e^{\ln F - M}{}_i$, assuming $f = 1$ and $S_p = 0$.

word in free recall, whereas in the recognition or serial-memory paradigms there is just one opportunity to recall the word. Because activation noise was independent from cycle to cycle, this meant that chances were good for recall unless the threshold was very high. The solution to this is to have the noise correlated from cycle to cycle in the simulation—something we did not pursue in the free-recall models. This can be achieved in ACT–R, utilizing the distinction between transient and permanent noise (see Base-Level Equation 3.6).

Although these studies reveal a general relationship between activation and the parameters τ and F, there is no reason to believe the relationship should be perfect, because there should be experiment and population differences in these parameters just as there should be in the s parameter. Differences in τ correspond to differences in levels of recall and bias. Some subjects in some experiments will show a greater recall and tendency to false alarm. This is captured by a lower value of the τ parameter. Similarly, it is reasonable to assume that there will be population differences in retrieval speed (e.g., Salthouse, 1991). Moreover, in some experiments subjects will have practiced more and so display higher activations. Thus, all differences in activation levels are not arbitrary and there should not always be compensating changes in τ and F. Nonetheless, Fig. 7.17 suggests that variations in the average activation levels are the main reason in the model fits for the large variation in the parameters τ and F.

Because τ and $\ln F$ both show an approximate linear relationship to mean activation, they should show a linear relationship to one another. In fact, one can do a pretty good job in predicting F from τ:

$$F = 0.348e^{\tau} \qquad \textbf{Speed-Accuracy Equation 7.4}$$

This equation accounts for 93.9% of the variance in the F parameter across the non-free-recall experiments where estimates of both τ and F were obtained.[17] So really in some cases only one parameter is being estimated per experiment. This parameter is τ, and the prediction is that retrieval time is about a third of a second when the activation is at the threshold τ. This equation also describes a situation where subjects can trade off increased accuracy for increased latency by lowering the threshold.

CONCLUSIONS

This chapter has shown that ACT–R is capable of accounting for a large range of phenomena in the field of list memory. As such, it has proven its

---

[17]The free-recall experiments provide very little constraints for the estimate of the F parameter, and it was just arbitrarily set at 2 for all of these experiments.

potential for being the integrating theory that Newell wanted (see Chapter 1). This effort at modeling has contributed to our understanding of ACT–R in that we have come to a better understanding of the parameters in ACT–R and the constraints on their variation. The parameter variation across experiments in this chapter has been exceedingly regular. The s parameter shows little variation, and the F and τ parameters are related by the Speed-Accuracy Equation just given. This regularity is a major piece of evidence for the underlying ACT–R theory. As a final note, the s parameter was always estimated to be less than 1. As Chapter 9 shows, this is a precondition for ACT–R's learning over a lifetime to converge on a stable knowledge base.

8

Choice

Marsha Lovett
Carnegie Mellon University

ELABORATING ACT–R'S THEORY OF CHOICE

For both humans and animals, choice is a necessary part of life. Some choices mark global decisions (e.g., for whom to cast a vote, whom to choose as a mate), but the majority of choices, encountered in daily life, have more immediate consequences and tend not to evoke explicit, deliberate reasoning (e.g., which route to take to work, in which patch to forage for food). This chapter focuses on the processes mediating the latter kind of choice—choice in service of a local goal—particularly when the chooser has repeated exposures to the same choice point. Problem-solving tasks offer many examples of choice in service of a local goal. For example, when working on a problem (e.g., solving an algebra equation), solvers often have multiple strategies available (e.g., graphing, quadratic formula) and must choose among these strategies in order to progress toward the local goal of reaching a solution. The same framework maps onto many animal choice situations. For example, in foraging, the animal's goal is to obtain some food, and the choices are the multiple patches in which food may be sought.

Making such choices involves facing two questions: (1) how to evaluate different options when the successful option cannot be known in advance, and (2) how to adapt one's choice tendencies to a potentially changing environment. The ability to evaluate options (and choose among them) in a way that is sensitive to the contingencies of one's environment is important for success. For example, people who choose more robust solution strategies will tend to solve more problems, and foraging animals who seek food in richer patches will tend to find more food. This sensitivity to environmental contingencies, however, is useless unless it adjusts to changing circumstances. For example, problem solvers need to be able to shift their choice tendencies when a strategy that was unsuccessful at first eventually outperforms other strategies once it is practiced. Similarly, ani-

255

mals need to adjust their foraging choices when a patch that was previously plentiful eventually becomes depleted, making it much less rewarding. In both situations, the choosers' goals are best served when their choice tendencies adapt to changing experiences of success and failure with the various alternatives.

ACT–R must face the same questions of evaluation and adaptation in choice situations. What does ACT–R do when more than one production applies to the current situation? The performance discussion in the third section of Chapter 3 specified how ACT–R's conflict resolution mechanism uses productions' parameter values to select the production with the highest expected utility. How does ACT–R adjust its choice tendencies to a changing environment? The learning discussion in the fourth section of Chapter 4 specified how ACT–R estimates production parameters from past experiences. Together, these performance and learning mechanisms allow ACT–R to choose adaptively within its environment. When the environment changes, the model learns new values for its productions' parameters, and its selection among those productions changes accordingly. As shown in various examples throughout Chapters 3 and 4, these ACT–R mechanisms do a good job of fitting problem solvers' choice tendencies in relatively stable environments.

In this chapter, we raise several issues regarding ACT–R's ability to adjust to rapidly changing environments and its applicability to choice situations beyond problem-solving choice. In particular, we focus on the predictions of ACT–R when time-based decay is incorporated into the computation of productions' success histories. This time-based adjustment was addressed briefly at the end of Chapter 4. Here we discuss in more detail how it affects the way productions' parameters are learned and how it influences the time course of choice among competing productions. Through a variety of examples, we demonstrate that the decay-based parameter-learning mechanism allows ACT–R models to account for a variety of learning and choice data at a fine-grained level of detail.

A Review of How ACT–R Learns to Choose

In ACT–R, each production rule i is chosen according to a probability that reflects its expected gain, E_i, relative to its competitors' expected gains, E_j. ACT–R chooses the production with highest gain, but because of noise in the evaluation, the production with highest expected gain is only chosen a certain proportion of the time. The Conflict Resolution Equation 3.4 describes the probability that a production with expected gain E_i will have the highest noise-added expected gain:

$$\text{Probability of } i = \frac{e^{E_i/t}}{\sum_j e^{E_j/t}} \qquad \textbf{Conflict Resolution Equation 3.4}$$

where t controls the noise in the evaluations. These evaluations of expected gain are computed as the quantity $E = PG - C$, where P is the estimated probability of achieving the production's goal, G is the value of the goal, and C is the estimated cost to be expended in reaching the goal. This chapter focuses on the impact of successes and failures on choice, so we take C as fixed and expand on P. Because P is the estimated probability of eventual success in attaining the goal, it is decomposed into two parts: $P = qr$, where q is the probability that the production under consideration will achieve its intended next state, and r is the probability of achieving the production's goal given arrival at the intended next state. For practical purposes, we can take q as 1, leaving r as the main quantity to estimate. Under this constraint, the r parameter is important for determining the choice among competing productions. When a production's r parameter is low, it implies that the production tends not to lead to the goal even when it leads to its intended next state; this low r value will be represented in a low P value, which will lead the production to have a low expected gain. In contrast, a production with a high likelihood of leading to its goal (i.e., high r value) will have a higher estimated probability of achieving the goal and hence a higher expected gain evaluation.

In ACT–R, the value of a production's r parameter is estimated as:

$$r = \frac{\text{Successes}}{\text{Successes} + \text{Failures}} \qquad \textbf{Probability Learning Equation 4.5}$$

where Successes and Failures refer to the number of eventual successes and failures that occurred when this production was used. This includes all prior such events (i.e., those before the beginning of the simulation) and experienced events (i.e., those during the current simulation). Thus, before a production has been used in the current simulation, these values represent a prior estimation of the production's successes and failures. As the current simulation runs and the production is exercised, the values of Successes and Failures will include more and more experienced successes and failures, and the ratio in Equation 4.5 will emphasize the experienced success rate of the production. A more explicit breakdown of experience into "prior" and "experienced" quantities rewrites Equation 4.5 as:

$$r = (\alpha + m)/(\alpha + \beta + m + n)$$

where α and β represent prior successes and failures and m and n represent observed successes and failures.

Two important ACT–R predictions stem from this basic mechanism:

1. As solvers experience success and failure, their choices will shift from initial tendencies to a preference of the more successful production(s).
2. Because success and failure information is maintained at the production level, solvers' preferences will be exhibited at the production level—that is, success with a certain production will generalize to all situations where it is applicable (even if the solver's successes with this production were limited to a small set of situations).

An Example of ACT–R's Mechanisms for Choice

The building sticks task (BST), described in the fourth section of Chapter 4, offers a problem-solving situation where solvers must learn to choose between various solution approaches. By studying how solvers' choice patterns change with different experiences in this task, we can test the preceding predictions and illustrate the basic ACT–R mechanisms described earlier. After doing so, the remainder of this chapter explores choice in ACT–R when the decay-based component is enabled.

Figure 8.1 (top) presents a typical problem that solvers face in the BST. It includes an unlimited supply of three different-sized building sticks that can be added together or subtracted from each other to build a new stick. The solver's goal is to build this new stick to be equal in length to the desired stick. There are two approaches to this task: The *overshoot* approach starts with a building stick that is longer than the goal stick and cuts it down using the other building sticks; the *undershoot* approach starts with a building stick that is shorter than the goal stick and lengthens it using the other sticks. (Note that the undershoot approach is generally initiated with the medium-sized stick; solvers almost never select the smallest stick for their first move.) If separate productions implement these two approaches, ACT–R will be able to keep separate records of the number of successes and failures associated with each and hence learn associated r parameters that estimate the probability of each production leading to achievement of the goal.

In the fourth section of Chapter 4, we described a model of the first experiment in Lovett and Anderson (1996). Table 4.7 described some of the

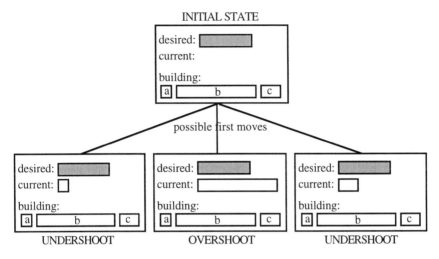

FIG. 8.1. The initial state (top) and three possible first moves (bottom) for a problem in the building sticks task.

basic productions for doing the task. To review, there were four critical productions:

1. *Decide-under.* This production decided to try undershoot for those problems where the difference between the goal and the medium-length building stick seemed less than the difference between the longest building stick and the goal.
2. *Decide-over.* This production decided to try overshoot for those problems where the difference between the longest building stick and the goal seemed less than the difference between the goal and the medium building stick.
3. *Force-under.* This production chose undershoot no matter how the differences appeared.
4. *Force-over.* This production chose overshoot no matter how the differences appeared.

Figure 4.4 reported a successful fit of this model to the first experiment of Lovett and Anderson (1996). Here we describe the fit of the model to their third experiment, which pushes the parameter-learning mechanism to account for choice learning across a longer sequence of problems.[1]

---

[1]The BST models presented in this book differ from th model specified in Lovett and Anderson (1996) in one important way: the models here conform to the ACT–R 4.0 conflict-resolution scheme which only allows separate production rules to compete: the Lovett and Anderson (1996) model instead allowed multiple instantiations of the same ...

In the third experiment, participants solved 90 BST problems while their solution choices were tracked. For each participant, one of the approaches (undershoot or overshoot) was more successful. This more successful approach was counterbalanced over subjects. The structure of the experiment was designed so that 10 out of each 30 problems looked like they could be solved by the more successful approach (i.e., the corresponding "decide" production would match the current goal), whereas the remaining 20 problems looked like they could be solved by the less successful approach (i.e., the less successful approach's "decide" production would match the current goal). The 10 problems that looked like they could be solved by the more successful approach were indeed solvable by that approach (and only that approach). However, depending on the condition, only 5 or 10 of the problems that looked like they could be solved by the less successful approach were actually solvable by that approach (i.e., a full 15 or 10 of these 20 problems were actually solved by the more successful approach). Thus, the two probability conditions in this experiment are labeled 83% and 67% (i.e., $10/10 + 15/20 \approx 83\%$ of problems solved by the more successful approach and $10/10 + 10/20 \approx 67\%$ of problems solved by the more successful approach). Note that each problem was solvable by one and only one of the two approaches (i.e., undershoot or overshoot), and subjects had to complete a solution of the current problem before they could advance to the next problem. In addition to these solved problems, subjects were given test problems on which they specified their first move but did not complete the problem (i.e., they could not see whether that move led to a solution). These test problems occurred before the first solved problems and between each block of 30 solved problems. The ten test problems varied along a dimension we call test problem bias (i.e., the relative closeness of an undershoot move versus an overshoot move to the desired stick length[2]). Specifically, the test problems ranged from strongly overshoot biased (overshoot was much closer) to strongly undershoot biased (undershoot was much closer) and included the three intermediate categories of weak

---

... production to compete based both on the production's overall success rate and on the specific instantiation's anticipated success rate. (A production instantiation is a production whose variables have been bound to certain values.) Conflict resolution in ACT–R 4.0 does not distinguish different instantiations of a production, so it is often helpful to represent different productions that will apply in situations where success rates are likely to differ. The BST model presented here exemplifies this practice by incorporating two productions each for undershoot and overshoot (a "decide" production applies when the corresponding approach looks closer for the current problem, and both "force" productions apply regardless of the current problem details).

[2]Specifically, we estimated a problem's undershoot bias to be $(b - g) - (g - c)$ where b and c are the big and medium-sized building stick lengths respectively and g is the desired stick length. The larger this quantity, the closer an initial undershoot move gets to the goal as compared to an initial overshoot move.

overshoot bias, weak undershoot bias, and neutral (undershoot and over-shoot were equally close to the goal).

Figure 8.2 presents a summary of subjects' choices on the test problems and the corresponding ACT–R 4.0 model predictions. These data are plotted as a function of test problem bias, where "High Against" test problems are those for which the less successful approach looked closer to the goal and "High Toward" test problems are those for which the more successful approach looked closer to the goal. The data points labeled 0 show solvers' initial choice tendencies (before the experimental trials began). The other data points (labeled 1 and 3) show solvers' choice tendencies on the same test problems after 30 and 90 problems of experience with the two approaches. The left panel presents average choice proportions of participants in the 67% condition, and the right panel presents average choice proportions of participants in the 83% condition.

In both conditions, solvers increased their tendency to choose the more successful strategy across subsequent test phases. Moreover, these shifts are greater for the condition experiencing a more extreme (83%) success rate. These results conform to the first prediction mentioned earlier, namely, that solvers adapt their choice tendencies to prefer the more successful strategy. Solvers also show a large effect of test problem bias, tending to choose the approach that appears to be more successful. A striking feature of the data is that the various curves are approximately parallel except where they run into the ceiling of 100%. This suggests that solvers increased their use of the more successful strategy across all problem types even though they had only solved problems that were similar to two of the five test problem types ("High Against" and "High Toward"). This general shift in solvers' choices thus conforms to the second ACT–R prediction mentioned earlier, namely, that solvers change their choice tendencies at the production level, not on a problem-by-problem basis. That is, solvers increased their choice of the more successful strategy for all problem types, not just the ones with which they had gained experience. This is consistent with the ACT–R notion that history-of-success parameters are stored at the production level.

As can be seen from the bottom of Fig. 8.2, ACT–R does a good job in accounting for this shift in probabilities. The ACT–R model was fit to this data by fixing the parameters α and β for the "force" productions and β for the "decide" productions at 0.5 and by estimating the remaining critical production parameter, the "decide" productions' α. The best-fitting value for the decide productions' α was 10.68. We also estimated the model's t parameter to be 8.17 (or, $s = 5.78$), which reflects the amount of noise added to productions' expected gain evaluations (with the value of the goal G set to 20.0). Finally, the perceptual noise added to stick length differences (used in determining which approach looks closer) was logistic with spread

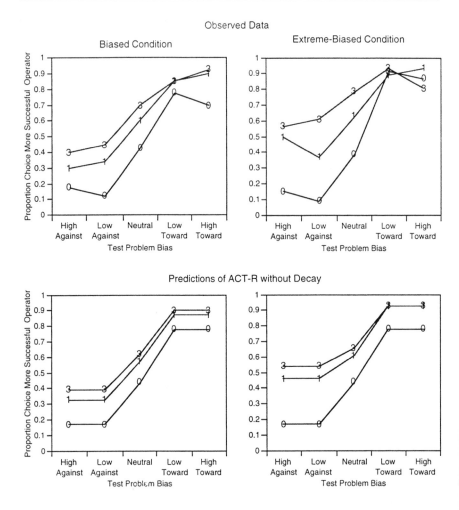

FIG. 8.2. Problem solvers' choice proportions as a function of the test problem type (plotted on the abscissa) and amount of experience in the task. Solvers were tested before solving any problems (test 0), after solving 30 problems (test 1), and after solving 90 problems (test 3). Test 2 data are not shown on the graphs, for clarity of presentation.

parameter $s = 2.5$. The resulting model predictions, based on these two free parameters, fit the data quite well with the best-fitting line being Observed $= 0.99 \times$ predicted $- 0.0005$, MSE $= 0.003$, $R^2 = .96$.

In terms of the critical production rules, what happens is that subjects decrease their evaluation of the less successful productions (e.g., **Decide-Undershoot** and **Force-Undershoot** when undershoot is the less successful approach) and increase their evaluations of the more successful productions (e.g., **Decide-Overshoot** and **Force-Overshoot**). Table 8.1 documents what happens to the r values of these productions. The first column of that table shows the initial r value for the "force" productions as 0.5 (based on the priors, $\frac{\alpha}{\alpha+\beta} = \frac{0.5}{0.5+0.5}$) and the initial r value for the "decide" productions as 0.96 (based on the priors, $\frac{\alpha}{\alpha+\beta} = \frac{10.68}{10.68+0.5}$). This represents an initial preference for using the "decide" productions, that is, choosing the strategy toward which the stick lengths are biased. Because the approach that looks closest will not always lead to a solution, however, the corresponding "decide" production will experience a certain number of failures (depending on the condition). Also, with expected gain noise, there is always some chance that a less successful production will be attempted; this allows the system to gather at least some information about the success of all of the four critical productions. After 90 trials of experience, the productions' r values will have been adjusted based on this information (see Table 8.1). Note that in both conditions, the production corresponding to the more successful approach (within both the "force" and "decide" pairs) had a higher evaluation. Moreover, in the 83% condition, this preference for the more successful production was even more extreme than in the 67% condition.[3]

TABLE 8.1
ACT–R Model *r* Values Before and After Problem-Solving Experience
in Experiment 3 (Lovett & Anderson, 1996)

Production	Initial Value	Final Value	
		67% Condition	83% Condition
MS "force"	.50	.60	.71
LS "force"	.50	.38	.27
MS "decide"[a]	.96	.98	.98
LS "decide"[b]	.96	.63	.54

Note. MS = more successful approach, LS = less successful approach.

[a]Production only competes when problem suggests more successful approach.

[b]Production only competes when problem suggests less successful approach.

---

[3]Note that the final r values for production p do not exactly correspond to $(\alpha_p + \text{success-rate}_p \cdot 90) / (\alpha_p + \beta_p + 90)$ because the number of successes and failures will tend to be less than the corresponding rate times 90 because a given production will not be attempted on all 90 problems.

Decay in ACT–R's Conflict-Resolution Learning

The preceding results suggest that ACT–R's general predictions concerning learning and choice are consistent with problem solvers' overall choice tendencies. These results, however, do not address choosers' potential sensitivity to the timing of successes and failures; instead, only intermittent test data, averaged by condition, were fit. ACT–R originally had no way to make its behavior sensitive to the timing of successes and failures. However, as explained in Chapter 4, this was changed to accommodate results such as the ones discussed in this chapter. Now one can optionally allow ACT–R to decay the success and failure experiences used in computing expected gain.[4]

There are a number of issues that motivate this switch to the decay-based version of the theory:

Issue 1. The ACT–R parameter-learning mechanism without decay cannot exhibit special sensitivity to a recent success or to a particular sequence of success. That mechanism will exhibit the same choice tendencies after m successes and n failures, regardless of different time delays or orderings of these experiences. This is because, without decay, ACT–R takes all experiences of success and failure as interchangeable in time and equal in weight.

Issue 2. Without decay, the information recorded in a production's r parameter is maintained perpetually. The estimation of r in Equation 4.5 only changes when there is an intervening experience, so a production that goes unused will maintain its parameter values indefinitely. This is not true of ACT–R Base-Level Learning Equation 4.1. And, as shown later, it is not true of production parameters when decay-based parameter learning is enabled.

Issue 3. Without decay, an ACT–R model with vast experience can change its choice tendencies only slowly. Because the basic learning mechanism estimates the r parameter as a ratio of successes to all experiences, this ratio will change more and more sluggishly with accumulating experience (i.e., when Successes and Failures are large, any additional experience exerts a very small change in r).[5] And yet,

---

[4]For nondecaying production parameter learning, the global :pl flag in the ACT–R simulation must be set to t. For decay-based production parameter learning, this flag should be set to the decay rate desired, that is, a non-negative number (usually around 0.5).

[5]The nondecaying learning mechanism makes a fairly extreme prediction in this regard. For example, when two productions' r parameters have complementary values based on n trials of experience (e.g., 0.7 and 0.3), it will take more than n *additional* trials of experience with the productions' success rates reversed (e.g., 0.3 and 0.7) for those r values to reflect the reversal.

there may be cases where choosers can adapt more quickly (even with vast experience).

Issue 4. The magnitudes of the prior values for Successes and Failures (α and β in the second version of Equation 4.5) affect the rate at which r can adjust to experience. Without decay, the larger these prior values, the smaller is the effect of a single experienced success or failure on r. Because ACT–R allows these prior parameters to be assigned separately for each production, there is no architecturally required commonality to the rate of production-parameter learning.[6]

This chapter considers the implications of enabling time-based decay in ACT–R's production parameter learning. This decay leads to a discounting of past experience and enables sensitivity to the timing of success and failure experiences. In particular, each experience of success and failure with a given production is decayed according to a power function. This function is similar to the decay of chunk activation after each access of a given chunk (see Base-Level Learning Equation 4.1). Equation 4.5 thus becomes:

$$r(t) = \frac{Successes(t)}{Successes(t) + Failures(t)} \qquad \textbf{Probability Learning Equation 8.1}$$

with Successes(t) and Failures(t) now defined as

$$Successes(t) = \sum_{j=1}^{m} t_j^{-d} \qquad \textbf{Success Discounting Equation 8.2}$$

$$Failures(t) = \sum_{j=1}^{n} t_j^{-d} \qquad \textbf{Failure Discounting Equation 8.3}$$

---

[6]This is a mixed blessing in that different learning rates may arise in situations where different prior weights provide a reasonable explanation for the difference, but they may also arise in situations where different prior weights do not make sense. For example, learning rates (measured in terms of change in choice tendencies per trial) for the same productions in different experiments are sometimes different even though subjects participating in the experiments would not be expected to have different prior histories. In particular, Lovett and Anderson (1996) modeled two experiments of different number of trials using the same productions. The learning rates observed in these two experiments differed (e.g., learning rates tend to be lower for longer experiments), leading to estimates for α and β that varied by an order of magnitude. These parameters allowed the same model to fit two experiments involving the same task, but the different values did not make sense, given the similarity of the task and subject populations.

where t_j is defined as how long ago each past success or failure was, (Equations 8.1, 8.2, and 8.3 correspond to Equations 4.5 and 4.7 from Chapter 4.) Like the nondecaying mechanism, these equations adjust a production's r values after each experience in the direction of that most recent experience (i.e., r increases after success and decreases after failure). With decay enabled, however, the size of the shift depends on the number and timing of previous experiences and the rate of decay d. For instance, the shift will be larger when d is larger and when the delay from previous experiences is longer. This decay-based learning mechanism thus allows a time-weighted ratio of successes and failures, with more recent experiences weighted more heavily than distant ones. (Note that this decay-based version of parameter learning decays both the prior and experienced components of Successes and Failures.)

Figure 8.3 shows how r changes in response to two different productions' histories of experience: SSSSFFFF for production A and SFFSFSFS for production B. The top panel shows the time-decayed $r(t)$, and the bottom panel shows the nondecaying r. Note that the experiences for these two productions contain the same number of successes and failures but in different orders. And yet, in the top panel of Fig. 8.3 (with decay), the r values of the two productions cross over at time $t = 5$, leaving production A with a lower r value at time $t = 8$. In contrast, in the bottom panel of Fig. 8.3 (without decay), r values are based on equally weighted experiences, so the two productions have equal r values at time $t = 8$. This example illustrates a new prediction of decay-based parameter learning—that the exact order and timing of successes and failures in a production's history impact choice.

Incorporating this decay function into ACT–R allows some responses to the issues raised earlier regarding the parameter-learning mechanism.

Issue 1. With the decay-based learning mechanism enabled, ACT–R can exhibit special sensitivity to a recent success or to a particular sequence of successes. Success and failure experiences that occur at different times or in different orders will contribute differentially to the r parameter (i.e., distant-in-time experiences contribute less than recent experiences). This enables models to differentially weight success information that is new versus old and to choose in a way that is sensitive to the timing of past experiences.

Issue 2. With the decay-based learning mechanism, the information recorded in a production's r parameter is not maintained perpetually. Success and failure information decays with the passage of time, changing r values, even when no experiences intervene. This kind of

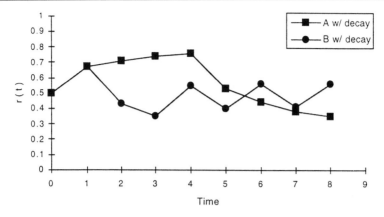

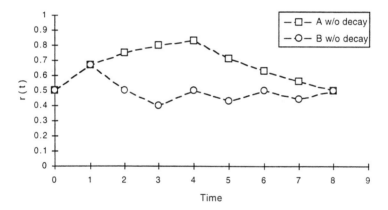

FIG. 8.3. Estimates of the success rates of two productions, A and B, when success and failure experiences are time-decayed (top) or equally weighted (bottom).

temporal weighting makes sense because success information is likely to be increasingly unreliable as time passes.

Issue 3. With its decay process enabled, an ACT–R model with vast experience can more quickly adjust to changes in environmental contingencies, even among productions that have long track records. This is because decay reduces the influence of a potentially large number of past experiences (by downweighting them) relative to the impact of a new success or failure.

Issue 4. Several factors affect the learning rate of production parameters when decay-based learning is enabled: the number and timing of prior successes and failures, the number and timing of experienced successes and failures, and the decay rate for parameter learning. Note, however, that because a single decay rate applies to all of the success and failure contributions, there is a more systematic theory of production-parameter learning.

Another advantage of adding a decay component to production-parameter learning is that it points to potential unification with other aspects of cognition such as memory and categorization. The power-law decay functions presented earlier are analogous to those used in ACT–R's declarative memory. A model of categorization by Elliott and Anderson (1995) also uses a similar power-law decay function to weigh recent exemplars more heavily than distant ones. With this new learning mechanism for production parameters, information regarding the statistical regularities of the environment is maintained in a similar fashion for declarative knowledge and for procedural knowledge.

Plan

In the remaining sections of this chapter, we explore how decay-based production parameters impact choice in the ACT–R theory. In particular, we use the decay-based mechanism to fit models to data in the following five areas:

- "Probability matching" behavior in probability learning.
- Overmatching under conditions of reward.
- Sensitivity to history of success during problem solving.
- "Ratio matching" behavior under concurrent variable interval schedules.
- Sensitivity to time delay in foraging.

Capturing this breadth of results is a challenge by itself. Where possible, we also attempt to capture these results at a fine-grained level of detail, that is, modeling trial-by-trial or subject-by-subject data. For each of the five phenomena, the presentation is organized as follows: First, we define the basic result, generalizing across multiple studies. Then, we describe a particular experiment that exemplifies the phenomenon. We devote considerable attention to the procedure of the highlighted experiment in each section because the same details (e.g., timing and ordering of trials) are used in fitting the model to that experiment's results. Finally, we present choice predictions for the experiment and discuss the goodness of fit.

PROBABILITY LEARNING

"Probability Matching" in Probability Learning

The phenomenon of probability matching occurs when people choose an option a proportion of the time equal to its probability of being correct. For example, in a simple binary choice task, if one of the two options has a 70% probability of being correct and the other has a 30% probability of being correct, probability matching occurs when people choose the first option 70% of the time, on average. This basic effect has been documented in many probability-learning experiments (e.g., Estes, 1964; Friedman et al., 1964; Hake & Hyman, 1953; Humphreys, 1939). These experiments support the importance of probability matching: The phenomenon has been observed among children, adults, and various patient populations, as well as across disparate situations—from word learning to spatiomotor tasks. One caveat, however, is that the label *probability matching* is some-times only an approximate characterization of the observed behavior. That is, subjects' choice behavior often deviates from the exact proportion that probability matching would predict. (For examples of this, see the third section of Chapter 3 and the following section on overmatching with reward.) Regardless of the accuracy of its name, however, probability matching (or probability-matching-like behavior) is a very robust phe-nomenon. Chapter 3 provided a very simple account of this literature as an introduction to ACT–R's conflict resolution mechanisms. Here, we provide a more detailed analysis that is additionally sensitive to issues of learning in the face of a changing environment.

Data from a study by Friedman et al. (1964) are used for the first test of the decay-based learning mechanism. In this study, college students com-pleted more than 1,000 choice trials over the course of 3 days. For each trial, a signal light was illuminated, participants pressed one of two buttons, and then one of two outcome lights was illuminated. A button press that matched the subsequent outcome light was considered "correct," and a button press that did not match the outcome light was considered "incor-rect." Task instructions encouraged participants to try to guess the correct outcome for each trial.

This study extended the standard probability-learning paradigm by changing the two buttons' success probabilities (p and $1 - p$) across 48-trial blocks during the experiment. Specifically, for the even-numbered blocks 2–16, p took on the values .1, .2, .3, .4, .6, .7, .8, .9 in a randomly permuted order. These were labeled the *variable-p* blocks. For the odd-numbered blocks 1–17, p was set to .5. These .5 blocks served to equilibrate the success probabilities of the two responses before the next variable-p block. We focus this analysis and modeling on the data from these 17 blocks because they are reported in greatest detail. In the experiment as a whole, however, there were additional .5 blocks and .8 blocks preceding and following the 17 blocks described here.

This experiment allowed for the test of several hypotheses with respect to probability matching. First, as Fig. 8.4 indicates, people were exhibiting probability-matching behavior within each block. Each small graph in this figure represents a 48-trial variable-p block during which participants' choice probabilities (filled circles) asymptoted to close to the outcome probabilities (horizontal lines). Second, the time course of probability matching was affected by the outcome probability that had occurred during the previous block. This result is also supported by Fig. 8.4, which shows that participants' choice probabilities tended toward .5 (the outcome probability of the preceding block) at the beginning of each block before climbing or falling to the probability associated with the current block. Third, choices were influenced by individual, recent outcomes. By inspecting the choice probabilities in Fig. 8.5, it is clear that participants' choices differed systematically, depending on the outcome of the previous one or two trials. For instance, the first-order conditional probabilities (AA and BA columns combined vs. AB and BB columns combined) show that participants were

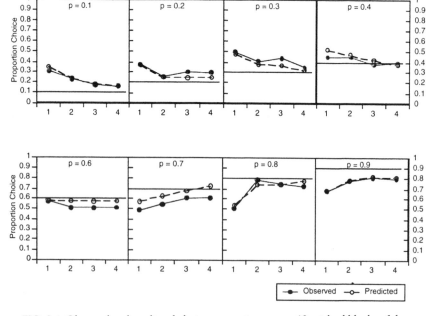

FIG. 8.4. Observed and predicted choice proportions across 12-trial subblocks of the variable-p blocks in the experiment by Friedman et al. (1964). Horizontal lines represent probability-matching values.

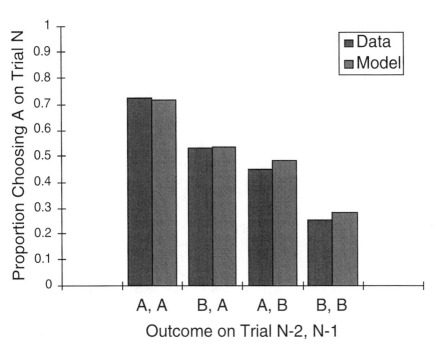

FIG. 8.5. Observed and predicted second-order conditional probabilities averaged over the variable-p blocks in Friedman et al. (1964)

more likely to choose the button on trial n that had been correct on the preceding trial than the button that had been incorrect on the preceding trial. Participants' choices were also somewhat influenced by the outcome that occurred two trials ago, as demonstrated by differences in the second-order conditional probabilities. For example, the probability of choosing A after the AA outcome sequence was greater than that after the BA sequence, and the probability of choosing A after the AB sequence was greater than that after the BB sequence. In sum, the data from this experiment demonstrate a sensitivity to past experience of success at three scopes—across block, within block, and trial-to-trial.

To compute model predictions for this experiment, we must first gather data on participants' history of success throughout the experiment. We take the two critical productions for this task as **Choose-Left-Button** and **Choose-Right-Button**. Both productions match at the beginning of each trial, but only one will be correct. For each of the variable-p blocks, Friedman et al. (1964) reported the exact sequence of outcomes experienced by participants.[7] This provides a sequence of successes and failures within each of the variable-p blocks. The same procedure is followed for the $p = .5$ blocks. Notice that the reported history of success information is only accurate within blocks; participants experienced the variable-p blocks in random orders. Therefore, we must approximate participants' exact history of success for trials preceding the current block. We take this average preceding experience to be 384 trials of evenly spaced successes and failures of the two options; 384 trials at $p = .5$ is the expected history before each variable-p block because, on average, participants have 8 blocks of experience preceding a variable-p block, and 384 trials = 8 blocks at 48 trials each. This approximation, together with the exact within-block histories, provides an explicit representation of participants' history of success preceding each trial.

This information serves as input to the computation of $r(t)$ (see Probability Learning Equation 8.1) for the two alternatives. (Note that we approximate the average time per trial as 1 sec.) For simplicity in model fitting, we took $G = 1$, $C \approx 0$, and $q = 1$ for both productions. Setting the value of the goal, G, equal to 1 merely sets a particular scale for expected net gain. The assumption that expected cost, C, equals 0 is made throughout the chapter, but it is not required by ACT–R.[8]

This leaves only two free parameters, d and t. To predict choice probabilities spanning the range [0–1], we constrained the noise parameter t to be 0.24 (which is equivalent to $s = 0.17$ and $\sigma^2 = 0.1$) and then estimated the decay rate d to minimize the SSE between the trial-by-trial observed choice proportions (computed as proportions of participants) and the predicted choice probabilities.[9] Thus, we are presenting a one-parameter fit to these data.

Figure 8.6 plots these observed choice proportions against the predicted choice probabilities, with $d = 0.714$. This fit has $R^2 = .88$, SSE = 8.697, and MSE = 0.01. The best-fitting line is Observed = 0.943 × predicted + 0.014, which is quite close to the "perfect prediction" line, $y = x$. The unique

---

[7]When ACT–R learns by experience in this task, it only records a single success or failure experience for the production responsible for the current trial's outcome. Thus, ACT–R's learning is not only specific to the actual sequence of outcomes, but also to its sequence of choices.

[8]In general, decay-based parameter learning affects the estimation of a and b, the two components of C in PG–C. By setting prior and experienced costs to 0 we eliminate their influence.

[9]Although Friedman et al. did not provide complete history of success information, their report contained the most precise information on participants' sequences of success and failure and the longest set of trial-by-trial choice data of all the studies we could find. Therefore, we use these data to derive an estimate for the decay parameter and then use the estimated value in as many model fits as possible throughout this chapter.

achievement here is that the ACT–R model is accurately predicting partici-pants' choice proportions trial by trial. Figure 8.4 presents these predicted values (as open circles) aggregated by 12-trial subblocks to give a better sense of how they would be ordered in time within the variable-p blocks. Here, one can see that the model exhibits within-block changes in choice

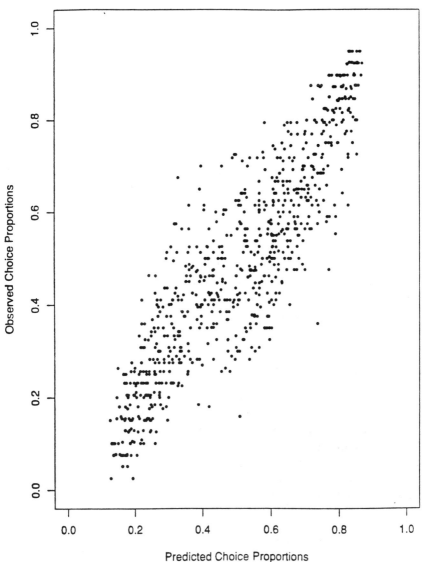

FIG. 8.6. Trial-by-trial observed versus predicted choice proportions for Friedman et al. (1964).

proportions that are similar to those of participants in the Friedman et al. experiment. At this level of aggregation, the fit has $R^2 = .95$, SSE $= 0.06$, and MSE $= 0.002$. Also, the model's conditional probabilities (computed based on the original trial-by-trial predictions) are very similar to the corresponding observed values (see Fig. 8.5). With decay, the model is coming very close to the observed data on several measures of choice, with only one free parameter in total.

The model's fit to these data shows that probability-matching behavior can arise from a basic mechanism that chooses based on individual, decaying experiences of success and failure. We used trial-by-trial data across the full time course of the experiment to model the gradual and systematic changes in choice. This approach thus promotes the view of probability matching as a natural by-product of choice processes that are sensitive to individual past experiences. In addition, the model's decay component is critical to achieving a good fit to the data from this experiment: When we fit an ACT–R model without decay to the preceding data set (i.e., decay fixed at 0), the trial-by-trial fit suffered greatly with R^2 dropping to .41; the best-fitting line was Observed $= 1.3 \times$ predicted $- 0.13$. This misfit is due to a lack of trial-by-trial sensitivity in the no-decay model, which even impacts the fit when these predictions are aggregated into 12-trial blocks. In that case, the best-fitting line is Observed $= 2.8 \times$ predicted $- 0.90$, $R^2 = .88$. Here, the slope of 2.8, which is significantly different from 1, suggests that, without decay, any new set of experiences with a new outcome probability cannot exert a big enough impact on choice (see Issue 3 given earlier). In contrast, as shown earlier, the decay-based model captures these data easily at both levels of aggregation.

Overmatching With Reward

Although the general characterization of choice during probability-learning experiments is that people tend to "match" the outcome probabilities, there is also evidence that, under certain circumstances, people will "overmatch" or even "maximize" in their choice behavior—that is, they will choose the more probable alternative a proportion of the time that is greater than the proportion it has been successful (e.g., Braveman & Fischer, 1968; Edwards, 1956; Myers, Fort, Katz, & Suydam, 1963; Myers & Atkinson, 1964; Myers & Cruse, 1968; Siegel & Goldstein, 1959). *Maximizing* occurs when people select the more successful alternative all (or almost all) of the time, and *overmatching* occurs when they select the more successful alternative with some probability p', where p' is less than 1 but greater than p, the experienced success probability of that alternative. When the experienced probability p is close to 1, it is clear that choices consistent with probability matching, overmatching, and maximizing will be hard to differentiate. In this section, then, we refrain from classifying results into these different categories and instead quantitatively study people's choice tendencies.

To evoke overmatching and maximizing behavior, experiments tend to employ monetary reward or specific task instructions. The instructional manipulations required to obtain significant levels of overmatching tend to be quite extreme. For instance, subjects might be told to "think of this task as a whole, and try to come up with one solution for the entire task." Given such instructions, it is likely that participants would view the task as qualitatively different from the standard discrete-trial choice situation. For this reason, we focus on how monetary reward, manipulated under standard instructions, leads people to overmatch.

Myers et al. (1963) performed an experiment in which they varied both (1) the probability that one alternative would be correct and (2) the amount of reward that participants would receive for each correct guess. Specifically, participants were assigned to conditions $p = .6$, $p = .7$, or $p = .8$ in which the better of two alternatives was correct with probability p and the other alternative was correct with probability $1 - p$. Crossed with this manipulation, people were assigned to conditions in which they would receive $\pm 10¢$ for each correct/incorrect guess, $\pm 1¢$ for each correct/incorrect guess, or $\pm 0¢$ (no reward or penalty) for each correct/incorrect guess.

The proportions of choices of the better alternative on the last 100 out of 400 trials are presented for each condition in Table 8.2. In general, choice of the better alternative is close to probability-matching levels (where probability matching equals the p for each condition). Notice, however, that an additional effect appears in these data: The greater the reward, the more the choice proportion exceeds the matching probability. Thus, it seems that under monetary reward conditions, exact probability matching is not the rule, but the exception. A subset of these data were fit in the second section of Chapter 3, but there only a performance model was fit to subjects' asymptotic choice behavior. Here, we show that an ACT–R model can learn production parameters through experience in such an experiment and produce the same quality of fit.

The model for this simple choice task (as in the previous section) has two critical productions, **Choose-Left** and **Choose-Right**. We model the reward manipulation from this experiment with different values for G, the value of achieving success. Because the monetary rewards were 0¢, 1¢, and 10¢, we would expect the values of G to be monotonically increasing for these three conditions, that is, $G_0 < G_1 < G_{10}$. The other parameter values, however, remain constant across conditions. Specifically, we fix $d = 0.714$, $t = 0.24$—the values from the previous model fit. This leaves three free parameters, G_0, G_1, G_{10}.

Because Myers et al. did not provide any sequence information with respect to history of success and choice, we approximate the temporal nature of participants' success and failure experiences by generating a random sequence of correct outcomes consistent with each condition's probability. As in the previous model fit, we represent each outcome as a success experience for the correct alternative or as a failure experience for the incorrect alternative. Based on this estimated history of success for each condition, we compute the model's predicted choice probabilities using the G values that minimize the SSE between the observed choice proportions and the model's average choice probability over the last 100 trials in each condition. These best-fitting G values are $G_0 = 0.753$, $G_1 = 1.039$, and $G_{10} = 1.165$. Note that as reward increases the G value increases, but that the increase is not proportional to or even linear with reward amount. This is consistent with other research on the psychological measurement of differential rewards (e.g., Kahneman & Tverksy, 1984). The predicted choice proportions from this fit are presented in parentheses in Table 8.2. The fit has $R^2 = .97$, SSE = 0.008, and MSE = 0.0009.

Again, a model that makes choices based on decaying success information achieves a good fit to the data with relatively few parameters. Notice that, just like the participants in this study, the model tends to overmatch and does so by a greater amount under higher reward conditions. This effect can be understood by examining ACT–R's basic choice mechanism. In this situation, choice depends mainly on the product PG for each alternative, so G can be viewed as scaling the model's sensitivity to differences in the alternatives' predicted probabilities of success, P. (Remember, when $q = 1$, $P = r$.) When G is large, the difference between two alternatives' P values

TABLE 8.2
Observed and Predicted Choice Proportions of the More Probable Option
Under Different Reward Conditions

	Probabilities		
Reward	$p = .6$	$p = .7$	$p = .8$
0 cents	0.624 (0.661)	0.753 (0.756)	0.869 (0.843)
1 cent	0.653 (0.715)	0.871 (0.829)	0.925 (0.917)
10 cents	0.714 (0.737)	0.866 (0.856)	0.951 (0.939)

Note: Predicted proportions for each condition are given in parentheses. From Myers et al. (1963).

will be magnified and (assuming a fixed amount of noise in the system) the alternative with higher P will more likely be chosen. In other words, with increasing reward, the model is more sensitive to the relative success rates of the alternatives and, hence, is more likely to choose the more successful option. This same result was captured in Chapter 3, where a standard ACT–R model was fit to a subset of these data.[10] However, in that case, the parameter learning mechanism was not invoked. Here, we have shown that giving the model a history of experience consistent with what participants experienced allows the model to learn production parameters that give an adequate fit. If more trial-by-trial information on subjects' experiences were available for this data set, we could have put the learning mechanism to a more stringent test. The next section uses a data set we collected with the intent of maintaining such trial-by-trial information.

Sensitivity to History of Success in Problem Solving

Probability learning does not just occur in simple, contextually sparse tasks like those already described. It also occurs in more complex, naturally occurring situations where a solver has multiple solution approaches, or strategies, for a particular problem. The different strategies available to the solver constitute the different choices, each of which may or may not lead to a successful solution. As solvers gain experience in these situations, they tend to use more successful problem-solving strategies more often and less successful strategies less often (Lemaire & Siegler, 1995; Lovett & Anderson, 1996; Reder, 1987, 1988; Wu & Anderson, 1993). Experiments in which the success rates of different strategies are varied across time reveal that problem solvers also distinguish between recent and global success rates when making strategy choices (Reder, 1988).

The building sticks task (BST) offers one example of probability learning in a complex task. Lovett and Anderson (1995) used it to study the relationship between problem-solving success on one trial and strategy choice on the next. For each problem, solvers were presented with three building sticks and a desired stick and were asked to use these building sticks to create a new stick equal in length to the desired stick (see Fig. 8.1). For a given problem in this task, solvers had to choose which strategy to use, Undershoot or Overshoot. The problems were designed so that (1) both strategies were applicable in the first move, (2) only one strategy led to a solution, and (3) all problems made the two strategies appear equally close

---

[10]Note that the current model's best-fitting values for G_0 and G_{10} are approximately one fourth those of the corresponding parameters in the performance-based fit from Chapter 3. This makes sense because the noise value used here is also approximately one fourth that used in the previous model. When G and the noise are similarly magnified, choice behavior remains the same.

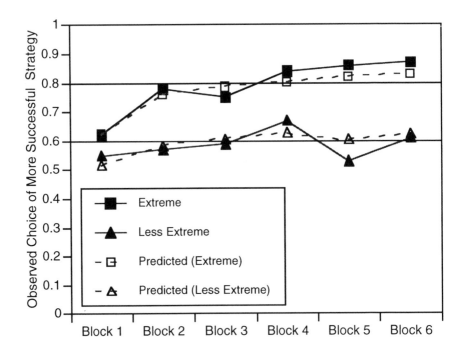

FIG. 8.7. Observed and predicted choice proportions of the more successful strategy for the experiment by Lovett and Anderson (1995).

to the goal. Because of this third constraint, all problems looked neutral and the **Decide** productions from the previous BST model were not necessary. Here, then, there are two critical productions that match at the beginning of every problem, **Force-Undershoot** and **Force-Overshoot**.

Participants in the different conditions received different sequences of problems that would lead them to experience certain histories of success and failure with these two productions. The overall success rates of overshoot versus undershoot were extreme for two conditions (80%:20% and 20%:80%) and less extreme for two other conditions (60%:40% and 40%:60%). Figure 8.7 presents the proportion of solvers choosing the more successful strategy (where "more successful" is defined by their condition), averaged over blocks of 15 problems. In both the extreme and the less extreme conditions, participants learned to prefer the more successful strategy as the experiment progressed, with the extreme conditions attaining a more noticeable preference. The two horizontal lines in the figure represent pure probability-matching behavior for the two conditions. In both cases, the observed proportions in the last three blocks are within 95% confidence intervals of the matching proportions.

Although the aggregate data suggest that probability matching occurs in this problem-solving context, the individual participant data presented in Fig. 8.8 belie that notion. Here, each individual's probability of choosing the more successful strategy (over the last 45 problems) is plotted against the proportion of problems actually solved by the more successful strategy (averaged over the last 45 problems).[11] The line $y = x$ represents probability matching, and yet many data points deviate from that line, $R^2 = .41$. If any trend can be found, it appears that the majority of solvers are overmatching relative to their experience. Nevertheless, only two participants show absolute "maximizing" behavior by choosing the more successful strategy on all of the last 45 trials of the experiment.

Even though overall probabilities of success were fixed for participants in

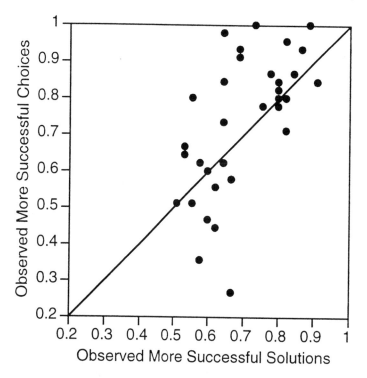

FIG. 8.8. Proportion of last 45 problems on which the more successful strategy (MS) was selected against the experienced proportion of success for the more successful strategy, computed for each participant based on the individual's solution history.

---

[11]As each subject's experience was randomly generated, they would not experience exactly 60% or 80% correct solutions.

a given condition, different problem solvers in this experiment had their own unique histories of success and failure with overshoot and undershoot because they could choose freely between the two strategies on each problem. We can use this history information to see if we can predict the aggregate choice tendencies in Fig. 8.7 and the individual differences in Fig. 8.8. In particular, we used the individual success and failure information to compute model predictions on a problem-by-problem, solver-by-solver basis. These probabilities were compared with the actual choices (i.e., overshoot or undershoot) made on the corresponding trials. For this fit, we constrained $t = 0.24$ and $d = 0.714$ (from previous fits), fixed G at 1, and allowed the prior experience for the two critical productions to vary. In particular, we constrained the prior experiences of success and failure for both productions to be equal in number (setting r initially to 0.5) and to be long ago in the past so that their decay would have asymptoted (i.e., the time lag for eventual-successes and eventual-failures was fixed at 100.0 sec before the beginning of the simulation). Thus, there was one free parameter to fit the data, the number of previous successes.

Estimating this parameter to fit the entire data set by individual subject-trials leads to 281 previous successes—an effective $\alpha = \beta = 11.2$ for both critical productions. The predicted choice proportions, aggregated and plotted with the observed values in Fig. 8.7, produce an R^2 of .92, MSE = 0.001, and best-fitting line is Observed = 1.1 × predicted – 0.08. This model fit successfully captures the trends and changes in solvers' choices during problem solving. Moreover, it helps to explain the lack of pure probability-matching behavior at the individual level in terms of the particular sequence of successes and failures experienced by each subject. Figure 8.9 plots the model's predicted choice behavior over the last 45 trials for each participant against their observed choice behavior on the last 45 trials. This individual-subject fit based on each participant's history of success is quite good, even though it used a single parameter set (with only one freely varying parameter) across the entire population of participants. In particular, the best-fitting line is Observed = 1.1 × predicted – 0.07, $R^2 = 0.52$, which is superior to the fit obtained by predicting probability matching behavior for each participant (Fig. 8.8).

Comparisons of this model, which decays success and failure experiences, with a nondecaying ACT–R model that treats all such experiences as equal does not show marked differences. For example, the no-decay model has only slightly lower R^2 of .90 for its fit to the aggregate data. However, by looking at a more fine-grained level of analysis than 15-problem blocks, the decay-based model's advantage becomes more apparent. Figure 8.10 shows the second-order conditional probabilities for the entire experiment (top panel) and for the second half of the experiment (bottom panel). Next to

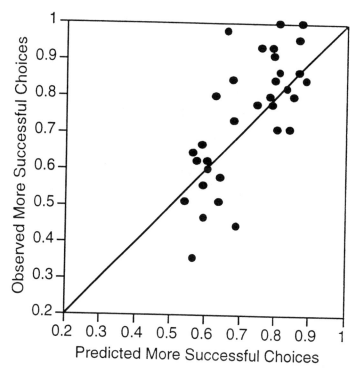

FIG. 8.9. Model fit and observed choice behavior for each participant on the last 45 trials of Lovett and Anderson (1995).

each conditional probability is the prediction of the decay-based model and the no-decay counterpart. In both panels, the decay-based model shows sensitivity across the four situations (UU, OU, UO, and OO) that is comparable to subjects' sensitivity, whereas the no-decay model shows insufficient sensitivity.

ANIMAL CHOICE

Concurrent Variable-Interval Schedules

The phenomena described thus far have all involved human choice. Nevertheless, choice behavior among animals has a vast literature of its own. The phenomenon described in this subsection is one of the classic results in operant conditioning. It consists of the basic result that animals tend to match their ratio of choices between two different options to the ratio of rewards they have received from those two options. For example, if an animal has experienced five times as many rewards from option A as from

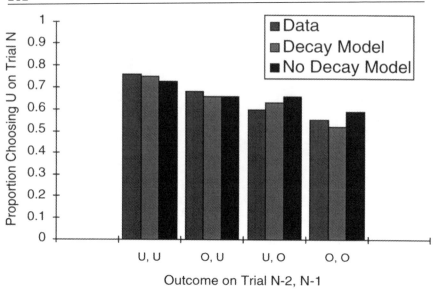

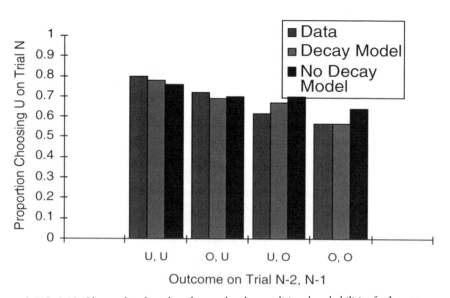

FIG. 8.10. Observed and predicted second-order conditional probabilities for Lovett and Anderson (1995). Top panel is for the entire experiment and the bottom panel is for the second half of the experiment.

option B, such ratio matching would imply that the animal would choose option A five times as often as B. This relationship has been named the *matching law* (Herrnstein, 1961):

$$\frac{\text{Number of A choices}}{\text{Number of B choices}} = \frac{\text{Number of A successes}}{\text{Number of B successes}}$$

Behavior that fits the matching law can be related to probability-matching behavior discussed earlier. Both imply that choice tendencies in some sense "match" environmental payoff tendencies. However, there are a few practical differences that we note briefly. First, the matching law is stated in terms of choice and success *ratios* that relate one option to the other (i.e., A/B), whereas probability matching is stated in terms of choice and success *proportions* that relate one option to the total of all options [i.e., A/(A + B)]. Second, in most probability-matching experiments, every trial produces a success (for one option or the other), whereas in matching-law experiments there tend to be many trials with no success. This difference implies that probability-matching computations of success take into account all trials, and matching-law computations of success focus on a subset of trials (success trials). Finally, matching-law behavior is usually observed in continuous-trial paradigms, where one choice is not necessarily equivalent to one trial, whereas probability-matching behavior is usually discussed in the context of discrete-trial paradigms (see the second section of this chapter). Therefore, in this section we explore how ACT–R's relatively discrete (at the production level) learning of success and failure can account for continuous-trial learning.

The matching law was first demonstrated with pigeons choosing between two concurrent variable-interval (VI) schedules (Herrnstein, 1961). In a variable-interval schedule, a reward is programmed to occur a certain number of seconds after the corresponding key has been pecked, regardless of the number of intervening pecks in that time interval. As the name suggests, however, this time interval is not fixed from reward to reward but varies about a central number of seconds. For instance, the time to each reward (assuming the triggering peck) in a VI-5 schedule would be 5 sec on average.

In Herrnstein's (1961) experiment, pigeons were placed in choice situations where they could peck on each of two keys programmed according to independent VI schedules. Figure 8.11 (top panel) presents the pigeons' proportion of choices of key A against their proportion of rewards from key A for each of several conditions. Each condition was specified by a certain pair of VI schedules (one schedule for each key), and each data point represents the average of the last five sessions under that condition. The data points of the same shape in Fig. 8.11 (top) represent choice behavior of a single pigeon. From this figure, it is clear that, across a variety of VI-VI schedules, the animals' choices asymptoted to match the experienced ratio of rewards.

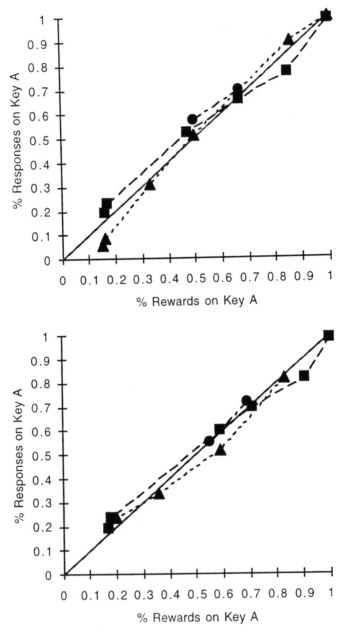

FIG. 8.11. Choice and reward proportions from Herrnstein (1961) (top panel) and those simulated by ACT–R with history-of-success information decayed (bottom panel). The VI-VI schedules used in this study were 5:25, 5:10, 5:5, 10:5, 25:5. These correspond to the first through fifth clusters of data points, reading from left to right. Different curves correspond to different pigeons (top panel) or different simulations (bottom panel).

To fit these data using the decay-based learning mechanism, we had to overcome a new challenge that had more to do with the nature of this experimental paradigm than with the model itself. The challenge was twofold. First, we had no specific information from Herrnstein's report on the timing or sequence of successes and failures that the animals experienced. Second, because success in a VI-VI environment is a complex stochastic process depending on both past rewards and past choices, we had no simple way to approximate a fixed history of experience for animals in the different VI-VI environments. Instead, we chose to emulate the VI-VI environments (using Lisp code) and then test the model's choice performance within these environments. Because both the ACT–R model and the VI-VI environments include their own sources of stochasticity and because the actions of each depend in a specific way on the output of the other, this is a highly interactive system. For example, even if the environment were set to represent a VI 5 VI 25 schedule, there is no guarantee that the rewards will be given in exactly a 5:1 ratio; the reward outcomes depend on the timing of the schedules relative to the timing of the animals' choices. For these reasons, the analytically based parameter-fitting techniques used in the preceding model fits were not much help in this case.

Therefore, we elected to run a set of simulations using the same schedules as in Herrnstein's experiment and to compare the model's output to the data. The simulation was endowed with separate productions for pecking on the left key, pecking on the right key, switching to the left key, and switching to the right key. The reason for the distinction between "pecking" and "switching" is that the two types of productions incur different costs; for example, switching requires that the pigeon actually walk around an obstacle to reach the other key, whereas pecking just involves pecking on the local key. In these simulations, the model made its choices among the four critical productions with the decay-based parameter-learning mechanism enabled. If the model chose to peck a certain key and did not receive a reward immediately on completion of the "peck" (according to the schedule that was running for that key), a failure was recorded for the productions leading up to that failure. Similarly, in the rare event that the model chose to peck a certain key and did receive a reward, a success was recorded for the productions leading up to that success. (Also, the timer for that key's schedule was reset.[12]) We ran this simulation under a few parame-

---

[12]In this environment, as in the conditions presented in Fig. 8.8, we included a change-over delay (COD), which prohibited the dispensing of a reward on a "new" key until 1.5 sec had passed after the animal switched to that key. The inclusion of a COD in this paradigm greatly affects the behavior of pigeons by decreasing their tendency to alternate between the keys with each peck. We simulated this (presumably learned) behavior by representing both the right and the left "pecking" productions as leading to pecking bursts. That is, when the "peck right" production is chosen, a certain amount of pecking time (fluctuating around …

ter settings and compared the model's choices from the end of each simulation run with Herrnstein's data. We also specified a certain amount of previous success with each of the four critical productions to represent the fact that these pigeons had previously been tested in this choice paradigm. Thus, the modeling results presented in this section are more qualitative demonstrations of ACT–R's ability to model the phenomenon under study using the decay-based parameter learning.

To constrain this parameter exploration, we fixed d and t to the values used in previous model fits, 0.714 and 0.24, respectively. Further, we set the prior successes and failures associated with the four critical productions to have approximately 50 past experiences of success out of either 250 past uses ("peck" productions for an initial r of .20) or 200 past uses ("switch" productions for an initial r of .25). This left one free parameter G, the value of achieving the goal. The bottom panel of Fig. 8.11 presents the model's choice behavior with G = 75 for all conditions, but other values provided similar results. (The main constraint on G in this simulation is that it be high enough such that all productions' $PG - C$ values do not fall below 0. This is an issue in any task where the probabilities of success are low as they are here.) Each data point in this graph plots the proportion of choices of key A against the proportion of rewards from key A during the last 300 out of 1,200 simulation cycles, for a particular VI-VI pair.

Because all of the model's predicted values in Fig. 8.11 lie close to the line $y = x$, these simulations demonstrate consistency with the matching law. Moreover, the similarity across the two panels in Fig. 8.11 suggests that the decay-based model exhibits the same choice tendencies as did the pigeons in Herrnstein's experiment. This demonstration is particularly important because it is the first example to show that ACT–R with decay-based parameter learning can capture real choice behavior in a continuous time environment. Gallistel and others (Gallistel, 1993; Mark & Gallistel, 1994) have claimed that this phenomenon arises because animals are estimating the rate parameter of a Poisson process (i.e., the time between successes). However, without explicitly recording or estimating the time interval between rewards, the ACT–R model was able to exhibit the same choice tendencies as did the pigeons. It accomplished this by virtue of its time-based decay of information on success. With the differential weighting of recent versus distant experiences, the model combined local and global differences in the two keys' success rates so that the richer key would be

---

...COD time) passed before the next choice was made. Although this solution sidesteps the issue of how such "staying" behavior arises, ACT–R could be used to study and model this learning process via the expected cost component. ACT–R is sensitive to the expected costs of different options and can adapt its estimates of expected cost based on experience. Because the COD manipulates (i.e., increases) the cost of switching keys, an ACT–R model would likely be able to adapt to it.

preferred but not selected exclusively. For example, a recent series of failures with the richer key could lead to a key switch, but this switch would not last long because the influence of those experiences would soon decay and be counterbalanced by the globally greater success of the richer key. Without decay of this success information, the thousands of trials typical in this paradigm would have led the model to become sluggish and unable to change its behavior based on recent experience.

We have demonstrated that the model can capture both ratio-matching behavior (this model) and probability-matching behavior (second section of this chapter). As mentioned earlier, matching-law and probability-matching behavior arise in different choice environments (VI-VI schedules and probability-learning paradigms). For example, probability-learning paradigms generally have one success per trial, which implies a complementarity among the options, which does not hold in VI-VI schedules (i.e., in VI-VI environments, one option failing does not imply that the other option succeeded). ACT–R can model the different adaptive behavior in these two cases by using the same decay-based parameter-learning mechanism in both situations. The key is that the different environments produce different histories of success to which the same decay-based learning mechanism is applied. ACT–R produces the appropriate behavior in the two types of choice environments because it bases its choices on the particular timing and sequence of past successes in their different histories.

Effects of Time Delay on Foraging

Another classic task for animal choice, studied from a more ecological approach, is foraging: In which of n different patches does the animal choose to forage for food? The generic result in the animal foraging literature is that animals, like humans, are sensitive to their past experiences of success, so they tend to forage in patches that have better records of leading to food. Further, as in the case of human problem solving, there are additional factors that contribute to this choice. For example, animals' patch choices suggest that they are also taking into account the effort they would have to expend to reach the different alternatives (Kamil, Lindstrom, & Peters, 1985), the danger involved in the trip (Wishaw & Dringenberg, 1991), and the "reliability" of success information gathered for each patch (Devenport & Devenport, 1993, 1994; Devenport, Hill, & Ogden, in press). Here, we focus on the last factor weighing into animals' foraging choices—the reliability of patch information.

By the term *reliability*, Devenport, Devenport, and their colleagues are referring to both the recency and durability of information on the past success of different patches. They have shown in both lab and field studies that animals make foraging decisions based on these factors. Specifically, animals tend to choose a patch that has been recently successful over one that was successful a long time ago, and they tend to choose a patch that has had a long history of success over a patch with a short-lived history of success. Both of these tendencies would seem effective for making choices in a potentially changing environment because they base choice on past success information that is more likely to be reliable now—either because that information was gathered recently or because it was found to be stable over a long period of time. This sensitivity to the reliability of past success information has been observed in studies with domestic dogs, ground squirrels, chipmunks, and rats (Devenport & Devenport, 1993, 1994; Devenport et al., in press).

In one experiment performed by Devenport et al. (in press), animals were presented with a series of foraging experiences in the laboratory and then, after various delays, they were tested in the same choice situation. Specifically, rats were run in a two-arm maze and were forced to experience a particular time-based sequence of successes (baited trials) and failures (unbaited trials) before the delay and testing. The experimental procedure included three phases after a preliminary familiarization phase. During the first phase, the rats went through 36 alternating trials on which they were forced to run down one arm and the other. This was accomplished by lowering a door that would block one arm of the maze at a time. For these trials, only arm A was baited, so half of the trials were success experiences with arm A, and the other half of the trials were failure experiences with arm B. The second phase began after a 30-min break. During the second phase, the same alternate arm-blocking procedure was used, but now only arm B was baited and there were only one third as many trials. Finally, after a variable time delay of 5 min, 25 min, 1 hr, 3.5 hr, 10 hr, or 2 days, the third phase began. In this "test" phase, both arms were unblocked and unbaited, and the animal was allowed to freely choose in a single test trial.

Table 8.3 shows the percentage of animals in each delay condition choosing arm B for the test trial. Note that the number of animals in each condition varied from 4 to 16 (see Table 8.3). After short delays, the animals chose B exclusively, suggesting a greater weighting of their recent successes with arm B. After long delays, however, the animals chose A almost exclusively, suggesting a sensitivity to the longer duration of this arm's success despite the greater time delay since its success. At an intermediate delay, approximately 40% of the rats' choices involved arm B, suggesting that at this delay the long duration of arm A's success weighed about equally against the more recent exposure to arm B's success. Devenport et al. concluded from these results that animals are temporally weighting success information in such a way that information is emphasized according to its reliability: Recent information is reliable because it is unlikely that the environment has changed in the small amount of intervening time, and stable (or long-lasting) information is reliable because it represents a good long-term estimate of success in the environment.

To fit the choice data observed in this study, we assumed two separate productions for choosing to travel down arm A versus arm B. Phase 1 trials were input as alternating arm A successes and arm B failures and phase 2 trials as alternating arm B successes and arm A failures (just as the animals experienced). With this history of experience and the "standard" decay rate of 0.714, the model predicts the switch in arm preference to occur after 25 min instead of after 210 min, as was observed. The decay parameter is most influential on the timing of this switch because it specifies the relative weighting of old versus recent experiences, which essentially balances the "A success" and "B success" phases in this experiment. Thus, to obtain a set of predictions that fit the exact switchover time in the observed data, we varied the decay parameter and found that with $2.0 \leq d \leq 8.0$, the crossover point occurs in the appropriate 210-min delay condition. For the best quantitative fit to the data, we fixed G at 3 (from the previous model) and estimated d, obtaining the best-fitting value of 4.61; this produces an almost perfect fit to the data ($R^2 = .99$, SSE = 0.03, and MSE = 0.005). Table 8.3 provides the predicted choice proportions for this fit.

Again, the model has provided an excellent fit to the data. However, this is the first case in which doing so required a decay parameter that was substantially different from the other model fits. What makes this experiment different? Two features stand out. First, during the training (phases 1 and 2) the animals were not given the opportunity to choose between the two arms. This could have affected their early representations of the task as well as what they learned from it; that is, they may not have distinguished

TABLE 8.3

Observed and Predicted Proportions of Animals Choosing the More Recently Successful Arm (Arm B) According to Delay Condition

Delay Condition (in min)	Number of Subjects	Proportion Choosing B	Predicted Proportion
5	7	1.00	0.99
25	4	1.00	0.98
60	5	1.00	0.90
210	16	0.38	0.40
360	8	0.13	0.26
2,880	8	0.13	0.14

Note: Adapted from Figure 1, Devenport et al. (in press).

the two arms of the maze as readily as if they had been in a free-choice training situation. In some sense, then, the model may be representing this "decreased learning" as "increased forgetting" relative to the other experiments' fits. Second, the choice data in this experiment were based on relatively few subjects (as low as four in one condition), which led to many choice measurements at the extremes of [0,1]. Such extreme choice proportions exert a strong influence on the model's "best-fitting" parameters. These distinguishing features suggest that we not take the exact parameter estimates from this fit too seriously.

The basic conclusion is that both the experimental data and the predictions suggest that, even in an adapted laboratory environment, these rats are choosing based on a time-weighted function of their past experiences of success and failure. Without the time weighting that the decay component implies, "test" performance in this experiment would forever favor the more often successful option over the more recently successful option. That is, a standard ACT–R model with no decay of past success experiences would be unable to show any shift in preference across time delays. In contrast, the decay component allows the model to capture the observed behavior across a variety of d parameter values.

CONCLUSIONS

Summary

We have fit a new version of ACT–R to five separate data sets that span a wide range of choice phenomena: choice by both humans and animals, choice in service of various goals, choice in rich and sparse contexts, choice in discrete-time and continuous-time situations, and choice in stable and variable environments. In all cases, models with decay-based parameter learning did a good job of capturing the observed choice behavior. Table 8.4 provides a quantitative summary of the model fits. In particular, notice that we have fit these disparate data sets while still maintaining a fairly consistent set of parameters.

It is interesting to note that the new decay-based feature incorporated into production-parameter learning for the models presented in this chapter is quite similar to the decay of declarative chunks in ACT–R. It is possible that declarative, example-based models of some of these tasks would be able to show a similar sensitivity to recent experiences. One difference between models involving the decay of declarative examples versus the decay of production-relevant information is that example-based models will tend to exhibit strong effects of sensitivity to specific problems, whereas rule-based models will tend to display similar behavior on new trials, regardless of their

TABLE 8.4
Summary of Parameter Values and Model-Fit Statistics Across Five Data Sets

Model Parameters	Friedman et al. (1964)	Myers et al. (1963)	Lovett & Anderson (1995)	Herrnstein (1961)[a]	Devenport et al. (in press)
d	**0.714**	0.714	0.714	0.714	**4.61**
t	0.24	0.24	0.24	0.24	0.24
$\alpha\ (= \beta)$	0	0	11.2	0	0
G	1	$G_0=0.75$ $G_1=1.04$ $G_2=1.17$	1	75	3
Model-fit statistics					
N	32	9	12	14	6
Free parameters	1	3	1	N/A	1
MSE	0.002	0.001	0.001	0.003	0.0005
R^2	.95	.97	.92	.97	.99

Note. Bold numbers indicate parameter values that were estimated. Model-fit statistics in the table are computed from aggregated data (as reflected in adjusted N) even though the parameters were estimated from individual data whenever possible.

[a]Due to the stochastic complexities in Herrnstein's (1961) task, this model fit was obtained via simulation (see text for details).

similarity to previous problems. Another difference is that the selection of relevant examples from declarative memory is based only on their activation (relative to some activation threshold), whereas the selection of which production to be fired is based on an evaluation of expected gain (that is sensitive to probability of success of the competing productions, estimated costs of competing productions, and current value of the goal). Past work (Lovett & Anderson, 1996) compared a rule-based model and an example-based model of choice in the BST and found the rule-based model provided a superior fit. However, the example-based model used in that case was not built within the ACT–R framework. Further research on choice may reveal whether the differences between ACT–R's example-based learning and this chapter's procedural learning are distinguishable in the data.

Relating ACT–R to Normative
and Other Theories of Choice

The models in this chapter show that ACT–R's learning and performance mechanisms are able to fit choice data of humans and animals quite accurately and at a good level of detail. This empirical approach still leaves open the question of the adaptiveness of the mechanisms employed by these models. In other words, even though these models fit the data, are there related models of choice that could perform better (i.e., better than people or animals do)? There are two features in ACT–R that might appear to be "imperfections" with respect to optimal choice. One is the noisiness of the choice mechanism: With expected gain noise, these models did not always choose the production with the highest expected gain. The second such feature is the decay of success and failure experiences that was the focus of this chapter. This decay process forces models to increasingly ignore information from the past. However, to judge these features as imperfections assumes certain things about the world. In particular, it assumes that the probabilities of success associated with various options stay constant over time. This is demonstrably not so in many environments. In foraging, patches become depleted and others blossom and become rich. Fortunes of companies change such that average performance over the last century tends not to predict performance in the next quarter. Problem solvers improve their execution of various strategies, so judging a strategy based on its early record of success may hide its new-found potential. In such a variable environment, it may actually be advantageous (1) to explore options that previously appeared suboptimal and (2) to downweight "old" information of the relative success of a certain option because things may have changed.

The noise in ACT–R's production evaluation process allows the system to occasionally choose poorer options and so allows the system to discover whether these other options have become more fruitful. The decay process for learning production parameters allows the system to weight its most recent experiences most heavily. Do these two features reflect the right combination of deviation from maximizing and discounting of the past? The answer to this question depends in part on what the correct characterization of the environment is. Anderson and Milson (1989) showed that power law decay gave the best estimate of probability of success in an environment where (1) options gradually became depleted and decayed away from original high levels and (2) options could occasionally undergo "revivals" and return to their original high levels. Moreover, they provided evidence that this characterized at least some environments. Thus, there may be some optimality in the power law decay proposed and used earlier.

Nevertheless, the situation faced by a chooser requires more than coming up with best estimates of the probabilities of success. It also involves deciding when it is worthwhile to choose the less-successful-appearing option to see if it has changed. This is basically the *n*-arm bandit problem that has been studied by statisticians (Berry & Fristedt, 1985). These problems are difficult, and suffice it to say there are no results on optimal strategies that begin to match the complexity of situations faced by typical organisms choosing in the real world.

In the absence of any results on optimality, then, we decided to compare a number of generic choice models that varied in their discounting of past information and maximization policy. Each model had a learning component that it used to estimate the value of each option based on past experience with the option, and each model had a choice component that governed how it used those values to choose. The learning component of each model used one of the two following schemes: equal weighting of all past events, or time-decay of past experiences with a decay parameter of *d* = 0.5. Crossed with this, the choice component of each model used one of the two following policies: Always choose the option with the highest estimated success rate (which we denote *maximizing*) or choose each option with a probability that matched its success rate estimate (which we denote *probability matching*). One could argue that the "perfect" choice model is the one that includes no decay of past experiences (equal weighting) and maximizing. In contrast, the ACT–R models explored in this chapter are consistent with the generic model that includes decay of past events and approximate probability matching.

Table 8.5 presents a 2 × 2 grid representing these four generic choice models. The table also places several specific models of choice in the appropriate cells. Note that each of the specific choice models included have been fit to various choice data and performed well. The fact that each cell is represented by an extant model of choice suggests that the field is still wrangling over the issues of choice policy and weighting of past information. This table also serves to place ACT–R in a larger context of theories of choice. Note that the lower right cell includes several models that share with ACT–R the features of time-based weighting of success information and probability-matching-like choice among options. Interestingly, these models were developed for and have primarily been concerned with modeling categorization tasks and simple choice tasks and have done so very well. In particular, ACT–R is the only model in that cell that has been applied to problem-solving choice. Based on the work presented in this chapter, we suggest that ACT–R can fit data from both humans and animals and that it can model both simple choice tasks and choice in service of problem-solving goals.

TABLE 8.5
Table of Choice Models According to Learning Component and Choice Policy

	Learning Component	
Choice Policy	No Weighting	Decay-Based
Maximizing	CE (Davis, Staddon, Machado, & Palmer, 1993)	TWR (Devenport et al., 1995)
Probability-matching	ASCM (Siegler & Shipley, 1995) Frequency array (Estes, 1986)	ACT–R (this volume) Adaptive network (Gluck & Bower, 1988) Rule competition (Busemeyer & Myeung, 1992) Rescorla-Wagner (Rescorla & Wagner, 1972)

With the four generic models now described, we decided to test them in a simulated world that approximated the environment formalized by Anderson and Milson. In this simulated environment, the probability of an option having a probability of success x was

$$f(x) = \frac{1}{4}x^{-0.5} + \frac{1}{4}(1-x)^{-0.5}$$

Figure 8.12 illustrates such a probability density. This distribution of probabilities has a mean of .5, which suggests that on average, options have success probabilities of .5. But the distribution tends to emphasize large and small probabilities (the edges of the U-shape), which suggests that most options have success rates near 0 or 1.0, meaning choice between two options will often be consequential. The environment we simulated did not have options with fixed probabilities taken from this distribution. Rather, we designed the environment so that on any trial there was a 10% chance that the success probability of one of the two options would switch to another value from this distribution. Thus, there were two options with independently varying probabilities of success, and the chooser had to try to maximize its wins.

In the simulated environment, random guessing would yield 50% success, and the expected maximum possible correct (if the chooser were omniscient

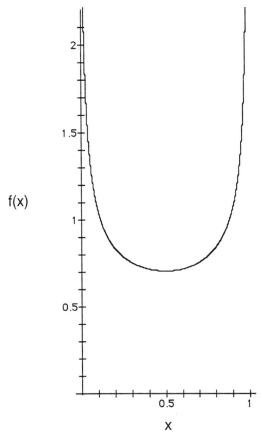

f(x)

X

FIG. 8.12. Probability density used in the simulation of different probabilistic environments.

and knew the true probabilities of the two options at all times) is 69.7%. How do the four different choice models described earlier fare? We ran all four generic choice models over 250 events in this simulated environment. All models started out assuming that each alternative had a .5 probability of success and then learned and chose according to their features in Table 8.5. All four models performed more closely to random than omniscient choice, but they were ordered as follows. The best was the probability-matching/decay combination, which returned 53.4% correct choices. The next best at 52.7% was the choice model that used a maximizing/decay combination. Then followed the "perfect" choice model of maximizing without decay at 51.7% correct. The worst choice model was probability matching without decay at 50.9% correct. One thousand Monte Carlo trials with each of the four options yielded standard errors of these estimated percentages between 0.2% and 0.3%. Thus, in the simulation of a variable world, the probability-matching/decay combination (representative of ACT–R's noisy choice and decay-based evaluation) is significantly better than the three other generic models.

It is rather difficult to choose well in an uncertain and variable world, so learning and adapting to one's environmental contingencies are critical. A decay-based and noisy set of learning and choice mechanisms produces an effective system for making choices in probabilistic environments. The decay and noise processes integrated in the ACT–R models given earlier fit a variety of choice phenomena, outperform other learning and choice processes in a simulated environment, and, perhaps most importantly, demonstrate a framework for unifying our understanding of choice across several tasks and species.

9

Cognitive Arithmetic

Christian Lebiere
John R. Anderson
Carnegie Mellon University

CHARACTERISTICS OF THE DOMAIN

Cognitive arithmetic studies the mental representation of numbers and arithmetic facts (counting, addition, subtraction, multiplication, division) and the processes that create, access, and manipulate them. Although the task is trivial for computers, it is quite difficult for humans to master, and presents a domain that is both propitious and challenging for ACT–R.

Arithmetic is one of the fundamental cognitive tasks (one of the three basic "Rs") that humans have to master. Children go through years of formal schooling to learn first the numbers and then the facts and skills needed to manipulate them. Many adults have not mastered and will never completely master the domain. Yet it is a task that is trivial for computer architectures to perform correctly. It is also trivial for ACT–R if we only consider its symbolic level. All one needs to do is give ACT–R the correct chunks representing arithmetic facts and productions encoding procedures to manipulate them, and perfect performance will result. This, however, ignores the impact of ACT–R's subsymbolic level and is not a very satisfactory model of human performance, especially that of children.

Some tasks, such as natural language processing or chess, are hard for both humans and machines to perform and require years of learning or engineering. Other tasks, such as vision, which seem to come naturally to humans, require much programming for computers to perform even poorly. One can attribute this to humans possessing complex systems for vision and other tasks which resulted from millions of years of evolution, but will require painstaking work to reverse-engineer and replicate in computers. But a task such as arithmetic seems so straightforward and easy to accomplish that it is surprising that it takes years of learning for humans to master. This suggests that human cognition at the subsymbolic level embodies some assumptions about its environment that are at odds with the structure of arithmetic as it is taught. Arithmetic, being a formal mathematical theory, assumes a set of precise and immutable objects (the numbers), facts, and procedures.

297

Human cognition, on the other hand, has evolved to deal with approximate concepts, changing facts, and adaptive procedures. Studying how such a system deals with a formal task such as arithmetic provides an excellent window to its assumptions and mechanisms.

This task is both well suited and challenging to ACT–R for a number of reasons. Unlike tasks artificially designed for the purpose of isolating a particular cognitive mechanism, the learning and performance of arithmetic involve almost every mechanism of the architecture. It is therefore an excellent test of whether these parts can perform together as well as separately. Unlike laboratory tasks, large amounts of data are available for every cross section of the population and every aspect of the task, making it easier to establish the trends being analyzed.

Although numbers can be seen as having a concrete interpretation (e.g., children learn the concept three by being shown three rabbits), the rest of arithmetic has an essentially abstract structure. It is much less likely that people have brain structures optimized to perform arithmetic than, for example, vision or language. This fact suggests a complete reliance on general-purpose learning mechanisms. Because each skill builds on the previous ones—for example, counting can be used to perform addition, which in turn can be used to perform multiplication—learning can be a mostly self-contained process, rather than entirely dependent on external factors such as teaching. Arithmetic also has an inherently clear, simple, and regular structure, with a systematic organization of knowledge into tables of immutable facts. This strong regularity, unlike, for example, the many exceptions of tasks such as natural language processing, also helps in reducing degrees of freedom in modeling the task and provides a good test of ACT–R's statistical learning. These factors lead to a simpler, more regular model that is more predictive than one with many unanalyzed degrees of freedom.

Basic Empirical Phenomena

There are two classes of empirical phenomena in the domain of arithmetic for which any model needs to account. One concerns the fact that children, and to a certain degree adults, approach arithmetic problems with two basic strategies. One strategy is simply to retrieve the answer. The second strategy, referred to hereafter as the *backup strategy* or *backup computation*, is to compute the answer. Thus, given a problem such as $3 + 4 = ?$, children may choose to count (perhaps 4, 5, 6, 7) to provide the answer, and given $3 \times 4 = ?$, they may choose to add to get the answer (perhaps $4 + 4 + 4$). One class of empirical phenomena involves how people choose between the computation strategy and the retrieval strategy.

The second class of empirical phenomena involves the problem-size effect. Children and adults take longer to answer problems involving larger numbers, and they also make more errors on these problems. In the case of backup computation, the reason for this is fairly obvious—one has to count more to add large numbers and one has to add more things when multiplying by a larger number. Although much reduced, the problem-size effect occurs for adults. It has been suggested that this is due to residual use of the backup strategy (LeFevre et al., 1996a), although recent research put those results in doubt (Kirk & Ashcraft, 1997). However, it has been argued that smaller problems also occur more often, offering greater practice. This is true in studies of textbooks (Ashcraft, 1987; Ashcraft & Christy, 1995; Hamann & Ashcraft, 1986; Siegler, 1988), but it is also true in the world at large. As many (Benford, 1938; Newcomb, 1881; Raimi, 1976) have noted, small numbers occur more often in the world generally. As just one interesting token of the ubiquity of small numbers, consider the addition problems created by adding the two rows in multiplication problems involving two-digit numbers. An example is:

$$
\begin{array}{r}
46 \\
\times\,83 \\
\hline
138 \\
368 \\
\hline
3818
\end{array}
$$

The problem creates a 3 + 8 addition problem and a 1 + 6 addition problem. If one looks at all such multiplication problems with multiplicands from 10 to 99, one finds that addition problems involving smaller addends occur more frequently. Figure 9.1 plots, as a function of the size of the addend, the frequency of all addition problems created by adding the tens digit from the top row (i.e., 138) with the ones digit from the bottom row (i.e., 368) or the hundreds digit from the top row with the tens digit from the bottom row. There is a clear drop-off with size of the addend.[1]

These effects of problem size and strategy are ubiquitous throughout the literature on cognitive arithmetic (for reviews of the field, see, e.g., Ashcraft, 1992, 1995; Campbell, 1995; Geary, 1996). Although these effects are not by far the only ones to account for, they constitute a good basis for a comprehensive model of cognitive arithmetic. In the Chapter 4 discussion of Zbrodoff's experiment, we showed that ACT–R had the ability to account for these effects in miniature. However, it is another question whether, when we turn on ACT–R's learning mechanisms and give it a lifetime of experi-

---

[1]The drop-off with size of addend in Fig. 9.1 is because the hundreds digit in these multiplication facts tends to be small, and the sawtooth pattern is produced because the ones digit of products is more often even.

1-Digit Addition from 2-digit Multiplication

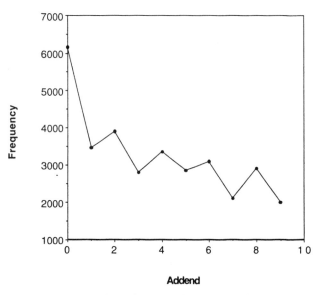

FIG. 9.1.   Frequency of one-digit addition problems created by two-digit multiplication problems.

ence, we will get behavior that looks at all like human behavior. This is the challenge that this chapter addresses.

In subsequent sections of this chapter, we describe the basic model and its ability to account for basic results in the performance and learning of cognitive arithmetic. These demonstrations are typical "minimodels," which assume a certain distribution of knowledge strength at a particular point in time. The final section describes a simulation in which we simulate the growth of arithmetic knowledge over a lifetime.

THE MODEL

This section sets forth our basic model for cognitive arithmetic. There is nothing particularly novel in the types of chunks and productions that we choose. They reflect the basic approach introduced in earlier chapters and are already used to model many phenomena.

Basic Representation and Productions

Arithmetic problems are represented as chunks with four slots: one for the operator, one for each operand, and one for the result. For example, the chunk representing the fact $2 + 3 = 5$ would be:

Fact-2+3=5
    isa arithmetic
    first 2
    operator +
    second 3
    result 5

where 2, 3, +, and 5 are other chunks representing the numbers and operator.[2] The most basic action that one can perform on knowledge chunks is to retrieve them. This is accomplished by the **Retrieval** production, which solves an arithmetic problem by simply retrieving the answer to the problem stored in long-term memory:

Retrieval
=goal>
    isa arithmetic
    first =first
    operator =operator
    second =second
    result nil
=fact>
    isa arithmetic
    first =first
    operator =operator
    second =second
    result =answer
==>
=goal>
    result =answer

This production simply retrieves a chunk (fact) matching the goal (problem), then copies the answer back to the goal. One can notice that the chunk retrieved from memory is of the same type as the goal representing the problem, and wonder how the fact was initially created. In ACT–R 4.0, there are only two possibilities. The first is that it results from the encoding of an environmental stimulus. This case would correspond to an external source of arithmetic knowledge such as a teacher, a table from a book, or a calculator. The second possibility is the long-term encoding of a past goal.

---

[2]Although addition and multiplication are commutative operations, this is not reflected in the declarative representation of facts; that is, $2 + 3 = 5$ and $3 + 2 = 5$ are represented as separate chunks. Of course, this does not prevent explicit procedures to exploit the inherent commutativity, such as a production which would solve the problem $2 + 3 = ?$ by retrieving the fact $3 + 2 = 5$.

If one cannot retrieve a fact, one can (re)generate the arithmetic knowledge by the use of backup computation strategies. An example of such a strategy, which is to perform an addition by repeatedly counting up from one argument a number of times equal to the second argument, can be implemented by the production **Iteration**:

```
Iteration
=goal>
   isa arithmetic
   first =first
   operator +
   second =second
   result nil
==>
=subgoal>
   isa iterate
   result =first
   counter 0
   limit =second
   increment 1
   result =answer
!push! =subgoal
=goal>
   result =answer
```

This production solves an addition problem by setting a subgoal to add the second argument iteratively to the first by increments of 1, using the basic counting skills. Table 9.1 shows the two production rules that were used to accomplish this iterative counting procedure. This counting subgoal is pushed on the stack, and its result will be returned to the current goal as the answer to the problem using the subgoal value return mechanism. When an answer to the problem has been found using either retrieval or one of the backup strategies, the answer is output and the goal is popped by the **Answer** production:

```
Answer
=goal>
   isa arithmetic
   first =first
   operator =operator
   second =second
   result =answer
==>
!output! =answer
!pop!
```

TABLE 9.1

Productions for Addition by Iterative Counting

Iterate-count	
=goal>	
isa	iterate
counter	=counter
- limit	=counter
result	=result
increment	1
=fact1>	
isa	count
number	=counter
next	=next-counter
=fact2>	
isa	count
number	=result
next	=next-result
==>	
=goal>	
counter	=next-counter
result	=next-result
Done	
=goal>	
isa	iterate
counter	=counter
limit	=counter
==>	
!pop!	

When the goal is popped, it becomes a fact in long-term memory. If this fact did not already exist, then the solving of this problem (presumably using the backup strategies) has added a new arithmetic fact to the knowledge base. If an identical fact already existed (modulo the chunk name[3]), then the new chunk is merged with the existing one, reinforcing it, and the duplicate copy is removed from declarative memory. If the problem could not be solved by retrieval, this reinforcement from the

---

[3]This, together with the rather dubious meaning of whichever name happens to be associated with such facts, suggests that chunk names are superfluous and that chunks could be best understood as the contents of their slots rather than referred to by name.

merging with the new problem will raise the activation of the fact until ultimately the problem can be solved by retrieval. If the problem was already solved by retrieving the fact, then it will receive two learning reinforcements: first, from its use in the retrieval production, and second, from being merged with the problem goal. This double reinforcement is not essential, but is a direct consequence of the separate rules for retrieval and merging. As seen in the Lifetime Simulation section, this simply speeds up the convergence to retrieval-based performance.

This technique of either directly retrieving the answer from the corresponding fact or using a number of backup strategies is a general ACT–R technique to model problem solving. By gradually raising the activation of the resulting goal with practice, it provides a general account of the transition from general problem-solving strategies toward more efficient ones. As noted in Chapter 4 in this regard, ACT–R implements Logan's (1988) proposal for transition from algorithmic solutions to direct retrieval.

Our discussion has focused on addition, but we have developed a parallel model for multiplication. The iterative addition procedure, corresponding to the counting procedure, is given in Table 9.2. The productions there try to retrieve the multiplication answers and, if they fail, call on a backup strategy of repeated addition.

Conflict Resolution

Because the retrieval and iteration productions (and possibly other backup strategies) share the same goal condition, conflict resolution is needed to determine which productions to attempt and in which order. Typically (and this may not be true for, say, small children), the retrieval production provides a high probability of producing a correct answer at low cost, and thus will have the highest evaluation and will be attempted first. If no arithmetic fact for that problem is above threshold, the retrieval production will time out and the next production in the conflict resolution order, such as iteration, will be allowed to fire.

A general observation is that children will choose to retrieve more often for smaller problems and choose to compute more often for larger problems (Siegler, 1988). The simplest explanation for this in ACT–R is that subjects cannot retrieve the answer in the case of large problems and fall back on computation. This would occur more often for larger problems because they have less practice (e.g., Fig. 9.1).

It is possible to have more sophisticated decision criteria in ACT–R. Thus, ACT–R might have a rule that chooses to calculate (perhaps on paper or with a calculator) for all problems that involved greater than one-digit numbers. Again, it might have a special rule of adding a zero for multiplication by 10. The exact special-case rules might vary from subject to subject.

TABLE 9.2

Productions for Multiplication by Iterative Addition

Iteration-times
=goal>
   isa   arithmetic
   first   =first
   operator   *
   second   =second
   result   nil
==>
=subgoal>
   isa   iterate
   result   0
   counter   0
   limit   =second
   increment   =first
   result   =answer
!push! =subgoal
=goal>
   result   =answer

Iterate-add
  =goal
   isa   iterate
   counter   =counter
  - limit   =counter
   result   =result
   increment   =increment
=fact>
   isa   count
   number   =counter
   next   =next-counter
==>
=subgoal>
   isa   arithmetic
   first   =result
   operator   +
   second   =increment
   result   =next-result
!push! =subgoal
=goal>
   counter   =next-counter
   result   =next-result

Note. The **Retrieval** and **Done** productions are the same as for addition.

Reder (1982, 1987; Reder & Ritter, 1992; Schunn, Reder, Nhouyvanisvong, Richards, & Stroffolino, 1997) presented evidence that subjects can be more strategic in their decision making than simply choosing to compute when retrieval fails. Her paradigm involved subjects being shown the same two-digit multiplication and addition problems, which they solved over and over again. Eventually, they got to the point where they could retrieve the answer, and Reder's interest was in the process by which they made the transition from computation to retrieval. She required her subjects to indicate very quickly (within 850 msec of seeing the problem) whether they would retrieve or compute the answer. She found they could make this decision with some reliability, even though it took them much longer than 850 msec to retrieve the answer. She found that they were making their decision on the basis of superficial features of the problem. Thus, if subjects had been trained on 34 + 47 they would false alarm and think that they could retrieve the answer to 34 × 47. We (Anderson, 1996) have suggested that subjects in Reder's task were making their decisions on the basis of memory for the problem rather than memory for the answer. Thus, subjects might be using productions like

> IF   the goal is to solve a problem involving n1 and n2
>   and n1 and n2 have been presented together
> THEN   indicate retrieve

This production has the advantage of not requiring that the problem be analyzed in detail before making a commitment to an answer strategy.

In general, people may evolve complex sets of strategies for making the decision between retrieve and compute. However, we ignore these complications and simply assume that the two strategies are retrieve and compute. Moreover, subjects will only choose to compute after they have failed to retrieve the answer.

Activation Processes and Errors

Clearly, the activation of chunks storing arithmetic facts is going to be very critical to ACT-R's performance in cognitive arithmetic. The activation of a chunk is given as a sum of a base-level activation and associative activation according to the Activation Equation:

$$A_i = B_i + \sum_j W_j S_{ji} \qquad \text{\textbf{Activation Equation 3.5}}$$

where B_i is the base-level activation (or strength) of the chunk i, W_j reflects the attentional weighting of the elements j that are slots of the current goal, and the S_{ji} terms are the strengths of association from the elements j. The B_i value will change with experience according to the Base-Level Learning Equation 4.1 in such a way that it grows approximately as a log function of amount of practice. The S_{ji} will change with experience according to the Posterior Learning Equation 4.3 such that it will come to vary approximately as a log function of the odds of the chunk i occurring when j is in the environment.

These activation quantities are converted into match scores, which reflect the effects of partial matching (Match Equation 3.8). In the case of a perfect match, the match score is just the activation, but in the case of a mismatch, a penalty will be subtracted from the match score. There is noise in these match scores because of activation noise. If the match score is above a threshold, the chunk will be retrievable and the probability of it being retrievable is described by the Retrieval Probability Equation 3.7. If there are multiple possible chunks that might match, the one chosen is the one with the highest match score and the probability of any one being chosen is described by the Chunk Choice Equation 3.9. Finally, match scores determine latency through the Retrieval Time Equation 3.10.

Errors can be committed whether the subject is computing or retrieving. Let us consider the example of the problem $2 + 3 = ?$. Because of ACT–R's partial matching process, it is possible for ACT–R to retrieve an arithmetic chunk (e.g., $2 + 4 = 6$) other than the correct one. Recall that chunks are retrieved on the basis of their match scores, which are calculated as their activation levels minus mismatch penalties. It is possible that even after the mismatch penalty is subtracted off, the wrong chunk will have the highest match score, be retrieved, and its answer stored in the current goal. In this model, the mismatch penalty between numbers increases linearly as a function of the difference between the two numbers. Thus, the mismatch penalty between numbers i and j is $D|i-j|$ where D is the scale factor to be estimated. The mismatch measure essentially encodes the representational similarity between numbers.[4,5] This assumption about the representation of numbers has been adopted in a number of other models of numerical memory (J. A. Anderson, Spoehr, & Bennett, 1992; Campbell, 1995; McCloskey & Lindemann, 1992).

---

[4]Past models have been relatively insensitive to the exact form of the mismatch measure, but Whalen (1996) argued that the internal representation of numerical magnitude is not uniform and influences performance of numerical tasks.

[5]The process of calculating these mismatch scores in the ACT–R simulation is more complex than this description implies, but it comes down to the same thing. In the ACT–R simulation, similarities range between 0 and 1 and if sim is the similarity, the mismatch penalty is MP($1 - sim$), where MP is a global parameter called the Mismatch Penalty.

Errors can also occur using the backup procedure when the iteration subgoal returns an erroneous answer because of a misretrieval, a procedural error, or any other reason. The erroneous answer will also be stored in the goal. In both cases of retrieval and computation errors, not only will the answer to this particular problem be wrong, but the goal holding the incorrect answer is popped and becomes an erroneous long-term fact (here, $2 + 3 = 6$)[6]. This fact can then be retrieved as the answer to future problems and perpetuate the error. This otherwise correct retrieval of an erroneous fact becomes another source of error. This competition between memories for both correct and erroneous answers is quite similar to Siegler's treatment (e.g., Siegler, 1988). It might seem possible that ACT–R could reach an unfortunate state where it has so practiced the wrong facts that it comes to believe them. Indeed this can occur, and we describe in the Learning section and the Appendix what must be true for ACT–R to avoid getting absorbed into such error states.

PERFORMANCE

This section examines how this ACT–R model can account for a wide range of effects in cognitive arithmetic, including the problem-size effect and the patterns of errors in retrieval and computation of addition and multiplication problems. Even though these effects typically have multiple, complex sources, we have chosen to make some simplifying assumptions for the sake of analytical simplicity. A more complex simulation could and will eliminate the simplifying assumptions and account for these effects in a more complex manner. The basic import of the results presented here is that even a fairly simple approach can successfully account for those effects.

The Problem-Size Effect

The most basic and robust effect in cognitive arithmetic is that larger problems are harder. This holds for measures of retrieval time and error rates, for the four basic operations, for production and verification tasks, and for the entire age span from children to adults and elderly (e.g., Ashcraft, 1992). Ashcraft (1987) reported the change in response time for addition problems in adults. Figure 9.2 illustrates the relationship between the sum of the digits and retrieval time. Although most problems exhibit an increase in response time roughly corresponding to the square of the sum of their operands,[7] the slope for problems involving a zero operand (squares in the graph) is approximately flat, and the increase in response time for tie problems (those

---

[6]This assumes that error correction, provided by another procedure, a teacher, or a calculator, does not take effect before the goal is popped and becomes a long-term fact.

[7]The product is in fact the best predictor (Siegler, 1988).

Problem Size Effect

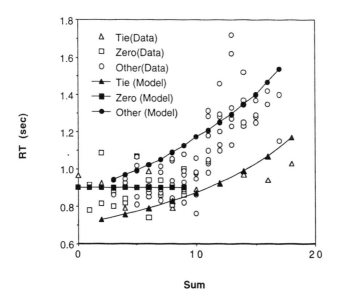

FIG. 9.2.   Problem-size effect for addition for adults: The data are the open points and the predictions of ACT–R are the closed points connected by lines.

having identical operands—triangles in the graph) is much smaller than for nonzero, non-tie problems (circles in the graph). The effect therefore reflects a more complex measure of problem difficulty than simply problem size.

The flat response time for problems involving zero is usually assumed to be the result of a special-purpose rule for those problems ("0 + x = x = x + 0 for all x"). We model it by use of the special **Zero** production. Two main explanations have emerged to account for the rest of the data. Groen and Parkman (1972) initially argued that the problem-size effect resulted from the use of backup strategies such as iterative counting. Larger problems involve more counting and therefore higher latencies and more errors. If the first number is always added to the second (or vice versa), then the latency will increase linearly with the sum of the numbers. A better fitting model, called the min model, assumes instead that the smaller number is always added to the larger one, thereby minimizing the number of increments necessary. Although this model certainly explains part of the problem-size effect for children and other poorly trained subjects, it has difficulties in fully accounting for the effect in well-trained adults as well as the better performance on tie problems.

The other category of models relies on the difference of presentation frequency between problems. As we noted earlier, smaller problems occur more frequently than larger ones. Smaller problems are therefore easier because they are presented and practiced more often. Ashcraft (1987) presented the frequency of presentation of addition facts by operand in Grades K to 3 and Siegler (1988) presented the frequency of multiplication problems in second- and third-grade workbooks. In each case, the frequency decreases roughly linearly with operand size, except for very small operands, which are special cases. It is generally assumed that the distribution in school books approximately reflects the real-life problem distribution. This frequency information was used in an ACT–R simulation whose results are illustrated as lines in Fig. 9.2. We assumed that the ratio of frequencies of the smallest (0 + 0) to the largest (9 + 9) was 4-to-1 and that intermediate problems had a frequency that varied linearly with each operand. Thus, if 0 + 0 occurred four times, 0 + 9 and 9 + 0 would occur twice, and 9 + 9 would occur once.[8] This distribution approximates closely the occurrence frequency in textbooks as described by Hamann and Ashcraft (1986). We assumed 500,000 problems presented according to these frequencies at an average of 100 problems per day. In the simulation, the underlying equation (based on Retrieval Time Equation 3.10) determining latency is

$$\text{Time} = I + Fe^{-A}$$

where I is an intercept reflecting encoding/answering times, F is the latency factor from the Retrieval Time Equation 3.10, and A is the activation of the chunk encoding the addition fact. The activation was determined by the half-million trials of experience in ACT–R. In our model, I was estimated at 0.4 sec and F was left at the default value of 1.0. We also estimated an additional latency of 0.5 sec for the Zero production. As can be seen in Fig. 9.2, the model does a pretty good job of capturing the effects in the data.

The basic increase in latency with problem size comes from ACT–R's base-level learning. It follows from the simplified form of the Base-Level Learning and Retrieval Time Equations (Equations 4.1 and 3.10) that retrieval time is a power function of frequency, and because frequency decreases roughly linearly with problem size, the response time for arithmetic retrieval grows as a power function of problem size.

The retrieval time for the zero operand problems is constant at 0.9 sec, whereas it increases slowly for tie problems to about 1.15 sec for the largest problem. Tie problems generate additional spreading activation in ACT–R because one of the arguments appears twice in the context. We explain next why, comparing the addition problems 3 + 3 and 3 + 4. Let us compare the S_{ji} values learned according to the Posterior Strength Equation 4.3 from the

---

[8]More generally, the relative frequency of a problem involving i and j was $(2 - i/9)(2 - j/9)$.

number 3 to a tie arithmetic fact $(3 + 3 = 6)$ and a non-tie arithmetic fact (e.g., $3 + 4 = 7$). In this case, j is the 3 and i is the fact. To review, that equation is

$$R_{ji} = \frac{(\text{assoc})R_{ji} + F(C_j)E_{ji}}{\text{assoc} + F(C_j)}$$

$$S_{ji} = \ln(R_{ji}) \qquad\qquad \textbf{Posterior Strength Equation 4.3}$$

With extensive experience, R_{ji} converges to E_{ji}, where (see discussion of the Posterior Strength Equation in Chapter 4):

$$E_{ji} = \frac{F(N_i \& C_j)F}{F(N_i)F(C_j)}$$

where $F(N_i \& C_j)$ is the frequency that i and j co-occur, $F(N_i)$ is the frequency that i is used, $F(C_j)$ is the frequency that j is a source in the goals, and F is the total number of retrievals (approximated by the number of production firings). Assuming for simplicity that the two facts ($3 + 3 = 6$ and $3 + 4 = 7$) are equally frequently needed, then all the components of the equation for the two facts are equal except for $F(N_i \& C_j)$, which is double for the tie fact because 3 is twice in the goal context for each retrieval so the frequency is also doubled, resulting in S_{ji} values larger by $\log(2)$ for tie facts. This additional activation spread to tie facts will in turn result in a decrease of their retrieval latency. Thus, the advantage of tie problems is a parameter-free prediction of ACT–R's mechanisms for associative learning.[9]

This simple model largely relies on differential presentation frequencies to produce the problem-size effect. As seen later, differential frequencies of rehearsal (small problems are retrieved and thus reinforced before larger ones) and backup strategies (recomputing larger facts is more error-prone than smaller ones) also contribute to the problem-size effect. Finally, even for adults, part of the effect may result from the residual use of nonretrieval procedures (LeFevre et al., 1996a, but see Kirk & Ashcraft, 1997). As

---

[9]It is also possible that subjects encode tie problems using a special representation to reflect their unusual character (data supporting this conclusion is presented by Eliaser, Siegler, Campbell, & Lemaire, 1997), which would affect the activation calculus as well as matching procedures. Finally, tie problems are often assumed to appear more frequently than indicated by their size alone, although that is not used in the simulation.

mentioned previously, a more complex simulation could take all these factors into account and determine their relative importance.

Errors in Addition Retrieval

Table 9.3a presents the pattern of retrieval errors of addition facts by 4-year-olds found by Siegler and Shrager (1984). The subjects were presented with addition problems ranging from $1 + 1$ to $5 + 5$ and were asked to state what they thought the answer was, without resorting to any overt strategy such as putting up fingers or counting. The main effect, similar to the problem-size effect, is an increase in errors for larger facts. The facts showing a comparatively low percentage of errors are those involving the operand 1, tie problems, and problems where the first operand is larger than the second one. Erroneous answers also tend to be smaller than the correct answer.

Because according to instructions the children were asked not to use any procedure other than retrieval, the computation productions in our model were disabled. Although guessing and other such procedures could be considered, the basic mechanism for producing an arithmetic error in ACT–R is the mistaken retrieval of another partially matching fact (see Match Equation 3.8). According to the Chunk Choice Equation 3.9, the probability of such commission errors is proportional to the scaled activation of the intruding facts relative to the correct fact. Because activation is related to frequency, the frequency difference between problems[10] is critical to explaining the patterns of errors. The other factor is that partial matching penalties will be smaller among similar addition facts.

In the case of the retrieval of addition facts, small sums (especially those involving 1, which can be reduced to the well-practiced skill of counting) are practiced at a higher frequency and are therefore more likely to intrude on another problem, leading to an error for that problem, than to be intruded on. This higher activation for smaller facts also explains why the errors for larger facts tend to be biased toward numbers smaller than the correct answer. Tie problems receive an additional amount of activation, as described in the previous section, and are therefore more likely to be retrieved correctly. Finally, we assume a small probability that, given a problem where the first operand is smaller than the second one (e.g., $2 + 4$), students reverse the order of arguments to simplify counting (the min strategy) and therefore also rehearse the reverse answer ($4 + 2 = 6$), giving it an advantage. The results are shown in part b of Table 9.3. The model generates answer probabilities that are very close to the data.

---

[10]Again, this difference can arise from presentation, rehearsal, and computation processes.

This model uses 1,000 problem presentations (an average of 40 for each of the 25 problems in Table 9.3) with a distribution frequency ratio (between smallest and largest problems) of 6.25,[11] an activation noise s parameter of 0.15, a scaling mismatch penalty factor D of 0.15 per digit difference,[12] and a retrieval threshold[13] τ of –2.25. The strategy of swapping arguments to make sure that the first is larger than the second (and therefore the extra rehearsals to facts of that type) is modeled by an additional probability of presentation of those problems that has been estimated at 6%.

Another way to examine this data is to plot the probability of correct retrieval for each argument, as in Fig. 9.3. Both plots show a fairly close match, with the jump in percentage correct for problems involving 1, and the greater slope of the addend curve resulting from the probability of swapping arguments to further favor smaller addends.

As was mentioned in the overview, this is a somewhat simplified model in that it assumes that only correct facts can be retrieved, albeit sometimes incorrectly. Of course, 4-year-olds may also hold some incorrect addition facts (at least weakly encoded), which if correctly retrieved will lead to error (or conversely if incorrectly retrieved could potentially yield a correct answer). In fact, the incorrect answers generated by the model's answer to this experiment would lead to just such incorrect facts. Another source of such errors could be results from past attempts at trying to reconstruct unavailable addition facts through counting (on their fingers or mentally) or other strategies. It is not necessary to specify such past history, however, because the basic assumptions of partial matching and a difference in rehearsal frequency can lead to a satisfactory model.

Errors in Multiplication Computation

Figure 9.4, from Siegler (1988), presents the percentage of errors in multiplication by repeated addition, a standard backup computation, for fourth graders. Subjects were given single-digit multiplication problems in the form of a column of numbers in which the multiplicand was repeated the number of times specified by the multiplier; for example, 8×6 was presented as a column in which 8 was written 6 times. Subjects were asked to add the columns of numbers and write down the answer. Analogous to the addition problems, the probability of error increases with the size of both the

---

[11]We used a ratio of 6.25 rather than 4 as in the previous simulation to reflect the assumption that young children have a steeper distribution of frequencies than do adults.

[12]This corresponds to the default value of ACT–R's mismatch penalty scaling parameter.

[13]Answers in the "other" category are assumed to be retrieval failures resulting in guessing outside the 0 to 10 range or simply failure to answer.

TABLE 9.3

Retrieval Percentages for 5 × 5 Addition Retrieval in 4-Year-Olds (Siegler & Shrager, 1994)

(a) Data

	0	1	2	3	4	5	6	7	8	9	10	11	Other
1+1	0	5	86	0	2	0	2	0	0	0	0	2	4
1+2	0	0	9	70	2	0	4	0	0	7	2	2	5
1+3	0	2	0	11	71	5	2	2	0	0	0	0	7
1+4	0	0	0	0	11	61	9	7	0	0	0	2	11
1+5	0	0	0	0	13	16	50	11	0	2	2	0	5
2+1	0	7	5	79	5	0	0	0	0	0	0	0	4
2+2	2	0	4	5	80	4	0	5	2	0	0	0	0
2+3	0	0	4	7	38	34	9	2	2	2	0	0	4
2+4	0	2	0	7	2	43	29	7	7	0	0	0	4
2+5	0	2	0	5	2	16	43	13	0	0	2	0	18
3+1	0	2	0	9	79	4	0	4	0	0	0	0	4
3+2	0	0	9	11	11	55	7	0	0	0	0	0	7
3+3	4	0	0	5	21	9	48	0	2	2	2	0	7
3+4	0	0	0	5	11	23	14	29	2	0	0	0	16
3+5	0	0	0	7	0	13	23	14	18	0	5	0	20
4+1	0	0	4	2	9	68	2	2	7	0	0	0	7
4+2	0	0	7	9	0	20	36	13	7	0	2	0	7
4+3	0	0	0	9	18	9	9	38	9	0	2	0	11
4+4	4	0	0	5	2	9	9	7	34	0	4	0	13
4+5	0	0	0	0	2	29	16	9	11	18	11	4	20
5+1	0	0	4	0	4	7	71	4	4	0	4	0	4
5+2	0	0	5	20	2	18	27	25	2	0	2	0	0
5+3	0	0	2	11	9	18	5	16	23	0	5	0	11
5+4	0	0	0	0	11	21	16	5	11	16	4	0	16
5+5	4	0	0	0	0	7	25	11	2	4	24	4	11

(b) Simulation

	0	1	2	3	4	5	6	7	8	9	10	11	Other
1+1	0	0	97	2	0	0	0	0	0	0	0	0	0
1+2	0	0	30	62	7	0	0	0	0	0	0	0	0
1+3	0	0	28	9	60	2	1	0	0	0	0	0	0
1+4	0	0	25	9	6	57	1	0	0	0	0	0	1
1+5	0	0	24	8	6	4	55	1	0	0	0	0	3
2+1	0	0	20	75	5	0	0	0	0	0	0	0	0
2+2	0	0	0	16	83	1	0	0	0	0	0	0	0
2+3	0	0	1	24	38	33	3	0	0	0	0	0	1
2+4	0	0	1	25	29	15	27	1	0	0	0	0	3
2+5	0	0	1	26	30	5	13	18	0	0	0	0	7
3+1	0	0	15	10	73	2	0	0	0	0	0	0	0
3+2	0	0	1	17	35	44	3	0	0	0	0	0	1
3+3	0	0	0	0	21	9	70	1	0	0	0	0	0
3+4	0	0	0	3	24	20	21	26	1	0	0	0	5
3+5	0	0	1	3	26	11	27	4	14	0	0	0	14
4+1	0	0	14	9	7	69	1	0	0	0	0	0	1
4+2	0	0	1	18	21	22	37	1	0	0	0	0	2
4+3	0	0	1	2	19	22	18	34	1	0	0	0	4
4+4	0	0	0	0	0	31	11	8	47	0	0	0	1
4+5	0	0	1	2	3	21	16	7	8	14	0	0	28
5+1	0	0	14	9	7	5	63	1	0	0	0	0	2
5+2	0	0	1	19	22	6	19	27	1	0	0	0	5
5+3	0	0	1	2	20	9	27	6	24	0	0	0	11
5+4	0	0	1	2	2	18	18	8	8	20	0	0	24
5+5	0	0	0	0	0	0	47	13	9	6	18	0	7

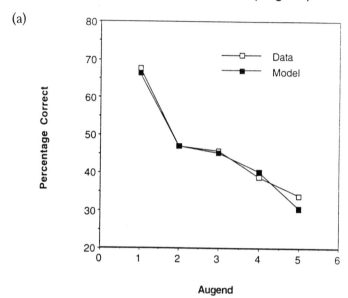

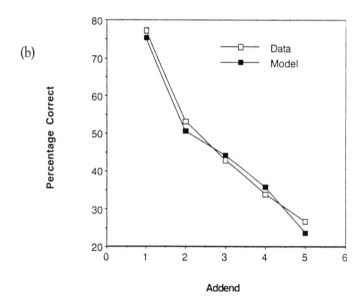

FIG. 9.3. Percentage of correct retrievals in addition: (a) augend; (b) addend.

multiplicand and the multiplier. Particularly remarkable is the very low percentage of errors for repeated addition of 5.

Because multiplication by repeated addition essentially involves the same retrieval of arithmetic facts (counting and addition), the same mechanism can also explain that pattern of errors. Error percentage increases with the size of the multiplier because of the increase in the opportunities for retrieval error, and with the size of the multiplicand because of the increased probability of error in the retrieval of larger facts. The particularly low percentage of errors for repeated addition by 5 is obtained because only two facts are needed ($0 + 5 = 5$ and $5 + 5 = 10$) and repeatedly reinforced, unlike other repeated additions where 5 or all 10 of the facts on that row of the addition table are needed.

Figure 9.4 compares the predictions of the model with the data. Because the subjects were fourth graders, this model assumes about 4 years of presentation of addition facts at a rate of 100 problems per day, for a total of about 150,000. The frequency ratio of this distribution was estimated at 16. In addition, it is assumed that subjects have previously solved a certain number of multiplication problems by repeated addition. The distribution of problems is the one reported by Siegler for second- and third-grade textbooks. About 1,000 multiplication problems are used, resulting in 5,000 additional addition rehearsals. The activation noise parameter s is 0.12, with the same standard mismatch penalty factor of 0.15 per digit as used in the addition retrieval model. The plot by multiplicand shows a general increase in error percentage with the size of the argument, resulting from the decrease in rehearsal frequency for larger problems, and very few errors for addition by 5, resulting from the limited set of facts needed (and, incidentally, the fact that they both contain the number 5 twice and therefore receive additional activation). The plot by multiplier also shows an increase in error for larger arguments, this time because the number of steps is directly proportional to the multiplier and each step introduces a new opportunity for error. One feature of the data that is not replicated by this model is the lower percentage of errors for even multiplier values. One possibility is that this may result from a hidden strategy of adding in pairs, such as adding 14 three times rather than adding 7 six times.

LEARNING

The previous section described a number of cognitive arithmetic perform-ance results at a particular point in the learning cycle and how to model them, assuming a specific state of knowledge at that time. This section examines how these skills improve with time and how ACT–R's learning mechanisms can account for that.

(a)

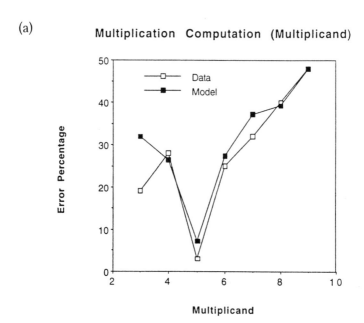

(b)

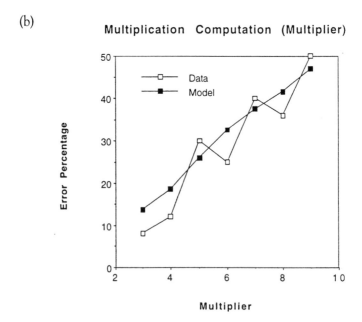

FIG. 9.4. Percentage of errors in multiplication by repeated addition: (a) multiplicand; (b) multiplier.

The Problem-Size Effect Over Time

Ashcraft (1987) described the decrease in response time to addition problems across grades, as well as the gradual flattening of the problem-size effect, from about a 2.5 to 1 ratio for large versus small problems (two-digit sum vs. single-digit sum) in first grade to about a 1.1 to 1 ratio by college. Figure 9.5a presents his data as a function of problem size and academic level of his subjects.

Although some of this effect may be due to the gradual adoption over time of more efficient strategies (e.g,. simply retrieving the fact instead of counting on one's fingers), the simplest way to account for it is by examining the increase in activation with practice and the resulting decrease in retrieval latency. Assuming that the frequency of presentation of each problem remains constant, the S_{ji} values in the Activation Equation 2.5 will also remain fairly constant and most of the effect of practice on activation will be reflected in the base levels of the facts. Thus, the critical equation is the Base-Level Learning Equation 4.1. If the number of references n in that equation is replaced by pL, where p is the presentation rate in terms of number of presentations per unit of time and L is the length of training, then as we noted in Chapter 4, the Base-Level Learning Equation 4.1 can be approximated as:

$$B_i = \ln \frac{pL^{1-d}}{1-d}$$

Then by substituting this quantity into the Retrieval Time Equation 3.10, the retrieval latency can be shown to be a power function of the life of the chunk:

$$T = cL^{-(1-d)}$$

where $c = Fp/(1-d)$ and so reflects the presentation rate p. Thus, we would expect that time to answer these addition problems would speed up as a power function of length of training (L). Figure 9.6 plots the data as a pair of small- and large-problem curves across grades with a log-log scale. It does appear roughly to speed up as a power-law function of grade.

The slope of the small-problem curve of about 0.5 is perfectly compatible with the default parameter values of 0.5 for the base-level decay d. The somewhat higher slope of about 0.75 for the larger problems can be explained by a switch from computation to retrieval in addition to retrieval speedup, because first graders are still likely to use computation for some

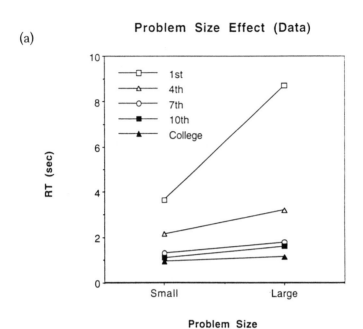

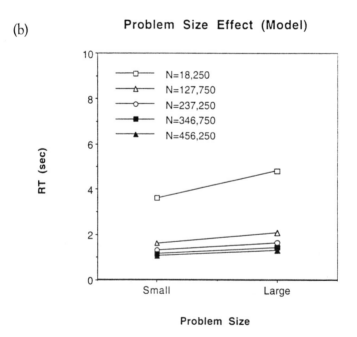

FIG. 9.5.   Effect of problem size across grades: (a) data; (b) model.

large problems. Another factor could be a leveling of the problem distribution over time, with large problems becoming gradually more frequent relative to small problems.

The results from the ACT–R model are displayed in Fig. 9.5b. All parameters were the same as those used for the problem-size effect model presented earlier in this chapter. The amount of presentations for each grade corresponds to that many years of training (minus a half, assuming that subjects were tested mid-year) at the usual average rate of 100 problems per day. This model fails to produce the degree of speeding up for the large problems. The most probable explanation is its failure to include computation. Children are probably using this backup computation extensively for the large problems and it is producing a considerable slow-down.[14] However, Fig. 9.5b shows how much of the effect we can account for purely in terms of speed up in retrieval.

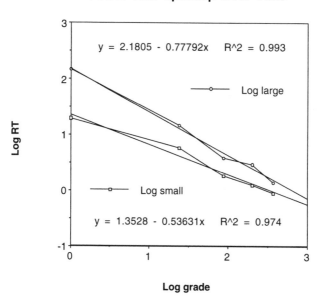

FIG. 9.6.   Power-law speed-up of response time.

[14]The final section of this chapter, on lifetime simulation, shows that this discrepancy goes away when we include a computation component.

Learning the Correct Answer

Cognitive arithmetic performance increases over the years from marginal (less than 50% correct retrieval of small addition facts among 4-year-olds as reported by Siegler & Shrager, 1984, and even much worse for larger ones) to almost perfect and efficient retrieval for most adults under normal circumstances. At some point, children largely stop using computation to answer their arithmetic problems and just retrieve the answer. They still make errors, and according to the model there are two sources for errors, which we call type-a and type-b, on a problem like $3 + 5 = ?$:

(a) They will have stored incorrect answers (e.g., $3 + 5 = 7$) from past miscomputations or misretrievals and these can be retrieved.
(b) They can partially match and retrieve a correct answer (e.g., $3 + 4 = 7$) to a different problem.

What happens when a child starts retrieving answers subject to these errors and stops getting regular feedback on the additions? Can these errors be reduced through sheer practice at retrieval? We examine this question separately with respect to these two types of errors in ACT–R.

First, will continued practice lead to a reduction in type-a errors? Every time the child retrieves the right answer or the wrong answer, it will increase the answer's base-level activation. Suppose p_1 is the frequency with which the correct answer is retrieved and p_2 is the frequency with which the incorrect answer is retrieved. Then from the earlier equation it follows that the difference in their base-level activations will be

$$B_1 - B_2 = \ln \frac{p_1}{p_2}$$

which is a function of their relative frequencies p_1 and p_2. Thus, the difference in base-level activations between a correct and incorrect fact will increase if and only if the ratio of their frequencies increases. Without a change in ratio of frequencies, the associative activation will not change because, according to the Posterior Strength Equation 4.3, the S_{ji} values only depend on the relative frequencies, not the amount of practice. Similarly, the other activation quantities (mismatch penalty, noise) do not change with practice. Under certain circumstances, the presentation frequencies and the base-level activations will diverge. This is essentially a rich-get-richer dynamics. Strong chunks (hopefully the correct ones) are more likely to be recalled, which will strengthen them further, whereas weak chunks (hopefully the wrong ones) will be increasingly less likely to be retrieved until they are gradually forgotten. The Appendix to this chapter presents a mathematical analysis of this situation. It turns out that the critical parameter in this is ACT–R's activation noise parameter, s. If the parameter s is set well below 1, ACT–R can "clean itself up," so to speak. Through repeated retrieval it will come more and more to retrieve the stronger answer and so strengthen its base-level activation.

The analysis of type-b errors is different. Under the assumption that the perfectly matching correct fact $(3 + 5 = 8)$ and the partially matching correct fact $(3 + 4 = 7)$ reflect problems that occur with a constant rate of frequencies, there will be no effect of practice on their relative base levels. Mismatch penalty and noise will not change with practice either. On the other hand, the critical factor concerns the associative strengths, S_{ji}, between the cue 5 and the two facts $3 + 5 = 8$ and $3 + 4 = 7$. Again, under the assumption of not too much noise in the system, 5 becomes an increasingly good predictor of the perfect matching fact and an increasingly bad predictor of the partial matching fact. Because association strength reflects log odds and because 5 is associated with multiple facts, there is a bound on how strong the association between 5 and $3 + 5 = 8$ can be. However, there is no bound on how negative the association between 5 and $3 + 4 = 7$ can become. As the odds go to zero, the associations can become unboundedly negative and so completely inhibit the mismatching fact. As the Appendix develops, this requires that the value of the noise parameter s be less than $1/3$.

Figure 9.7 illustrates some results from a simulation in which the system starts out making a fair number of errors and eventually cleans itself up. The odds of commission errors decrease approximately as a power function of practice for a range of low noise values. The odds start at about 2.0 for the first block independently of the noise, but decrease by the hundredth block to about 0.02 for a noise variance of 0.1 and to 0.2 for a variance of 0.4. The decrease is roughly linear on a log-log scale, confirming the power-law nature of the process.

ACT–R's behavior with s values as in Fig. 9.7 can be seen as the middle ground between two extreme strategies to deal with conflicting information, also known as nonmonotonic knowledge (e.g., Bobrow, 1980). One strategy would be to consider all facts to be immutable (as is the case for arithmetic knowledge) and reject any information that conflicts with accepted knowledge. Although this may be the right thing to do in the case of cognitive arithmetic, in general it leaves one overly determined by one's initial knowledge state and incapable of dealing with a changing, evolving world. The opposite strategy is to immediately reject previous knowledge when faced with conflicting information. Although this may again be the right thing to do in situations where information is absolutely reliable, it could lead to catastrophic imbalance in many cases, including cognitive arith-

Retrieval of 10x10 Addition Table

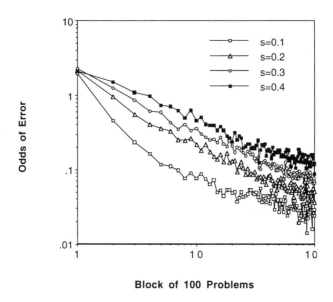

FIG. 9.7.   Power-law decrease of retrieval errors (model).

metic. Consider the consequences of trying to instantly rearrange your knowledge base if someone told you that $2 + 2 = 5$. Gradually shifting the strength of each piece of knowledge to reflect its strength of evidence (practice) is ACT–R's way of gracefully coping with conflicting knowledge.

Comparisons to Other Models

A number of cognitive arithmetic models have been proposed (e.g., Ashcraft, 1987; Campbell, 1991; Siegler, 1988; Siegler & Shrager, 1984). Although they differ in their focus, their details, and their complexity, they share a similar approach: They are based on the retrieval of facts from long-term memory, they employ a network-type approach where activation is spread and decays, and they control those processes using strengths that reflect past patterns of use.

ACT–R, an activation-based production system with Bayesian statistical learning of underlying real-valued parameters, is highly compatible with this approach. One of the details about which these models differ is the precise form of the decrease in error probability over time. Ashcraft (1987) increased the network strength values for correct associations (percentage of correct retrievals) yearly according to the formula:

$$\Delta\text{strength} = g(100 - \text{strength})$$

where g is the growth rate, estimated at 0.2. This equation originates from the incremental learning theory (e.g., Estes, 1964). It implies that the probability of error decreases exponentially with time:

$$\text{Prob(error)} = ce^{-gt}$$

Siegler and Shrager (1984) and Siegler (1988) used a reinforcement rule that increments associations between problems and correct answers twice as much as associations between problems and erroneous answers. Although the exact form of the learning curve was not discussed, graphs in Siegler and Shrager (1984) suggest that the increase in the probability of a correct answer is roughly linear through most of the range until ceiling effects are encountered.

ACT–R's prediction of power-law decrease in retrieval errors differs from linear and exponential predictions. Error percentages in arithmetic retrieval from childhood to adulthood would enable us to choose among these theories, assuming that reliable data exist. As another data source, one could use error curves from artificial substitutes such as alpharithmetic.

Finally, the analysis presented here is entirely consistent with reports that convergence to perfect retrieval occurs at sharply different speeds among individuals and indeed may sometimes not happen at all. Goldman, Pellegrino, and Mertz (1988) concluded from data on the learning of addition facts by learning-disabled students that the performance of most of these children is developmentally delayed (rather than developmentally different) relative to that of normally achieving children. An obvious explanation to account for this result would be through the use of a larger noise value. LeFevre et al. (1996b) also reported that some undergraduate college students have not entirely switched to retrieval of multiplication facts and occasionally still use nonretrieval procedures. Again, this is consistent with this analysis, including a strong sensitivity of the convergence time to initial performance.

THE LIFETIME SIMULATION

The simulations presented earlier in the Performance section all shared the same simplifying approach. To focus on a particular effect at hand, they assumed a certain distribution of knowledge strength at a particular point in time and proceeded to model the results given that state of knowledge and a particular set of parameter values. For example, the simulation of the problem-size effect assumed a distribution of strength for each arithmetic fact and derived the retrieval latency from these strengths. The simulation of the retrieval of addition facts by 4-year-olds assumed the distribution of strengths of those facts given the distribution of problems and backup procedures such as counting, and derived the probability of correct retrieval and errors for each fact. The simulation of multiplication by repeated addition by fourth graders assumed a distribution of strengths for the addition facts used and derived the probabilities of errors for each problem. Even the evolution of the problem-size effect over time, in the Learning section, relied on assumptions about the growth of strength of facts over time.

Although this method is widely used in cognitive science and produces both tractable analyses and often excellent simulation fits, it suffers from a number of disadvantages. It requires additional assumptions about the state of knowledge at particular points in time. It allows different parameter values to be estimated for each fit. And it provides only an incomplete understanding of how each part fits with the others. For example, errors in the computation and retrieval of addition problems will lead to permanent erroneous facts, which in turn should have an impact on the computation of multiplication by repeated addition. The only way to account for those interactions is to develop a single simulation to trace the evolution of knowledge and performance through the hundreds of thousands of problems of the entire development cycle, from childhood to adulthood, all with the same set of parameters. That is the goal of the lifetime simulation described in this section.

The Model

The model of the lifetime simulation is essentially an assembly of the partial models described previously, with a few modifications. It models the impact of a lifetime of solving addition problems. Although we present some results about multiplication by repeated addition, we do not model experience with subtraction, multiplication, or division problems.

Table 9.4 presents the basic productions of the model. Part a of the table displays the productions that are responsible for performing arithmetic by retrieval. The main production, **Arithmetic-Retrieval**, solves an arithmetic problem by retrieving the corresponding fact. Addition problems of type "x + 0" and "0 + x" are solved by the special-purpose productions **First-Plus-Zero** and **Zero-Plus-Second**, respectively. Part b of Table 9.4 displays the productions that do addition by backup computation. The production **Addition-Counting** generates a subgoal to iteratively count up to the answer from the first operand to the second. The production **Iterate-Count** counts up with **Count-Up** doing the actual counting, and the production

TABLE 9.4
Production Rules in the Lifetime Simulation

(a) Basic Arithmetic Productions

Arithmetic-Retrieval
IF	the goal is to solve an arithmetic problem of the type X OP Y and there is a fact stating that X OP Y = Z
THEN	set the answer as Z

Done-Arithmetic
IF	the goal is to solve an arithmetic problem and the answer has been found
THEN	output the answer and pop the goal

First-Plus-Zero
IF	the goal is to solve an arithmetic problem of the type X + 0
THEN	set the answer as X

Zero-Plus-Second
IF	the goal is to solve an arithmetic problem of the type 0 + X
THEN	set the answer as X

Double-Recoding
IF	the goal is to solve an arithmetic problem of the type X + X
THEN	recode the problem as X + Double

(b) Productions for Addition by Repeated Counting

Addition-Counting
IF	the goal is to solve an arithmetic problem of the type X + Y
THEN	set a subgoal to count from X a number of times equal to Y

Done-Count
IF	the goal is to count Y times and the counter is Y
THEN	return the result and pop the goal

Iterate-Count
IF	the goal is to count from X and the counter Z is less than the limit Y
THEN	set a subgoal to increment X and a subgoal to increment Z

Count-Up
IF	the goal is to increment the number X and the number following X is Y
THEN	return the number Y

Double-Counting
IF	the goal is to solve an arithmetic problem of the type X + Double
THEN	set a subgoal to count from X a number of times equal to X

(c) Productions for Multiplication by Repeated Addition

Iterate-Add

IF	the goal is to add Y a total of X times and the counter Y is less than X
THEN	set subgoals to increment the counter
	to add Y to he units digit
	to split the result to extract the carry
	and to increment the tens digit with the carry

Construct-Result

IF	the goal is to add X times and the counter is X
THEN	set a subgoal to merge the tens and units digits

Done-Add

IF	the goal is to add X times and the counter is X
	and the tens and units digits have been merged
THEN	return the result and pop the goal

Split

IF	the goal is to split the number X
THEN	return the tens and units digits of number X

Merge-Numbers

IF	the goal is to merge the tens digit T and units digit U
THEN	pop the goal with answer TU

Done-Count recognizes that the limit has been reached and pops the answer. Similarly, part c of Table 9.4 displays the productions that solve a multiplication problem by iteratively adding the multiplicand a number of times equal to the multiplier. The production **Iterate-Add** subgoals the operations to execute one step of repeated addition. Because we do not model multiplication otherwise, there is not a production corresponding to **Addition-Counting** in part b, which converts multiplication into repeated addition. Rather, we assume the subject starts with the goal of repeated addition. When all the steps have been completed, the production **Done-Add** pops the answer. Because only single-digit addition facts are systematically stored, the **Iterate-Add** production performs multidigit addition by splitting the numbers into tens and units digits using the **Split** production, incrementing tens and units digits separately, then finally reconstituting the digits into a single number using the **Merge-Numbers** production and returning the result as the answer.

Two features of this model are worth mentioning, both of which are related to the functioning of the S_{ji} values. As developed in the previous section, the S_{ji} values become increasingly differentiated as the simulation progresses given the right parameters. Numbers are the basic components of goals and chunks, and as such they will be the sources of activation (i.e., the j terms). The S_{ji} values between numbers and related facts (e.g., 3 and 3 + 4 = 7) become large positive numbers, and the S_{ji} values between numbers and unrelated facts (e.g., 5 and 3 + 4 = 7) become increasingly and unboundedly negative. The latter results from the increasingly infrequent retrieval of the fact given the unrelated number, and is the essential condition to achieving asymptotically perfect performance given initial error-prone performance.

The first feature that we want to note concerns an interaction between these S_{ji} values and our subgoal structure. In complex computational goals such as to perform addition by repeated counting and multiplication by repeated addition, the source activation will be divided among many sources such as counters and intermediate results, only a subset of which are involved in any given retrieval. For example, the following goal to compute the sum of 4 and 3 by iterative counting starts as:

Goal
    isa ITERATE-COUNT
    count Zero
    limit Three
    Result Four

The first step is to increment the intermediate result Four and counter Zero by retrieving the appropriate counting facts. However, if those retrievals are done directly, then Zero, Three, and Four will all be sources when the counting facts Four $\rightarrow$ Five and Zero $\rightarrow$ One are retrieved. The S_{ji} values between those numbers and facts will all be reinforced, including incidental ones such as between Four and Zero $\rightarrow$ One, and Three and Four $\rightarrow$ Five. This would have two undesirable consequences. The first is interference errors, such as retrieving Four $\rightarrow$ Five instead of Three $\rightarrow$ Four, because the extra spreading activation from the source Three overcomes the mismatch penalty between Three and Four. Although the errors produced by this type of interference do occur, in this case the interference leads to an excessively deterministic pattern of errors. An even more fundamental problem is that because of these accidental reinforcements between unrelated facts and numbers, the S_{ji} values between them will not become increasingly negative but instead settle at some base value that will prevent further improvement in performance. The solution is to subgoal retrievals instead of performing them directly. This corresponds to moving the retrievals from the left-hand side of productions to the right-hand side and pushing subgoals to perform them on the stack. This operation focuses on the retrieval to be performed by creating a new goal, which only includes the activation sources necessary to the retrieval. Examples of this technique can be found in productions **Iterate-Count** (which subgoals a count) and **Iterate-Add** (which subgoals a number of operations). Once the retrieval patterns have been subgoaled, a production must fire to perform the actual retrieval, complete the pattern, and pop the goal. These productions are **Count-Up** and **Arithmetic-Retrieval** for counting and arithmetic facts, respectively. This technique, in addition to allowing S_{ji} values to achieve optimal predictiveness, has the advantage of increasing the modularity of knowledge. Instead of having to generate separate productions for retrieval and backup computation in each situation in which an arithmetic fact would be needed, a single production would be needed to set up a subgoal of that type, which could be solved by either retrieval or backup computation without the need to duplicate those productions.

The second feature of the model is the introduction of the production **Double-Recoding** (see part a of Table 9.4 and the corresponding **Double-Counting** in part b) to recode tie problems in a way that explicitly recognizes the special character of the problem. The reason that this recoding is necessary is quite subtle. After all, the additional S_{ji} strength from numbers such as 4 to tie problems such as $4 + 4 = ?$ over other problems such as $3 + 4 = ?$ is sufficient, in the simulations developed in the previous sections, to provide enough of an activation boost to tie problems to reproduce the tie effect. However, in the lifetime simulation, that additional strength is ultimately overcome by the lack of distinctiveness of the basic tie-problem representation. Although non-tie problems such as $3 + 4 = ?$ include two distinct number sources, at least one of which will develop over time a very negative S_{ji} value to tie facts such as $4 + 4 = 8$ (in this case, from the number 3), tie problems such as $4 + 4 = ?$ only have one number source, and thus cannot develop a negative S_{ji} link to non-tie facts that involve that number, such as $3 + 4 = 7$. Therefore, over time, errors of non-tie facts being retrieved for tie problems will become increasingly more common than vice versa, and tie problems develop a worse error performance than non-tie problems. To prevent that, tie problems such as $4 + 4 = ?$ are recoded into a form such as $4 +$ Double $= ?$ where the chunk Double explicitly recognizes the number duplication and presents a form for tie problems distinct from non-tie problems. Attributing the extra strength of tie problems to an explicit recoding step rather than (only) to a built-in advantage is consistent with results such as those reported by Eliaser, Siegler, Campbell, and Lemaire (1997). They found that subjects spend more time encoding tie problems and that non-tie problems exhibit better performance than tie problems in artificial problem sets where tie problems are the rule rather than the exception, as they are in arithmetic.

Finally, the parameters for the lifetime simulation include an activation noise $s = 0.25$ and a retrieval threshold $\tau = -1.0$. As argued in Whalen (1996), we also introduced a similarity measure that was sensitive to the magnitude of numbers. We used perhaps the simplest such measure, in which the similarity between the numbers i and j is proportional to the ratio between those numbers, that is, i/j, where i is the smaller of the numbers and j is the larger. This similarity measure has the advantage of scalability—that is, the similarity between 3 and 5 is the same as the similarity between 30 and 50, an intuitively desirable property. The mismatch penalty is proportional to one minus the similarity—that is, $D(1 - i/j)$. The mismatch scale, D, was set to the default ACT–R value of 1.5.

The Results

In the previous section, we described the structure of the lifetime simulation model, which is essentially the same as the previously introduced partial models, except for a few minor changes. Although the models themselves fit together nicely, an important question was whether the different parameter values used to model each separate result could be unified in a single parameter set with which the lifetime simulation could reproduce the entire set of results. The answer is affirmative, and this section describes each result and how it was obtained.

The first result presented was the problem-size effect in adults. As in the model for Fig. 9.2, the latency factor F was left unchanged at the default value of 1.0 sec, the constant latencies for the input and output procedures were 0.4 sec, and the latencies for the zero productions were 0.5 sec. Because the latency of backup computation is now taken into account, a constant action latency of 0.5 sec for the **Iterate-Add** production is added. The purpose of this parameter is to account for the context-switching part of the counting task, either in the form of subgoal creation and pushing, or external strategies such as finger counting. Another set of parameters concerns the distribution of problems over time. Because when retrieval becomes the dominant strategy each problem results in two rehearsals of the solution fact, one from the retrieval and one from the merging when the completed goal is popped, the frequency is lowered to about 55 problems a day, or 20,000 problems a year. A 3 to 1 ratio between most frequent (0 + 0) and least frequent (9 + 9) problem is assumed, which is slightly smaller than the 4 to 1 ratio assumed previously. The reason is that because smaller problems are solved and thus reinforced more consistently than large ones, the actual reinforcement distribution is steeper than the problem-presentation distribution.

Altogether this simulation has to go through 250,000 addition problems to simulate the experience of a human through college. On our 180-MHz PowerMacs, this experience can be covered in about 16 hr of simulation.

The fact that we can perform this degree of compression is testimony to the considerable efficiency of the ACT–R simulation language, even with all of its real-valued computations enabled.[15] Even if someone did nothing but addition, we estimate that it would take them in the order of 50 hr to cover 250,000 addition problems.

Figure 9.8 presents the results of this simulation in terms of the problem-size effect at various ages. The results of the lifetime simulation are even better than those of the previous simulation, because the additional latency of backup computation provides a closer fit to the long response times for large problems in the early grades (see Fig. 9.5). The response times are decreasing not only because the answers are getting stronger but also because the model is increasingly switching from computation to retrieval.

We also modeled the early retrieval accuracy data displayed in Fig. 9.3. In this case the distribution is restricted to problems from $0 + 0$ to $5 + 5$, again on the assumption that 4-year-olds did not have much exposure to double-digit facts. Twenty-five hundred previous problem presentations are assumed, which is more than the thousand presentations assumed by the previous simulation because the retrieval threshold ($\tau = -1.0$) of the lifetime simulation is significantly higher than the threshold used in that simulation ($\tau = -2.25$). The probabilities of correct retrieval as a function of argument

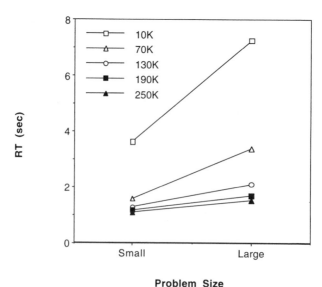

FIG. 9.8.   Problem-size effect as a function of practice (lifetime simulation).

---

[15]This is with the optimized-learning flag on, which allows the summation in Equation 4.1 to be approximated.

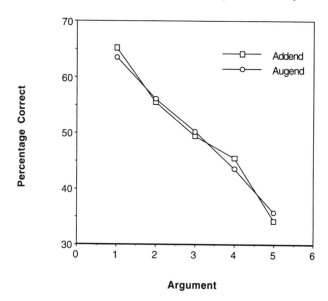

FIG. 9.9.   Percentage of correct retrievals in addition (lifetime simulation).

size are given in Fig. 9.9. Because at that age addition problems are still solved mostly by counting, the use of that backup procedure is reflected in the slightly steeper pattern for addend than augend, reflecting the increased error rate, and therefore weaker reinforcement, for problems that required a larger number of counting cycles. Therefore, although the simulation is fired to solve the problems by retrieval instead of counting (as were the subjects), the past computation errors are reflected in the retrieval performance.

The multiplication computation data are obtained by running 1,000 multiplication problems after 70,000 addition problems, which at a rate of about 20,000 problems per year corresponds to the middle of the fourth grade, as was the case for the subjects. The results are given in Fig. 9.10 (compare with Fig. 9.4), which reproduces the problem-size effect for both multiplicand and multiplier. The slightly noisy nature of the effect is compatible with the noise in the data. This is just one run of the simulation (corresponding to one child), and different runs would yield different results. The decreased error rate for the multiplicand 5 is present, resulting from the lower error rate for the two main single-digit addition facts used in counting by 5, that is, $0 + 5 = 5$, which is solved by the zero rule, and $5 + 5 = 10$, which is a tie problem. The overall error rate of about 25% also corresponds closely to the fourth graders.

Finally, one can look at the detailed latency pattern for addition facts at the end of the simulation, which here corresponds to about 20 years of training, or 400,000 problems. These results are displayed in Fig. 9.11, which can be compared to the earlier Fig. 9.2. Although an occasional computation is performed (0.1% of all answers are by computation), the latencies here overwhelmingly reflect the retrieval latencies for the correct fact, or the constant time (0.5 sec) of application of a rule for the problems involving zero, plus a constant time for encoding the problem and outputting the result (0.4 sec). The curve for tie facts is lower and flatter than the curve for nonzero, non-tie facts. This is due not only to the increased spreading activation to those facts, but also to the fact that because those problems could be retrieved earlier and more reliably than the others, they have received a comparatively higher amount of reinforcement.

We ran two simulations, one with a noise of $s = 0.25$ and another with a noise of $s = 0.35$ (see Retrieval Probability Equation 3.7 and Chunk Choice Equation 3.9). The results from these two runs are displayed in Fig. 9.12. For the relatively low noise value ($s = 0.25$), the error percentage for addition problems decreases from 16.7% in the first grade to 6.7% in the fourth grade, 1.5% in the seventh grade, 0.6% in the tenth grade, and 0.4% in the first year of college. For a slightly higher noise value ($s = 0.35$), however, the error curve starts at a somewhat higher error level of 23.7% in

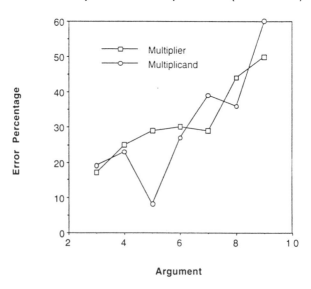

FIG. 9.10.   Percentage of errors in multiplication computation (lifetime simulation).

Problem Size Effect (Simulation)

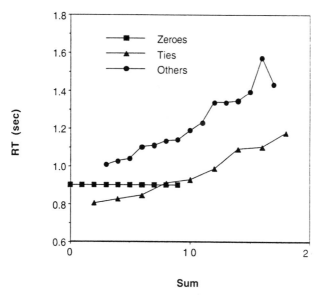

FIG. 9.11.   Problem size effect for zero, ties, and other problems (lifetime simulation).

Errors as a function of practice and noise

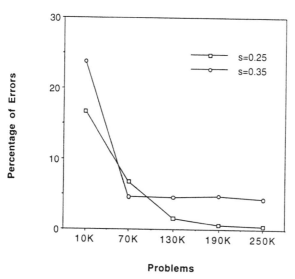

FIG. 9.12.   Percentage of addition errors as a function of practice and noise (lifetime simulation).

the first grade, then drops quickly to 4.5% in the fourth grade, but stabilizes at that level and does not improve further. This confirms our earlier theoretical analysis (and see the Appendix) on the effect of noise on learning. This fundamental performance difference under slightly different parameter sets may explain why under similar sets of circumstances (teaching, presentation schedule, etc.) some people attain perfect knowledge whereas others get stuck at some suboptimal performance level.

Discussion

Although the model presented here focused on the problem-size effect, it is clear that it should be able to account straightforwardly for a number of other results in the field. As previously mentioned, human errors tend to be close to the correct answer, and in verification tasks close foils tend to be more difficult to reject. As seen in the model of addition retrieval, ACT-R can account for that error pattern through the use of both computation and retrieval procedures. Because of its iterative nature, backup computation tends to produce errors that are close to the actual answer, and those errors, if not immediately corrected, become facts that can later be retrieved directly. Partial matching of correct answers, too, tends to produce close misses because the degree of mismatch increases with the difference between numbers.

Another type of error is cross-operator confusion, which is particularly common in verification problems such as $3 + 4 = 12$ (Miller, Perlmutter, & Keating, 1984; Winkelman & Schmidt, 1974). The activation spread from the number sources 3, 4, and 12 may be enough to overcome the mismatch penalty between + and ×, and the misretrieval of the $3 \times 4 = 12$ fact would then produce a "correct" answer. Of course, the error can always be detected if the operator of the fact retrieved is explicitly compared to the original operator, and the mismatch between × and + noticed, but for a number of reasons, such a procedure is fairly unlikely. First, the extra step taken and its associated latency are undesirable factors in situations where the subject is implicitly or explicitly pressured to minimize response time. Second, there is the need for extra slot(s) in the goal structure to hold the retrieved operator and operands for comparison. These extra slots would diffuse activation spreading and would typically be used only in situations where error correction is critical. However, it is quite possible that this error-checking procedure could account for people's ability sometimes to correct their own errors and prevent error propagation.

For multiplication facts, a pervasive effect is the dominance of table errors; that is, the most likely error when solving a multiplication problem is a number that is the answer to a fact in the same row or column in the multiplication table, usually close to the original problem. This effect is predicted in the ACT–R model by the form of the mismatch penalty. Facts in the same table row or column will only incur one mismatch penalty—for instance, 3 × 7 mismatches 3 × 6 only in the 6 versus 7 discrepancy. The size of this mismatch penalty is smaller the closer the retrieved number is to the actual number in the problem. In contrast, facts that are neither in the same row nor column as the problem will incur two mismatch penalties, one for each argument, resulting in a much reduced probability that the fact's activation after penalties will be the highest of all the competing facts. In addition, facts that are neither in the same row nor column will not receive spreading activation from either argument.

Another phenomenon is error priming (Campbell, 1991), which results when the answer to a particular problem (e.g., 3 × 8 = 24) tends to generate errors in subsequent trials (e.g., 4 × 7 = 24). This can be accounted for through base-level activation decay, because a fact that has been recently retrieved maintains for a short time a significant activation advantage that may be sufficient to overcome mismatch penalties. It is not clear, however, how to explain such priming errors when only the answer (e.g., 24) is presented as the prime, because no arithmetic fact is (at least explicitly) accessed. The fact that a number (e.g., 24) was recently activated has no impact on the activation spreading for a separate problem (e.g., 4 × 7), because only the components of this problem are activation sources at the time. Perhaps the solution would be to assume that when the new problem is presented, the previous activation source (24) only decays away gradually and thus still produces some interference effect.

CONCLUSION

Up to now, ACT–R has been understood as an adaptive system tuned to the statistics of its environment. Although this is certainly still the case for this model, our results suggest a certain generalization of that view. Cognitive systems are driven not only by external statistics but also by their internal dynamics. There are two sources for chunks in ACT–R. The external environment can introduce new declarative knowledge to ACT–R's long-term memory or reinforce existing facts. But the system itself, running in isolation from the external world, constantly affects its own statistics through retrieval and creation of new chunks when each new goal is popped off the stack.

This view can be carried further. Each model can be decomposed into a set of skills, composed of the production(s) acting on a certain set of goals and the declarative knowledge that they use. The retrieval of addition facts and the computation of multiplication by repeated addition are two such skills. We saw in a previous section how one could be used to solve the other, with the multiplication imposing in the process a different set of statistics on the addition problem (e.g., the high retrieval of facts such as 0 + 5 and 5 + 5) and therefore altering their performance (latency, error probability) in the process. Each set of problems can be viewed as imposing a statistical pattern on the knowledge structures of the skills that it uses just as the external environment does.

Like physical systems, cognitive systems are partly determined by the boundary conditions imposed by their environment. But they also share enough complexity to exhibit internal dynamics of their own.

APPENDIX

Basic Dynamics of Retrieval Odds

To formalize the dynamics of retrieval, let us first assume that the two chunks C_1 and C_2 are competing for retrieval without any context. The Chunk Choice Equation 3.9 can be rewritten to express the odds of chunk C_1 being retrieved as a function of the two chunks' activations and the activation noise level:

$$\text{Odds}_1 = e^{(A^1 - A^2)/s}$$

Ignoring the contribution of associative activation and considering only base-level activation, the difference between the activations of C_1 and C_2 can be expressed using the equation in the main chapter giving the difference in base-level activation as the logarithm of the ratio of their presentation frequencies. This yields:

$$\text{Odds}_1 = \text{Ratio}_1^{1/s} \qquad \textbf{Dynamic Odds Equation 9.1}$$

where $\text{Ratio}_1 = p_1/p_2$ is the past ratio of the frequencies of retrieving C_1 and C_2. This equation shows that the current odds of retrieval are sensitive to the activation noise level. If $s > 1$, the current odds of retrieval are closer to even odds (Odds = 1) than past history. This will ultimately lead to each chunk becoming equally likely to be retrieved. If $s = 1$, the current odds of retrieval are equal to the past odds of retrieval. This does not imply that the retrieval odds will be fixed, but rather that they will drift randomly with experience, driven by chance and external events. If $s < 1$, then the odds of retrieval become more extreme, with one becoming arbitrarily large and the other becoming infinitesimal. This is the winner-take-all dynamics mentioned previously. The noise level thus behaves much like the temperature in a Boltzmann machine: If it is too high, then the system is very disorganized and its entropy is maximized. If the noise is low enough, however, the system settles down into a fixed answer pattern.

Each new experience will be added by the declarative learning mechanisms to the statistics of past history. This incremental change in the history of retrieval odds can be expressed by a differential equation, which for the $s < 1$ case admits of two approximate solutions:

$$\text{Ratio}_1 \approx (cn)^{\pm 1} \qquad \textbf{Rehearsal Ratio Equation 9.2}$$

which means that the past frequency ratio of retrieving either chunk gradually diverges according to a power law in the amount of practice of exponent -1 for the loser and $+1$ for the winner (c is a constant that depends on initial conditions and n is the total amount of practice). Combining this with the Dynamic Odds Equation 9.1, the current or observed odds of retrieving either chunk, and therefore the odds of commission errors, are a function of the amount of practice to the power of the inverse of the noise measure:

$$\text{Odds}_1 \approx (cn)^{\pm 1/s} \qquad \textbf{Retrieval Odds Equation 9.3}$$

The Retrieval Odds Equation implies that the noise will determine the speed of convergence. But whereas a lower noise level implies a faster emergence of the winning, although not necessarily correct, answer, a higher noise level (still smaller than 1) causes slower convergence but a higher probability of the right answer emerging as the winner because the slower convergence lowers the impact of initial randomness.

Another way to view the Retrieval Odds Equation is in terms of the number of training examples needed to reach a particular accuracy. The number n of presentations of a particular problem needed to lower the odds of confusion errors below some threshold ε is:

$$n = \frac{1}{c\varepsilon^s}$$

As a final comment, the power law form of the Rehearsal Ratio and Retrieval Odds Equations (or the sigmoidal form of the equivalent probabilities) can also be found in the evolution of biological and technological systems between states of equilibrium (e.g., West & Salk, 1987). This is probably related to the fact that these systems follow power-law distributions similar to those of the cognitive environment (Anderson & Schooler, 1991).

Context and Complexity

The previous section analyzed what is described in the main chapter as type-a errors, that is, the competition between correct and incorrect answers through base-level strength. A similar analysis can be applied to type-b errors, the competition between two correct answers for different problems. Each will continue to be rehearsed because they are correct answers, but they will gradually become more sensitive to the exact features of the problem through the S_{ji} values, which control spreading activation. Based on our discussion of the Posterior Strength Equation 4.3 in the main text of this chapter, the difference between the S_{ji} values from the context C to chunks N_1 and N_2, respectively, is:

$$S_{CN_1} - S_{CN_2} = \ln \frac{F(N_1 \& C)}{F(N_2 \& C)} - \ln \frac{F(N_1)}{F(N_2)}$$

Assuming a total source activation level W of 1 (the ACT–R default), then when adding base-level strength to spreading activation, the base level difference will cancel the second term of the previous equation and the difference in total activation between the chunks N_1 and N_2 is:

$$\Delta A = A_1 - A_2 = \ln \frac{F(N_1 \& C)}{F(N_2 \& C)}$$

which means that the results derived in the previous section still hold, that is, that the odds of retrieving either chunk in a given context is the same function of the past odds to the power of $1/s$ that was obtained in the context-free condition, but this time specific to the context.

But usually the context is not composed of a single chunk, and only part of the context can be used to differentiate between competing chunks. For example, if the problem is $3 + 4 = ?$, 4 is the only part of the context which can differentiate between $3 + 4 = 7$ and $3 + 5 = 8$. Because W must be divided among all three features (goal slots holding 3, +, and 4) the 4 will only receive a 1/3 weighting. Thus, the difference in activation between those chunks is:

$$\Delta A = \frac{1}{3} \ln \frac{F(\text{"}3+4=7\text{"} \& 4)}{F(\text{"}3+5=8\text{"} \& 4)}$$

It can be shown that the 1/3 factor multiplies the noise level s and the odds equation becomes:

$$\text{Odds} = \text{Ratio}^{1/3s}$$

This implies that the more complex the problem, the lower the noise level needs to be to guarantee convergence. Note in Fig. 9.12 that the lifetime simulation achieved convergence for $s = 0.25$ but not for $s = 0.35$.

Mismatch Penalty

This analysis focused on the influence of past rehearsal frequency through base-level and spreading activation. An additional component of the Activation Equation is the mismatch penalty. The mismatch penalty P biases the system in favor of one particular fact by adding or subtracting from the difference in activation between chunks:

$$\Delta A = \ln \text{Ratio} \pm P$$

This introduces a factor proportional to the exponential of the penalty in the odds equation:

$$\text{Odds} = (e^{\pm P}\, \text{Ratio})^{1/s}$$

Although strongly biasing the initial odds toward the correct answer, the mismatch does not directly affect the speed of convergence.

Multiple Alternatives

Until this point we have only discussed the odds of retrieval when two competing chunks were involved. It can be shown from the Chunk Choice Equation 3.9 that the odds of retrieving one of many alternatives is a direct function (the harmonic average) of the pairwise odds:

$$\text{Odds}(i) = \frac{1}{\sum_{j \neq i} \dfrac{1}{\text{Odds}(i \text{ over } j)}}$$

The same dynamic therefore applies in which the strongest alternative will get increasingly dominant over all others since it dominates each independently. This result is a variant of Luce's Choice Axiom (Luce, 1959).

External Feedback Sources

The analysis up to here assumed a closed system following its internal dynamics. Human cognition, of course, constantly interacts with the outside world. A particularly salient form of interaction in the case of cognitive arithmetic is teacher instruction. It can be shown that although teacher correction has a major impact on the dynamic odds equation early on in the process, it becomes overwhelmed by the weight of experience if one allows the system to run uncorrected for a long time. This may be why ingrained errors are so hard to root out from human cognition.

Error correction will still be possible later on, but a much larger amount of correct feedback will then be necessary to reverse the odds in favor of the correct solution. This need to keep the system relatively stochastic early on in the learning to prevent the odds from growing large (and therefore less susceptible to correction) suggests a positive effect of activation noise on long-term accuracy. Keeping the process sufficiently random early on prevents an occasional error (random or otherwise) from being locked in as the dominant answer too quickly and allows more time for the correct answer to emerge. Noise therefore performs a function similar to simulated annealing in a Boltzmann machine. In other words, noise is not (only) a shortcoming of the system but an essential contribution to its robustness in an imperfect environment. This reinforces a theme of Chapter 8.

10

Analogy

Dario D. Salvucci
John R. Anderson
Carnegie Mellon University

THEORIES OF ANALOGY

Anology is one important way in which people acquire new information. Most knowledge acquisition by analogy is rather mundane, as when a student learns to solve a physics problem by analogy to an example presented in a textbook. This type of analogical problem solving is the focus of this chapter. Occasionally, knowledge acquisition by analogy can be more profound, as when a scientist discovers a new theory by analogy to an existing theory. Our general view is that all forms of analogy, mundane or profound, involve the same basic processes. Given the importance of learning by analogy and the peculiar role of analogy in the history of the ACT–R theory, we aim in this chapter to formulate a detailed understanding of analogy in ACT–R 4.0. This both significantly extends the scope of what can be modeled in ACT–R and helps complete our understanding of production compilation as introduced in Chapter 4.

Changing Conceptions of Analogy in ACT–R

The ACT–R view of analogy has evolved greatly since the days of ACT–R 2.0 and its predecessor PUPS system (Anderson & Thompson, 1989). In ACT–R 2.0 and PUPS, the "analogy mechanism" served as both a theoretical account of behavioral phenomena associated with analogy and the sole mechanism for production creation. The mechanism operated by finding a mapping between the current problem and a previously solved problem and creating a production rule that implemented this mapping. The analogized production rule typically solved large problems in a single step—the left-hand side matched a full description of the problem and the right-hand side created or modified all chunks needed for the response. It has become clear that such productions are not in keeping with the new "atoms of cognition" conception of production rules; these productions could not account for the

343

low-level, multistep processing evident in many problem-solving tasks. For this reason and others outlined in Chapter 4, the analogy mechanism has been eliminated in ACT–R 4.0. Production creation is now handled by the simpler production compilation mechanism. The new ACT–R view of analogy is that analogy is no different than other problem-solving skills and can be modeled as a standard production system without a dedicated analogy mechanism.

The goal of this chapter is to illustrate this new ACT–R view of analogical problem solving. We develop two models of how people take a complex example, decompose it into its components, and use it analogically to solve new problems. Each of the two models represents a different approach to modeling analogy in a production-system architecture. The first model stores the analogical mappings in declarative chunks and strengthens these chunks through repeated retrieval. The second model represents mappings with production rules that are created and strengthened through production compilation. Both models represent detailed process models of analogical problem solving that decompose analogy into a fine-grained temporal structure. Interestingly, both models fit the observed data equally well, highlighting the need for further investigations into whether declarative or procedural representations are more appropriate.

We begin our exposition by outlining several existing theories of analogy and their similarities and differences with our approach. We then describe empirical results and two ACT–R models for a task in which students solved physics problems by example. We conclude by attempting to place ACT–R's view of analogy in context with other existing theories and by describing implications of the ACT–R approach for future analogy research.

Other Theories of Analogy

Numerous theories of analogy and analogical reasoning have emerged in the past two decades (e.g., Gentner, 1983, 1989; Holyoak & Thagard, 1989a, 1989b; Hummel & Holyoak, 1997; Keane, Ledgeway, & Duff, 1994). These theories approach analogy in its most general sense, describing how some process of *mapping* can infer relations between concepts. Colloquially, people often use the term *analogy* to refer to this process of mapping, or finding correspondences between two conceptual structures; for instance, students often think of analogy in terms of problems like

herd : buffalo :: school : ?

for which the student must infer the relation between the first and second objects and apply it to the third to obtain the solution (in this case, *fish*). Researchers have overwhelmingly agreed that mapping is the core component of analogy, although each has taken a slightly different approach to the problem. Gentner (1983, 1989) postulated that mapping centers on finding structural relations among concepts, with a systematicity that favors higher-order relations. Holyoak and Thagard (1989a) used similar ideas to implement an analogy mechanism based on constraint satisfaction. Keane et al. (1994) presented a mapping engine that operates incrementally on the components of the given analog. Hummel and Holyoak (1997) used distributed patterns of activation and dynamic binding to perform analogical mapping. Regardless of their particular approaches, these and other theories have considered mapping the centerpiece of the analogy process.

Successful problem solving by analogy requires more than just mapping, however. It is also necessary to represent the problem in a way that allows or facilitates analogical mapping. *Representation*, or encoding, of the mental structures that participate in mapping is crucial to the ability of any theory to construct analogical mappings (e.g., Novick, 1992). Of course, representation is important not only for analogy, but for all problem solving. As just one example, Hinsley, Hayes, and Simon (1977) discussed the importance of representation for word-problem solving. Representation is pervasive in the analogy process, and although it is sometimes labeled as the first subprocess of analogy (Reeves & Weisberg, 1994), we may more appropriately think of it as a precondition for successful analogizing.

Another key element of analogical reasoning is the *retrieval* of an appropriate source analog for mapping (Gentner & Forbus, 1991; Thagard, Holyoak, Nelson, & Gochfeld, 1990). The source may constitute some mental structure stored in memory (e.g., Anderson & Thompson, 1989) or may come from the external world in another form, such as written text (e.g., VanLehn & Jones, 1993). In tasks involving a mentally recalled source analog, successful retrieval can be extremely difficult; for instance, using a hint/no-hint paradigm, Gick and Holyoak (1980) found that only 20% of subjects who received no hint recalled the appropriate source analog for Duncker's (1945) tumor-ray problem. Such studies provide strong support for the contention that the retrieval stage is crucial to the analogy process and can provide substantial difficulty in certain situations.

Researchers have identified several other components of the analogy process. After the retrieval and mapping processes have been completed, the mappings can be applied to generate new conjectures about the target analog. This process of *inference* allows for the formation of new concepts based on existing ones. Inference is not necessarily an automatic consequence of successful mapping; *adaptation* is sometimes needed to modify the source analog to fit the requirements of the target analog (Novick & Holyoak, 1991). Furthermore, *schema induction* often occurs during the analogy process (Gick & Holyoak, 1983; Novick & Holyoak, 1991; Ross &

Kennedy, 1990). The literature is somewhat undecided on whether schema induction occurs during mapping, as a separate stage, or along with some other component of analogy. Nevertheless, further use of analogical mappings after the initial application seems to involve inference of some schematic knowledge.

Comparison of Existing Theories and the ACT–R Approach

The approach to analogy taken in this chapter and that taken by existing theories of analogy are different in several ways. Our approach has two primary foci: developing a fine-grain process model of analogy that addresses its detailed temporal structure, and placing analogy within the larger context of problem solving. Rather than stressing one particular model of analogy, we emphasize the framework for analogical models that ACT–R 4.0 provides and the ways in which ACT–R models can be developed for analogical problem-solving tasks. Although existing theories have addressed these issues to some extent, their primary focus has been on other issues, such as generality to many domains and incorporation of all the components of analogical processing. We believe that our approach provides an interesting complement to existing theories and sheds light on areas that have not been emphasized in previous research.

The first major difference between our approach and that of others is our emphasis on the process and subprocesses involved in analogy. Most theories have tended not to use detailed empirical data concerning what happens *during* the analogy process, focusing instead on the *results* of the analogy process; in other words, they have focused on analogy at the computational level rather than at the algorithmic level (Marr, 1982). For example, Keane et al. (1994) presented empirical data on subjects' performance in an attribute-mapping task. They compared their empirical data to the predictions of three analogical theories: SME (Falkenhainer, Forbus, & Gentner, 1989), ACME (Holyoak & Thagard, 1989a), and their own IAM. Because none of the theories make predictions about latency, Keane et al. were forced to a crude evaluation of the theories by comparing subjects' total time for completion to the number of mappings generated by the models. For comparison purposes, this metric works in showing how IAM captures several aspects of analogical problem solving in the attribute-mapping task. However, arguing for the plausibility of such metrics in general could be difficult, and the metrics may not generalize when considering observables during the analogy process. Ideally, we would like the theory to make predictions about both observable events during the analogy process and observable results of the process. Some work has been done in this vein (e.g., R. J. Sternberg, 1977; R. J. Sternberg & Gardner, 1983), but there have not been detailed process models of analogical strategies. We feel that existing work on the computational level of analogy has provided a necessary basis for work on the algorithmic level and we are now at a stage where we can analyze the algorithmic level of analogy in a rigorous manner.

The second major difference between our approach and others' is our emphasis on placing analogy within a larger problem-solving context. Analogy in the real world arises in various forms, each of which has unique aspects to its solution, just as any problem-solving task may have domain-specific components. As such, analogy encompasses a broad spectrum of tasks that involve not only analogical reasoning but a great number of other skills. Existing theories of analogy have typically been developed as a basis for future work on more general theories of problem solving. We take the opposite approach: We start with an existing general theory, ACT-R, and attempt to account for analogy within this theory. Such an approach allows us to combine our model of analogy with models that are specific to the particular task domain. In addition, it provides a framework for higher level goals to influence when analogy takes place. Our approach also allows for different models of analogy that implement different analogical strategies, modeling the strategy variability in analogy that many researchers have found (Chi, Feltovich, & Glaser, 1981; Grudin, 1980; Novick, 1988; Spellman & Holyoak, 1993; Whitely & Barnes, 1979). Any theory of analogy must lie within a more general processing system, and the ACT-R theory provides an excellent opportunity to explore how analogy interacts with other problem-solving skills.

Because of our emphasis on low-level algorithmic details and interaction with general problem solving, we do not stress certain other issues that existing theories of analogy have. For instance, we have little to say about retrieval and adaptation in analogy, or the application of our models to typical analogy test problems (such as the solar system and atom analogy). Thus, we do not attempt to achieve the breadth of empirical support that other studies have achieved (e.g., Hummel & Holyoak, 1997). However, our investigation demonstrates that ACT-R is capable of successfully modeling the detail of analogical problem solving, and develops an approach in which broader empirical and modeling studies can be done in the future. We certainly believe that ACT-R can model these other aspects, and indeed it has a lot to say about issues such as the retrieval of sources.

A STUDY OF ANALOGY
IN THE PHYSICS TASK

We decided to examine the analogical strategies utilized by subjects in solving physics problems. We consider data that allow us to trace the detail of the information processing that occurs during the use of analogy. The experimental task involved solving several sets of physics problems by analogy to a given sample problem and solution. We chose this task for several reasons. First, many researchers have used physics problems in exploring the role of analogy (e.g., Chi, Bassock, Lewis, Reimann, & Glaser, 1989; Chi et al., 1981; VanLehn & Jones, 1993); thus the physics domain is a familiar one in the literature, facilitating comparison of other work to our own. Second, the task allowed relatively terse problems and solutions with a small natural-language component, allowing us to ignore language comprehension to a large extent. Third, the task is representative of real-world physics problem solving from a textbook; we can imagine the student doing a test problem at the end of the chapter, referring back to a worked out example in an earlier section.

The Physics Paradigm and Display

In the physics task, problems were presented to subjects on computer screens like Fig. 10.1. The left half of the screen contained the worked out sample. The sample problem first gave a description of the problem situation, then listed the relevant quantities (in short phrases) with their respective values. The sample solution used variables (e.g., f for flux), operators (e.g., *), and constants (e.g., c for speed of light, not shown in Fig. 10.1) in the first step, and values (e.g., 4), operators, and constants in the second step. The right half of the screen contained the test problem to be solved and an editable text field in which to enter the answer. The test problem had a structure similar to the sample problem, except for different

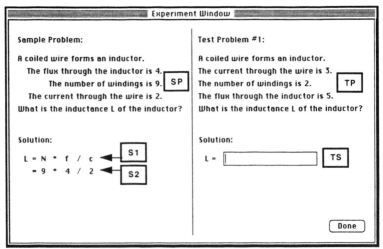

FIG. 10.1.   Physics experiment screen, without blocks. The labels in grayed boxes indicate the names of the visual areas.

quantity values and a possibly different ordering of quantity–value pairs. For future reference, we define the screen's visual areas (labeled in Fig. 10.1 in boxes) as sample problem quantities and values (SP), sample solution step 1 symbols (S1), sample solution step 2 symbols (S2), test problem quantities and values (TP), and a test solution block (TS).

Subjects were asked to solve sets of five problems in each of eight topics, all dealing with basic physics and all involving instantiation of a single equation. Table 10.1 shows the equations used for each topic; the first three equations are of equal complexity, whereas the others range in difficulty from fairly easy to fairly difficult. All topics and equations were taken from a standard physics textbook (Halliday & Resnick, 1988), massaged in some cases to fit the task, but still mathematically correct. The program presented the eight sets and the five problems within each set in the same order. The same sample problem and solution were used for all problems within a particular set, but the order of the quantities in each test problem varied from screen to screen. The numeric values used were constrained to one-digit integers so that typing times would be comparable across all problems. Subjects were to type their answers as instantiated equations, without simplifying; for example, they were to type answers such as "3*6/2" instead of simplifying this quantity and entering "9." Thus, the task involved learning a schematic equation such that values could be plugged in for quantities to produce the desired answer. The sample problems and solutions used in each of the eight topics can be obtained from this chapter's Web page (accessible from the book's home page, which is in turn accessible from the *Published ACT–R Models* link available from the ACT–R home page, http://act.psy.cmu.edu/).

Because we wished to examine the step-by-step nature of subjects' analogical behavior in detail, we needed some method of recording subjects' activity *during* the analogy process, specifically their visual scanning and

TABLE 10.1
Experiment Topics and Equations

Set	Topic	Equations	PC	NC
1	Capacitance	*area/spacing*	A/s	s/A
2	Thermal resistance	*thickness/conductivity*	T/c	c/T
3	Contracted length	*length/factor*	L/f	f/L
4	Force	*− constant*distance*	− c*d	− d*c
5	Velocity	*c/index*	c/i	c/i
6	Slit width	*number*wavelength/ sin angle*	n*w/S a	w*a/S n
7	Volume	*R*temperature/pressure*	R*T/p	R*p/T
8	Inductance	*number*flux/current*	N*f/c	c*N/f

typing activity. To accomplish this, we modified the stimulus presentation so that parts of the screen were covered with opaque blocks, which would disappear when clicked on and reappear on release of the button. An actual experiment screen, namely, the screen in Fig. 10.1 with blocks included, is shown in Fig. 10.2. The program concealed each symbol in S1 and S2, allowing us to examine which equation and symbol subjects were scanning. Blocks also covered the SP quantities and the TP values, but left the SP values and TP quantities uncovered. The reason for leaving the latter pair uncovered centered on the strategies expected of subjects. When a subject reads a value in S2, we expect the subject to search for that value in SP; to facilitate the search and to obtain simpler data, we left the SP values uncovered so that subjects can quickly locate the desired value. Similarly, when typing the solution equation, subjects search for a TP quantity to obtain its value; we thus uncovered the TP quantities. It is possible that the setup of the blocks changes the character of the task, because the blocks may alter the strategies that subjects utilize during the analogy process. Nevertheless, it does not change the fact that the task is fundamentally analogical and can provide rich empirical data concerning strategies of analogy.

The block approach for recording scanning activity is an adaptation of a common information-search paradigm where text or pictures appear on the backs of cards, such that subjects must turn the card over to reveal the information. For example, Payne (1976) used this paradigm in studying strategies of gathering evidence for decision making. Our technique differs from Payne's in that the information is reconcealed after being looked at, whereas the information in Payne's experiment remained visible for the duration of the task. We used the reconcealing technique to record not only

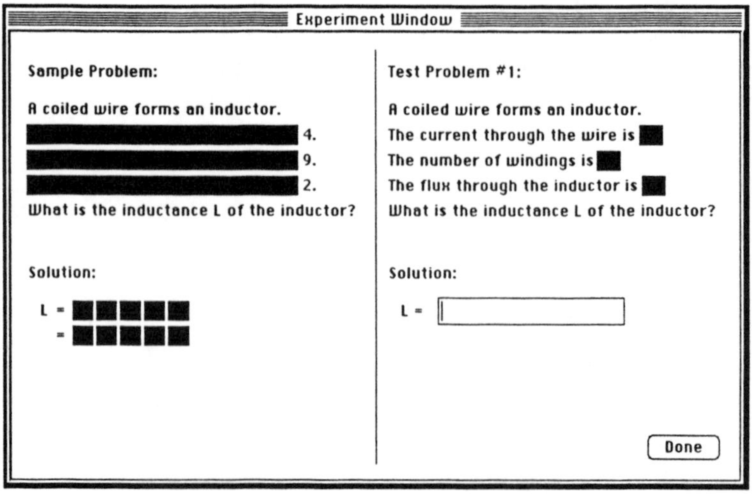

FIG. 10.2.   Physics experiment screen, as seen by subjects.

the order in which symbols are scanned, but also how often they need to be scanned. A third option for uncovering blocks would not require the subject to click on the block, but only move the pointer to it (e.g., Anderson, Matessa, & Douglass, 1995). We decided against this option to avoid an inevitable flux of unintended references in the data, when subjects incidentally uncover blocks as they move to the intended block.

During an experiment, the program recorded two types of information: the time, location, and duration of each mouse click, and the time and identity of each key press. Therefore, the program not only logged subject responses after each problem, but also much of how subjects went about solving the problem. In fact, the experiment program (in a different mode) can read subject data files and simulate all mouse clicks and key presses, allowing the experimenter to "watch" the subject at work.

In order to induce subjects to learn different analogical strategies, we manipulated the presentation of variables in S1. Subjects were randomly assigned to one of two conditions. In the positive-correlation (PC) condition, each variable was named using the first letter of the quantity it represented; for instance, m would represent mass and L length. In the negative-correlation (NC) condition, each variable was named using the first letter of a quantity it *did not* represent; for example, L might represent mass and m length. Thus, the PC variables suggested correct relations, whereas the NC variables deliberately misled the subject by suggesting incorrect relations. The equations used in each condition appear in Table 10.1. Note that in both conditions, the S2 values did correspond to the correct quantities, so the solutions remained correct—the only discrepancy between conditions is the mapping from variable to quantity.

Because of the different variable namings in the conditions, we can predict different strategies for the two groups. PC subjects, encountering names they would likely expect, should utilize a *solve-by-variable* strategy. That is, they should eventually tend to focus on S1 rather than S2, using variables more heavily than values for inferring the correct schema.[1] Indeed, the most efficient strategy for PC subjects involves looking only at S1; the subject can infer mappings from variable to quantity by referring to the visible TP quantities. NC subjects should utilize a *solve-by-value* strategy, relying more heavily on SP and S2. Here the most efficient strategy involves finding a corresponding SP quantity for each S2 value and storing the mapping from value to quantity. Of course, because the S1 variable names are misleading, NC subjects can get no (or little) useful information from the variables in the sample solution. In addition, because we expect NC

---

[1]It is possible that PC subjects might use the S2 values exclusively when analogizing, which would in fact yield correct results. However, the empirical results indicate that very few subjects did this.

subjects to be deceived initially by the incorrect namings, we also expect them to make more errors in the initial sets of the experiment.

The cross-mapping manipulation in the physics task is reminiscent of Ross's (1989) work on superficial similarities. Ross showed that superficial similarities between the sample and test problems can affect the quality of solution by analogy. In several studies, he manipulated the similarity between corresponding objects in probability problems presented to subjects. To summarize his results, performance on the problems increased with high similarity between corresponding objects and decreased with high similarity between noncorresponding objects. We expect our physics task to lead to similar subject behavior. The variable namings used in each condition hint at superficial similarities between variables and quantities; for instance, subjects are more likely to associate the variable m with the quantity mass rather than length, although there is no structural justification for such reasoning. In the PC condition, we expect high initial performance because of the similarity between corresponding objects. In the NC condition, we expect poor initial performance because of the similarity between noncorresponding objects. Note that there are also differences between Ross's work and our own that we discuss in a later section.

In summary, the physics task involves analogy in the learning of problem mappings and the application of the mappings to new problems. The mapping process produces a schematic equation that describes the quantities and values that belong in the desired answer expression. The schema is then applied to a new problem to infer the problem's solution. Admittedly, the task does not capture all the complexities of analogy that have been discussed in other work. However, we feel that the task is complex enough to allow for interesting analogical strategy differences in a problem-solving context, yet simple enough to facilitate analysis at the level of visual encoding of analog components. This balance of complexity and simplicity helps to achieve the primary goal in this study—to demonstrate how ACT–R can be used to model the detailed step-by-step process of analogical problem solving.

Overall Results

Data were collected from 19 subjects in the PC condition and (a different) 19 subjects in the NC condition. We discuss the results in two stages. First, we consider high-level data for the entire task, examining total latency and correctness per set of problems. Second, we look at low-level data for the final set, because we expect fairly stable behavior by the end of the experiment. Because the sets were presented in the same order, the final set always corresponded to the final topic in Table 10.1. On average, subjects required approximately 20 min to complete all 40 problems.

We begin by analyzing the correctness summary in Fig. 10.3, where solid lines represent subject data in each condition (dashed lines, representing model predictions, are discussed later). PC subjects worked essentially at ceiling, hovering around 95% correct for all sets. NC subjects exhibited more numerous errors in the initial sets, but eventually approached ceiling as well. A two-factor analysis of variance (ANOVA) shows that the effects of set, $F(7,288) = 2.59$, $MSE = 5.63$, condition, $F(1,288) = 20.0$, $MSE = 43.50$, and their interaction, $F(7,288) = 2.50$, $MSE = 5.44$, are all significant, $p < .02$. Particularly, PC and NC errors differ significantly in earlier sets, namely, in the first, second, and fourth sets,[2] $t(36) = 3.63$, $t(36) = 3.52$, $t(36) = 2.75$, respectively, $p < .01$; the differences between PC and NC errors on other sets are not significant, $p > .1$.

We explain the correctness results as follows. Both PC and NC subjects initially rely on the S1 variables to induce the meaning of the equations and to solve the test problems. For PC subjects, this method works well, because the variables correspond directly to the first letters of the quantities they represent. For NC subjects, however, this strategy leads to incorrect solutions, given that the variables are mismatched. Eventually, NC subjects experience an epiphany; they notice the discrepancy in the S1 variable namings, and begin to use the S2 values and SP quantities for mapping. The aggregate correctness graph reflects how subjects one by one arrive at this epiphany, and eventually NC subjects too perform at ceiling. It is important to note that when subjects made errors, they typically made them across all

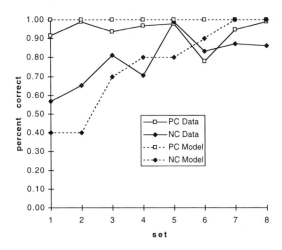

FIG. 10.3.   Average correctness for all sets. Correctness denotes the percentage of the five set problems answered correctly. Solid lines show subject data; dashed lines show learning model predictions.

---

[2]All t-tests conducted are two-tailed.

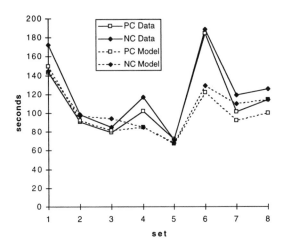

FIG. 10.4. Average set latency for all sets. Set latency denotes the time needed to complete all five problems in the set. Solid lines show subject data; dashed lines show learning model predictions.

five problems in a particular set, so singleton errors appear infrequently.

We can also examine the total latency per set of five problems. The solid lines in Fig. 10.4 show the average time (in seconds) taken by subjects to complete the five problems in sets 1 through 8. The first three points manifest the beginnings of the familiar power learning curve (Newell & Rosenbloom, 1981); recall that the problems in these sets have the same complexity, each having an equation with two variables and one operator. Subjects here were both familiarizing themselves with the system and honing their analogy skills as they pertain to these problems. For the other sets, the total latency corresponds roughly to the complexity of the problems in the set. The sixth and most complex set has the highest latency; in fact, the latency is unexpectedly high given that the complexity difference between the sixth and eighth sets is only one operator (the sine operator—see Table 10.1). The fifth and least complex set[3] shows the lowest overall latency. A two-factor ANOVA shows a very significant effect of set, $F(7,288) = 48.85, MSE = 56193.80, p < .001$. The ANOVA also shows a significant effect of condition, $F(1,288) = 8.36, MSE = 9615.60, p < .01$. This effect arises primarily because NC subjects required additional time to reach their epiphanies and additional mouse clicks to analogize. There is no set–condition interaction, $F(7,288) = .72, MSE = 828.12, p > .6$.

As expected, the results of the physics study corroborate the results of Ross (1989): We see high initial performance in the PC condition with

---

[3] It has only one variable—c is a constant.

similar corresponding objects, but poor initial performance in the NC condition with similar noncorresponding objects. If we look more closely at the cause of high versus poor performance, though, we can see subtle differences in the origin of subjects' behavior. In the physics task, the misleading variable names almost certainly lead to a mistaken schematic structure for the equation. Subjects seem to map variables to quantities incorrectly, thus remembering the schematic equation with the quantities in the wrong places. Errors in Ross's probability problems arose from superficial similarities between the sample and test problems, rather than between the sample problem and sample solution. Thus superficial similarities can affect both the mapping process that produces a schema (our research) and the use of the schema (Ross's research).

Final Set Results

We now focus on subjects' performance in the eighth and final set, which, roughly speaking, reflects asymptotic performance in the task. We first examine the average latency per problem in the final set, shown as solid lines in Fig. 10.5. Not surprisingly, the subjects took more time in the first problem, as they needed to study the sample and understand the meaning of the equation before solving the test problem. The latency curves flatten out quickly in later problems, most notably in the PC condition; subjects were essentially just checking the TP values and entering the solution equation. The problem effects are very significant, $F(4,180) = 1.72$, $MSE = 10876.01$, $p < .001$, whereas the effects of condition, $F(1,180) = 2.64$,

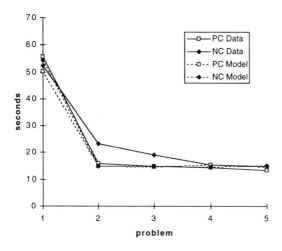

FIG. 10.5.   Average problem latency for final set. Problem latency denotes the time needed to complete a single problem. Solid lines show subject data; dashed lines show terminal model predictions.

$MSE = 231.18$, and of the interaction of problem and condition, $F(4,180)$ $= 1.72$, $MSE = 150.92$, are not, $p > .1$.

Subject latency data illustrate approximately when and how often subjects analogized. Visual scanning data, on the other hand, give important clues to *how* subjects analogized. We first consider our original hypothesis that PC subjects would rely more heavily on the S1 variables, whereas NC subjects would favor the S2 values. Table 10.2 contains the number of references[4] per area item in the final set, across all subjects. From the table we see that PC subjects did indeed scan S1 more often than NC subjects, who exhibited more references to SP and S2. The effects of area, $F(3,144)$ $= 29.31$, $MSE = 761.38$, and the area-condition interaction, $F(3,144) = 8.21$, $MSE = 213.25$, are very significant, $p < .001$, whereas the effect of condition is not, $F(1,144) = 1.42$, $MSE = 37.01$, $p > .2$. The values across conditions for SP, S1, and S2 differ significantly, $t(36) = 2.23$, $t(36) = 3.18$, and $t(36) = 3.31$, $p < .05$.

Although subjects' area references correspond to our predictions, it is interesting to note that overall subjects do not utilize what would be the most efficient strategy for our class of problems. On the one hand, PC subjects could have safely ignored the S2 values if desired and looked only at the S1 variables, yet they still scanned the S2 values. On the other hand, NC subjects did not need to look at the S1 variables, because the variables were always misleading; nevertheless, they clicked on the S1 variables approximately half as often as they did on the S2 values. Of course, subjects were not aware that the experimental condition would not change during the task, so these extra clicks can be viewed as checking that mapping conventions remained the same.

We can also analyze the time taken to look at objects in each area, as shown in Table 10.3. The *reference time* corresponds to elapsed time between the click on some item and a subsequent click or key press; note that duration of a click may not be an accurate measure, because some subjects

TABLE 10.2
Subject References per Area Item

	SP	S1	S2	TP
PC	1.74	2.11	1.13	1.11
	(1.75)	(2.40)	(0.85)	(1.00)
NC	2.96	1.05	2.22	1.11
	(2.95)	(0.80)	(2.20)	(1.00)

Note. Values represent average number of references per item in each area. Unparenthesized values represent subject data; parenthesized values represent terminal model predictions.

[4]In these and all other reference data reported, multiple references to a single block with no intervening actions were collapsed into one reference. This adjustment was made because of subjects who tended to click several times on the same block.

TABLE 10.3.
Subject Reference Times per Area Item

	SP	S1 Variables	S1 Operators	S2 Values	S2 Operators	TP
PC	2.74	1.77	0.94	1.57	0.79	1.38
	(2.84)	(1.81)	(0.75)	(1.82)	(0.80)	(1.20)
NC	2.76	1.76	0.97	1.59	1.12	1.45
	(2.69)	(1.87)	(0.75)	(1.50)	(0.60)	(1.20)

Note. Values represent average reference times, in seconds, per reference in each area. Unparenthesized values represent subject data; parenthesized values represent terminal model predictions.

may hold the button down while processing information, whereas others may release the button. The reference times shown in the table reveal no significant effect of condition, $F(1,189) = .78$, $MSE = 0.27$, $p > .3$, or of the interaction between condition and area, $F(5,189) = .35$, $MSE = 0.12$, $p > .8$. The effect of area, however, is very significant, $F(5,189) = 47.80$, $MSE = 16.67$, $p < .001$. This effect arises partly because of the high latency for the SP area; the SP times reflect the fact that the SP quantity blocks covered not only letters or words but partial sentences. Other significant differences occur in the times between S1 variables and S1 operators and between S2 values and S2 operators, $t(34) = 4.46$ and $t(28) = 3.98$ for PC, $t(21) = 3.11$ and $t(35) = 3.90$ for NC, $p < .01$. Subjects took only half as much time to process an operator in comparison with a variable or value.

These data give us a general sense of subjects' strategies of analogical behavior during the task, but we can characterize their behavior in more detail. We define a *reference path* as the sequence of area scans or area groupings that a subject accesses during a problem. An area scan, denoted by a single area such as S1, represents a scan of all objects within the area, hitting each at least once. An *area grouping* enclosed in parentheses, such as (S2 SP), indicates a "bouncing" scan between two or more groups. A bouncing scan does not necessarily hit every object within the groups. For example, assume we observe the following subject behavior: scan all S1 symbols, bounce between the S2 symbols and the SP quantities, and bounce between the TP values and the test solution block TS. We can characterize this behavior in the reference path S1 (S2 SP) (TP TS). Area groupings with a single area, such as (S2), indicate an incomplete scan of a single area bracketed by complete scans of other areas; such groupings that represent only one item access are considered spurious and are omitted from our analyses.

Table 10.4a shows the reference paths for each PC subject in the five final-set problems. The variability between subjects is quite striking; even with this rough characterization of analogical strategies, very few used identical strategies. Only one subject (PC1) used the most efficient strategy, scanning only S1 before proceeding to enter the solution. Approximately half the subjects began with a scan of SP, and generally continued by scanning S1. It seems that these subjects read top-down from the sample problem until they reached the relevant equation for mapping (the S1 equation for PC subjects). Also, most subjects exhibited some bouncing scans between SP and S2 after scanning S1, apparently checking the quantity equation derived from S1 by mapping S2 values to their respective SP quantities. Only one subject (PC15) seemed to use a solve-by-value strategy, scanning SP and S2 exclusively; this fact provides evidence that subjects tend toward the more efficient (solve-by-variable) strategy in the PC condition. Finally, PC subjects showed very little dependence on the sample problem and solution after the first problem. They seem to have abstracted out the solution during the first presentation.

Table 10.4b lists the reference paths for NC subjects. We see a fair number of scans of the S1 equation, even though the S1 variables are misleading. Again the subjects seem to manifest the top-down reading behavior, frequently reading SP and S1 before using the variable equation S2. NC subjects also exhibited the (S2 SP) bouncing, but presumably for the purpose of inferring the correct equation rather than for checking the variable equation. Several subjects inferred a mapping by scanning SP and S2 separately rather than bouncing between them. As in the PC condition, only one NC subject (NC16) exhibited the most efficient strategy, scanning SP and S2 once. Use of the test problem and entering of the solution are fairly similar across conditions. Both PC and NC subjects prefer to bounce between the test problem TP and the solution TS, as the behavior (TP TS) lightens working memory load. However, a minority of subjects showed the behavior TP TS, scanning all the test values first, then entering the entire equation into the solution block.

In summary, PC subjects generally followed the solve-by-variable strategy, whereas NC subjects followed the solve-by-value strategy. We have also seen that subjects exhibited a great deal of variability in analogizing, and adapted their strategy of analogy to either solve-by-variable or solve-by-value according to experimental condition. In the discussion of the model for these empirical data, we characterize subjects' behavior more formally and investigate how well ACT–R can fit these data.

DECLARATIVE MODEL
FOR THE PHYSICS TASK

We developed two models of the physics task that are capable of predicting the high- and low-level data presented earlier. The first model, described in this section, learns declarative chunks that represent the schematic knowl-

TABLE 10.4
Subject Reference Paths

a. PC Subjects

	Problem 1	Problem 2	Problem 3	Problem 4	Problem 5
PC1	S1 (TP TS)	(TP TS)	(TP TS)	(TP TS)	(TP TS)
PC2	SP S1 (S2 SP S1) (TP TS)	(SP S1 TP TS)	(TP TS)	(TP TS)	(TP TS)
PC3	SP	(TP TS)	(TP TS)	(TP TS)	(TP TS)
PC4	SP S1 (S2 SP S1 TP TS)	(TP TS)	(TP TS)	(TP TS)	(TP TS)
PC5	S1 SP S1 TP TS	TP (TP TS)	TP TS	TP	TP TS
PC6	(SP) S1 SP (S2 SP S1 TP TS)	(S1 TP TS	(S1 TP TS)	(TP TS) TS)	(TP TS)
PC7	SP S1 (S2 SP S1) (TP TS)	(TP TS)	S2 (TP TS)	(TP TS)	(TP TS)
PC8	SP S1 SP S1 (TP TS)	(TP TS)	(TP TS)	(TP TS)	(TP TS)
PC9	SP S1 (TP TS)	(TP TS)	(TP TS)	(TP TS)	(TP TS)
PC10	SP S1 S2 (S2 SP) (TP TS)	SP S2 (TP TS)	(TP TS)	(TP TS)	(TP TS)
PC11	S1 SP S2 TP TS	TP TS	TP (TP TS)	TP TS (S1)	TP TS
PC12	SP (S2 SP S1) TP (TP TS) S1 TS	TP TS TP TS	TP TS (TP)	TP TS	TP TS
PC13	SP S1 (TP TS)	(TP TS) (S2) S1	TP	TP	(TP TS)
PC14	(S2 SP S1) (TP TS)	TP TS	TP TS	TP	TP TS
PC15	S2 SP S2 TP TS	TP TS	TP TS	TP	TP TS
PC16	S1 (S2 SP) (TP TS)	(TP TS)	(TP TS)	(TP TS)	(TP TS)
PC17	SP S1 (S2 S1) S1 (S1 TP TS)	S1 (TP TS)	(TP TS)	S1 (TP TS)	(TP TS)
PC18	SP (S2 S1) SP S2 S1 (TP TS)	(TP TS)	(TP TS)	S1 (TP TS)	(TP TS)
PC19	SP S1 S2 (S2 SP) (TP TS)	(TP TS)	TP (TP TS)	(TP TS)	(TP TS)

359

b. NC Subjects

	Problem 1	Problem 2	Problem 3	Problem 4	Problem 5
NC1	SP S2 (SP TP) TP TS	TP TS	TP TS	TP	TP TS
NC2	(S2 S1) SP (S2 SP TP TS)	SP (S2 SP TP TS)	(S2 SP TP TS)	(TP TS)	(TP TS)
NC3	S1 (TP TS)	(TP TS) (S2 SP)	TP (S1) S2 (S2 SP TP TS)	(TP TS)	(TP TS)
NC4	SP S1 (S2 S1 TP TS)	S1 (TP TS)	(TP TS)	(TP TS)	(TP TS)
NC5	SP (S2 SP) SP (S2 SP TP TS)	(TP TS)	(TP TS)	(TP TS)	(TP TS)
NC6	SP (S2 SP S1 TP TS)	(S1) (TP TS)	(TP TS)	(TP TS)	(TP TS)
NC7	SP (S2 SP TP TS)	(S2 SP TP TS)	(TP TS)	(S2 SP TP TS)	(TP TS)
NC8	SP (S1) S2 (SP TP TS)	(S2 TP TS)	(SP TP TS)	(TP TS)	(TP TS)
NC9	S2 SP S2 SP (TP TS)	(TP TS)	(TP TS)	(TP TS) TS (TP TS)	(TP TS)
NC10	S2 (S2 SP TPTS)	S2 (S2 SP TP TS)	(S2 SP TP TS)	S2(S2 SP TP TS)	(S2 SP TP TS)
NC11	SP S2 (SP TP TS)	(SP TP TS)	(S2 SP TP TS)	TPTS	TP TS
NC12	SP (S2 SP TP TS) TP	(TP TS) S1 TP	(TP TS)	(TP TS)	(TP TS)
NC13	SP S1 (S1) S2 (S1) TP TS	TP TS	TP TS	TP TS	TP TS
NC14	S1 (S2 SP) TP TS	TP TS	TP (TP TS)	TP TS	TP TS
NC15	(S1) S2 (S2 SP) (TP TS)	(TP TS)	(TP TS)	(TP TS)	(TP TS)
NC16	SP S2 (TPTS)	(TP TS)	(TP TS)	(TP TS)	(TP TS)
NC17	SP (S2 SP S1) SP (S2 S1) (TP TS)	(TP TS)	(TP TS)	(TP TS)	(TP TS)
NC18	SP S1 (S2 SP TP TS)	(S2 SP TP TS)	(TP TS)	(S2 SP TP TS)	(TP TS)
NC19	SP S1 (S2 SP S1) S2 SP (TP TS)	(S2) (S2) (SP TP TS) S2 SP TP	(TP TS)	(TP TS)	(TP TS)

edge necessary to solve the problems. The second model, described in the next section, learns similar schematic knowledge in procedural form using the production compilation mechanism. Because the final models are quite large (over 120 production rules each), we cannot simply present the rules as they are. However, we give a sense of how we designed and implemented the models at a high level and illuminate their most crucial elements.

This section outlines the declarative model for the physics task and discusses how well the model fits the observed data. For ease of exposition, we introduce the model as two *terminal* models that represent the asymptotic behavior of subjects (for each condition). That is, the terminal models capture the behavior of subjects after the subjects have optimized their strategy for a particular condition. Thus we present one terminal model that executes the solve-by-variable strategy (for the PC condition), and another that executes the solve-by-value strategy (for the NC condition). After describing the terminal models and their predictions, we merge the two terminal models into a single *learning* model. The learning model can account for the evolution to the appropriate terminal model based on the condition (PC vs. NC) of the simulation.

The Basic Declarative Terminal Model

As the first step in creating the terminal models, we need to perform a task analysis to determine the overall strategy that subjects undertake in analogizing. The data support our original predictions that PC subjects focus on S1, whereas NC subjects focus on S2 and SP. The correctness data suggests that subjects begin using the solve-by-variable strategy, and eventually adjust to the appropriate strategy for their condition. The reference paths manifest, for some subjects, a tendency to read the sample problem from the top down to the area relevant for analogy. Finally, the data show that PC subjects seem to look at the S2 equation to check that the equation derived from the variables is correct. Taking all these facts into account, we can propose a general strategy for subjects on first seeing the problem. The general strategy applies to both the PC and NC terminal models, but is implemented slightly differently for each model.

The overall model strategy is illustrated in Fig. 10.6, where the control flow for the initial problem in a set appears on the left and the graph for subsequent problems appears on the right. Before examining the stages of the model in detail, let us briefly outline its general control flow. First, subjects either read top-down to the relevant area, or skip directly to the area. For PC subjects, the relevant area is the S1 equation; for NC subjects, it is the S2 equation. Second, in the study-mapping stage, subjects use the equation to build a mental representation of the schematic equation. This schematic equation, which we call the *quantity equation*, contains quantity names in place of the variables or values, such that the representation could be used to solve the test problem. For instance, for the induction problem shown in Fig. 10.1, the equation $L = N*f/c$ would map to the quantity equation $L = number*flux/current$. The quantity equation is the essential product of the analogy process from which all subsequent problem solving flows. Third, in the check-mapping stage, subjects either check the quantity equation or skip the check. PC subjects would check the quantity equation against the equation represented by the S2 equation, whereas NC subjects cannot perform any check, because the variable names are known to be misleading. Fourth, in the solve-problem stage, subjects solve the test problem using the quantity equation and the TP values. For subsequent problems, the quantity equation may need to be reviewed before solving the problem, and this review would constitute restudying the equation.

The first stage allows two options, reading top-down to the study equation or skipping ahead. Reading top-down means reviewing material in the problem that appears before the critical material, that is, the S1 equation for PC subjects and the S2 equation for NC subjects. To decide between

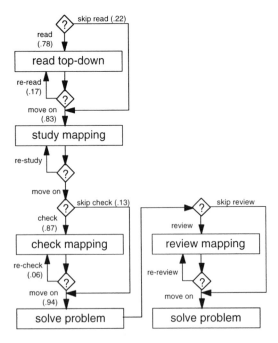

FIG. 10.6. Main control flow graph for the physics model. The graph on the left illustrates the control flow for the initial problem, and the graph on the right represents the flow for subsequent problems. Percentages in parentheses indicate statically computable frequencies for their respective paths.

reading top-down and skipping ahead, the model has two productions that compete through conflict resolution. If the model opts to read top-down, this subgoal is pushed onto the goal stack. For PC subjects, reading top-down involves simply reading the SP quantities and values in order. For NC subjects, reading top-down involves reading SP and S1.

The second stage, study mapping, requires inferring the quantity equation. The PC terminal model uses S1 to infer the quantity equation. The model performs a different action for each S1 symbol type (variable, constant, or operator). For each S1 variable, the model scans TP for the quantity that begins with the variable letter.[5] It then creates a knowledge chunk that stores the quantity name along with its position within the equation. For each S1 constant, the model similarly scans TP, but finds no quantity with the same first letter. Thus it assumes that the letter is a constant and stores the constant along with its position. For each S1 operator, the model simply stores the operator with its position. In contrast to the PC terminal model, the NC terminal model focuses on S2 and SP to infer the quantity equation. For each S2 value, the model finds the value in SP and clicks on its covered block, exposing the corresponding SP quantity. Constants and operators are immediately recognized, and all three types are again stored with their position.

The study-mapping stage thus uses either S1 or SP and S2 to build a declarative representation of the quantity equation, of which each element (quantity, constant, or operator) is associated with its position in the equation. The first component of this declarative representation is the EQUATION chunk, which acts as a tag for the current type of problem being studied. For instance, for inductance problems with the quantity equation $L = number*flux/current$, we have the following EQUATION chunk:

Inductance-Equation
    isa   EQUATION
    type   Inductance

Each element of the quantity equation is then represented as an EQUATION-SYMBOL chunk that contains its equation tag, type (quantity or constant), position, and value. For example, the third and fourth positions of the preceding quantity equation would be represented by the following chunks:

---

[5]We could ask why subjects would scan TP for the quantity names, rather than SP. Because the SP quantity names are covered by blocks, searching them would take more time, and thus searching TP is more efficient. The reference paths for PC subjects exhibit little bouncing between S1 and SP, supporting these conclusions.

Equation-Symbol-3
    isa   EQUATION-SYMBOL
    equation   Inductance-Equation
    type   Quantity
    position   Three
    value   Flux

Equation-Symbol-4
    isa   EQUATION-SYMBOL
    equation   Inductance-Equation
    type   Constant
    position   Four
    value   /

Note that a value of Constant in the type slot can represent operators, integers, or constant variables, all of which are simply typed out at response time with no additional processing. This representation is very similar to the chunk representation for serial lists in Chapter 7. It is one instance of the convergence that is occurring in representation for different ACT–R models.

After the model studies the equation, it must decide whether to stop studying or to review. If the equation can be readily retrieved, the model advances to the checking stage and studying terminates. Otherwise, the model reviews (or restudies) the equation. Base-level learning (see Base-Level Learning Equation 4.1) controls how easily the quantity equation can be retrieved; as the equation is reviewed, its activation increases steadily, facilitating retrieval on the next attempt. Thus more reviews make it more likely that the model can recall the equation and move on.

The third stage, check mapping, allows the models to check the quantity equation created in the study stage. Because NC subjects can use only the S2 equation to solve the problem correctly, only PC subjects can actually check their equations. As before, the model contains two competing productions, one for checking and one for skipping the check. To check, the PC model goes through the same steps as the NC model does for studying, bouncing between S2 and SP. By definition in the PC case, the check will never fail, so after the check the model simply continues to the next stage. We modify this check stage later when we merge the terminal models into a single learning model.

The fourth stage, solve problem, where the terminal models solve the current test problem, is relatively straightforward. The model traverses the mental representation of the quantity equation, beginning with the first symbol. If the symbol is a quantity, the model searches TP for that quantity, clicks on its corresponding value, and types the value. If the symbol is an operator, the model simply types it in. Finally, when the model has traversed the entire equation, it clicks on the lower right button to indicate that it has finished with the problem. For subsequent problems, the model enters a review-mapping stage in which the quantity equation is reviewed until it can be readily retrieved (just as in the study stage). When this review finishes, the model shifts back to the solve-problem stage to enter the solution.

The stage descriptions just given refer to many subprocesses, such as scanning the sample problem for a particular value or searching the test problem for a quantity. Each of these processes is implemented by a separate subgoal and a set of production rules. In this sense, the models are rather low-level, because they describe what the model is "looking at" during all stages of the analogy process. The leaf subprocesses are primarily visual- or motor-related, such as clicking on a block or typing in a number. The model executes these visual and motor actions via the ACT–R visual interface (see Chapter 5). The model can also be made to produce a trace that can be compared directly with experimental results, or even run through the experiment program in simulation mode.

Parameter Setting

At this point, we have provided a broad overview of the models at the symbolic level. However, we still need to define the subsymbolic, real-valued parameters associated with chunks and productions. Important parameters for the performance of the model are the levels of activation of the chunks encoding the quantity equation. These activations were not estimated but determined by the base-level learning model, which in turn depends on the default setting of the activation and decay parameters. For productions, we used the default settings[6] for all parameters except the a and r parameters for certain conflicting productions.

We set all productions to have the standard ACT–R default effort time of 50 msec. In setting the latencies for the visual and motor actions, we found that we could work with very approximate assumptions. Moving the mouse a short distance (less than 50 pixels on the Macintosh screen) has a latency of 300 msec, whereas long movements require an additional 500 msec. To model the adjustment to a new screen when starting a trial, the initial reading for a new screen takes 2 sec. Reading the SP quantities takes 1 sec, due to the difficulty of reading partial sentences as opposed to simple numbers and letters. Finally, typing a value requires 1 sec, which includes time needed for the subject's hand to move from the mouse to the keyboard.[7]

---

[6]The default settings for these parameters are strength $= 0$, $a = .05$, $b = 1$, $q = 1$, and $r = 1$.

[7]This typing speed is slower than continuous typing speed, but justifiably, because subjects are entering numbers and operators rather than words in text.

We manipulated the a and r parameters in order to adjust conflict resolution between productions in the cases where we design the model to have competing productions. Recall that the a parameter denotes the estimated effort spent executing the production (Cost of Goal Equation 3.3) and the r parameter determines the production's estimated probability of success (Probability of Goal Equation 3.2). Both parameters in turn help determine the expected gain of the production rule (Expected Gain Equation 3.1). The probability of selecting a production during conflict resolution is a function of its expected gain (Conflict Resolution Equation 3.4). For most productions, setting the production parameters is straightforward, merely reflecting which rule we prefer over others. However, the a and r parameters for certain crucial decision points need to be estimated using empirical data. The points where we estimated these parameters are the decision points shown in Fig. 10.6. These decision points generally represent a trade-off between further work in executing a subgoal (e.g., checking the equation) versus the probability of failure if the subgoal is not executed (e.g., not noticing the incorrectness of the variables when skipping the check). Fitting the model to the data was essentially a hill-climbing search manipulating these crucial parameters. We performed the search manually; that is, we ran several simulations, examined the output, and adjusted the parameters accordingly. We repeated this process until the parameters produced satisfactory results.

Stating the actual values of the estimated a and r parameters would not be highly illustrative, because it is not obvious how they correspond to the probabilities of firing the respective productions.[8] However, we can actually derive the expected probabilities using the parameters and the amount of expected-gain noise using the Conflict Resolution Equation 3.4. Thus, we can compute the probability of choosing each path in the general control flow graph. There is one caveat, however: The likelihood of firing a production that retrieves the studied (quantity) equation depends not just on its being selected during conflict resolution, but also on retrieval of the quantity equation. This dependence means we cannot statically compute the probabilities for these paths. The control flow graph in Fig. 10.6 includes probabilities for all statically computable paths. The probabilities displayed in the figure are intuitively reasonable.

From our presentation, one might get the impression that so many parameters could easily fit almost any data set. This is far from true. Although the two terminal models (for the PC and NC conditions) are indeed distinct models, they actually differ in only a few productions. Specifically, we vary only the specific subgoals pushed for the read top-down, study-mapping, check-mapping, and review-mapping productions; all other

---

[8]The values of these and other parameters are available with the Web models.

productions, and all continuous parameters, are kept the same across models. This high degree of overlap allows us to combine the models into one learning model, as we show later. More importantly, though, the overlap manifests the real predictive power behind these models. It highly constrains the predictions of one terminal model given the parameters of the other. Thus, if both models provide good fits to their respective data sets, we have strong evidence to support our underlying theory.

Declarative Terminal Model Results

Let us now examine the predictions and behavior of the terminal models in comparison with the final set data. Given the two models, we can run repeated simulations that model individual subjects performing the final set of five problems. To compare the models' results with the experimental data, we ran 20 simulations for each model and examined the resulting traces.[9] Overall, the models produced good fits to many aspects of the data.

We first compare the total latencies to complete each problem, for both the models and subjects. Figure 10.5 includes the models' predictions (dashed lines) with the experimental data (solid lines) for the PC and NC conditions. Both models' latency curves fit their respective data nicely. Most of the analogizing is completed in the first problem, with the latencies flattening out quickly in later problems. The fit is especially good considering our rigid demand that every production's action time be set at the ACT–R default of 50 msec (with the exception of the visual and motor actions).

Regarding the visual data, Table 10.2 shows the predicted (parenthesized) and observed (unparenthesized) number of references per item. Again, the models capture many of the nuances of the data. For example, recall that NC subjects scanned S1 almost half as much as S2, even though the S1 variables were misleading. The NC model reproduces this phenomenon in the read top-down stage (Fig. 10.6), predicting that many subjects read S1 on the scan from the top of the screen down to the relevant equation for analogizing (S2 for the NC condition). Also, the PC model explains why PC subjects referred to the S2 equation, namely, to check that their inferences from the S1 equation are correct.

Table 10.3 shows the empirical data and model predictions for reference times across the two experimental conditions. The model captures several aspects of the data, including the fact that latencies vary little across conditions. The high latency for reading SP quantities stems from a higher

---

[9]Terminal model simulations were run with base-level learning enabled (decay rate of 0.5), strength learning disabled, an expected gain noise variance of 0.2 ($t = .247$), and an activation noise variance of 0.1 ($t = .174$)—see discussion of Conflict Resolution Equation 3.4 in Chapter 3.

production latency for reading sentences rather than single words or symbols. The models also predict that reference latencies for S1 variables and S2 values are significantly longer than those for S1 or S2 operators. The extra time spent arises from the visual scans necessary for variables and values; for instance, after reading a value, the model must scan SP for that value. On the whole, the models account for much of the time spent looking at and processing the items in the various visual fields.

The reference paths for the experimental data revealed some variability in the strategies of analogy during the task. Because of ACT–R's activation and expected gain noise, the models are able to account for this variability. Although the models do not exhibit as much variability as the subjects, they are able to produce some of the important facets of these differences. Tables 10.5a and 10.5b illustrate the reference paths for the 20 simulation runs for each model. For both models, we see varying amounts of studying and reviewing across simulations. Also, many of the simulations begin by reading SP, just as many subjects did. We can observe several reviews of the equation in later problems, although the reviews are less frequent than in the empirical data. Interestingly, only one simulation (MNC9) executed the most efficient strategy; recall that of our 38 subjects, only 2 (PC1 and NC16) did the same. Thus the models not only reproduce the latency and visual data present in the experiment, but also much of the qualitative variability in the detail of subjects' scanning behavior.

The Declarative Learning Model

We have seen how the PC and NC terminal models operate to fit the final set data. However, there is still the question of how these terminal models might evolve. We would like for the models to arise from a single initial model, which would itself evolve into one of the terminal models. That is, we desire a learning model that runs on the entire task (i.e., all eight sets) and, depending on the problems presented to the model, would shift to either the solve-by-variable strategy (the PC terminal model) or the solve-by-value strategy (the NC terminal model).

Because the terminal models were designed with the learning model in mind, merging them is fairly straightforward. The learning model retains a single chunk that describes the current strategy to utilize, either solve-by-variable or solve-by-value. The few productions that differ between the terminal models are modified to retrieve this chunk and determine the current strategy. If the strategy dictates to solve by variable, the productions push the subgoals corresponding to the PC terminal model; otherwise, they push the subgoals corresponding to the NC terminal model. Initially, the strategy chunk is set to solve by variable. As the model simulates the task, it will frequently check the S2 values to ensure that they correspond to the

Table 10.5
Terminal Model Reference Paths

a. PC Terminal Model

	Problem 1	Problem 2	Problem 3	Problem	Problem 5
MPC1	SP S1 S1 (TP TS)	(TP TS)	(TP TS)	(TP TS)	(TP TS)
MPC2	SP S1 S1 S1 S1 (SP S2) (TP TS	(TP TS)	(TP TS)	(TP TS)	(TP TS)
MPC3	SP S1 (SP S2) (TP TS)	(TP TS)	(TP TS)	(TP TS)	(TP TS)
MPC4	SP S1 S1 (SP S2) (TP TS)	(TP TS)	(TP TS)	(TP TS)	(TP TS)
MPC5	SP SP S1 (SP S2) (TP TS)	(TP TS)	(TP TS)	S1 (TP TS)	(TP TS)
MPC6	SP S1 S1 S1 S1 S1 (TP TS)	(TP TS)	(TP TS)	(TP TS)	(TP TS)
MPC7	SP S1 S1 (SP S2) (TP TS)	(TP TS)	S1 (TP TS)	(TP TS)	(TP TS)
MPC8	S1 (SP S2) (TP TS)	(TP TS)	(TP TS)	(TP TS)	(TP TS)
MPC9	S1 S1 (SP S2) (TP TS)	(TP TS)	(TP TS)	(TP TS)	(TP TS)
MPC10	SP S1 S1 (SP S2) (TP TS)	(TP TS)	(TP TS)	(TP TS)	(TP TS)
MPC11	SP S1 S1 S1 (SP S2) (TP TS)	(TP TS)	(TP TS)	(TP TS)	(TP TS)
MPC12	SP SP S1 (SP S2) (TP TS)	(TP TS)	(TP TS)	(TP TS)	(TP TS)
MPC13	SP S1 (SP S2) (TP TS)	(TP TS)	(TP TS)	(TP TS)	(TP TS)
MPC14	SP S1 S1 S1 S1 S1 (SP S2) (TP TS)	(TP TS)	(TP TS)	(TP TS)	(TP TS)
MPC15	SP S1 (SP S2) (TP TS)	(TP TS)	(TP TS)	(TP TS)	(TP TS)
MPC16	SP S1 (SP S2) (TP TS)	(TP TS)	(TP TS)	S1 (TP TS)	(TP TS)
MPC17	SP S1 S1 (TP TS)	(TP TS)	(TP TS)	(TP TS)	(TP TS)
MPC18	S1 (SP S2) (TP TS)	(TP TS)	(TP TS)	(TP TS)	(TP TS)
MPC19	SP S1 S1 (SP S2) (TP TS)	(TP TS)	(TP TS)	(TP TS)	(TP TS)
MPC20	S1 S1 S1 S1 (SP S2) (TP TS)	(TP TS)	(TP TS)	(TP TS)	(TP TS)

b. NC Terminal Model

	Problem 1	Problem 2	Problem 3	Problem 4	Problem 5
MNC1	(SP S2) (SP S2)	(TP TS)	(TP TS)	(TP TS)	(TP TS)
MNC2	SP S1 SP S1 (SP S2) (TP TS)	(TP TS)	(TP TS)	(TP TS)	(TP TS)
MNC3	SP S1 SP S1 (SP S2) (SP S2) (SP S2) (TP TS)	(TP TS)	(TP TS)	(TP TS)	(TP TS)
MNC4	SP S1 (SP S2) (TP TS)	(TP TS)	(TP TS)	(TP TS)	(TP TS)
MNC5	(SP S2) (SP S2) (SP S2) (SP S2) (SP S2) (TP TS)	(TP TS)	(TP TS)	(TP TS)	(TP TS)
MNC6	SP S1 (SP S2) (SP S2) (SP S2) (TP TS)	(TP TS)	(TP TS)	(TP TS)	(TP TS)
MNC7	SP S1 (SP S2) (TP TS)	(TP TS)	(TP TS)	(TP TS)	(TP TS)
MNC8	SP S1 (SP S2) (SP S2) (TP TS)	(TP TS)	(TP TS)	(TP TS)	(TP TS)
MNC9	(SP S2) (TP TS)	(TP TS)	(TP TS)	(TP TS)	(TP TS)
MNC10	(SP S2) (SP S2) (SP S2) (TP TS)	(TP TS)	(TP TS)	(TP TS)	(TP TS)
MNC11	(SP S2) (TP TS)	(TP TS)	(SP S2) (TP TS)	(TP TS)	(TP TS)
MNC12	SP S1 (SP S2) (TP TS)	(TP TS)	(TP TS)	(TP TS)	(TP TS)
MNC13	SP S1 (SP S2) (TP TS)	(TP TS)	(TP TS)	(TP TS)	(TP TS)
MNC14	SP S1 (SP S2) (SP S2) (SP S2) (TP TS)	(TP TS)	(TP TS)	(TP TS)	(TP TS)
MNC15	SP S1 (SP S2) (SP S2) (SP S2) (TP TS)	(TP TS)	(TP TS)	(TP TS)	(TP TS)
MNC16	SP S1 (SP S2) (TP TS)	(TP TS)	(TP TS)	(TP TS)	(TP TS)
MNC17	(SP S2) (SP S2) (TP TS)	(TP TS)	(TP TS)	(TP TS)	(TP TS)
MNC18	SP S1 (SP S2) (SP S2) (TP TS)	(TP TS)	(TP TS)	(TP TS)	(TP TS)
MNC19	SP S1 (SP S2) (SP S2) (SP S2) (SP S2) (SP S2) (TP TS)	(TP TS)	(TP TS)	(TP TS)	(TP TS)
MNC20	SP S1 (SP S2) (TP TS)	(TP TS)	(TP TS)	(TP TS)	(SP S2) (TP TS)

S1 variables. In the PC condition, the variables and values always correspond, so the learning model continues to use the solve-by-variable strategy.
In the NC condition, the check detects a discrepancy with a probability of
.5. The model should sometimes fail to detect the discrepancy during a
check because subjects sometimes performed the sequence of clicks for a
check but apparently did not notice the discrepancy in variable namings;
when the discrepancy is discovered, the model switches to the solve-by-
value strategy. The learning model thus adjusts to the condition in which
the simulation is run, shifting in the NC condition from the solve-by-variable to the solve-by-value strategy.

The other form of learning that takes place over the course of the
problems is the strengthening of the productions that are responsible for
creating and applying quantity equations. We thus enable strength learning
in the learning model simulations, as defined by the Production Strength
Equation 4.4. This learning increases the production strength for frequently
fired productions, resulting in lower firing latencies.

We now present the results of 10 learning model simulations of the entire
task in each condition.[10] The learning model correctness results are included
in Fig. 10.3. Comparing the model's predictions (dashed lines) with the
empirical data (solid lines), we see that the model captures several aspects of
subjects' behavior. The PC model, like PC subjects, performs at ceiling. This
behavior arises from the fact that the learning model always tries initially to
solve by variable, which is the correct approach in the PC condition. In the
NC condition, the model requires some number of trials before it notices the
discrepancy between the sample solution variables and values; recall that
subjects exhibited similar epiphanies. The NC error curve then essentially
maps out when the model simulations reached their epiphanies.

Figure 10.4 shows the average set latencies for the model (dashed lines)
and the experiment (solid lines). We see that the learning model nicely
reproduces the shape of our empirical data—namely, the sets involving more
complex problems require more time to complete. In the three initial sets
(which have identical complexities), we observe a steady decrease in latency,
due primarily to the strengthening of relevant productions. Also, the model
requires slightly more time in the NC condition than in the PC condition,
because the NC times include an overhead for epiphanies that occur during
the sets.

Generally, the learning model captures the important aspects of the data.
Nonetheless, we can point to two incompletenesses of the model. First, the

---

[10]As with the terminal model, the learning model simulations were run with base-level
learning enabled (decay rate of 0.5), strength learning enabled (decay rate of 0.5), an
expected gain noise variance of 0.2 (t = .247), and an activation noise variance of 0.1 (t =
.179).

model does not account for the acquisition of productions specific to the task. Second, there may be other strategies that subjects utilize when first attempting the task. Our model assumes that subjects begin with the solve-by-variable strategy, and sometimes (i.e., in the NC condition) shift to the solve-by-value strategy. It is possible, though, that subjects initially use a different strategy, perhaps a hybrid of solve-by-variable and solve-by-value or perhaps an altogether different approach.

PROCEDURAL MODEL
FOR THE PHYSICS TASK

The previous section described how the declarative model learns schematic knowledge for the physics task as declarative chunks that represent the quantity equation. The schematic knowledge was then used by interpretive productions to perform the task. Rather than involving this indirect process of interpretation, an alternative approach would acquire new productions that directly apply schematic knowledge to solve problems in the domain. This section describes a procedural model for the physics task that implements this direct approach. The procedural model learns schematic productions that represent the quantity equation through production compilation. In essence, there is a one-to-one correspondence between schematic chunks in the declarative model and schematic productions in this model. The declarative and procedural models have few differences, both in the models themselves and in their simulation predictions. The similarity between these models is one token of what is increasingly becoming an issue in the ACT–R community—when to represent knowledge declaratively and when to represent knowledge procedurally.

Before turning to the actual procedural model, we digress briefly to evaluate one idea that initially may seem reasonable but fails to capture low-level subject behavior. This idea is that we learn single production rules that solve each problem in one instantiation. We could learn such rules if we represent the entire sample problem as a single chunk with values for each quantity and the sample solution as a single chunk with the appropriate answer values and operators. We could then form a dependency with a blank solution chunk as the goal, the sample solution chunk as the modified goal, and the sample problem as the given constraint. Given this dependency, production compilation would form a single production that can solve any new problem of that equation type. Such a model would have been typical of the grain size of modeling used in previous versions of ACT–R, such as ACT–R 2.0 (Anderson, 1993). However, as a model of the information processing of actual subjects, the model is woefully inadequate: Only a single production rule is created and executed in one atomic step. The model ignores the process by which subjects inspect the problem, inspect the equation, build up a representation of the two, and relate them. There is no representation of how subgoals must be set to execute the individual steps. Clearly subjects take a much more piecemeal approach to analogy, and the advantage of the new ACT–R theory of analogy in this chapter is that it captures this piecemeal approach.

The Procedural Learning Model

The procedural model we now describe is more in keeping with the current "atoms of thought" approach by having ACT–R learn smaller productions that map and apply each of the equation symbols separately. In fact, the procedural model is identical to the declarative model with one modification: With repeated practice of a particular equation, subjects no longer retrieve the declarative representation of the quantity equation but rather "just do it" by means of productions that step through the solution symbol by symbol. Instead of creating a declarative representation for each equation symbol that encodes its position in a particular equation, the model creates a declarative dependency that encodes the action(s) taken for that symbol. When this dependency is pushed onto the goal stack and subsequently popped, the production compilation mechanism uses the dependency to create a specific production for that symbol. With further study of that symbol, the production is strengthened through repeated production compilation and strength learning.

The actual productions created during production compilation act on the SOLVE-PROBLEM subgoal, which signifies the intention to determine and type out the solution. The productions have one of two forms depending on the type of equation symbol needed, that is, whether the symbol represents a quantity whose value must be determined or a constant that can be immediately typed. For quantities, the new production would resemble the following example:

```
Solve-Problem-3
  =goal>
    isa          SOLVE-PROBLEM
    equation     Inductance-Equation
    position     Third
  ==>
  =subgoal>
    isa          FIND-TEST-PROBLEM-VALUE
    quantity     Flux
    result       =result
  =subgoal1>
    isa          TYPE-SYMBOL
    symbol       =result
```

```
=goal>
  position    Fourth
!push! =subgoal1
!push! =subgoal
```

The production first matches the SOLVE-PROBLEM subgoal for the current equation and the third position. It then sets two subgoals to find the value of the quantity Flux in the test problem and to type the resulting value. The goal is then reset to continue solving the problem at the fourth position. For constants (integers, operators, and constant variables), the new production would resemble this example:

Solve-Problem-4
```
=goal>
  isa         SOLVE-PROBLEM
  equation    Inductance-Equation
  position    Fourth
==>
=subgoal>
  isa         TYPE-SYMBOL
  symbol      /
=goal
  position    Fifth
!push! =subgoal
```

Here the production matches the equation in the fourth position, sets a subgoal to type the symbol /, and resets the goal to continue to the fifth position.

Thus, we now have a procedural model that closely resembles the declarative model, except we have a shift from declarative knowledge of the equation symbols to a proceduralized version of this knowledge. The only differences from the declarative model are the addition of two productions to create each type of dependency (quantity and constant), slight changes to existing productions to subgoal to these productions, and the removal of the existing interpretive SOLVE-PROBLEM productions, because the necessary productions are generated from the appropriate dependencies. All other productions and parameter settings are identical across the two models.

Because the procedural model so closely resembles the declarative model, it may not be surprising to discover that they produce almost identical predictions, modulo the variability inherent in both models. The two models are almost indistinguishable in terms of their fits to set latencies and correctness, problem latencies, area references per area, and area reference times. Thus, we omit the specifics of these simulation results, because examining them in detail would provide little insight into the model. Instead, we proceed to a more qualitative evaluation of the two models.

Evaluating the Declarative and Procedural Models

Of the two models, declarative and procedural, which better captures the nature of subject behavior in the physics task? The quantitative fits of the two models reveal little in the search for an answer to this question. We now give a brief qualitative evaluation of the models to help provide an answer. Because the models are similar in so many respects, we focus our discussion on two issues: the representation of schematic knowledge, and the model's decisions about when to review this knowledge.

Because the declarative and procedural models represent schematic knowledge in different ways, one interesting aspect of the models is how well each lives up to the "atoms of thought" goal in this book. In the creation of schemata, the declarative model produces equation symbol chunks that represent each item in the quantity equation. The chunks are created in a straightforward manner, with the creating productions and the chunks themselves being small and psychologically reasonable. The procedural model produces dependencies that, through production compilation, are transformed into appropriate production rules. The compiled production rules, like the chunks in the declarative model, are atomic and psychologically plausible. To ensure that the productions that create the dependencies are also atomic, the procedural model includes several productions that build up the dependency incrementally. The model unfortunately requires the use of lists in its dependencies, a problem that seems to us more rooted in the syntax of the production compilation mechanism than in this particular model. With this possible exception, both models seem equally plausible and consistent with ACT–R 4.0's "atoms of thought" principle.

Another interesting aspect of the two models is how and when the models decide to review previously studied schematic knowledge. At the highest level, both models decide to review the equation in the same way: The model attempts to retrieve the equation chunk to solve the problem, and if the chunk cannot be retrieved, the model reviews the sample problem and solution to strengthen the studied schemata. This flow of control seems reasonable in that the decision to review is based on whether studied knowledge can be recalled. However, retrieval of the equation chunk does not guarantee that the problem can be solved: The declarative model must still retrieve an EQUATION-SYMBOL chunk for each equation position, and the procedural model must have SOLVE-PROBLEM productions of sufficient strength to fire. Thus, both models rely solely on the equation chunk as an indicator of when to review and ignore the possibility of failure in using lower level schematic knowledge (i.e., equation-symbol chunks or solve-problem productions). As it turns out, such a failure never occurs in simulation, but this possibility does raise the issue of what subjects do when failures occur. Although the empirical evidence shows that subjects usually review the entire equation, surely they have more sophisticated methods of dealing with failure to use individual schemata components and reviewing just those components. The declarative and procedural models thus capture overall reviewing behavior for the entire equation but cannot account for reviewing behavior for components of the equation.

Overall, this brief evaluation sheds little light on which model better captures subject performance in the physics task. The models, through declarative learning of schematic chunks and procedural learning of schematic productions, seem to capture the quantitative and qualitative aspects of the task equally well. Our own intuition is that subjects are using a declarative representation for the five problems they solve for each physics equation. However, with enough practice they would transition to a procedural representation. Further empirical work would be needed to help establish whether our intuitions about such a declarative-to-procedural transition for this task are correct. In other tasks (Anderson, Fincham, & Douglass, 1997), we showed evidence for this sort of transition with extended practice.

The juxtaposition of both a procedural and a declarative model of knowledge compilation reflects the now complete separation in ACT–R of issues of analogy from issues of production formation. We see that we can equally model analogy formation with or without creating production rules.

GENERAL ISSUES IN ANALOGY

In this section, we address issues about analogy that go beyond the physics example. First, we show that the basic ideas apply to a different experimental paradigm where detailed latency data were collected. Second, we examine the relationship between this theory of analogy and other theories of analogy in the literature.

Generalizing the Physics Model:
The People-Piece Model

We have seen how an ACT–R model can capture many aspects of the physics task. Nevertheless, we might reasonably question how useful the model is when considering the broader picture of problem solving by analogy. Can we generalize the physics model to make predictions about other analogical tasks? More generally, can production-rule models for specific analogical tasks assist in modeling similar tasks? The answer is yes, and centers on our earlier claim that models for similar analogical tasks share common production rules that implement analogy. We now provide evidence for this claim by presenting a rule model for a similar analogical task, where the model uses specific productions taken from the physics model.

Sternberg (1977) used a "people-piece" analogy task and, as we did, systematically investigated the latency structure of analogy formation. Sternberg presented subjects with picture analogies of the form A:B::C:D. The elements of the analogy were drawings of people varying four binary attributes: sex (male or female), color (blue or red), height (short or tall), and girth (fat or thin). Sternberg asked subjects to respond whether the analogy was true or false. Figure 10.7 shows a sample correct people-piece problem where the A–B and C–D pairs differ in sex and color and the A–C and B–D pairs differ in height. Sternberg's data showed that subject response latencies increased as elements A and B differed by more attributes; the data showed a similar effect for differences between A and C. The solid lines in Fig. 10.8 graph Sternberg's results for differences of one and two attributes for both the A–B and A–C pairs. The data thus suggest that subjects consider both A–B and A–C mappings, and take more time as these mappings become more complex.

We can further characterize subject behavior in the people-piece task by considering the process models of Sternberg (1977) and Grudin (1980). Sternberg provided four distinct process models for solving people-piece analogies. Although the models differ in specifics, each requires encoding of the elements, mapping between source and target elements, and application of the mapping to derive a solution. Sternberg proposed that subjects map both A to B and A to C during the process. Grudin suggested a change

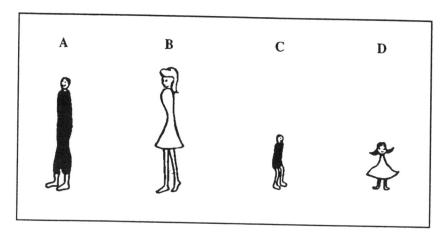

FIG. 10.7. Sample people-piece problem from Sternberg (1977). The problem is a correct analogy in which the A–B and C–D pairs differ in sex and color and the A–C and B–D pairs differ in height.

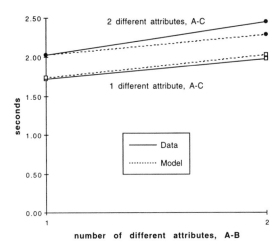

FIG. 10.8. People-piece data and model predictions. The solid lines show the empirical data from Sternberg (1977) for one and two attribute changes from A to B and A to C. The dashed lines show the people-piece model predictions.

to Sternberg's model: Subjects map *either* A to B *or* A to C, but do not infer both mappings. We combine the ideas of both researchers into our process model for the people-piece task. Our process model first decides to execute one of two strategies, either the one using the A–B mapping or the one using the A–C mapping. If the model chooses to use the A–B strategy, it runs through the following sequence of steps: Encode A and B, infer the A–B mapping, encode C and D, apply the mapping to C to create D′, compare D and D′ for equality, and respond. If the model chooses the A–C strategy, it follows the same steps with B and C switched.

We can frame this process model within the general strategy for the physics task (Fig. 10.6). Our model for this task induces an attribute mapping, which serves the same role as the quantity equation in the physics experiment. The study-mapping stage of the physics model handles the encoding of the sample and the formation of the mapping. Similarly for the people-piece model, we bundle the encoding and mapping of A and B (or C) into a study-mapping stage. The solve-problem stage of the physics model corresponds to the application of the mapping. For the people-piece model, the solve-problem stage similarly involves the application of the A–B or A–C mapping. The read top-down and check-equation stages in the physics model have no analog in the people-piece model, so they are omitted. Thus, the two models share the study-mapping and solve-problem stages.

The production-rule specification for the people-piece process model utilizes this overlap between models. The common stages allow us to borrow productions from the physics model and insert them directly into the people-piece model. Specifically, the people-piece model uses the productions in the physics model that implement the study-mapping and solve-problem stages in Fig. 10.6. We also insert productions that skip over the read top-down and check-equation stages, because they are not applicable here. Other productions are also added to implement subprocesses specific to the people-piece task. Before analogizing, the rule model decides (by choosing among competing productions in conflict resolution) whether to use the A–B or A–C strategy. It encodes people-piece drawings as chunks with four slots for each of the binary attributes. The model handles mapping by examining the four attributes sequentially and creating a declarative linked list of attribute mapping chunks. Each mapping chunk indicates a single attribute, which changes from source to target. To apply this attribute mapping, the model first copies the source person chunk into a target person chunk. It then runs through the list of mapping chunks and changes each mapped attribute. The model finally compares the target chunk to the solution chunk and responds true or false.

We set production parameters for the people-piece model by following the basic assumptions of the physics model. Productions that were copied from the physics model maintained similar parameter settings, although the a and r parameters changed to more accurately reflect the task at hand. For other productions, action times were again set at the ACT–R default of 50 msec. The only crucial parameters are those for the competing productions that choose the A–B or A–C strategy; in that case, the r parameters were given identical values so that the model would choose each with equal likelihood. We also increased the productions' strength parameters to model repeated trials, because subjects solved over 1,000 people-piece analogies in the original Sternberg task; we estimated these strengths to have a value of 3.5.

Figure 10.8 includes the predictions of the model averaged from 10 simulations (dashed lines) along with Sternberg's empirical data (solid lines). The model provides an excellent fit to the data. The model predicts increasing latencies as the number of differing attributes between A and B (or C) increases. This behavior arises from both the mapping and application stages. In the mapping stage, different attributes call for several extra productions that handle the creation of a new mapping chunk. In the application stage, each attribute that must be mapped requires several additional production firings to change values in the target person chunk. Because the model chooses the A–B and A–C strategies with equal likelihood, the effects are the same for attribute changes in the A–B and A–C pairs.

We have thus shown that it is possible to transfer the implementations of analogical skills between models for different analogical tasks. The physics and people-piece models share several analogy productions, and also incorporate domain-specific knowledge relevant to the particular task. Both models also illustrate how production-rule models can account for multiple strategies of analogy: The physics model can use either a solve-by-variable or solve-by-value strategy, and the people-piece model can choose between the A–B and A–C strategies. Presumably, if one of the A–B or A–C strategies proved more effective (which is not the case in Sternberg's experiment), the people-piece model could incorporate learning of that strategy similar to the learning in the physics model.

Related Theories of Analogy

In understanding how ACT–R's theory of analogy relates to other theories of analogy, it is important to realize that ACT–R addresses the steps of analogy at a much finer grain size than most theories. As such ACT–R is often not in contradiction with other theories and often could actually implement these theories. The one strong assumption it makes in contradiction with a number of theories is that the steps of mapping occur serially in time. Several other theories, including the analogy mechanism in ACT–R 2.0, assume that mappings are computed in parallel. However, in research that has inspected the temporal structure of the analogy, such as ours or Sternberg's, the evidence seems strong that the mapping is indeed computed serially, step by step over time.

Although ACT–R addresses analogy at a finer grain size, there are other senses in which the ACT–R account is not as complete as these theories. One issue that arises is the trade-off between the generality of the model and the specificity of its predictions. Although most theories of analogy operate over many domains, our theory posits distinct but similar models for each domain, which overlap usually in only the high-level productions. Although certain ideas and productions carry over directly from existing models, some domain-specific skills must be added for models in any particular new domain. On one hand, this has the disadvantage of a loss of generality, because each model operates over a specific domain; on the other hand, the inclusion of some domain-specific skills seems more accurate characterization of analogy in many contexts and allows us to make finer grained predictions to compare to empirical data. Another issue on which our model clearly needs further elaboration concerns the mapping process. We assume that the problem involves a fixed number of roles (quantities in the physics task or attributes in the people-piece task) and the system simply determines what fills these roles in the current problem. A number of existing theories have addressed the question of what happens when more complex mapping relationships are required, and we review some of these theories here.

The mapping process is the heart of Gentner's (1983) structure-mapping theory of analogy. Gentner proposed three principles for inferring mappings between a source and target analog: discard attributes of objects, preserve relations between objects, and prefer systems of relations (i.e., systematicity; see also Gentner & Toupin, 1986). Using these principles, analogy then forms a mapping between structures expressed in a predicate language comprising relations and objects. Gentner's theory does not contradict the ACT–R account of analogy; in fact, it is quite feasible that an ACT–R model could implement such a theory. To build a production-rule model of the theory, we would need to represent the relevant concepts as hierarchical structures of declarative chunks. The model would contain production rules that can traverse such a structure and build up a representation of a mapping. These rules would implement Gentner's three principles and would produce a structure mapping from source to target. Such a production-rule model would decompose analogy into a number of discrete steps rather than treating it as a single act. As such, it would be possible to predict observables like the sequence of visual scanning actions that subjects would make in performing the analogy. Decomposing the overall process into a number of rules would also enable us to make predictions about how the analogy process would improve with practice. Such predictions could be made by ACT–R's strength learning mechanism, as we have seen with respect to the physics learning model in Fig. 10.4.

The structure-mapping theory has been the foundation for several computational models of analogy, such as SME (Falkenhainer et al., 1989) and IAM (Keane et al., 1994). We believe that the empirical support for such models could be strengthened in at least two ways. First, the empirical support is based on comparisons using metrics that correspond only indirectly with empirical data; for instance, Keane et al. compared subject latencies to the number of alternative mappings computed by the model. Although the comparison works adequately in this context, such metrics may not generalize well to other theories and make it difficult to evaluate the models with real data. Second, those models that address working memory constraints (such as IAM) do not actually incorporate a dedicated limited-capacity working memory, again complicating evaluation of their ability to handle such constraints. Production-system architectures can help address such problems. Because architectures like ACT–R have a limited-capacity memory built into the system, any analogy model developed in the architecture must necessarily deal with working memory constraints. Also, production-system models produce traces that can be directly compared with empirical evidence, avoiding the problem of determining suitable metrics for comparison.

Like the mechanisms just described, Holyoak and Thagard's (1989a) ACME model considers analogy as the creation of mappings between structures, but takes a slightly different approach. ACME builds up a network of mapping propositions with excitatory and inhibitory connections, and uses constraint-satisfaction methods to arrive at a solution. Although some work has linked network-based systems to rule-based systems (Cho, Rosenbloom, & Dolan, 1991; Lebiere & Anderson, 1993), fitting ACME into a production rule framework seems awkward and certainly nontrivial. It is also the case that the parallel constraint-mapping process is fundamentally different than our serial mapping. We can discuss, however, how our framework addresses some of the same issues as ACME. Holyoak and Thagard emphasized three constraints that affect analogical behavior: structural, semantic, and pragmatic. Structural constraints state that the system can form correspondences between the objects and relations of the source and target analogs; the mappings are usually one-to-one. Semantic constraints add a similarity metric between objects and predicates that allow the system to prefer certain mappings over others. Finally, pragmatic constraints guarantee that analogy is relevant to the current context—that is, that the current goal directs the mapping process.

Production-rule models of analogy can implement each of these constraints. Structural constraints arise from the particular rules that implement the mapping process. These rules can map relations to relations and objects to objects; for instance, the physics model contains rules that find one-to-one correspondences between the symbols in the solution equation and the schematic quantity equation, mapping operators to operators and operands to operands. Semantic constraints fall out of the spreading activation process for facts in declarative memory. During rule matching, the source facts being considered help to activate similar target facts, thus facilitating retrieval of similar target objects and relations. Pragmatic constraints arise from the fact that we handle analogy within a general problem-solving framework. Within such a framework, all actions are purpose directed, taking into account the current goal and context. Thus production-rule systems are well suited to address all three constraints.

A recent entry into the field of analogical models, Hummel and Holyoak's (1997) LISA model, embodies arguably the most comprehensive theory of analogy to date. LISA implements a theory of both analogical access and mapping, which represents propositions as distributed patterns of activation and learns mappings through the process of dynamic binding. Like ACME, LISA's distributed nature makes it difficult for the model to be expressed as a production system. Nevertheless, LISA begins to address several of the problems we noted in earlier models by focusing closely on working memory constraints and by discussing (to a limited extent) implications of the LISA model for analogical processing at the algorithmic level. However, the empirical support for LISA still concentrates on the computational level of analogical processing with model-specific metrics for evaluation. Overall, we view LISA as a comprehensive model of analogy at the computational level and as a promising step toward understanding analogy at the algorithmic level. However, a transition to a more process-oriented theory like ACT–R would eventually be needed to account for the moment-by-moment computation of analogy.

It is important to emphasize two major differences between the ACT–R theory and related theories. First, all of the preceding models, with the exception of LISA, use a single deterministic mechanism to represent the analogical process. Therefore, as discussed earlier, these theories cannot predict variability in analogical strategies, nor can they predict adaptation of these strategies during learning. Second, the theories as presented are not incorporated into a more general processing system, although the current trend seems to indicate a move toward this incorporation (e.g., Gentner, 1989). Production-system models of analogy do not have these limitations, as evidenced in the physics and people-piece models.

CONCLUSIONS

This chapter has described the new ACT–R 4.0 view of analogy, namely, that analogy can be modeled by a standard production system without the need for a specialized analogy mechanism. ACT–R models of analogy share higher-level productions for general analogical processing but contain different lower-level productions for domain-specific skill knowledge. In contrast with most existing computational models, ACT–R models of analogy predict both the results and the intermediate steps of the analogical process, account for variability and learning of analogical strategies, and generate predictions that can be compared directly to empirical data without the need for model-dependent metrics. ACT–R thus provides an excellent theoretical framework for the development and exploration of models of analogical processing.

We view this study as having two major implications for future analogy research. First, our study has demonstrated how low-level data for analogical tasks can elucidate the step-by-step process of analogy. Given our now thorough understanding of analogy at the computational level, we should focus our attention on analogy at this algorithmic level. Second, our study has shown that models of analogy implemented in general problem-solving architectures can successfully account for analogical behavior at both the computational and algorithmic levels. We believe that modeling analogy within ACT–R and other general theories of cognition will prove to be a fruitful direction for future analogy research.

11

Scientific Discovery

Christian D. Schunn
John R. Anderson
Carnegie Mellon University

Overview

Earlier chapters demonstrated how ACT–R can do a good job of accounting for the microlevel of cognition. This emphasis on the lower level, however, raises the question of whether ACT–R can scale to very complex cognitive tasks—can ACT–R models of very complex tasks be developed at this microlevel of detail both in a reasonable amount of time and without being overwhelmed by microdetail? Moreover, does this microlevel bring any advantages or new insights to the modeling of very complex tasks?

As an existence proof that the new ACT–R can scale to very complex tasks, we present an ACT–R model of one of the most complex tasks that we know of: designing and interpreting experiments in psychology. We present no proof of the relative complexity of this task, but expect that most of the readers will agree, based on their own experiences, that scientific discovery is a very complex task.

In addition to providing another test of ACT–R, this chapter seeks to provide further understanding of scientific discovery behavior and expertise in general. Two particular questions are at the center of attention. First, how much of scientific discovery behavior can be understood by examining the microlevel processes? Second, what skills underlie expertise in scientific reasoning? Addressing these questions will involve a mixture of new empirical and modeling work. But before we present this work, we expand on this issue of expertise in scientific discovery.

There is a mix of claims about the nature of scientific discovery skills. On the one hand, there are claims that it primarily involves very general skills (Qin & Simon, 1990; Shraagen, 1993; Voss, Tyler, & Yengo, 1983). For example, scientific discovery is typically thought to involve two primary activities: developing (and evaluating) hypotheses and designing experiments (cf. Klahr & Dunbar, 1988). At this basic level, it is similar to the exploratory activities of children as they interact and learn from their

385

environment (Klahr, Fay, & Dunbar, 1993; D. Kuhn, 1989; Piaget, 1952) and the way many adults learn to program VCRs (i.e., by means other than reading the manual). Along those lines, some research has found that scientists do not have improved general-reasoning skills (Griggs & Ransdell, 1986; Kern, Mirels, & Hinshaw, 1983; Mahoney & DeMonbreun, 1977). On the other hand, there are claims that it, like any other area of expertise, primarily involves many specific skills that are acquired through extended experience in the domain. For example, each scientific discipline has specific experimental paradigms (Baker & Dunbar, 1996; T. S. Kuhn, 1970; Schunn & Klahr, 1995) and specific methods for evaluating evidence (e.g., statistical tests).

To investigate the role of expertise in scientific reasoning, we conducted an experiment that attempts to assess empirically the skills available to expert and novice scientists. In the next section, we describe this experiment and its results. Following the experiment, we describe an ACT–R model of the task and data. Of particular importance is the issue of whether the model can further illuminate the origins and nature of expertise in a complex task like scientific reasoning.

AN EXPERIMENTAL STUDY OF PSYCHOLOGICAL EXPERIMENTATION

Method

The experiment used two groups of experts (4 Domain Experts and 6 Task Experts) and two groups of novices (14 High-Ability and 16 Mid-Ability undergraduates). These groups were used to tease apart the effects of domain expertise (i.e., declarative and procedural knowledge specific to a particular domain of scientific inquiry) and the effects of task expertise (i.e., the procedural knowledge general to scientific inquiry in many domains). The logic of the experiment was that skills for which the two groups of experts perform equally are domain-general skills and skills for which the Domain Experts outperform the Task Experts are domain-specific skills (or at least require domain-specific declarative knowledge). The relative performance of the novices would testify as to whether the domain-general skills were learned through the experience of being a scientist or whether they were shared by most adults. To examine the influence of general reasoning ability, the undergraduates were divided into two groups (High-Ability and Mid-Ability[1]) using a median split on Math SAT scores. If the

---

[1]Because the novices were undergraduates were from Carnegie Mellon University, we thought it unrepresentative to call any of them Low-Ability.

differences between the undergraduates and the Task Experts were due to task expertise and not general reasoning ability differences, then there should be no differences between the two groups of undergraduates.

We chose a particular scientific task that simultaneously satisfied three constraints:

1. The solution was unknown to the Domain Experts, as science involves the discovery of previously unknown solutions.
2. The problem was free of domain-specific jargon and easily understandable to even the novices.
3. The solution was obtainable through experimentation.

A problem that seemed to meet these constraints was taken from the domain of cognitive psychology. In particular, the problem was to find the cause of the spacing effect in memory—that items with longer intervening intervals tend to be better remembered.

Because the domain was memory research in cognitive psychology, the Domain Experts were cognitive psychology faculty doing research in memory. The Task Experts were social and developmental psychology faculty not doing research in memory. The novices were undergraduates who had not yet had courses in psychology research methods.

The subjects were given a description of the spacing effect as well as two theories about the cause of the spacing effect. These theories were simplified forms of actual theories from the literature. The first theory was the shifting-context theory, which stated that memories are associated with the context under study and that context gradually shifts with time. Under this theory, the spacing effect occurs because spaced practice produces associations to more divergent contexts, which in turn are more likely to overlap with the test context. The second theory was the frequency-regularity theory, which states that the mind estimates how long memories will be needed based on regularities in the environment and, in particular, adjusts forgetting rates according to the spacing between items. Under this theory, items learned with short intervening spaces are forgotten quickly because they need not be remembered for very long, whereas items learned with long intervening spaces are forgotten more slowly because otherwise they would be long forgotten before they were needed again.

The subject's goal was to develop experiments that could determine that explanation of the spacing effect was correct. The subjects used a computer interface called the Simulated Psychology Lab (SPL) to design experiments. The interface provided a set of variables that could be manipulated, as well as the facility to conduct factorial-design experiments easily. The use of the computer interface allowed the subjects to observe the outcomes of their experiments and iterate through several experiments—important aspects of scientific discovery.

In the interface, the subjects could manipulate six different factors:

1. Repetitions—the number of times that the list of words was studied.
2. Spacing—the amount of time spent between repetitions.
3. Source context—whether the studying occurred in the same context for each repetition or whether the context changed on each repetition.
4. The test task—free recall, recognition, or stem completion.
5. Delay—the amount of time from the last study repetition until the test was given.
6. Test context—whether the testing occurred in the same context or a different context at test relative to the study context.

For each variable, the subjects could either hold the variable constant or vary it. Values had to be selected on all dimensions, including the dimensions that were held constant in the given experiments; no default values were used. There was no restriction on the order of value selection, and subjects could go back to change their selections for any of the variables at any point in time up until they selected to run the experiment. Figure 11.1 shows the six variables that could be manipulated as they appeared on the screen and their current settings. In this example, the experiment is only partially specified, with only the repetitions and spacing variables determined—repetitions was not manipulated (it was held constant at 3) and spacing was manipulated (5 min vs. 20 min). An experiment was not complete until values for all six variables were specified.

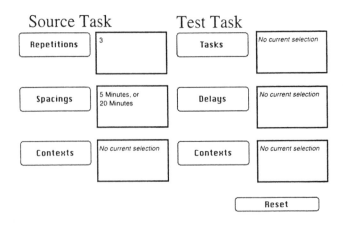

FIG. 11.1.   The interface used for displaying the variables that could be manipulated and their current settings in the experiment being designed.

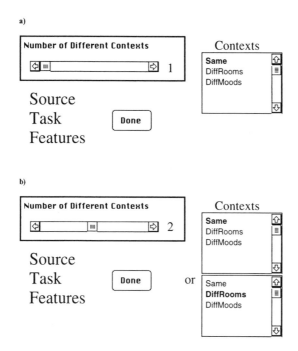

FIG. 11.2.   The interface used for selecting how many levels of an independent variable and the values for each level. In (a), only one level is selected (i.e., this variable is held constant), and the constant value is "Same." In (b), two levels are selected (i.e., this variables is manipulated), and the values are "Same" and "Diff-Rooms."

Subjects selected variable settings by clicking on sliders and scrolling lists using a mouse. Figure 11.2 provides an example of how values were selected for the source context variable. The slider on the left was used to select whether the variable was held constant (by setting it to 1—Fig. 11.2a) or whether the variable was manipulated (by setting it to 2 or 3—Fig. 11.2b). Values for repetition were selected using a slider, which varied from 2 to 5. Values for context and test task were selected from a scrolling list of three options. Values for spacing and delay were selected using a slider (which varied from 1 to 20) and a scrolling list of units (minutes, hours, or days).

The subjects made predictions and were given outcomes in a table format with all cells being shown at once. A table format was used rather than a graphical format because it was thought that the table format was less difficult to understand and manipulate for the undergraduate subjects. Before being given the table, subjects had to decide on which dimension each manipulated factor would be plotted. After deciding on the table structure, subjects made numerical predictions for their tasks. After completing their predictions, the subjects were shown the results of their experiment in table format (see Fig. 11.3). In addition, the outcome tables also displayed the subject's predictions for each cell in italics. To facilitate comparison across rows, columns, and tables, the row, column, and table marginals were also provided. To provide a rough evaluation of the quality of the predictions, the subjects were shown the Pearson correlation between the predictions and outcomes. The actual results displayed were generated by a mathematical model that is roughly consistent with results from research on memory and the spacing effect.

Subjects worked at the task until they felt that they had found out what the cause of the spacing effect was. The primary data gathered in this experiment was the keystroke data generated as the subjects designed experiments, chose the table structures, and interpreted experiments. To provide additional information about the processes they used, the subjects were asked to give a think-aloud verbal protocol throughout the task, and at the end of the task they were asked to report verbally their conclusions about the two theories for the spacing effect and their conclusions about the effects of each of the six variables.

It is important to note that the SPL environment and the structure of the experiment simplified many aspects of scientific discovery that a scientist would often have to accomplish. Just to name a few: The subjects did not have to work in groups (e.g., with collaborators, advisors, students, or

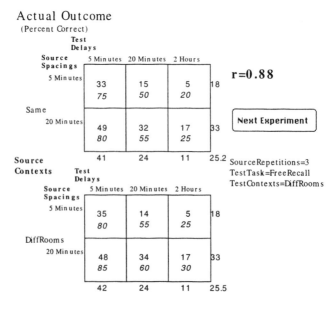

FIG. 11.3. The interface used for displaying the outcomes of experiments. Actual outcomes are the main entry in each cell. Predicted outcomes are in italics. The r value is the Pearson correlation between the predictions and actual outcomes.

research assistants), they did not have to propose the theories to test, they did not have to propose which variables might be manipulated, they did not have to decide on the general experimental paradigm (i.e., they were forced to use a between-subjects factorial design involving a study of words followed by a single test), there were many other variables for which values would have to be selected (e.g., subject Ns) and yet were not mentioned, the subjects did not have to compute inferential statistics, and the subjects did not have to publish their results. In part, these components of scientific discovery had to be removed for practical considerations (e.g., in order to be able to present the subjects with experimental outcomes and allow them to iterate through the process of experiment design and outcome evaluation).

It is equally important to note that many of the important and difficult aspects of scientific discovery were maintained in this task. First, subjects designed experiments to test theories and evaluated those tests, two very basic and important aspects of scientific discovery. Second, the subjects were given a real scientific phenomenon, real scientific theories, and real experimental variables. In particular, the mapping of the two theories for the spacing effect onto these six variables was not simple. This is typical of the relationship between theory and operational variables in most psychological theories and experiments. Third, there were many complex experiment design decisions that remained, as we will see in the results. Fourth, the stopping criterion for when the theories were adequately tested was not well defined. Thus, it is fair to say that the subjects were presented with a complex and relatively ill-defined problem.[2]

Results

Comparisons of the different groups of subjects revealed several kinds of skills that were common to experts but were lacking in undergraduates. Schunn and Anderson (1997) gave a more complete listing of skills that were examined. In this chapter we focus on five skills that involved clear expert-novice differences. Later in the chapter, we discuss how these differences can be understood within ACT–R.

Design Experiments to Test the Given Theories. Using the verbal protocols, we classified the participants according to whether or not they mentioned either of the two theories (frequency regularity and shifting context) during the course of design experiments, either during the first experiment or during any experiment. Note that this is a very lax criterion for measuring use of theories in experiment design—only one theory need be mentioned and the theory need only be mentioned in passing, thereby

---

[2]In fact, many of the experts complained that the task was unfairly complex.

ensuring that the understanding of both theories was not required to be successful under this measure. All of the Domain Experts and Task Experts mentioned the theories, starting with the very first experiment (see Fig. 11.4). However, only 64% of the High-Ability undergraduates and 6% of the Mid-Ability undergraduates mentioned the theories during *any* of the experiments, significantly fewer than the Task and Domain Experts. Thus, it appears that not even all of the brighter undergraduates understood that theories are used to guide experiment design. Instead these undergraduates simply designed experiments to explore the effects of the various factors.

How did these differences in orientation toward the overall task impact the choice of factors to include in the experiments? Focusing on the undergraduates, Fig. 11.5 presents the proportion of undergraduates including each of the factors in their first experiment as function of whether they were trying to test theories (mentioned the theories during the design of the first experiment) or simply exploring the factors (did not mention either theory during the design of the first experiment). Although the undergraduates testing theories focused on the factors relevant to the theories under test (spacing and source context), the undergraduates exploring the factors selected among the factors using a simple visual strategy, preferring leftmost and topmost variables (as shown in Fig. 11.1).

Keep General Settings Constant Across Experiments.   Another general heuristic of experimental design is to use the same constant values across experiments—it makes comparisons across experiments easier, and it capitalizes on the success of previous experiments. Note that this is subtly different from the focus of previous psychological research on variable variation (e.g., Schauble, 1990; Tschirgi, 1980). Previous research examined whether individuals vary one factor at a time within their experiments (i.e., avoid confounding variables). In the SPL environment, the interface forces

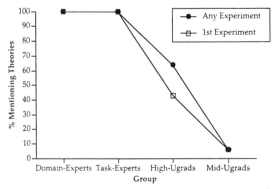

FIG. 11.4.   Proportion of subjects in each group who mention the theories during experiment design (during the first experiment or during any experiment).

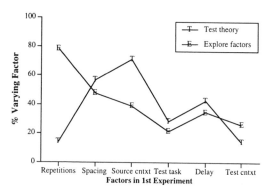

FIG. 11.5. Percentage of undergraduate subjects varying each of variables in the first experiment as a function of whether they were explicitly testing the given theories or simply exploring the factors.

valid, factorial designs. However, there remains the issue of consistency across experiments.

Consider the following example. Suppose that in the first experiment the individual decides to vary only repetitions, selecting 2 versus 3 repetitions. The remaining variables are held constant, and the particular constant values are shown in Table 11.1. Then suppose that in the second experiment the individual decides to vary repetitions again, but this time using a stronger manipulation of 2 versus 5 repetitions. The issue of interest here is what constant values the individual selects for the other variables. The individual could select all the same constant values as in the first experiment (see Experiment 2 in Table 11.1). Alternatively, the individual could select different constant values (see Experiment 2′ in Table 11.1). Both permit logically valid conclusions regarding the effects of repetitions. However, Experiment 2 is more conservative; varying all the factors as in Experiment 2′ increases the risk of producing a useless experiment (e.g., producing floor or ceiling effects).

TABLE 11.1
Example Experiments Illustrating the Difference Between Holding General Settings Constant (Experiment 2) and Varying General Settings (Experiment 2′)

Variable	Experiment 1	Experiment 2	Experiment 2′
Repetitions	2 vs. 3	2 vs. 5	2 vs. 5
Spacing	10 min	10 min	2 days
Source context	Same room	Same room	Different room
Test task	Recall	Recall	Recognition
Delay	1 day	1 day	20 min
Test context	Same room	Same room	Different mood

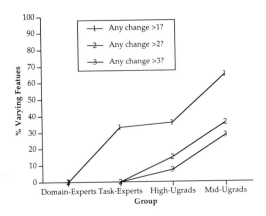

FIG. 11.6.   Percentage of subjects varying more than one, two, or three values.

Violations of this heuristic were counted by examining the situations in which a variable was not manipulated in consecutive experiments and then determining whether the same constant value was used in both experiments (e.g., hold spacing constant at 10 min across multiple experiments). Three measures of the tendency to keep values constant were used: whether the subject ever changed more than one unmanipulated variable value (i.e., minor violations that might even have a justification), whether the subject ever changed more than two values, and whether the subject ever changed more than three values (i.e., major violations). Across the different measures of value variation, the Domain Experts, Task Experts, and High-Ability undergraduates did not differ significantly (see Fig. 11.6). By contrast, the Mid-Ability undergraduates were higher on all measures of value variation, with almost one third of them varying three or more constant values, suggesting that many of them did not understand this heuristic.

Avoid Floor and Ceiling Effects.   In designing experiments, it is a good heuristic to try to avoid floor and ceiling effects because they make the interpretation of null effects and interactions very problematic. To examine whether the groups were differentially effective at avoiding floor and ceiling effects, we coded which experiments produced all outcome values over 90% correct or all outcome values less than 10% correct. Figure 11.7 presents the proportion of participants with any such floor or ceiling effect experiments. The Domain Experts never produced such experiments, indicating that domain knowledge could be used to avoid floor and ceiling effects. The High-Ability undergraduates were just as likely as the Task Experts to produce a floor or ceiling effect experiment, and the Mid-Ability under-

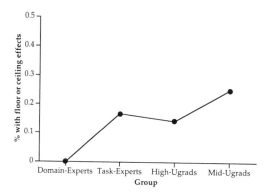

FIG. 11.7. Percentage of subjects with floor- or ceiling-effect experiments.

graduates were even more likely to produce such an experiment—possibly a result of being less conservative in their value selections.

How did subjects respond to these potentially invalid experiments? Of the seven subjects producing floor or ceiling effects, five changed the delay values appropriately on the next experiment (i.e., decreasing it if there was a floor effect and increasing it if there was a ceiling effect). One subject changed the spacing values, which was also effective. The remaining subject held delays constant (at 1 min) and, consequently, had frequent ceiling-effect problems—in six of nine experiments. In sum, the majority of the subjects who produced floor and ceiling effects were able to react appropriately. This, combined with the previous result, suggests that they understood at some level what floor or ceiling effects were and that they should be avoided, but did not initially have sufficient domain knowledge to avoid them.

Keep Experiments Simple (When Necessary).   Another general principle of experiment design is to keep experiments simple, especially as a first approach. Figure 11.8 presents the mean experiment complexity for participants in the various groups (the mean number of factors per experiment). The Domain Experts designed more complex experiments than did the Task Experts, and both groups of undergraduates designed more complex experiments than did the Task Experts. The High- and Mid-Ability undergraduates produced equally complex experiments. From the verbal protocols, it was clear that the Domain Experts were able to interpret their complex experiments, whereas the undergraduates were often overwhelmed with the large tables they produced. Thus, it appears that Domain Experts do not need to keep experiments simple, and that undergraduates do not know that they should keep experiments simple.

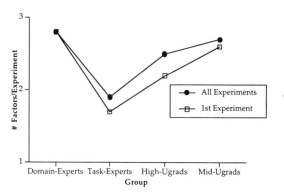

FIG. 11.8.   The mean number of factors varied per experiment.

Encode Interactions and Ignore Noise Levels.   An important general outcome-interpretation skill is the ability to encode the main effects and interactions within a table. All groups of subjects were able to correctly report the main effects of the variables at the end of the task (if they had run an experiment manipulating the variables). Therefore, we can assume that the groups were all capable of encoding main effects. However, there were differences in ability to encode interactions. In this task, there were two two-way interactions. First, there was a quantitative Spacing × Delay interaction, such that the spacing effect was larger at longer delays. Second, there was an effect/no-effect Spacing × Test Task interaction, such that there was no spacing effect with stem completion. As with the main effect analysis, subjects' final hypotheses were coded for correctness on these two interactions, and only those subjects who had conducted the relevant experiments were included in this analysis. Overall, the Domain Experts and Task Experts were equally able to correctly encode these interactions (see Fig. 11.9). By contrast, the High-Ability undergraduates were less able to encode the interactions, and the Mid-Ability undergraduates rarely encoded the interactions.

In addition to being able to encode interactions when they exist, there is also the skill of noting noninteractions (i.e., not being deceived by small levels of noise). To see whether the groups differed in their ability to note noninteractions, the subjects' final conclusions were coded for descriptions of nonexistent interactions. The Domain Experts and Task Experts almost never made such errors, whereas the undergraduates made a significant number of such errors (see Fig. 11.9). In fact, the undergraduates are just as likely to report nonexistent interactions as to report existing interactions.

In sum, this experiment found several skills that are common across Domain and Task Experts, but that many undergraduates are missing. The differences between experts and undergraduates suggests that this task tapped aspects of expertise in science. The lack of differences between

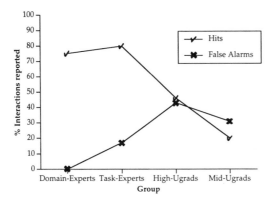

FIG. 11.9.   Percentage of subjects making correct conclusions about each interaction given opportunity to observe the interaction (hits) and percentage of subjects making extraneous interaction conclusions (false alarms).

Domain Experts and Task Experts further indicates that some aspects of this expertise are general to scientific reasoning (at least within trained psychologists). Given that bright undergraduates are missing these competencies, they must have been acquired through the practice of doing science. In the next section we present an ACT–R model of the SPL task, which may further illuminate this issue of generality of expertise.

THE ACT–R MODEL OF THE SPL TASK

Overview

We had three primary goals in building an ACT–R model of the Simulated Psychology Laboratory (SPL) task. First, as discussed in the introduction to this chapter, we wanted to see whether we could build a model of a complex task in the new, smaller grain size ACT–R. Second, we were interested in what kinds of general modeling styles would emerge from building a model of this task. Many subtasks had to be solved and the methods for solving these subtasks may generalize to modeling other phenomena. Third, we were interested in what insights a detailed process model might provide for understanding the group differences observed in the SPL task. The model as presented focuses on capturing Domain Expert performance, but we also discuss how it can be modified to capture the group differences. We touch on each of these three goals throughout the description of the SPL model.

Although the model is by no means a complete model of all the aspects of behavior in the SPL task, the model is quite complex, reflecting the complexity of the task. There are 48 chunk types and 116 productions. Consequently, we sketch the functionality of the model rather than simply presenting the productions.

Much of the model is concerned with interactions with the environment. That is, at many points the model has to encode information from the visual array or perform actions in that array. Although we could have, we did not make the model interact with the actual SPL interface (because it would have to be reimplemented in LISP). Nonetheless, we were careful to put into the model the necessary rules for interacting with the interface. Most importantly, the model distinguishes between internal and external memory, and productions do not directly access external memory. Thus, the model could be hooked up to a LISP reimplementation of the interface without having to modify the core productions. The details of these rules are discussed relatively little in this report, but they can be examined by following the *Published ACT–R Models* from the ACT–R home page (http://act.psy.cmu.edu/).

The top level goal of the task is a DISCOVERY goal. It specifies that the goal of the task is to discover whether a given hypothesis is correct. To implement the full goal of the task—discover which of two hypotheses is correct—we push two DISCOVERY goals onto the stack, one for each hypothesis. From the verbal protocols, it appears that this divide-and-conquer strategy was used by many of the subjects.

The DISCOVERY goal leads to repeated pushing of EXPERIMENT goals to perform individual experiments and EVALUATE-EVIDENCE goals to examine whether these experiments have produced results that satisfy the DISCOVERY goal. The terminating condition that EVALUATE-EVIDENCE seeks is that some consequence of the hypothesis under test has been directly proven true or false. For example, the shifting-context hypothesis (that source context mediates the spacing effect) has as a consequence that there should be an effect of source context. When source context is found to have no effect, then the shifting-context hypothesis is assumed to be false, and the DISCOVERY goal for that hypothesis is achieved. Currently these consequences are not derived via inductions or deductions, but are simply retrieved from memory. Because the subjects were given consequences of each theory in the explanations of how the theories explain the spacing effect, retrieval of such consequences from memory is a reasonable model of subjects' behavior.

Each hypothesis for a variable consists of an effect direction (greater-than, less-than, or equal-to), and a belief level (true and maybe). Each experiment can:

1. Create a new hypothesis with initial truth level of maybe (if no prior hypothesis for the given variable existed).
2. Move the belief level from maybe to true (if the same effect direction was observed).

3. Move the belief level from true to maybe (if a different effect direction was observed).
4. Change the effect direction, holding the belief level at maybe (if the belief level was maybe and a different effect direction was observed).

Thus, three consistent outcomes will lead the model to either accept or reject any hypothesis even if the prior beliefs were in the opposite direction, two consistent outcomes are required if no prior hypothesis exists, and only one if the prior knowledge is consistent with the outcome.

Each EXPERIMENT goal leads to the design, running, and encoding of one experiment (see Fig. 11.10). There are three different subtypes of EX-PERIMENT goal, which can be thought of as different experimental paradigms: HYPOTHESIS-TESTING, EXPLORE-SYSTEM, and TEST-FAC-TOR.[3] The HYPOTHESIS-TESTING and EXPLORE-SYSTEM subtypes correspond to the two general approaches that subjects took toward the task: designing experiments relevant to the hypotheses, versus simply investigating the effects of the six factors. Previous models of scientific discovery have also distinguished among such different approaches to experimentation (e.g., Cheng, 1990; Klahr & Dunbar, 1988; Shrager, 1985, 1987). The TEST-FACTOR is produced as a consequence of an experiment that produced an ambiguous result that needs to be explored further. The three types of goals lead to similar experiment design behaviors, although there are some critical differences. In the next subsection, we first describe experimental design for hypothesis testing. Then we discuss the differences for the other two types of goals.

Experimental Design

The experimental design process is similar for the three EXPERIMENT goal subtypes in Fig. 11.10. We describe the experimental design process with respect to the HYPOTHESIS-TESTING goal, which produces the overall structure of designing an experiment to test a hypothesis. A HYPOTHE-SIS-TESTING goal pushes two primary goals: to vary the hypothesis factors, and to fix the remaining variables. The goal to vary hypothesis factors selects whether to vary one or two factors relating to the hypothesis and which factors to vary. The goal to fix the remaining variables then iterates over the variables visually and selects the remaining unselected variables.

The content of the hypothesis under test drives the selection of factors to vary. The hypothesis has three components: the variable causing the effect, the direction of the effect of the variable (greater-than, less-than, equal-to),

---

[3]Note that these are different types of experiment goal, not subgoals of the experiment goal. ACT–R allows for different types of a general chunk type.

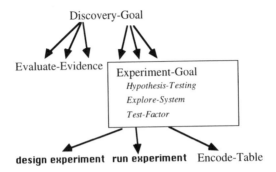

FIG. 11.10.   The model's top-level goal structures.

and the current belief level (true or maybe). To select a variable to manipulate, the simulation searches for a consequence of the hypothesis under test, which names a variable and an expected effect direction. For example, a consequence of the shifting-context theory is that source context should have a greater-than effect (i.e., varying study contexts should improve retention). The simulation then sets a goal to vary that consequent variable.

A series of productions are responsible for setting the factors. They start with task-specific productions of the form, "if you want to vary some factor and you are looking at the main screen then press the button relating to that factor." When the screen relating to the desired factor is achieved, a VARIABLE-SETTING goal is created and pushed on the stack. This VARIABLE-SETTING goal serves as both a control structure and a memory for details of the experiment design. The VARIABLE-SETTING goal initially contains only information about which variable is being considered. Incrementally, slots are filled regarding the number of levels of that variable and what value each level has. For example, if the repetitions variable is to be varied, then the number of levels is set at 2, the first value may be set to 3, and the second value may be set to 5. Alternatively, if the repetitions variable is not to be varied, then the number of levels is set at 1, the first value may be set to 3 repetitions, and the second value is left empty.

By default, if the simulation does not have a goal to vary this particular factor, it chooses not to vary the factor. However, there is one exception. If the simulation is planning on varying some other factor B and can retrieve an INTERACTION hypothesis involving that factor B and the current factor A, then the simulation chooses to vary the current factor A. In other words, the simulation prefers to vary only the one selected factor unless it expects to find interactions with that factor. More is said about these INTERACTION hypotheses when it comes to encoding the results of experiments.

How are particular values selected for each variable? Knowledge of possible selections for a particular variable is presented in the form of

POSSIBLE-SELECTION chunks. At first, when the simulation has not previously considered a variable, it has no POSSIBLE-SELECTION chunks in memory for that variable, and must create POSSIBLE-SELECTIONS by conducting a visual search of the options available in the interface. This visual search creates a POSSIBLE-SELECTION chunk for each possibility. Given a set of POSSIBLE-SELECTION chunks, there are four alternative schemes for selecting a particular one. The alternative schemes are implemented as productions competing in conflict resolution. The first scheme is to choose the visually leftmost (or topmost) selection. The second scheme is to choose randomly among the POSSIBLE-SELECTIONS, which favors the most active one in memory. The third scheme is to specifically retrieve the value that was used for that variable in a prior experiment (and activation differences will favor the just previous experiment). The fourth and final scheme is to retrieve specific knowledge of what values must be avoided and find a value that satisfies these constraints. For example, a previous experiment may have determined that short delay values lead to ceiling-effect problems. Therefore, short delay values will be avoided.

The alternative EXPERIMENT goal types in Fig. 11.10 have similar goal structures as the HYPOTHESIS-TESTING goal. The most similar is TEST-FACTOR, which pushes a goal to vary the factor it desires to test and another goal to fix the remaining variables. In contrast, EXPLORE-SYSTEM simply conducts a visual search for the variables not yet set, and then pushes a goal to vary the first such factor found.

Encoding the Table

After the experiment is designed and run, the resulting table must be encoded. The ENCODE-TABLE goal initializes and directs the search over the table, setting ENCODE-DIMENSION subgoals for each of the table dimensions. The slots of ENCODE-TABLE are method, start-cell, current-dimension, and searched-dim. All of these slots start out empty and are filled in that order. The method slot encodes the method that will be used to search the table. The LtR-scan method is the default method and searches tables from left to right and top to bottom. The start-cell indicates the reference cell to initiate all dimension searches. It is set by default to the upper leftmost cell in the upper leftmost table. The current-dimension slot encodes which physical dimension is currently selected to be searched (i.e., horizontally vs. vertically vs. across tables vs. down tables). When its value is nil, it is initialized to be dimension-1 (searching down within a table). The searched-dim slot encodes whether the selected dimension has been searched yet. If its value is nil, then an ENCODE-DIMENSION goal is pushed for that subgoal (and the searched-dim slot is then set to true). If its value is true, then the next search dimension is sought (by visually searching the table) and the searched-dim slot is reset to nil. If no more unsearched dimensions can be found, then the table is assumed to be fully encoded, and the ENCODE-TABLE goal is popped.

The ENCODE-DIMENSION goal directs the search for a main effect of a particular dimension. Its slots are dimension, variable, current-cell, current-value, prev-value, value1, value2, feature, and prev-feature. The dimension and current-cell values are initialized with the values taken from the ENCODE-TABLE goal. The next slot to be filled is the variable slot, which encodes the name of the dimension being searched. Value1 and value2 encode the names of the factor levels of the dimension (or factor) being encoded (e.g., same and different room levels on the source-context dimension).

The current-cell slot encodes the physical location in the table where the search is currently focused. The current-value slot encodes the value of that cell and the prev-value slot encodes the prior value on that dimension. When the current-value and prev-value slots are both filled, the feature slot is used to encode the pattern formed by these two values. The relationship between the two values is encoded as greater-than, less-than, or equal-to. An equal-to feature is immediately created only when exact equality is found. However, when the size of the difference is below some threshold (5 in this simulation), the feature is recoded to be equal-to as well. For example, the comparison between prev-value = 65 and current-value = 63 would result in an equal-to feature (after first encoding a less-than feature).

Once the feature is encoded, the search for effects of that dimension continues in the next row (or column) of the table. For example, in a 2 × 2 table, the first column is searched first, followed by the second column. When the search of the second column begins, the value of the feature slot is placed in the prev-feature slot, and the feature slot is reset to nil. At the end of the search of the second column (and all subsequent ones) of a given dimension, the values of the feature and prev-feature slot are compared. If the two values are the same, then the search continues. When there are no new columns to search, the simulation assumes there is a consistent main effect of the dimension and the ENCODE-DIMENSION goal is popped. When the two values are not the same, then the simulation assumes there is an interaction and no consistent main effect and the ENCODE-DIMEN-SION goal is popped even if there are more columns to encode on that dimension.

In either case (consistent or no consistent main effect), a TEST-GENERALITY goal is pushed, with the name of the examined variable and the found feature, in the consistent case, or with an equal-to feature, in the inconsistent case. The generality of the feature is tested by comparing it to the current hypothesis regarding that variable. If no such hypothesis exists, it is created and the truth level is set to maybe. If the hypothesis for that variable exists and is consistent with current outcome, then the hypothesis truth level is strengthened (i.e., is changed from maybe to true). However, if the hypothesis is inconsistent with the current outcome, then a subgoal to explain the inconsistency is pushed.

The subgoal to explain the inconsistency initiates a search for possible design problems in the current experiment that might have lead to misleading results. The simulation can currently detect three types of problems. If the values in the table are above 90% and there was no effect of the variable, then the simulation proposes that there was a ceiling effect. If the values in the table are below 10% and there was no effect of the variable, then the simulation proposes that there was a floor effect. If the two values of the variable were too close together (e.g., 1 min and 2 min) and there was no effect, then the simulation proposes that the manipulation was too weak. In the case of the floor and the ceiling effects, the simulation examines the details of the experiment design to see what might have caused those effects.

A discovered experiment problem is stored in a chunk (called EXPERI-MENT-PROBLEM), which then can be used to influence later experiment designs. In the case of a weak manipulation, the next experiment will use the TEST-FACTOR paradigm to design the experiment (instead of TEST-HYPOTHESIS or EXPLORE-SYSTEM). For all three types of problems, when that particular variable is being considered during the design of the next experiment, a production will set a subgoal to try to find a value that avoids the problematic values found in the previous experiment. Thus, although the simulation is conservative in that it prefers to pick the same variable values as in the previous experiment, it will specifically avoid values that were found to be problematic.

When interactions are found, an INTERACTION chunk is created and pushed as a goal. Its slots are variable1, variable2, feature1, feature2, cell, and prev-cell. Variable1 encodes the variable that was being searched when the interaction was found. Feature1 and feature2 encode the two inconsistent features that were found. Cell encodes the table location that was last viewed when the interaction was found (and was associated with feature2). To determine what the interacting variable (variable2) was, the simulation first retrieves a cell that was associated with the other feature (feature1), and then determines which dimension differentiated the two cells.

In sum, experiments are designed by considering factors one at a time, focusing on the theory-relevant ones first. Experiment outcomes are interpreted by scanning the table, noticing main effects and interactions, and testing the generality of these effects. The simulation iterates through these processes until the hypothesis under test has been either confirmed or disconfirmed.

General Features of the Model

There were a number of general approaches adopted in this model that are useful in developing ACT–R models for many domains. We mention three here. Performance in this task required interleaving productions that were not specific to the interface with productions that were (cf. Gray, 1997). For instance, experimentation-general productions selected which variables were relevant to the hypothesis, but device-specific productions chose to initiate manipulation of the variable by pressing the button for that variable. The experimentation-general productions represent what subjects knew about designing experiments before our task whereas the device-specific productions represent what they had to learn to perform our task. The critical problem is to enable the general productions to transfer from scientific discovery to our task without having the specific productions learned in our task transfer back to other environments. For example, our expert subjects would not want to return to their offices, try to design an experiment, and then be looking for a particular factor button on the screen. This delimitation of transfer was achieved by giving all goals a looking-at slot that referred to the general contents of the current screen. The device-specific productions contained tests for the value of the slot and so would not generalize to other contexts.

Second, we used a context slot to bind together in memory all the chunks representing a particular experiment. For example, there were VARIABLE-SETTING chunks encoding the values selected for each factor and EN-CODE-DIMENSION chunks encoding the outcomes for each variable that was varied. The model could tell when they referred to the same experiment by seeing if they had the same value in the context slot. This allows the model to distinguish between the current experiment and previous experiments, all of which must be maintained in declarative memory. This use of the context slot is similar to the list slot used in the simulations of the list memory experiments (see Chapter 7) and is an idea that can be traced back to the list memory models of Anderson and Bower (1972). In the SPL simulation, the context slot is always the number of the current experiment. This context value is automatically updated when a new experiment is begun.

A third feature of the simulation is the distinction between memory retrieval and visual retrieval. In many instances, information can be obtained either by doing a memory retrieval or by setting a VISUAL-SEARCH goal to retrieve the information from the interface. For example, in the design of experiments after the first one, either the POSSIBLE-SELECTION chunks can be retrieved from memory from the design of the previous experiment, or new ones can be created again by another visual search of the interface. With production parameter learning turned on, the productions tune themselves to switch from visual retrieval to memory retrieval over time.

A TRACE OF THE RUNNING MODEL

We now step through a trace of the running model. We do not, however, present every step, since a full run requires over 1,000 cycles and contains many repetitive aspects. Moreover, we suppress the steps relating to motor activities. A full trace can be found by running the model available on the Web.[4] The snippets of trace that we provide take advantage of the user feature (!output!) to print out a message in a production to announce what it is doing. This produces something with the flavor of a verbal protocol.

Setting Variables

Our general exposition strategy in this section is to present a fragment of protocol and follow it by an explanation. The protocol for one run begins:

Looking for a screen_type
    Found screen_type object Main_Screen
   Evaluate evidence for hypothesis Shifting_Context.
    Found consequence Source_Context Greater_Than.
  Design an experiment to test hypothesis Shifting_Context
   Vary hypothesis factors and fix remaining variables.
    Found consequent variable Source_Context of the hypothesis
      Shifting_Context
   Vary variable Source_Context
   Click on the button relating to factor Source_Context
ACTION: Click button 3LEFT
NEW SCREEN: Choose Variable

The model begins by looking to environment to uncover what screen type is on the screen and finds that the environment is in the MAIN_SCREEN state. Then the model evaluates the current evidence for the hypothesis under test by considering when one of its consequences is true. It cannot retrieve any knowledge about the truth of this consequence and so returns to designing an experiment. At this point, the model chooses to design an experiment to test the shifting-context hypothesis (i.e., push a HYPOTHESIS-TESTING subgoal). This in turn pushes goals to vary factors relevant to the hypothesis and fix the remaining factors. With respect to varying factors relevant to the hypothesis, the model selects to vary the

---

[4]Please note that because of random choices the path (and trace) taken by the model will vary from run to run. To see this trace, turn on *action trace* and *experiment trace* for the Fig. 11.2 simulation. This will produce a novice and expert sequence of experiments.

variable identified in one of the consequences of the hypothesis. The model
then clicks on the button relating to that factor.[5] The protocol continues:

> Looking for a screen_type
>> Found screen_type object Source_Context
>> On the right screen to pick Source_Context
>> How many levels are we currently at for Source_Context?
>>> Found nlevels One
>> Source_Context is at 1, but we want 2, so change it
>>> Clicking slider Source_Context
> ACTION: Update nlevels for Source_Context to Two
>> Look for options for variable Source_Context
>>> Visually found option Same
>>> Visually found option Diff_Room
>>> Visually found option Diff_Mood
>> Pick the top value (Same) as a default.
>>> Making selection One for Source_Context
> ACTION: Update value One for Source_Context to be Same
>> Picking Diff_Room as second value.
>>> Making selection Two for Source_Context
> ACTION: Update value Two for Source_Context to be Diff_Room
>> Done picking values for Source_Context
> ACTION: Click Done
> NEW SCREEN: Main Screen

After clicking on the source context button, the model discovers that it
is now on the correct screen to actually modify source context. It then
creates a VARIABLE-SETTING goal for source context and proceeds to
fill in the slots for that goal. The first slot to be filled is how many levels is
the variable currently set at, which it discovers is currently 1. However,
because the goal was to vary this variable, this must be updated to 2. Then
the model looks to the environment to discover which possible selections
there are. Three are found (Same, Diff-Room, and Diff-Mood), and Same
is selected for the first value (because it is the topmost value in the interface),
and Diff-Room is selected randomly for the second value (because it
happened to be the most active in memory, other than Same). Thus, this
aspect of the experiment is designed without significant amounts of knowledge. The protocol continues:

> Looking for a screen_type
>> Found screen_type object Main_Screen
>> Look for first unselected variable.

---

[5]As a note about the trace formatting: When the model takes a physical action, the LISP
code implementing this action states which action was taken (ACTION:) and what new
screen is displayed if there is a screen change (NEW SCREEN:).

       Found variable Repetitions
       Consider factor Repetitions
         Click on the button relating to factor Repetitions
ACTION: Click button 1LEFT
NEW SCREEN: Choose Variable
      Looking for a screen_type
        Found screen_type object Repetitions
      On the right screen to pick Repetitions
       How many levels are we currently at for Repetitions?
         Found nlevels One
      Search memory to see if Source_Context is an interacting variable
          with Repetitions
      Look for options for variable Repetitions
        Visually found option Two
        Visually found option Three
        Visually found option Four
      Pick the top value (Two) as a default.
        Making selection One for Repetitions
ACTION: Update value One for Repetitions to be Two
      Done picking values for Repetitions
ACTION: Click Done
NEW SCREEN: Main Screen
   ...

Back at the MAIN_SCREEN, the model looks for the nextmost unselected variable and finds repetitions. For this variable, the number of levels
is left unmodified at 1 as a default, and the topmost value of 2 is selected as
the value. This process continues until values for the remaining four
variables are selected.

Interpreting an Experiment

We resume the protocol when the experiment design is complete:

   ...
Looking for a screen_type
      Found screen_type object Main_Screen
     Look for first unselected variable.
     Finished selecting variable values.
   Finished designing the experiment, click on run
ACTION: Click Run
NEW SCREEN: Outcome Table
Exper1
   Repetitions — Two
   Spacing — One_minute
   Source_context — Same Diff_room

```
Test_task — Stem
Delay — One_minute
Test_context — Same
Source_Context
Same        100
Diff_Room   99
```

When no more unselected variables can be found, the experiment design is complete and the experiment is run. The simulation of the SPL task prints the designed experiment and outcome of the experiment. In this case, only source context was varied, and the results were 100% for Same and 99% for Diff-Room. Then the interpretation of these results begins:

```
Looking for a screen_type
  Found screen_type object Outcome_Table
Encode table.
  Try scanning left-to-right.
  Visually find starting place — top left.
    Found top-left cell   1111
  Start with dimension dim1.
  Push goal to encode dimension Dim1
    Visually get cell value
       Found value 100
    Look for value1 visually
       Found dimension value Same
    Visually locate dimension variable.
       Found dimension name Source_Context
```

To encode the outcomes, the model first selects the default scanning strategy—top-down, left-to-right. Then the model locates the table reference cell (upper leftmost—encoded as 1111) to begin the search. Finally, the model looks for a dimension to search, beginning with dimension1 (going down). Because this dimension has not yet been searched (i.e., no ENCODE-DIMENSION chunk for that dimension can be retrieved), the model pushes an ENCODE-DIMENSION goal to search that dimension. At this point, the model could either look to find the name of dimension variable, or encode the contents of the first cell. In this case, it happens to encode the contents of the first cell (100%). Then it searches for the value on that dimension that corresponds to the cell (Same). Finally, it looks for the name of the dimension variable (Source_Context).

```
Move in desired direction.
  Found location below, 2111
Visually get cell value
```

```
Found value 99
Look for value2 visually
  Found dimension value Diff_Room
  Notice less than pattern.
Difference -1 in Dim1 is not significant.
Finished first row of dimension Dim1
```

The model then moves to the next cell in the direction of the search dimension, encodes the cell contents, and discovers what variable value is associated with that cell (Diff-Room). Comparing the table cell values of 99 and 100 (encoded in the earlier trace fragment), the model creates a pattern chunk encoding a less-than relation. This feature is elaborated to note that the difference of 1 is not significant, thereby changing the feature to an equal-to relation. Then the first pass at dimension 1 is complete, and the model attempts to move to the next row (or column in this case) in this dimension.

```
Finished encoding dimension. See if main effect generalizes.
Hypothesize that Source_Context may have no effect and check for
              problems.
  Pop hypothesis.
  Rehearsing hypothesis involving Source_Context
Suspect a ceiling effect.
  Delay One_Minute too short.
Rehearsing experiment_problem involving Delay
  ...
```

Because there are no more rows to search on that dimension, and no interactions have been found, the model assumes that the found effect (equal-to) is the main effect for that dimension and tests the generality of that effect. No previous hypotheses for that variable are found, and so a new hypothesis is proposed that it may not produce an effect. This hypothesis is also rehearsed once to insure that it will be remembered later. Because there was no effect of the variable, the model also looks for problems in the experiment that might have lead to an artifactual null result. Because the values were above 90%, the model suspects a ceiling effect, and guesses that the delay of 1 min was too short. This proposed experiment problem is also rehearsed once to insure that it will be remembered during the design of the next experiment.

Designing a Second Experiment

The first steps in the design of the second experiment begin:

...
   Evaluate evidence for hypothesis Shifting_Context.
     Found consequence Source_Context Greater_Than.
   Design an experiment to test hypothesis Shifting_Context
    Vary hypothesis factors and fix remaining variables.
      Found consequent variable Source_Context of the hypothesis
            Shifting_Context
    Vary variable Source_Context
ACTION: Click button 3LEFT
NEW SCREEN: Choose Variable

Again, the model evaluates the evidence for the hypothesis under test, and finds no definite evidence for or against. For the next experiment, the model chooses again to vary source-context because it is involved in a consequence of the shifting-context theory:

   Looking for a screen_type
    Found screen_type object Source_Context
   On the right screen to pick Source_Context
   Already know options for Source_Context
   How many levels are we currently at for Source_Context?
    Found nlevels One
   Source_Context is at 1, but we want 2, so change it
ACTION: Update nlevels for Source_Context to Two
   Pick previous value Same.
    Making selection One for Source_Context
ACTION: Update value One for Source_Context to be Same
   Picking previous value2 (Diff_Room)
    Making selection Two for Source_Context
ACTION: Update value Two for Source_Context to be Diff_Room
   Done picking values for Source_Context
ACTION: Click Done
NEW SCREEN: Main Screen
...

Because this is no longer the first experiment to be designed, the process is changed. Because the model can remember the possible options presented previously, it no longer has to look externally to find these options. Moreover, instead of choosing values arbitrarily, the model specifically chooses the same values for source context as in the previous experiment. Although it is not shown, the process for picking the other variables is similarly shortened. However, we look at the critical selection of the delay variable:

   On the right screen to pick Delay
   Already know options for Delay

How many levels are we currently at for Delay?
   Found nlevels One
Look for something greater than One_Minute
Failed finding something for value1. Look for more options.
   Visually found option One_Minute
   Visually found option Five_Minutes
   Visually found option Ten_Minutes
Look for something greater than One_Minute
   Found Ten_Minutes to be greater than One_Minute
   Making selection One for Delay
ACTION: Update value One for Delay to be Ten_Minutes

The process of selecting a value for the delay variable is changed in one additional manner. Because there was an experiment problem associated with delay in a previous experiment, the model explicitly sets a goal of avoiding this problematic value (1 min). However, the model forgot about values other than 1 min, and must do another visual search of the available options. Then a delay of 10 min is selected instead of the previously selected 1-min delay. Consequently, the resulting experiment no longer suffers from ceiling effects (both Same and Diff-Room produce 64% recall). The search process through the table, not shown in the preceding material, is the same as in the previous experiment. Once again, the model finds no effect of source context, and therefore concludes that it definitely has no effect:

   ...
   Evaluate evidence for hypothesis Shifting_Context.
     Found consequence Source_Context Greater_Than.
     Found consequence to be false. Therefore reject hypothesis Shifting_
      Context.
     Examined consequence. Therefore done testing hypothesis Shifting_
      Context.

When the evidence is evaluated again, the shifting-context hypothesis is rejected because its consequence involving source context is found to be false. The model then turns to examining the frequency-regularity hypothesis.

Testing the Frequency Regularity Theory

The design of the third experiment begins:

   Update context for Start2 to be Exper3
   Looking for a screen_type
     Found screen_type object Main_Screen
   Evaluate evidence for hypothesis Frequency_Regularity.

Found consequence Spacing Greater_Than.
Design an experiment to test hypothesis Frequency_Regularity
   Vary hypothesis factors and fix remaining variables.
      Found consequent variable Spacing of the hypothesis Frequency_
         Regularity
      Vary variable Spacing
   ...

The model decides to vary spacing, a variable implicated in a consequence. The critical portion of the variable selection is reproduced here:

On the right screen to pick Spacing
 How many levels are we currently at for Spacing?
   Found nlevels One
Spacing is at 1, but we want 2, so change it
ACTION: Update nlevels for Spacing to Two
   Already know options for Spacing
   Pick previous value One_Minute.
      Making selection One for Spacing
ACTION: Update value One for Spacing to be One_Minute
   Failed finding something for value2 in memory. Look for more options.
      Visually found option One_Minute
      Visually found option Five_Minutes
      Visually found option Ten_Minutes
   Picking Five_Minutes as second value.
      Making selection Two for Spacing
ACTION: Update value Two for Spacing to be Five_Minutes
   Done picking values for Spacing
ACTION: Click Done
NEW SCREEN: Main Screen
   ...

In selecting values for spacing, the simulation chooses the same first value
from the previous experiments. However, in selecting the second value, it
must reexamine its options visually because it has forgotten what the other
options were. Five minutes is selected as the second value (because it
happens to be most active in memory). The model selects the other values
as before, but when it comes to selecting test task something interesting
happens:

   ...
On the right screen to pick Test_Task
Already know options for Test_Task
How many levels are we currently at for Test_Task?

Found nlevels One
Search memory to see if Spacing is an interacting variable with Test_Task
   Found interaction between Spacing and Test_Task.
Test_Task is an interacting variable with Spacing, so set nlevels to 2
ACTION: Update nlevels for Test_Task to Two
   Pick previous value Stem.
      Making selection One for Test_Task
ACTION: Update value One for Test_Task to be Stem
   Failed finding something for value2 in memory. Look for more options.
      Visually found option Recall
      Visually found option Recog
      Visually found option Stem
   Picking Recall as second value.
      Making selection Two for Test_Task
ACTION: Update value Two for Test_Task to be Recall
   Done picking values for Test_Task
ACTION: Click Done
NEW SCREEN: Main Screen
...

When it examines test task, it find the prior belief that test task may interact with the spacing variable. This reflects the sort of knowledge we might expect of a memory expert. Also, when it comes to the variables of delay, it retrieves the fact that the frequency regularity theory implies an interaction of spacing and delay. Therefore it chooses to vary that, too (this decision is not shown in the protocol). The experiment finally designed is shown here:

NEW SCREEN: Outcome Table
Exper3
  Repetitions — Two
  Spacing — One_minute Five_minutes
  Source_context — Same
  Test_task — Stem Recall
  Delay — Ten_minutes One_minute
  Test_context — Same
Delay

Ten_Minutes	Test_Task	
Spacing	Stem	Recall
One_Minute	65	11
Five_Minutes	63	31

One_Minute	Test_Task	
Spacing	Stem	Recall
One_Minute	100	93
Five_Minutes	99	92

...

Experiment 3 results in a three-dimensional table, whose results show the interaction of spacing with test task.

Interpreting an Interaction

The interpretation of this table is interesting because it contains an interaction:

```
...
Start with dimension dim1.
Push goal to encode dimension Dim1
    Visually get cell value
        Found value 65
    Visually locate dimension variable.
        Found dimension name Spacing
    Look for value1 visually
        Found dimension value One_Minute
    Move in desired direction.
        Found location below, 2111
    Visually get cell value
        Found value 63
    Look for value2 visually
        Found dimension value Five_Minutes
    Notice less than pattern.
    Difference -2 in Dim1 is not significant.
    Finished first row of dimension Dim1.
```

The model begins with the first dimension as before, encodes the first column, and finds an equal-to relation. Then it searches the second column:

```
    Visually get cell value
        Found value 11
    Move in desired direction.
        Found location below, 2211
    Visually get cell value
        Found value 31
    Notice greater than pattern.
    Found interaction. No main effect? Investigate interaction.
        Found the cell 2111 with the Equal_To effect.
        Search for variable which separates 2211 from 2111.
        Found separating dimension, Test_Task
    Done investigating interaction of Spacing with Test_Task.
```

This time, however, the search over that dimension is not finished. The next column is searched, and a greater-than relation is found. Note that the dimension name and dimension values must only be examined for the first column that is searched—that information is simply carried over for the other columns. Because the greater-than effect is different from the equal-to effect found in the first column, the model assumes no main effect and investigates this interaction. This involves looking for the cell that produced the other effect (equal-to), and then searching for the dimension that separates that cell from the current one. The resulting dimension (test task) is assumed to interact with the current one (spacing).

> Hypothesize that Spacing may have no effect and check for problems.
>   Pop hypothesis.
> Rehearsing hypothesis involving Spacing
> Insufficient range One_Minute Five_Minutes
> Rehearsing hypothesis related to Spacing
> Rehearsing experiment_problem involving Spacing
> ...

Because an interaction was found, the search of that dimension halts and the variable (spacing) is assumed to have no main effect. The generality of this relationship is tested. Because there are no priors for this variable, the model tentatively assumes there may be no effect of spacing and checks for possible experiment problems that may have produced an artifactual null result. It suspects that the difference of 1 min versus 5 min (in the spacing manipulation) may have been an insufficient range. The hypothesis for spacing and this experiment problem is rehearsed to insure that it will be remembered later.

Note that the model's reasoning about the absence of a main effect is not the same as what would be produced by an analysis of variance (ANOVA). Even though there may be an effect of spacing overall, the model reasons (as did the Domain Experts) that because there is a case in which there is no spacing effect, then the prediction of a consistent main effect of spacing is falsified (and hence the frequency regularity is falsified). In general, the model reasons about main effects and interactions qualitatively rather than quantitatively. In fact, purely quantitative interactions (same effect direction but different magnitudes) are ignored.

The rest of the examination of the table is not shown but we briefly summarize it. Because there is a second dimension (and it has not yet been searched), the model turns to this second dimension (going across within a table). The values 65 and 11 are encoded, along with the less-than relationship. The search continues over this dimension and completes all four rows because the same effect (less-than) is found in all cases. Because no interactions are found, the model assumes there is a consistent less-than main effect of test task, and creates a new hypothesis for this belief (which is rehearsed).

The model then searches dimension three (going down across tables). Note that in selecting the next dimension to search, the dimensions are always considered in the same order until one is found for which no matching ENCODE-DIMENSION chunk can be found. This third dimension is also searched exhaustively because the same relation (greater-than) is found in all cases.

The Final Experiment

Because an insufficient range problem was found for the spacing variable in experiment 3, experiment 4 is designed to retest the effect of that variable. This involves pushing a TEST-VARIABLE goal, which then bypasses the need to evaluate the current evidence or choose which factor to vary. In selecting a value for spacing, the model retrieves its previous experiment problem and thus chooses a second value that is further apart from 1 min than 5 min, which in turn involves searching visually again to find more options. Once again, the test task and delay variables are also varied because they are suspected to interact with spacing, although in this case both values for each variable are selected from memory without having to search visually for options. The rest of the variables are also held to the same values as in the previous experiment. The resulting experiment is displayed here:

```
...
Exper4
    Repetitions — Two
    Spacing — One_minute Ten_minutes
    Source_context — Same
    Test_task — Stem Recall
    Delay — Ten_minutes One_minute
    Test_context — Same
Delay
    Ten_Minutes                    Test_Task
      Spacing          Stem          Recall
        One_Minute      64            12
        Ten_Minutes     63            39
    One_Minute                     Test_Task
      Spacing          Stem          Recall
        One_Minute      99            92
        Ten_Minutes    100            92
...
```

The exact same search path over the table is followed as in experiment 3, and the same conclusions are drawn. The differences are that the conclusions are now believed more strongly and no experiment problems are sought (because the null effect is found as expected).

> ...
> Evaluate evidence for hypothesis Frequency_Regularity.
>   Found consequence Spacing Greater_Than.
>   Found consequence to be false. Therefore reject hypothesis
>   Frequency_Regularity.
>   Examined consequence. Therefore done testing hypothesis Frequency_
>   Regularity.
>   Top goal popped.
> ...

When evaluating evidence this time, the model discovers that the frequency-regularity theory has been falsified because there is no main effect of the implied variable spacing. Thus the goal to test that theory is popped, and the task is done. Table 11.2 summarizes the experiments that were designed and the conclusions that were reached from each of them.

RELATING MODEL TO DATA

How does the model account for the group differences data presented earlier in the chapter? In this section, we step through the relationship between the model and each of the five skill differences. The model that is on the Web allows one to set structural variables to produce these individual differences. The experimentation traces produced are correspondingly different.

First, there is the issue of using the theories to design the experiments. In the model, there are productions that create and push the TEST-HY-POTHESIS goal and there are other productions that create and push the EXPLORE-FACTORS goal. Moreover, there is a set of productions relevant to achieving each of these two goals. Thus, by selecting either one goal or the other, the model is able to simulate the experts and theory-oriented undergraduates or simulate the non-theory-oriented undergraduates. There are many ways of implementing this preference. For example, it could be that some undergraduates do not have the production for proposing the TEST-HYPOTHESIS goal or the productions for attaining that goal. Alternatively, it may be that some of the undergraduates simply prefer to select the EXPLORE-FACTORS goal (i.e., the expected utilities of the EX-PLORE-FACTORS productions are higher than those of the TEST-HY-POTHESIS productions).[6] Whichever of these schemes is used, they all capture the important underlying difference of theory-orientedness be-

---

[6]We capture these differences in the Web model by varying utilities.

TABLE 11.2
The Experiments Designed in the Example Model Trace, Their Outcomes,
and the Conclusions Regarding Them Reached by the Model

Number	Design	Outcome	Conclusions
1	Repetitions=2	Source-context	
	Spacing=1 min	Same 100	• Maybe no effect of
	Source-context=	Diff-Room 99	source context
	Same vs. Diff-room		• 1min delay too short
	Test-task=Stem		
	Delay = 1 min		
	Test-context=Same		
2	Repetitions=2	Source-context	
	Spacing=1 min	Same 64	• Definitely no effect of
	Source-context=	Diff-Room 99	source context
	Same vs. Diff-room		
	Test-task=Stem		
	Delay=10 min		
	Test-context=Same		
3	Repetitions=2	Delay	
	Spacing=	10 min Test-task	• Maybe no effect of
	1 min vs. 5 min	Spacing Stem Recall	source context
	Source-context=Same	1 min 65 11	• 1 min vs. 5 min too close
	Test-task=	5 min 63 31	• Maybe effect of delay
	Stem vs. Recall	1 min Test-task	• Maybe effect of test task
	Delay=	Spacing Stem Recall	
	10 min vs. 1 min	1 min 100 93	
	Test-context=Same	5 min 99 92	
4	Repetitions=2	Delay	
	Spacing=	10 min Test-task	• Definitely no man effect
	1 min vs. 10 min	Spacing Stem Recall	of spacing
	Source-context=Same	1 min 64 12	• Definitely effect of delay
	Test-task=	10 min 63 39	• Definitely effect of test
	Stem vs. Recall	1 min Test-task	task
	Delay=	Spacing Stem Recall	
	10 min vs. 1 min	1 min 99 92	
	Test-context=Same	10 min 100 92	

tween the groups. That is, the difference is not just whether the theories are mentioned; rather, there are also large changes in which variables are varied. Figure 11.11 presents a comparison between the performance of the undergraduates (as a function of whether they mentioned the hypotheses during experiment design) and the model with and without the production that proposes the TEST-HYPOTHESIS goal.[7] The measure of performance is the set of variables that are varied in the first experiment. We see that, with the relevant production, the model focuses (as do the subjects) on the spacing and shifting context variables, whereas without the relevant production, the model focus (as do the subjects) on the repetitions variable.

Second, there were group differences in the number of general settings held constant across experiments. The Experts and High-Ability undergraduates were much more conservative in their selections than were the Mid-Ability undergraduates, who seemed to select these general settings randomly on each experiment. In the model, there is a specific production that retrieves the value used in previous experiments. By simply removing this production (or reducing its expected utility), the model transitions from an Expert model to an undergraduate model on this dimension (see Fig.

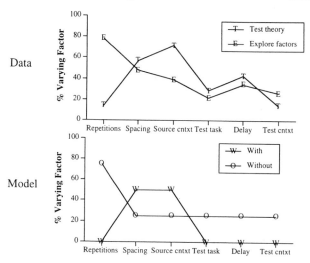

FIG. 11.11. Top: Percentage of undergraduate subjects varying each of variables in the first experiment as a function of whether they were explicitly testing the given theories or simply exploring the factors. Bottom: Percentage of model runs in which the model varies each of the variables in its first experiment as a function of whether the model is run with or without the production that sets the TEST-HYPOTHESIS subgoal.

---

[7]Because this comparison is to different undergraduate groups, prior knowledge of plausible interactions was first removed (for both cases).

11.12).[8] It is interesting the model does not produce as many extreme feature variations (i.e., >3) as did the Mid-Ability undergraduates. Because the model was essentially choosing values randomly from one experiment to another (unless an EXPERIMENT-PROBLEM motivated a particular value), it appears that some of the Mid-Ability undergraduates were purposely picking entirely different values rather than simply selecting values randomly.

Third, there were group differences in the ability to avoid floor and ceiling effects. Here the model begins like the worst undergraduates—it avoids floor and ceiling effects only by chance selections of the spacing and delay variables. However, from feedback in the outcomes, the model is able to quickly learn to avoid delay values that produce floor and ceiling effects—as did the majority of the undergraduates who produced floor and ceiling effects. To account for the initial group differences, one might posit that the Experts and High-Ability undergraduates already had this declarative knowledge (or were more likely to use this knowledge), which the model had to learn through experience with the task.

Fourth, there were differences in the number of variables varied within experiments. Domain Experts and undergraduates varied more variables per experiment than did the Task Experts. The model as described behaved like a mixture of Domain and Task Experts. By default it preferred to vary

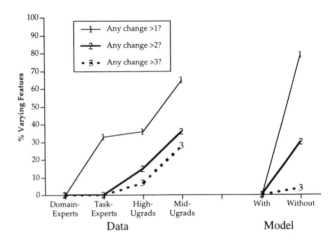

FIG. 11.12.   Left: Percentage of subjects varying more than one, two, or three values. Right: Percentage of model runs in which the model varies more than one, two, or three values as a function of whether the model is run with or without is run with or without the production to retrieve from memory and use values from the previous experiment.

[8]The model means were produced by running 100 simulations.

only one variable per experiment (as in Experiments 1 and 2 in the example trace). The default preference for varying only one variable occurred because, in considering the other variables, there was a default production that proposed to hold the variable constant. A model of the undergraduates might not have such a default production, randomly selecting whether to vary or hold a variable constant. Also, when the model is using the EXPLORE-SYSTEM goal rather than the TEST-HYPOTHESIS goal, the decision as to which and how many variables to vary is arbitrary. Thus, the model can reproduce the undergraduate behavior in two different ways. To account for the Domain Expert behavior, there are productions that access domain-specific knowledge. This domain-specific knowledge is hypotheses about which variables are likely to interact with the variables currently being varied. If such a hypothesis can be retrieved, then the interacting variable is added to the experiment (as in Experiments 3 and 4 in the example trace). Thus, to model the Domain Experts, we simply add the prior knowledge of INTERACTION hypotheses that the test task variable may interact with the spacing effect and that spacing may interact with delay. These are plausible hypotheses for an expert on memory. Figure 11.13 presents the subject data as well as the performance of the model with these interaction hypotheses (modeling Domain Experts), without these interaction hypotheses (modeling Task Experts), and both without the interaction hypotheses and without the production that proposes the TEST-HYPOTHESIS goal (modeling High- and Mid-Ability undergraduates). Although the model overall generates simpler experiments than all four groups, the model does capture the magnitude of the group differences.

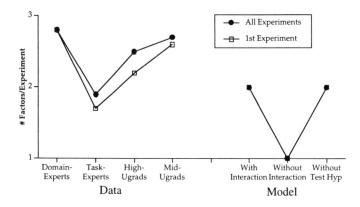

Figure 11.13. Left: The mean number of factors varied per experiment by the subjects. Right: The mean number of factors varied by the model as a function of whether the model was run with or without prior INTERACTION chunks, or both without prior INTERACTION chunks and without the production that sets the TEST-HYPOTHESIS subgoal.

Fifth, the Experts were better able to encode interactions and ignore noise levels in the data. Here we saw that encoding interactions was a complex process. Many productions were required to successfully encode interactions, and the absence of even a small subset of these productions would greatly limit performance. The ability to generate the exhaustive search path over the multiple dimensions is a likely skill that the undergraduates were missing. Another important component of table encoding is the ability to ignore small noise levels. The model is able to ignore small differences in the data through a production that recategorizes a small difference as no difference. By simply removing this production, the model's performance would become more undergraduate-like on this dimension.

In addition to capturing many aspects of the data described thus far, the model also makes new predictions for other group differences. For example, with respect to the order in which subjects select variables to consider, the model predicts (1) that the order for all groups will usually follow the left-to-right, top-to-bottom sequence, and (2) that the experts, because they are more focused on testing the theories, should be somewhat less likely to follow this sequence. The most interesting aspect of this prediction is that the experts should show both aspects of the overall trend (because the model predicts that aspects of the visual interface determines search order of a variable when theory does not implicate the variable) and important violations of the trend (because the model predicts that variables implicated by the theory should be selected first). Table 11.3 reveals that these predictions are confirmed. It displays the order in which variables were set in the interface in terms of what variables were set after what other variables. For Undergraduates, the most frequent transitions in the design of the first experiment are from the left-to-right, top-down sequence: Repetitions to Spacing, Spacing to Source Context, Source Context to Test Task, Test Task to Delay, and Delay to Test Context. These transitions are also common for the Experts but they show two marked deviations—the Experts prefer to set repetitions after spacing and test context after source context. Undergraduates were more likely to follow the left-to-right, top-down pattern, with 68% of their transitions following with the five cells that define this pattern, in contrast to only 47% for the Experts. Similar patterns are found when the transitions are aggregated across just the first experiment, or when one focuses on the frequency with which each variable is selected first.

CONCLUSIONS

The modeling effort presented in this chapter served three primary goals. First, it served as an existence proof that models of complex cognition can still be built in the smaller grain size ACT–R 4.0. Although the construction of this model was not the task of a single afternoon, it was certainly no more difficult than our previous modeling efforts using the larger grain size ACT–R 2.0. Also, although there is much to be added to the model to account for the full range of behaviors and strategies displayed by the different faculty and undergraduate subjects, the model was sufficiently detailed to account for the data described earlier in the chapter. With simple changes in the model, the model could provide an account of the differences in expert and novice performance. Moreover, focusing on the smaller grain size led to many insights regarding the source of various behaviors (discussed later).

It is important to note that there were many aspects of scientific discovery that were not modeled, some because the task being modeled did not include all aspects of scientific discovery (as noted in the introduction to the task), and others simply not yet included in the model. The goal of this modeling effort was not to produce an exhaustive model of scientific discovery, but rather to show whether and how some important aspects could be modeled in the ACT–R 4.0 cognitive architecture and be understood in terms of that architecture.

TABLE 11.3
During the Design of Each Experiment, the Proportion of Transitions from One Variable (Rows) to Another Variable (Columns) Including Returns to the Same Variable and Finishing of the Experiment Design (Stop), Separately for Experts and Undergraduates

Experts	Repetition	Spacing	Source Context	Test Task	Delay	Test Context	Stop
Repetition	4	52	11	16	11	1	5
Spacing	38	5	41	9	7	0	0
Source context	4	17	7	32	5	29	6
Test task	3	0	12	3	60	9	14
Delay	3	2	3	19	11	51	11
Test context	13	0	16	6	18	5	43
Under-grads	Repetition	Spacing	Source Contex	Test Task	Delay	Test Context	Stop
Repetition	3	77	6	7	2	1	4
Spacing	12	5	65	6	8	0	3
Source context	1	6	4	62	4	19	4
Test task	4	3	6	5	72	3	8
Delay	4	4	4	9	7	62	10
Test context	5	5	8	11	13	8	49

The second goal of the modeling effort was to further illuminate the cognitive processes underlying scientific discovery behavior. In fact, building this model did produce several insights for us regarding the nature of scientific discovery processes. First, we found that the experimental design process was controlled by a goal structure for specifying which subgoals must be achieved to design an experiment. Different design paradigms involved slightly different goal structures. For example, a hypothesis-testing, factorial-design experimental paradigm consists of selecting which factors to vary and then fixing the remaining variables. By contrast, the explore-system paradigm specifies a slightly different goal structure. A paradigm other than factorial design would involve yet another goal structure. Although it might be argued that the artificial structured interface used in the SPL task favored the use of such a goal structure and that real scientific discovery would not involve such a goal structure, we would argue the opposite. Because the SPL task presented so much information about the experiment design visually, the individual could rely somewhat on the visual interface (rather than a goal structure) to control search in experiment design. By contrast, in real scientific discovery, with less information contained in a simple visual interface, the individual would have to rely more heavily on a regular goal structure to control search in experiment design.

As another insight gathered from the modeling process, we found that the process of encoding the results in even simple tables is much more detailed and complex than we expected. There must be a careful coordination of table cell and table dimension information to encode main effects and interactions. Relatively little past research has been conducted on how people encode information from tables, which is surprising given how commonly scientific information is presented in tabular form. By developing a better understanding of how tables are read, we may learn how table organization influences when and how discoveries are made.

As a third insight regarding scientific discovery processes, the model illuminated the relationship between performance and the external aspects of the SPL interface in the way that it relied heavily on information in the interface to guide experiment design. Although cognitive science in general has long understood the role of external information in guiding problem space search generally (e.g., Anzai & Simon, 1979; Larkin, 1989) and hypothesis generation and revision specifically (e.g., Cheng, 1990; Shrager, 1987, 1990), past research on scientific discovery has placed little emphasis on the external world for understanding experiment design. This new-found emphasis on the external aspects of the interface led to new predictions about group differences, which we found to be confirmed. Of particular note was that even the experts showed some tendency to rely on the visual interface to order experiment design.

Why should the model rely on external aspects of the interface? First, the environment provided a convenient method for organizing search (Larkin, 1989). Second, the declarative memory decay aspects of ACT–R made this reliance on the external aspects especially important to model performance. For information that could not be found in the environment (hypotheses and previous experiment problems), the model had to engage in extra memory rehearsals to insure that the information would be remembered later. Recall that the analogy model of the previous chapter had to similarly rehearse its hypotheses as to formula structure. When information was obtainable externally, it was often easier and more reliable to simply retrieve it from the external world. Related to this point, another difference (not modeled) between the Experts and undergraduates in the SPL task was that the Experts were much more likely than the undergraduates to use external memory aids like paper and pencil during the task—Experts in the task were aware that forgetting is a common occurrence in scientific discovery. The model was not committed to relying on the interface exclusively—it was capable of using different strategies for retrieving information and making choices, and it adapted its strategy use over time.

Did these three insights derive from specific aspects of ACT–R, or would we have come to these insights in modeling performance using any cognitive architecture? Although such questions are invariably difficult to answer in models of complex problem solving, we believe that the learning and forgetting equations embedded in ACT–R combined with the new restrictions placed on production complexity in ACT–R 4.0 had a strong impact on the final structure of the model. For example, when the model was first written with very little reliance on the external interface or environment, model performance was very poor because things were constantly being forgotten. Other consequences of using ACT–R are explored in our modeling styles comments that follow. However, it is likely that some of our insights were simply a result of having to think through all the detailed steps involved in making decisions in this complex task—and that such insights could have been obtained from using other architectures as well.

The third and final goal of the modeling effort was to examine the modeling styles that emerge from building a model of a complex task. In other words, what features of this model might be useful for ACT–R models in other domains? Several features come readily to mind. For example, making use of information in the environment is likely to be a general feature of human behavior. Cognitive models in earlier versions of ACT–R have represented internally all information that is available to the subject externally, and thus these models have not examined how the organization of the environment can structure behavior. Chapters 5 and 6 of this book describe how ACT–R models can be fully integrated with the external environment.

This chapter and the previous one have shown the importance of such integration.

Another feature that is likely to be general is the use of contextual indexing. Many complex tasks require keeping track of both what has occurred thus far in the current situation and what has happened in previous situations. In order to access both types of information reliably and separately, chunks need to have some form of a context slot. Similar context indexing was seen in the chapters on list memory (Chapter 7) and analogy (Chapter 10). One might further speculate that episodic and semantic memory distinctions might be related to chunks that have or do not have such context slots.

A third general feature is the use of multiple strategies and transitioning between strategies over time. As Reder (1982, 1987) and Siegler (1996) demonstrated, performance in most domains involves multiple strategies within even the same individual. Just as our model can transition from testing a hypothesis to testing the effects of a particular variable, so did the subjects in the SPL task. Chapter 8, on choice, illustrated the details of ACT–R's views on strategy selection, and this chapter merely instantiates the use of multiple strategies within a complex domain.

A fourth feature is that the model was able to improve its performance by storing constraints on future behavior. Specifically, certain outcomes of experiments cued search for experiment problems, and experiment problems that were found produced specific recommendations for subsequent experiments. This use of stored constraints is likely to be another general feature. A yet unresolved issue is whether such constraints are best stored declaratively and used by productions that try to retrieve them later during design (as in our SPL model), or whether these constraints are better viewed as new productions created by production compilation, which essentially act as "demons" to monitor the design of later experiments. A similar issue was raised in the earlier analogy chapter.

As a final point, we would like to address what this model says about the nature of the scientific enterprise itself. When all is said and done, our model is just composed of production rules and chunks like all the other models in this book. There are certainly more knowledge units and the model is incomplete in ways that would require adding many more knowledge units. However, there is none of the "magic" that many associate with the scientific process. There is just a lot of knowledge required. The model can take different paths in solving a problem, depending on momentary differences in activation levels and conflict resolution. Maybe this is what is meant by insight and intuition in science. That is, perhaps scientists are sometimes lucky and have random fluctuations in the subsymbolic quantities that cause them to explore a particularly profitable line of experimentation. However, this does not convey much credit to the scientist. What brings credit to the scientist is to have more of the right knowledge (chunks and productions), just as this is what separated our undergraduates from domain experts. In the end, we think this ACT–R model instantiates Simon's (1989) characterization of science:

> Moreover, the insight that is supposed to be required for such work as discovery turns out to be synonymous with the familiar process of recognition; and other terms commonly used in the discussion of creative work—such terms as "judgment," "creativity," or even "genius"—appear to be wholly dispensable or to be definable, as insight is, in terms of mundane and well-understood concepts. (p. 376)

12

Reflections

John R. Anderson
Christian Lebiere
Carnegie Mellon University

This book has reported the results of our efforts to make ACT–R a theory capable of modeling a wide range of phenomena. The key step in that development has been reducing the size of ACT–R's knowledge units to what have been advertised as the *atomic components of thought*. As a result of this commitment to a consistent, atomic grain size in knowledge representation, modeling in ACT–R has become much more principled and there has been a substantial convergence on the values for the subsymbolic parameters that control the system. This book described some of the in-house applications of ACT–R as demonstrations of the productivity of this approach. However, these application are but a few of the many that researchers have developed. As a better representation of the range of applications of ACT–R, Table 12.1 lists the research papers presented at the 4th Annual ACT–R Workshop in August 1997. The range of applications is truly gratifying in that it indicates that ACT–R is becoming a useful tool for modeling many aspects of human cognition. This breadth of application is a sign that the ACT–R theory is capturing significant generalizations about the nature of human cognition.

The major function of this chapter is to recapitulate and to speculate about the future. It has four sections. The first serves the role of recapitulation in stating the theoretical assumptions of ACT–R and discussing how these assumptions have evolved from past theories. On the view that one can best appreciate the force of these assumptions by comparing ACT–R to its near cousins, the second section provides a comparison of the ACT–R, 3CAPS, EPIC, and Soar architectures. The third section presents our current speculation about the neural realization of ACT–R. Ever since ACT* (Anderson, 1983) we have been concerned with the issue of how ACT might be realized neurally. Such considerations have influenced current developments and will influence future developments. The fourth and last section presents some thoughts about possible directions for the future development of the ACT–R theory.

TABLE 12.1
Papers Presented at the 1997 ACT–R Summer Workshop

Saturday, August 2

Session 1

Bruno Emond	Models of natural language comprehension and parsing
Eric Scott	Implementing a schema theory in ACT–R
Mike Matessa	Focused learning in linguistic role assignment

Session 2

Kevin Gluck	Learning to learn from a computer-based tutor: An ACT–R model as proof-of-concept
Chris Schunn	Psychologist in a box: An ACT–R model that designs and interprets experiments
Brian Ehret	ACT–R models of submariner situation assessment
Wayne Gray & Erik Altmann	Dynamic microstrategies as an explanation of cognitive workload

Sunday, August 3

Session 1

Tony Simon	Computational evidence for the nonnumerical basis of number competence
Todd Johnson	Computation and retrieval in alphabet arithmetic
Christian Lebiere	Lessons from cognitive arithmetic

Session 2

Marsha Lovett, Lynne Reder, & Christian Lebiere	Modeling working memory effects at the individual level
Dieter Wallach	Modeling complex problem solving
John Anderson & Jonathan Betz	Modeling categorization in ACT–R
Niels Taatgen	Explicit learning in ACT–R

Monday, August 4

Session 1

Joyce Tang Boyland	Modeling syntactic priming in ACT–R
Todd Johnson	Multistrategy learning and transfer in tic-tac-toe
Ken Koedinger & Ben MacLaren	Modeling strategy learning in early algebra

Session 2

Frank Lee	Eye tracking in the air traffic controller task
Dario Salvucci	Relating ACT–R models and eye movement protocols
Tony Simon	Modeling a functional limit to the subitizing phenomenon
Mike Byrne	ACT–R and PRP

TABLE 12.1 (contd.)

Tuesday, August 5

Session 1

Raluca Vasilescu	An ACT–R model for learning anaphoric metaphors
Peter Brusilovsky	ACT–R on the Web
John Anderson, Dan Bothell, Scott Douglass, & Christian Lebiere	ACT–R models of the navigation task

ACT–R'S ASSUMPTIONS

There has been a tradition of laying out the foundation of the ACT theories as a set of about 12 assumptions. Although the segmentation of the theory into a small number of assumptions is both a bit arbitrary and uneven, it provides a useful way to succinctly describe the theory and address the question of what is new. This section uses the same assumptions numbered 0 to 13 that were used by Anderson (1993) to describe ACT–R 2.0. We can use the same ACT–R 2.0 structure because the basic assumptions have largely stayed the same. Most changes have been in the implementation details. We state the position of ACT–R 4.0 on each assumption and describe how it has changed from ACT–R 2.0, if it has. This discussion makes reference to the ACT–R Equations, which are collected together in Table 12.2. These equations make use of the ACT–R parameters and variables defined in Table 12.3 (which is similar to Appendix D to Chapter 3).

Assumption 0: Technical Time Assumption

Time is continuous. This assumption has been part of the ACT theory since ACT*. With each iteration of the theory our assumptions about timing have become more detailed. One step in this direction was the addition in ACT–R 4.0 of 50 msec as the default time for a production action. Perhaps the high point on the real-time nature of cognition is Chapter 6 on the perceptual-motor interface. There we coordinated ACT–R's real-time cognitive timing with parallel timing occurring in various perceptual and motor systems.

Assumption 1: Procedural-Declarative Distinction

ACT–R has a procedural component that operates on a declarative component. Both declarative and procedural representations are permanent. This has been the unchanging assumption of all ACT theories.

TABLE 12.2
The Fundamental Equations in ACT–R

(a) Performance-Procedural

Expected Gain $= E = PG - C$ Expected Gain Equation 3.1

$P = qr$ Probability of Goal Equation 3.2

$C = a + b$ Cost of Goal Equation 3.3

$$\text{Probability} = \frac{e^{E_i/t}}{\sum_j e^{E_j/t}}$$ Conflict Resolution Equation 3.4

(b) Performance-Declarative

$$A_i = B_i + \sum_j W_j S_{ji}$$ Activation Equation 3.5

$$B(t) = \beta - d * \ln(t) + \varepsilon_1 + \varepsilon_2$$ Base-Level Equation 3.6

$$\text{Probability} = \frac{1}{1 + e^{-(A-\tau)/s}}$$ Retrieval Probability Equation 3.7

$$M_{ip} = A_i - D_{ip}$$ Match Equation 3.8

$$\text{Probability} = \frac{e^{M_{ip}/t}}{\sum_j e^{M_{jp}/t}}$$ Chunk Choice Equation 3.9

$$\text{Time}_{ip} = F e^{-f(M_{ip} + S_p)}$$ Retrieval Time Equation 3.10

(c) Learning-Declarative

$$B_i = \ln\left(\sum_{j=1}^{n} t_j^{-d} \right) + \beta$$ Base-Level Learning Equation 4.1

$$R_{ji}^* = (1/n)/(1/m) = m/n$$

$$S_{ji}^* = \ln(m/n) = \ln(m) - \ln(n)$$ Prior Strength Equation 4.2

TABLE 12.2 (contd.)

$$R_{ji} = \frac{\text{assoc } R_{ji}^* + F(C_j)E_{ji}}{\text{assoc} + F(C_j)}$$

Posterior Strength Equation 4.3

$$S_{ji} = \ln(R_{ji})$$

(d) Learning-Procedural

$$S_{\text{p}} = \ln\left(\sum_{j=1}^{n} t_j^{-d}\right) + \beta$$

Production Strength Equation 4.4

$$q, r = \frac{\text{Successes}}{\text{Successes} + \text{Failures}}$$

Probability Learning Equation 4.5

$$a, b = \frac{\text{Efforts}}{\text{Successes} + \text{Failures}}$$

Cost Learning Equation 4.6

$$\text{Successes, Failures} = \sum_{j=i}^{m,n} t_j^{-d}$$

Event Discounting Equation 4.7

$$\text{Efforts} = \sum_{j=1}^{m,n} t_j^{-d}\text{Effort}_j$$

Effort Discounting Equation 4.8

Assumption 2: Declarative Representation

As in ACT–R 2.0, the declarative representation consists of a set of chunks. A chunk consists of a limited number of elements (about three) in specific relationships or slots. ACT–R 4.0 has elaborated these assumptions in two ways. First, we have become more serious about the size limitation by eliminating lists of elements as slot values. Such lists previously had provided a means of giving chunks unlimited capacity. Second, ACT–R has begun to address the question of the origin of chunks with the assumption that all chunks are either popped goals or encodings of objects in the environment.

Assumption 3: Procedural Representation

Production rules are the basic units of skills. This is the representational assumption that has evolved the most in ACT–R 4.0. There is now a very restricted sense of a production rule that involves

TABLE 12.3
ACT-R's Variables and Parameters

α^{**}	prior number of successes in instantiation of Probability Learning Equation 4.5
a^{**}	expected cost of matching and firing a production, typically measured in seconds. The default value is 50 msec
A_i	activation of chunk i; see Activation Equation 3.5
$assoc^*$	weighting of prior strength in Posterior Strength Equation 3.1
β^{**}	prior number of failures in instantiation of Probability Learning Equation 4.5
β^*	base-level constant in Base-Level Equation 3.6
b^{**}	expected cost, measured in seconds, from the firing of a production to the resolution of the goal
B_i	base-level activation of chunk i
C	cost incurred in trying to achieve the goal if a particular production is selected, typically measured in seconds; see Cost of Goal Equation 3.3
d^*	decay rate which appears in Equations 3.6, 4.1, 4.4, 4.7, and 4.8. The default value is .5
D_{ip}	mismatch penalty for match of chunk i to production p
ε_1	permanent noise in base-level activation—settable as s parameter
ε_2	temporary noise in base-level activation—settable as s parameter
E	expected gain of a production; see Expected Gain Equation 3.1
f^*	latency exponent in Retrieval Time Equation 3.11; given default value of 1.0
F^*	latency scale factor in Retrieval Time Equation 3.11
G^*	value of the goal
m	total number of chunks in Prior Strength Equation 4.2
m	number of experienced successes in instantiation of Probability Learning Equation 4.5
M_{ip}	match score for chunk i in production p
n	number of associated chunks in Prior Strength Equation 4.2
n	number of failures in instantiation of Probability Learning Equation 4.5
P	probability of the goal should the production be chosen; see Probability of Goal Equation 3.2
q^{**}	probability of a production succeeding, including matching of condition and achievement of subgoals
r^{**}	probability of achieving the goal if the production succeeds
R_{ji}	$e^{S_{ji}}$
s^*	parameter controlling noise in ACT-R logistic noise distributions for utilities and activations; it is related to the variance of the noise distribution by the formula $\sigma^2 = \pi^2 s^2/3$
S	estimated constant in setting S_{ji}—see discussion of strengths of association
S_{ji}^{**}	strength of association between source j and chunk i
S_p^{**}	production strength
τ^*	retrieval threshold of activation in Retrieval Probability Equation 3.7

TABLE 12.3 (contd.)

t	temperature used in Conflict Resolution Equation 3.4 and Chunk Choice Equation 3.9. $t = \sqrt{2}s$ where s is the parameter of the logistic distribution—settable as s parameter
t	variable for time
W_j	attentional weighting of the source j in Activation Equation 3.5; typically set to 1/number of filled goal slots
z^{**}	total prior cost in instantiation of Cost Learning Equation 4.6

* Global parameters that can be set in the ACT-R simulation.
** Parameters that can be set for specific chunks and productions.

1. In the condition, a specification of a goal to which the production can match.
2. In the condition, a specification of retrievals from declarative memory.
3. In the action, a transformation of the goal structure on the basis of these retrievals.

In ACT–R 2.0 it was possible to have complex interdependent retrievals with backtracking for pattern matching and complex computations in the action side. These computations were unrealistically powerful. ACT–R 4.0 has instituted a substantial limitation on the complexity of production rules. This has been part of an overall move to have production rules that model cognition at a finer grain size.

Assumption 4: Goal-Directed Processing

Goals are ordered on a last-in-first-out (LIFO) goal stack. Productions can push goals on the stack or pop goals off the stack. Goals have specific values associated with them. Every production that fires must respond to the top goal on the stack. This assumption has not changed since ACT*.

Assumption 5: Sources of Activation

The slots of the current goal are the sources of activation—the j terms in Activation Equation 3.5—which have source activations W_j. Earlier versions of ACT–R allowed for arbitrary elements to be sources of activation with the goal itself being the default source of activation. As a further constraint in ACT–R 4.0, the W_j are bounded to sum to 1.[1] Although the assumption of a bound on source activation is a strong theoretical claim, the setting of this bound at 1 just serves to establish the scale for associative activation.

---

[1]However, Lovett, Reder, and Lebiere (in press) have speculated that this bound might be an individual difference parameter.

Assumption 6: Activation in Declarative Memory

Chunks have activation levels, which reflect the log odds that they will match a particular production instantiation. On each production cycle the base-level activation of a chunk is combined with activation from associated sources according to Activation Equation 3.5. This equation is identical to the original formulation in ACT–R 2.0 (it was Equation 3.1 in Anderson, 1993). In ACT–R 2.0 there was noise in the base-level activations. This has been elaborated in ACT–R 4.0 with the potential for separate permanent and temporary noise (see Base-Level Equation 3.6).

Assumption 7: Production Pattern Matching

The chunks in a production condition are matched sequentially. The quantity controlling matching of a chunk is the match score, defined by Match Equation 3.8. This equation involves a partial matching component, which was not part of the original formulation of ACT–R 2.0. The retrieval latency function (Retrieval Time Equation 3.10) is the same as in ACT–R 2.0 except that the quantity controlling time in ACT–R 2.0 was the chunk activation whereas now it is the match score (which combines the chunk activation and the mismatch penalty). In ACT–R 4.0 a chunk is retrieved if its activation is above threshold (probability described by Retrieval Probability Equation 3.7) and greater than the activations of other chunks (probability described by Chunk Choice Equation 3.9). The other fundamental change is that the pattern matcher no longer backtracks and only one instantiation is computed for any production: Each chunk pattern is matched by the chunk with the highest match score. If one chunk pattern is matched in a way that makes it impossible to match later patterns then the production fails. If everything succeeds a single instantiation results. ACT–R is moving in the direction of productions with a single chunk retrieval, so this backtracking limitation is often not relevant.

Assumption 8: Production Selection

A major change in ACT–R 4.0 is that productions are selected for the conflict set based solely on whether the top goal matches the goal pattern in the condition. In contrast, in ACT–R 2.0 they were selected for the conflict set only if all of their condition chunks matched. Because the pattern matching of all condition chunks was done in parallel in ACT–R 2.0 this led again to excessive pattern-matching power. Productions in the conflict set in ACT–R 4.0 are selected according to the expected gain PG–C (Expected Gain Equation 3.1) where P is their expected probability that they will lead to the goal, G is the value of the goal, and C is the expected cost of the path. P is defined by the Probability of Goal Equation 3.2 and C is defined by the Cost of Goal Equation 3.3. These equations are the same as in ACT–R 2.0, but in ACT–R 2.0 each instantiation of a production had its own $PG–C$ evaluation, which could be different from other instantiations of the same production. In contrast, in ACT–R 4.0 each production has a single $PG–C$ because productions are selected before they are instantiated by retrieving chunks to match to condition pattern. Noise in the evaluation of productions results in probabilistic selection described by the Conflict Resolution Equation 3.4. Only if a production is selected from the conflict set will an attempt be made to retrieve chunks to match the rest of its condition.

Assumption 9: Strength in Declarative Memory

The activation of a chunk is a sum of its base-level activation and the weighted strengths of association to it from the sources (Base-Level Equation 3.5). Chunks acquire base levels of activation, which reflect their log prior odds of matching a production. Similarly, associations among chunks acquire strengths, which reflect the log-likelihood ratios of one chunk being a source if the other chunk is going to match. The growth in base-level activation is described by Base-Level Equation 4.1 and the change in associative strength is described by Posterior Strength Equation 4.3. These are the same strength adjustment functions as in ACT–R 2.0. In these equations a chunk is considered to have been used (the j terms in the summation in Equation 4.1) if it is retrieved by a production or created anew.

Assumption 10: Production Strength

Production strength grows and decays according to the Production Strength Equation 4.4, which is the same as Base-Level Equation 4.1 that describes changes in base-level activation. In this equation a use (the j terms in the summation) of a production is defined as a firing of an instantiation of that production or an attempt to recreate it.

Assumption 11: Interpretive Application of Declarative Knowledge

In the ACT theories one way to get behavior is to have general productions interpret declarative knowledge as in instruction following or problem solving by analogy. Until the current ACT–R 4.0, there always was the further assumption that this interpretive use of declarative knowledge resulted in the creation of new productions. However, as Chapter 10 on learning from examples illustrated, this is no longer the case. Declarative knowledge can be interpreted without being compiled into production rules or, as we discuss in the next assumption, declarative knowledge can be directly compiled into production rules without first being used. Thus, interpretation application of declarative knowledge no longer has any implications for production formation.

Assumption 12: Knowledge Compilation

Production rules are created from declarative structures called dependencies through a process called production compilation. Dependency structures represent the goal transformations and any deviations from the default variabilization rule. Dependency structures are formed when a goal is set to understand a problem-solving step. When the dependency goal is popped a production rule is created along with the dependency chunk. Production compilation derived from the analogy process in ACT–R 2.0 but has become much more controlled and produces the smaller grain size productions of ACT–R 4.0.

Assumption 13: Learning Production-Rule Utilities

The parameters q and r (underlying P) and a and b (underlying C) are all estimated by Bayesian methods as a weighted combination of a prior and the empirical quantities. The probabilities, q and r, are defined through the Probability Learning Equation 4.5 and the cost quantities, a and b, are learned through the Cost Learning Equation 4.6. These equations are unchanged from ACT–R 2.0 but there has been a change in the scope of the parameters. In ACT–R 4.0 the r and b parameters are associated with the set of productions that fire until the current goal is popped (see Fig. 3.1) whereas they had arbitrary scopes in ACT–R 2.0. Similarly, the scope of the q and a parameters has been extended from the action side of the production to its matching condition side as well as any production cycles to solve the subgoal(s) pushed by the action side. Another change is that the experiences shaping these estimates can decay with time, as described by Event Discounting Equation 4.7 and Effort Discounting Equation 4.8.

Summary

Although the changes from ACT–R 2.0 to ACT–R 4.0 have been in the details, the cumulative impact of these changes has resulted in a qualitative change in the theory. These changes are responsible for the emergence of ACT–R chunks and productions as the atomic components of thought and for the broad range of applicability of the theory as documented in Table 12.1. The devil is in such details. If we were to point to where changes in the details have been most critical it would be Assumptions 7 and 8 about production selection and matching and Assumptions 12 and 13 about production learning. The first pair of assumptions have been tuned to make ACT–R much more applicable to addressing a wide range of performance data. The second pair of assumptions have been tuned to give ACT–R a more realistic theory of production learning.

COMPARISONS OF PRODUCTION-RULE ARCHITECTURES

As noted in the introductory chapter, there are four current production system architectures: ACT–R, 3CAPS[2] (Just & Carpenter, 1992), EPIC (Meyer & Kieras, 1997), and Soar (Newell, 1990). This section does not provide an exposition of the other three architectures. The reader can go to the original sources for this.[3] Rather, the goal of this section is to help the reader of this book place ACT–R by drawing comparisons between these architectures and ACT–R. This can be achieved without complete descriptions of the other architectures because they all share the same basic conception of cognition. Thus, in describing ACT–R we have established the basis for making relevant comparisons to the other architectures. This description is organized around a set of criteria established at the Cognitive Science Meetings in 1995 (Anderson, John, Just, Carpenter, Kieras, & Meyer, 1995) for comparing the production systems. The participants in that symposium agreed to compare the production systems with respect to a set of issues that can be organized into three main categories: their architectural features, their relationship to data, and their practical considerations. These categories form the three subsections of this section. We should say in advance that we are not attempting an artificial sense of neutrality in our description. We think that at many points ACT–R represents the right decisions and we say so and why. One may look at this section as motivating the ACT–R assumptions by looking at the near misses. The reader should also consult Johnson (1997b) for a comparison of Soar and a slightly older version of ACT–R.

Architectural Features

Parallelism. The first architectural feature on which we agreed to compare the production systems was their stance on parallelism. All production systems allow for some degree of parallelism but ACT–R allows for the

---

[2]As this book goes to press, we understand that 3CAPS is to be replaced by a new system, 4CAPS.

[3]Bonnie John's Chapter 9 in Pew and Mavor (1998) offers a general review of these and related cognitive architectures.

least. The other production systems have a fixed cycle time in which it is possible to match many production rules and fire these in parallel. A major problem with this stance is that it allows an unbounded amount of computation to be compacted into a single production cycle. This was also a problem with ACT–R 2.0 in which all productions could be matched in a single cycle even if only one was fired. As Wallach (1998) showed, it is possible to embed in a single production match a solution to the traveling salesman problem, which is known to be NP-complete.[4] The next section, on ACT–R's possible neural realization, describes some of the unrealistic assumptions about neural computation that this kind of parallelism would imply.

In ACT–R 4.0, production rules are processed in parallel only with respect to their match to the goal chunk. As the next section of this chapter discusses, this is an amount of parallelism that the nervous system can support. Any declarative retrievals to instantiate the selected productions must be performed serially. Perhaps the complete serialization of declarative retrievals is too extreme, but it is not possible to process in parallel unboundedly many declarative retrieval requests. On the other hand, there is a great deal of parallelism in ACT–R's processing of a specific retrieval request. All of the declarative chunks of a particular type are accessed in parallel to see if any match the retrieval request. As the next section of this chapter shows, this is a reasonable amount of parallelism to expect from the brain.

An additional reason for wanting to have only one production fire at a time is the problem of coordinating potentially contradictory actions, such as when requests are made to move the hands in two incompatible directions. We discuss this issue further under conflict resolution.

Activation Processes.   The second question we agreed to address was whether there were continuously varying, real-valued quantities modulating performance. The answer in the case of Soar and EPIC is that there are not. This creates serious problems for these theories in accounting for the continuously varying graded character of human behavior, which has been constantly referenced throughout this book. It also creates something of a mystery as to how such discrete computation can arise out of something as continuous and stochastic as the human nervous system. ACT–R and 3CAPS have taken the stance of hybrid systems in which continuously varying quantities modulate the performance of the symbolic system. They can also be seen as systems in which their symbolic structure is really an approximation achieved from the subsymbolic processes.

---

[4]NP-complete problems are generally considered not to be solvable in bounded time but rather to require solution times that grow exponentially with their size. Thus, they are not candidates for "atoms of thought."

In ACT–R, continuously varying quantities modulate performance of procedural memory as well as declarative memory. However, for comparison with 3CAPS we will focus on the activation processes in ACT–R's declarative memory. Here the similarities are substantial. In both, activation of a declarative element underlies its retrieval, that activation is a sum of a base-level activation plus activation spread from sources, and the base-level activation reflects the log frequency of the declarative element. However, the conception of spreading is substantially different. In ACT–R activation is spread from slots in the goal, whereas in 3CAPS activation is spread by the actions of production rules. The role of activation in retrieval is also different. In ACT–R level of activation determines rate of retrieval, whereas in 3CAPS productions have to fire repeatedly until some threshold of activation is reached. This makes the effect of activation on latency more like a step function in 3CAPS. If there is not quite enough activation to fire a production, a whole additional cycle must be spent in building up activation. It is not always possible in 3CAPS to get the number of steps to match up with the observed timing effects.

Declarative Memory.   The third architectural question is whether there is a long-term declarative memory separate from the long-term procedural memory created by the production rules. All production systems require at least a temporary declarative memory because this is what the production rules match to. However, in Soar this working memory is attached to the goals and disappears as the goals are achieved. The other three production systems all have separate long-term declarative memories. Soar can encode the effect of a long-term declarative memory by productions like

> IF   George Washington appears
> THEN   note that George Washington is the president of the United
>   States

This creates declarative memories (called "data chunks" in Soar) that are asymmetric in their access. For instance, the production rule just given can go from *George Washington* to the fact but not from *United States* to the fact.

The process of learning such production rules is one of the most problematic aspects of the Soar architecture, which was solved by a mechanism called data chunking. It was a major discovery within the Soar architecture and is a very complex mechanism, which would be too long to recount here (but see Newell, 1990). The contrast between its complexity and the ease people have in learning new declarative facts is evidence, in our view, that data chunking reflects a confluence of mistaken assumptions in the Soar architecture.

The origins of ACT–R in the HAM (Anderson & Bower, 1973) theory of memory has meant that it has always had an elaborate theory of declarative memory. It is fair to say that it is the only production-system architecture that has taken seriously the task of modeling results from the human memory literature. This book does represent some of that effort. Within the human memory literature ACT–R has sometimes been criticized for its complexity because it has not been clear to many in the memory community what the contribution of the production-system architecture is to accounting for the basic effects of the field. We hope that this book has demonstrated some of the integration that is possible by adopting a production-system framework.

Conflict Resolution.   The fourth architectural question concerned how decisions are made about which path to follow at points of non-determinism. EPIC and 3CAPS are parallel-firing production systems that do not have any conflict-resolution principles. In both systems the programmer must make sure that contradictory actions are not taken. Control issues seem not to have been a focus of attention in 3CAPS but have been a major concern in the EPIC system, where modeling dual processing has been an important topic. The actual control regimens that have been programmed in published EPIC models are very difficult to understand, and it stretches credibility to believe that such control structures could ever have been learned. Moreover, as Chapter 6 displayed, the degree of parallelism predicted by EPIC does not appear to occur.

Although Soar is a parallel-firing production system, it does not have the problem of contradictory actions firing because production-rule firings do not actually determine control of cognition. Rather, Soar operates in an elaborate-decide cycle. In the elaboration phase productions do fire in parallel, bringing information to bear in deciding what operator to apply. Then in a decision cycle a single operator is applied. As Johnson (1997b) noted, Soar operators are really the equivalent of ACT–R productions and the elaborate-decide cycle is the equivalent of an ACT–R cycle. At the level of selecting operators that control cognition, Soar is every bit as serial as ACT–R. In some ways, the discrete accumulations of elaborations play the same role as continuous ACT–R subsymbolic computations.

ACT–R, by placing its conflict resolution at the subsymbolic level, is capable of modeling many of the continuously varying properties of human choice. It can also adapt itself to the statistics of the environment. Chapter 8, on choice, displayed the virtues of this approach.

Goal-Oriented Behavior.   As Chapter 2 noted, it is remarkable that all of these architectures have converged on using goal structures to control production-rule firing. It is remarkable in part because none of the original production systems (including ACTE—Anderson, 1976) had such a goal structure. The need for a goal structure was a lesson learned in all of these systems. Although all architectures have goal-factored production rules, it is in Soar and ACT–R that one finds an elaborate set of architectural assumptions to support this goal-based processing. Both involve a goal stack, but in Soar, productions can respond to any goal on that stack, whereas in ACT–R, only the current goal can control behavior. Although this is a significant distinction, data do not seem to be available that are relevant to the distinction.

The principles for the creation of subgoals are quite different in Soar versus ACT–R. In ACT–R production rules explicitly set subgoals at appropriate times. In contrast, in Soar subgoals are only created when an impasse is encountered. An impasse occurs when there is not a basis for making a decision in a decision cycle. At such points Soar automatically creates a subgoal to obtain relevant knowledge for making a decision. For instance, a classic example would be when Soar is trying to make a move in a game, cannot decide, creates a subgoal to get information for deciding, and tries look-ahead as a method for deciding. Although this is a different mechanism for subgoaling, in practice Soar production rule systems are designed so that they often subgoal just at the points where ACT–R productions would deliberately set a subgoal.

The issue of what to do at true impasses is a profound one for any cognitive architecture. What does one do when one comes to a problem state for which there is no relevant knowledge about how to proceed? For instance, suppose a subject in an experiment suddenly finds that the computer administering the experiment has died and the screen has gone blank. Assume, for the sake of making this a true impasse, that this subject is totally computer naive and so has no knowledge relevant to the state. What would the subject do? If the subject were Soar it would impasse to a new subgoal and could potentially impasse forever going into ever deeper problem states. ACT–R's architectural primitive is to abandon the subgoal[5] and return to the higher goal that set it. Thus, if the subject were ACT–R it would return to its goal of getting experimental credit and seek out the experimenter with the problem.

Learning. The final architectural question concerned what kinds of learning and self-improvement the systems could achieve. All production systems allow themselves to add declarative elements.[6] However, the only production system other than ACT–R with a serious theory of learning is

---

[5]Recall that ACT–R 4.0 will abandon a subgoal whenever there are no productions that apply with positive expected utility. Note that the utility threshold is settable in the ACT–R 4.0 simulation system.

[6]However, in Soar these are lost when the goal context is lost.

Soar. In contrast to ACT–R, Soar has only a single mechanism for learning, called chunking, and it is a symbolic mechanism for learning production rules. Chunking compiles the computation that was done to resolve an impasse. It compares the state of working memory before an impasse occurred and a subgoal was spawned, with the state after the subgoal was popped. It notes the knowledge that was added to this state by the subgoal and creates a production rule that will directly provide this knowledge without going into a subgoal. Thus, the chunking mechanism finds the knowledge that was relevant to making that decision and provides it directly in a single elaboration production. For instance, if a look-ahead subgoal in a game situation found some principle for selecting a move, that principle will be available the next time without look-ahead.

Chunking has similarities to the production compilation mechanism in ACT–R. For instance, Soar's chunking incorporates a similar default variabilization rule to the one in ACT–R and has similar problems as ACT–R in terms of occasions when a different variabilization is needed. The major difference is that the dependencies, from which productions are compiled in ACT–R, are created by deliberate computation and so the default variabilization rule can be tuned, whereas variabilization occurs automatically in the Soar architecture.

A general problem with Soar chunking is that it creates too many productions. The ACT theory has evolved, from mechanisms in ACT* that created production rules much too promiscuously, to the more focused analogy mechanism of ACT–R 2.0, to the deliberate production compilation of ACT–R 4.0. This need to control and direct production creation has been a lesson learned in the ACT systems.

In addition to symbolic learning, ACT–R has subsymbolic learning mechanisms that play a major role in the adaptiveness of the system and its ability to account for data as was displayed throughout this book. In particular in this context, ACT–R's ability to learn conflict-resolution parameters allows it to learn that a production rule is bad and so recover from a mistake. In contrast, there is no direct way to get rid of a bad production rule in Soar.

Relationship to Data

The second major issue discussed at the Cognitive Science Symposium was how these theories related to data. There were four subtopics.

Time.   With respect to latency predictions the four architectures offer interesting similarities and contrasts. All four have converged on 50 msec as the minimum cycle time for processing. In all but Soar this is the minimum time for a production firing. In Soar this is the approximate time for an elaborate-decide cycle. The actual length of the cycle depends on the number of rounds of elaboration, with each round of elaboration taking about 10 msec.

In all the models except ACT–R, time progresses in discrete ticks. These are 50-msec ticks in EPIC and 3CAPS and 10-msec ticks in Soar. Human behavior does not occur in discrete time ticks, so these models would have to add some variability in the timing of the cycles to obtain the latency distributions observed of human subjects. Such variability is built into EPIC simulations. In our view the continuous nature of human timing is not just a matter of noise rounding off the corners of a discrete process but is a fundamental property of human cognition (at least at the level at which it is usually measured). For instance, the problem-size effect in cognitive arithmetic (Chapter 9) shows that latency increases relatively continuously with the size of operands. It would be difficult to produce such effects in the other production-system models. As another example from Chapter 9, the gradual improvement with practice is not easy to capture. The gradual slowing that occurs with delay and disuse is even harder to capture without recourse to a subsymbolic level.

Errors.   An important question for production-system models of human cognition, which goes to the issue of whether they are "computer" models or cognitive models, is whether and how they can make errors. One kind of error in production systems and humans is what is called knowledge errors. That is, errors occur because the system has the wrong production rules or wrong declarative chunks. These are the kinds of errors that all systems can make, including the most non-human-like computer programs, as anyone knows who has received an error in a banking statement.

Other kinds of errors occur infrequently and randomly and are more uniquely human. For instance, errors can occur because of loss of relevant declarative information. In 3CAPS or ACT–R, errors in processing can occur because needed declarative information is not sufficiently active. Adding some stochasticity to activation levels in ACT–R enables it to model the graded error rates that are characteristic of human cognition and that one cannot get from the EPIC or Soar architectures.

In addition, and unique to ACT–R, there is a partial-matching process that produces the kind of confusion among declarative chunks that is critical in modeling other slips that people make that are not just errors of omission. Such slips also cannot be knowledge errors because they tend to occur infrequently and probabilistically. So, for instance, the false alarms that are characteristic of human memory in many situations depend on some sort of partial matching (see Chapter 7).

Connections to the External World. The presence of EPIC at the symposium assured that we all addressed the issue of what the connection was between our architectures and the external world. As Chapters 5 and 6 argued, it is not possible to give truly principled predictions about human cognition without addressing the issue of how these systems sense and act on the external world and the consequences of these operations for the flow of cognition. The data and model in Chapter 10 are striking evidence for the importance of understanding such details for high-level models. That chapter showed that essentially all existing models of analogy were wrong because they incorporated mistaken assumptions about how the development of an analogy was interleaved with external access to information about the problem.

EPIC established a high-water mark for concern with the external world, but we think that the ACT–R/PM system (Chapter 6) has reached and surpassed that mark. In part this is because it incorporates the best ideas from the EPIC system. Recently, there has been an effort to directly tie together EPIC's system with the Soar architecture (Chong & Laird, 1997). Such efforts enable these production systems (ACT–R, EPIC, Soar) to interact with the actual software that runs experiments (see the discussion of ACT–R's no-magic doctrine in Chapter 1). This is an important demonstration of the sufficiency of the system, and it is also an important aid to applications where interaction with an external piece of software is critical. We have more to say about this when discussing practical applications.

Individual Differences. The presence of 3CAPS at the symposium likewise assured that we all addressed the issue of individual differences. One way to deal with individual differences in a production-system architecture is in terms of knowledge differences. Different individuals bring different sets of knowledge (productions and chunks) to bear in solving a task and so show differences in behavior. This is the only kind of account EPIC or Soar can give of individual differences. This was also basically the account offered in Chapter 11 of differences in scientific discovery. On the other hand, 3CAPS and ACT–R can also relate individual differences to system parameters that reflect performance differences in the individuals' cognitive architecture. So, for instance in ACT–R, Lovett, Reder, and Lebiere (in press) have explained differences in working memory capacity in terms of the total amount of source activation, the sum of the W_j terms, available for activation spread in the Activation Equation 3.5. They called this total capacity W.

3CAPS has another dimension to individual differences in that it postulates distinct activation resource pools for performing different activities like spatial versus linguistic processing. Thus, it can explain different patterns of individual strengths as different capacities for these resource pools. In

ACT–R, the parameters are global and do not allow for the potential of different values in different content domains. Although one could always elaborate the ACT–R theory with such distinctions, Lovett et al. speculated that the domain-specific differences might be due to differential practice that would affect things like base-level activation. The source activation, W, captures domain-general effects that do not depend on practice. This domain-general W would be like Spearman's (1904) g in theories of intelligence.

Practical Considerations

It is significant that practical considerations were one of the categories of evaluation at the Production System Symposium. This reflects an emerging consensus that production systems should serve as useful modeling tools. The following were the issues we considered.

Applications. What are the potentials for practical applications? Each system has its own strengths here. EPIC, Soar, and ACT–R all have some investment in providing cognitive models for human-computer interaction domains. In the case of ACT–R, the system has also provided cognitive models for intelligent tutoring systems. In this regard, it should be noted that the cognitive models that exist in our current tutoring systems (Anderson, Corbett, Koedinger, & Pelletier, 1995) reflect a production-system architecture that actually predates ACT–R 2.0 and served as a source of many of the ideas for ACT–R 2.0. As such, it models cognition at a much larger grain size than is done in ACT–R 4.0. It remains to be seen how much instructional leverage can be gained from the finer grain size of analysis in ACT–R 4.0.

Our deepest hopes for the practical applications of the ACT–R architecture are to education. Education is a domain where psychology should be making greater contributions and where there is a real lack of applications with good theoretical foundations (Anderson & Schunn, in press). Applications of cognitive architectures to education need not be confined to development of tutoring systems, however. Cognitive architectures should have implications for all aspects of instruction.

In the case of Soar, the major domain of application of the architecture has been to building artificial intelligence systems. Given the increasing standards for success both in artificial intelligence applications and cognitive modeling, it is becoming increasingly difficult to have one system serve both domains. In recent years the cognitive modeling use of Soar has been receiving less attention.

Model Re-Use.   The presence of Soar at the symposium assured that we all addressed the issue of model re-use. One of the admirable attributes of the Soar community is that models for one application use models developed in another application. Thus, for instance, the NASA Test Director model (Nelson, Lehman, & John, 1994) used NL Soar (Lehman, VanDyke, & Rubinoff, 1995) to model language processing. This means that constraints developed in one model are preserved in another. EPIC is only used by Kieras and Meyer and is not publicly available, so re-use has not been a major issue. The amount of re-use in 3CAPS is modest and of the same pattern and degree as described next for ACT–R.

There is some modest model re-use in the ACT–R system. So, for instance, the PRP model reported in Chapter 6 used the arithmetic facts and parameters developed in the cognitive arithmetic model in Chapter 9. However, in ACT–R there has been relatively little wholesale re-use of models from one task to another. This is related to the issue of the size of ACT–R models. Because ACT–R models are relatively small there is little need or opportunity to re-use exact productions or chunks. What has transferred across models, as illustrated throughout the book, is a style of knowledge representation and a set of constraints on the global parameters.

Scalability.   Again, the presence of Soar at the symposium raised the question of whether our models would scale up. The artificial intelligence (AI) applications of Soar with learning of new productions have involved as many as a million production rules (Doorenbos, 1992, 1995). In contrast, ACT–R, EPIC, and 3CAPS models have had at most a few hundred production rules. This difference reflects at least three factors. First, as already noted, it takes many Soar production rules to implement an operator that is the equivalent of one ACT–R production rule. Second, again as noted, there is the overfecundity of Soar's chunking mechanism in creating too many production rules. Most of the production rules learned are not particularly useful.[7] Third, the emphasis on large-scale AI application in Soar require coding more knowledge than modeling detailed human data from a particular cognitive task. With respect to cognitive models with detailed concern for correspondence to data, there is not a difference in the complexity of the tasks to which ACT–R and Soar have been applied.

However, it does seem reasonable to assume that human cognition does involve millions of chunks and at least tens of thousands of ACT–R style production rules. ACT–R 4.0 has been designed to have its efficiency not be impacted much by scale. Much of this comes from the use of chunk types in the implementation. Production rules are selected by matching the chunk

---

[7]For instance, in Altmann's (1996) dissertation, 63% of the learned production rules were never used.

type of the goal. This goal factoring of production rules allows the system to efficiently focus on the relevant production rules without having to match them all. Similarly, retrievals must specify the chunk type, again allowing the system to focus on a small subset of its declarative knowledge. The elimination of backtracking in matching has eliminated the danger of any combinatorics involved in production-rule matching. Typically, ACT–R simulations run many times faster than subjects.[8] The elimination of expensive pattern matching not only means that ACT–R simulations are efficient but, as the next section of the book will review, also means that ACT–R avoids inconsistencies with what we understand about the neural basis of cognition. The same is not true of Soar production rules, which can potentially be quite expensive to match (Tambe, Newell, & Rosenbloom, 1990).

Most of ACT–R's computation time is actually spent performing real-valued mathematics to simulate subsymbolic computations. This is not an issue in a symbolic system like Soar. However, the costs of these real-valued computations are bounded for the same reasons that the symbolic computation is bounded. ACT–R performs calculations on an as-needed basis for the simulation and so is not always updating all the quantities in the database. There is one notorious "hole" in the bound that ACT–R places on subsymbolic computation. This occurs in computing the sums defined in Equations 4.1, 4.4, 4.7, and 4.8. The past references can increase linearly with time, and the sum needs to be computed anew each time the quantities are needed because the power-law decay equation is not open to simplification, unlike, say, exponential decay. As a consequence, the long simulations have been known to grind to a halt. There is an Optimized Learning option in ACT–R that enables these sums to be approximated in a manner that is usually quite satisfactory (e.g., see Fig. 4.1). When this is set there is not significant slowing of ACT–R simulations.

Modeling Effort. The question here is, how easy is it to develop models in the architecture? As the first chapter discussed, ease of model development is a major goal in the ACT–R system. Of course, an added constraint is that the models that are easy to develop also have to be the models that give accurate accounts of the data. Although model development is never easy, model development in ACT–R by researchers other than the original developers is easier than in any of the other competitive architectures. This is both because of the structure of ACT–R and because of the set of facilities that we have put in place to support model development. Moreover, reflecting our major commitment to this goal, we are continually improving the situation in this respect.

---

[8]This is time for the simulation to deliver its predictions. Predicted times are, of course, on the same scale as the human times.

Time to Learn. We have also continually refined the teaching of ACT–R. In 1994 we taught the first ACT–R summer school. As an instructional effort it was frankly a disaster, although some students still managed to learn. However, we constantly try to absorb the lessons of our teaching experience to improve the instruction of ACT–R. Each year, the ACT–R summer school has improved and in 1998 we hope to reach a major point in ACT–R instruction. We plan to take students in 10 days to the point where they understand all the aspects of ACT–R and have begun to model some of their own data. The 10 days will be very busy and students will still have much to learn (as indeed we do), but we will have reached the point where cognitive scientists can learn to use ACT–R in their research with a modest investment of time. The instructional material for this summer school is generally available and is also used for other summer schools and to teach courses at other universities. With respect to university courses, the experience seems to be that students can get a basic "feel" for ACT–R in less than a month,[9] can come to master all of the basics of ACT–R in a quarter course, and can also complete a significant project in a semester course. Researchers can come up to speed in modeling in ACT–R faster than in any of the other production-system formalisms. Furthermore, when one considers the range of tasks to which students can apply ACT–R after mastering the material, we can confidently say that learning is much more efficient now in ACT–R than in any other modeling formalism (i.e., not just production systems).

ACT–R'S POSSIBLE NEURAL REALIZATION

Two lines of research in cognitive neuroscience are currently receiving a lot of attention. One is concerned with how cognition might be achieved by computation that is neurally plausible. The second is concerned with how cognition is mapped onto regions of the brain and the functional consequences of this mapping. We have given thought to how ACT–R relates to both of these issues. This section describes ACT–RN (Lebiere & Anderson, 1993), which is a potential connectionist realization of ACT–R and addresses the first cognitive neuroscience issue. This has served to help us think through a number of the changes that transitioned from ACT–R 2.0 to ACT–R 4.0. It also serves as the basis for thinking about how ACT–R might map onto neural structure—the second cognitive neuroscience issue, which we speculate about as we describe ACT–RN.

The end of the ACT–R 2.0 book (Anderson, 1993), described some ideas for realizing the computation in a neurally plausible manner. That served as

---

[9]ACT–R has been used for this period in "Comparative Architectures" or "Introduction to Cognitive Science" courses.

a starting point for the development of ACT–RN. However, as we went down that path we recognized a number of unnecessary complexities. Therefore, in the Lebiere and Anderson (1993) conference paper we described a version of ACT–RN that was much simpler, easier to imagine neurally implemented, and much closer to the current version of ACT–R 4.0. ACT–RN has never been a very practical system for simulating cognition because it requires specifying a fair amount of connectionist detail to create a model, in addition to what has to be specified for ACT–R. It is also much less efficient to run simulations. It also suffers from some shortcomings typical of connectionist simulations, in particular the difficulty in interpreting and analyzing what is happening. ACT–R has served as a more useful level of abstraction for developing cognitive models. However, ACT–RN has served as an existence proof that ACT–R could be achieved in a current connectionist architecture. ACT–RN has also served as an inspiration for many of the ideas that led to the development of ACT–R 4.0. We describe later the implementation of ACT–RN and how it has influenced the development of ACT–R 4.0. In writing this section we are assuming that the reader knows the basic concepts of connectionist models (as are found in McClelland & Rumelhart, 1986; Rumelhart & McClelland, 1986).

As was illustrated in Fig. 1.2, there are three major memories in ACT–R: declarative memory, procedural memory, and goal memory. The next three subsections describe how ACT–RN implements each memory. The actual running code for ACT–RN can be obtained by following the ACT–R Software link from the ACT–R home page, http://act.psy.cmu.edu.

Declarative Memory

Figure 12.1 illustrates how ACT–RN implements declarative chunks. A chunk in ACT–R consists of a unique identifier called the header, together with a number of slots each containing a value which can be another chunk. Retrieval of chunks in ACT–R involves specifying some of these elements and retrieving other elements by activating the declarative network. To implement this kind of associative memory, ACT–RN uses a simplified version of a real-valued Hopfield network (Hopfield, 1984). Each slot, as well as the chunk identifier itself, is represented by a separate pool of units. The unit pool for the chunk identifier is called the header in Fig. 12.1. Instead of having complete connectivity among all pools, the slots are only connected to the header and vice versa. Therefore retrieval works not by energy minimization on a recurrent network but through a forward-backward mapping mechanism. Retrieval involves activating patterns in some of the pools and trying to fill in the remaining patterns corresponding to the retrieved chunk. If some slot patterns are activated, they are mapped to the header units to retrieve the chunk identifier that most closely matches these

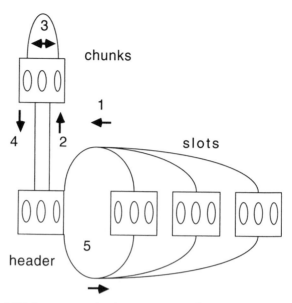

FIG. 12.1. ACT–R represents chunks as connections between a header module and slot modules with a chunk module to perform the cleanup.

contents (path 1 in Fig. 12.1). Then, the header is mapped back to the slots to fill the remaining values (path 5). If the header pattern is specified then the step corresponding to path 1 is omitted.

To insure optimal retrieval, we found it necessary to "clean" the header. This can be achieved in a number of ways. One would be to implement the header itself as an associative memory. We chose instead to connect the header to a pool of units called the chunk layer in which each unit represented a chunk, achieving a localist representation (path 2). The header units are connected to all the units in the chunk layer. The pattern of weights heading to a particular localist unit in the chunk layer corresponds to the representation of that chunk in the header. By assembling these chunk-layer units in a winner-take-all network (path 3), the chunk with the representation closest to the retrieved header ultimately wins. That chunk's representation is then reinforced in the header (path 4). A similar mechanism is described in Dolan and Smolensky (1989). The initial activation level of the winning chunk is related to the number of iterations in the chunk layer needed to find a clear winner. This maps onto retrieval time in ACT–R. (See the neural model in Appendix B of Chapter 3.)

Every time a new chunk is created, a new representation appears in the header pool, and a new unit is initialized in the localist chunk layer with the proper connections. One-step Hebbian learning is then used to add the correlation between header units and slot units (paths 1 and 5) to the connections between header and slots. If header representations are orthogonal, such one-time learning is sufficient (Hinton & Anderson, 1981). If rather than using orthogonal header representations we use random representations, we get interference between representations that decreases with the size of the representation (number of units in the header).

The other possibility is to allow chunk representations to be correlated to the extent they are similar. This would both increase interference and promote generalization. To learn this type of representation, an iterative supervised learning algorithm such as the generalized Delta Rule (Rumelhart & McClelland, 1986) would be necessary. Such representations can be directly specified in ACT–RN but cannot be learned.

For those chunks that we regard as symbolic, we used either random or orthogonal representations for identifiers. For those chunks that we regard as analog, we encoded their similarity in the patterns of correlations among their identifiers. For instance, in a simulation of the multicolumn addition model, we had symbolic chunks representing the addition columns but we specified for the integers a representation encoding their magnitude. That allows the addition table to be represented compactly and to generalize well. This was the beginning of the partial-matching mechanism that is now part of ACT–R.

ACT–RN uses separate connectionist modules like Fig. 12.1 to implement each chunk type. This segregation of memory by chunk type plays a major role in terms of optimizing the storage requirements of ACT–RN. It is widely assumed that the capacity of associative memories grows linearly with their size (Hopfield, 1982). If full connectivity is used, however, the number of connections grows with the square of the number of units. By breaking up declarative memory into type memories, ACT–RN preserves capacity while considerably decreasing the number of connections necessary. Separate type memories can also learn better the representational structure of each chunk type without being perturbed by the other types. Finally, because various types have different numbers of slots and therefore different lengths, having separate memories for each type improves memory efficiency.

We suspect that each type in ACT–RN corresponds cortically to a hypercolumn or small cortical area of 10,000 or more cells. There are tens of thousands of such cortical areas that could more than support the implementation of the different types in ACT–RN. These cortical regions have the sort of interconnectivity to support the iterative processing and cleanup described with respect to Fig. 12.1. Note that we are assuming that declarative memories are stored cortically in ACT–RN. As noted in Chapter 2, the hippocampus seems to be involved in the creation of new declarative memories, but it is not the permanent long-term repository of declarative memory.

Procedural Memory

ACT–R is a goal-oriented system. To implement this, ACT–RN has a central memory, which at all times contains the current goal chunk (Fig. 12.2), with connections to and from each type memory. Central memory consists of a pool of units where each pool encodes a slot value of the goal. With this system we implemented productions that retrieve information from a type memory and deposit it in central memory. Such a production might retrieve from an addition table the sum of two digits held in central memory. For example, given the goal of adding 2 and 3, a production would copy to the addition-fact type memory the chunks 2 and 3 in the proper slots, let the memory retrieve the sum 5, and then transfer that chunk to the appropriate goal slot. This operation implements the basic goal transformation by retrieval that has been characteristic of many ACT–R 4.0 productions throughout this book.

To provide control over production firing, we needed a way to decide not only what is to be transferred where, but also under what conditions. That is the role of the conflict-resolution mechanisms in ACT–R. In ACT–RN, that task is achieved by gating units. Each gating unit implements a particular production and has incoming connections from central memory that reflect the goal constraints on the left-hand side of that production.

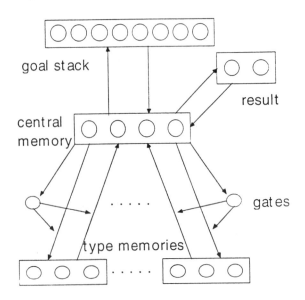

FIG. 12.2. The realtionship among the various memories in ACT–RN (compare with Fig. 1.2). Production rules are basically implemented as gates to control flow of information between the memories.

For example, suppose goal slot S is required to have as value chunk C in production P. To implement this the connections between S and the gating unit for P would be the representation for C, with an appropriate threshold. At each production cycle, all the gating units are activated by the current state of central memory, and a winner-take-all competition selects the production to fire. This is similar to the scheme in ACT–R 4.0 of only testing against the goal in selecting which productions to try.

Connections between central and type memories describe the patterns of transfer to and from central memory. The winning gating unit is used to turn on the connections used by that production with all other connections left off. Each gating unit is restricted to enabling paths back and forth between central memory and a particular type memory.[10] Thus, the basic production type is:

Type I: Lookup-Fact
goal
fact
==>
transformed goal

This looks up some fact and copies some slot value(s) (or header) back into the goal, thus transforming the goal. It is possible to replace the goal with the fact itself. In this case the production rule is:

Type II: New-Goal
goal
==>
fact as new goal

Although this syntax is a severe restriction over ACT–R 2.0, it anticipated the format of production rules in ACT–R 4.0 (see Chapter 2).

It is worth noting that production rules in ACT–RN are basically rules for enabling pathways back and forth between a central goal memory and the various declarative memory modules. This makes it clear than production rules are not really structures that are stored in particular locations but are rather specifications of information transfer. Neurally, they would correspond to pathways between cortical areas.

---

[10]This is the origin of the constraint in ACT–R 4.0 restricting the condition to independent chunk retrievals, preferably just one chunk retrieval.

Goal Memory

The goal stack is an important construct in ACT–R. It is implemented in ACT–RN by using a dedicated type memory of the same character as Fig. 12.1 but with enough slots to encode the slots of both the new goal G and parent goal PG. The header representation is chosen at random in order to minimize interference. To push the new subgoal, both G and PG are copied in the appropriate slots of the stack memory, and the correlations between the slots and the header are memorized, just as type memories are encoded.[11] When G is to be popped, it is copied from central memory to the stack memory and PG is retrieved, just as for any other type retrieval, and restored back to central memory. The association between G and PG is erased from the stack memory through explicit unlearning. Weight decay would be a less exact but perhaps more psychologically plausible technique to accomplish this.

ACT–RN introduced a variant of the mechanism, currently in use in ACT–R 4.0, for returning a result from a subgoal to its parent goal. We had long felt that the inability to do this led to rather awkward production rules in past ACT theories. In addition, this facility avoids a problem that would otherwise arise in ACT–RN: When the goal has been restored to its previous value, the production that initially pushed the subgoal would fire again and the system could be caught in a loop. The appearance of the result value changes the goal and so prevents the old production from firing. The subgoal return mechanism serves a similar refraction role in ACT–R 4.0.

This goal stack mechanism is implemented by gating the transmission of values back and forth between central memory and the result memory, just as information is gated between type memory and central memory. This is represented in the syntax of ACT–RN by augmenting it with a push and a pop command. The push command specifies a slot of the parent goal in which the result returned by the subgoal is to be copied. The pop command in turn specifies a value to be returned when the subgoal is popped. That value is copied to a result memory, which is then restored in the proper goal slot after popping. These commands modify the second production type, **New-Goal**, given earlier to add the push command and the pop command:

Push-Goal
    goal
    ==>
    [push goalslot]
    subgoal

---

[11]Because it has double the slots of goal memory, it is a particularly large type memory.

Pop-Goal
  goal
  ==>
  pop value

The ACT–R 4.0 production rules given in Chapter 2 bear a close relationship to these ACT–RN rules.

In this context one is led to speculate about the neural location of goal memory. Given that damage to the prefrontal cortex results in deficits in executive function (Luria, 1965; Milner, 1963), it is natural to associate goal memory with the prefrontal cortex. Indeed, Kimberg (1994) and Kimberg and Farah (1993) developed a version of ACT–R that models frontal patients in terms of goal-memory deficits that can be conceived as of loss of source activation from the goal (the W_j in Activation Equation 3.5). Similarly, Lovett, Reder, and Lebiere (in press) have modeled individual differences in working memory capacity in terms of source activation. However, goal memory is not associated with a circumscribed small area of prefrontal cortex, because damage to many areas of prefrontal cortex results in similar deficits. Rather, goal memory is probably distributed over large areas of prefrontal cortex.

The Status of ACT–RN

ACT–RN does not perfectly mirror the performance of ACT–R 4.0. For one thing, the connectionist learning algorithms used in ACT–RN do not perfectly mirror the activation processes in ACT–R 4.0 nor the activation learning processes. More substantially, ACT–RN did not address the issue of the learning of new production rules or the tuning of production rules to reflect their expected gain. Still, ACT–RN serves as an existence proof that the basic conception of cognition in ACT–R 4.0 is neurally plausible. At a future time we may work further at improving the correspondence between ACT–R and ACT–RN. Maybe new versions of each system will result. And this takes us to the last point in this book, the future of ACT–R.

THE FUTURE OF ACT–R

ACT–R is not an unchanging theory, and it will be tuned and elaborated as experiences with it warrant. However, we are keenly aware that the cognitive science community does not profit by a rapidly changing theory, especially when it is a complex cognitive architecture. The architecture acquires increased impact and credibility as additional successful models are implemented within the same system without ad hoc changes from one model to another. Researchers who are developing theories of subdomains in ACT–R do not want to see the basis for their theories change under them nor the syntax of ACT–R change capriciously. Researchers who want to perform some critical test or analysis of ACT–R want assurance that their efforts will still be relevant when they are completed. Researchers want a basis for sharing their modeling experiences. Students and scholars who study ACT–R for general edification want some assurance that their knowledge will be relevant. Therefore, for all of these reasons, we have adopted a deliberate strategy of being conservative in changes introduced into the theory. The rate of change from ACT–R 2.0 to ACT–R 4.0, although not rapid, is probably more rapid than in the future, as many of the changes reflect the early growing experiences of ACT–R.

We have made the ACT–R 4.0 code less restrictive than the theory. For instance, although the theory does not perform backtracking in pattern matching, one can get the simulation system to do so.[12] In fact, at a symbolic level almost[13] anything that worked in ACT–R 2.0 can work in ACT–R 4.0. Also, researchers can and do change the code to suit their needs. When we published ACT–R 2.0 we had anticipated more people would have taken the code and produced modified theories to suit their needs. There has been relatively little of this, and we suspect this reflects the value researchers place on having their research in a context similar to that of other researchers. We have offered to produce variants of ACT–R for users that are having problems with some feature, and they have declined to use the variants unless we assured them that these would become part of the common ACT–R.

Although we want to maintain a stable official version of ACT–R 4.0, there will be pressures for change. There will inevitably be discussions in the ACT–R community about strengths and weaknesses of ACT–R 4.0 and researchers trying out variations. Undoubtedly, an idea will arise that is so good that we will be compelled to incorporate it into the official ACT–R. We would like to assure that any such changes will constitute cumulative progress. To help achieve this, we have decided to commit to a conservative policy for entering any significant changes into the official ACT–R 4.0 over the next 5 years. This policy involves a commitment to support all of the running ACT–R models that are available from the published models link in the ACT–R home page. This repository contains running ACT–R models that are described in generally available written papers (they do not actually have to be published but the papers have to be available to the public), including all of the models described in this book. We have also included a

---

[12]This is the behavior of ACT–R when the flag Enable Rational Analysis is off, which essentially disables all subsymbolic computations in ACT–R.

[13]The exceptions are string matching to lists, and generalized negation.

number of other models by other researchers, and we encourage and support more submissions. Our commitment for 5 years is to not introduce any modifications to ACT–R 4.0 that negate the successful behavior of these models. If we do introduce a change that hurts a model's account of some behavioral phenomena, it is our obligation to find some transformation of the model that will allow it to provide at least as good an account. As we will not introduce any changes to ACT–R unless they allow the system to account for some new data, this published models repository becomes a way of guaranteeing that all changes to ACT–R constitute cumulative progress.

For the intermediate term, we are committed to the idea that these published models will be the principal instrument for the evaluation of ACT–R 4.0. ACT–R 4.0 will be successful to the degree that models are built in it that cover a wide range of phenomena in a broad range of domains. Although ACT–R researchers are engaged in this process of model accumulation, undoubtedly new and important issues will arise and be discussed. What might the future directions be for the development of the ACT–R system? We have learned from past experience the perils of predicting the future of the ACT theory, but nonetheless we will describe the dimensions that currently seem most prominent to us, as follows.

Probably, the aspects of ACT–R that seem most problematic are the assumptions surrounding its goal stack. This is curious because, as mentioned throughout this chapter and the book, a goal structure is critical to the success of modern production systems. However, as Chapter 2 noted, the perfect-memory feature of the goal stack seems unrealistic. The research described in this book has not really focused on that assumption. Another important function of the goal structure is localizing conflict resolution and credit assignment to small spans of information processing in service of a goal (see Fig. 3.1). However, again the research to date has not focused on the particulars of these assumptions. Future research may indicate modifications that maintain what ACT–R's goal structure has achieved in terms of focus but are more accurate in terms of details of implementation that have yet to be stressed in ACT–R modeling.

There are a number of issues in our mind surrounding partial matching. For one, the similarity metrics that determine it are currently ad hoc and could use constraint. Also, the mismatch penalty and the associative S_{ji} terms in ACT–R have similar effects and there may be a possible unification. Note that in ACT–RN the S_{ji} terms are represented in the associations between slots and header, but similar inputs (j terms) will evoke similar header representations. Thus, mismatch and association are not simply added as they are in ACT–R. Perhaps related is the fact (noted in Chapter 7) that ACT–R does not have a mechanism for producing continuously varying answers like confidence ratings, similarity judgments, or magnitude estimates. Wallach and Lebiere have explored mechanisms for converting degree of match into such quantities. Whether partial matching is the right mechanism or not, a major hole in ACT–R is the lack of some principled mechanism for producing continuously varying answers. Much psychological research involves such dependent measures, and the relationships involving these measures can be quite systematic.

Finally, there are a number of issues involving production-rule learning. The production compilation mechanism described in Chapter 4 is basically a research proposal, and most of that research has yet to come in. Another issue is the process of production-rule strength learning and the role of production-rule strength in rule execution. Again, the research in this book did not stress those assumptions. For instance, although it is clear some rule-strengthening mechanism is needed, it is unclear whether it should play the role it does in determining retrieval speed (Equation 3.10) but not accuracy (Equations 3.7 and 3.9). Perhaps related to this is the fact the ACT–R community is still working out when learning should be implemented declaratively and when it should be implemented procedurally. This was a major theme of the most recent ACT–R Workshop (Table 12.1). This issue is also reflected in the contrast between the declarative and procedural learning models in Chapter 10 on analogy.

We conclude by reiterating our commitment that ACT–R will continue to grow as a system for developing models in cognitive science and that any further changes will move it even closer to capturing an emerging consensus about the nature of human cognition. Indeed, our hope for ACT–R is that it ceases to be "our" theory of cognition and that it comes to formalize the common wisdom about how to integrate and organize the research and theory in cognitive science. To return to the opening theme of this book, this is what Allen Newell would have wanted.

References

Aaronson, D. (1968). Temporal course of perception in an immediate recall task. *Journal of Experimental Psychology, 76,* 129–140.

Abelson, R. P. (1981). Psychological status of the script concept. *American Psychologist, 36,* 715–729.

Ackley, D. H., Hinton, G. E., & Sejnowsky, T. J. (1985). A learning algorithm for Boltzmann machines. *Cognitive Science, 9,* 147–169.

Altmann, E. M. (1996). *Episodic memory for external information.* Doctoral dissertation, Carnegie Mellon Univerisity, Pittsburgh, PA.

Anderson, J. A., Spoehr, K. T., & Bennett, D. B. (1992). A study in numerical perversity: Teaching arithmetic to a neural network. In D. Levine & M. Aparcio (Eds.), *Neural networks for knowledge representation* (pp. 331–335). Hillsdale, NJ: Lawrence Erlbaum Associates.

Anderson, J. R. (1972). FRAN: A simulation model of free recall. In G. H. Bower (Ed.), *The psychology of learning and motivation* (vol. 5, pp. 315–378). New York: Academic Press.

Anderson, J. R. (1974). Retrieval of propositional information from long-term memory. *Cognitive Psychology, 5,* 451–474.

Anderson, J. R. (1976). *Language, memory, and thought.* Hillsdale, NJ: Lawrence Erlbaum Associates.

Anderson, J. R. (1983). *The architecture of cognition.* Cambridge, MA: Harvard University Press.

Anderson, J. R. (1983). Retrieval of information from long-term memory. *Science, 220,* 25–30.

Anderson, J. R. (1987). Skill acquisition: Compilation of weak-method problem solutions. *Psychological Review, 94,* 192–210.

Anderson, J. R. (1990). *The adaptive character of thought.* Hillsdale, NJ: Lawrence Erlbaum Associates.

Anderson, J. R. (1991). The adaptive nature of human categorization. *Psychological Review, 98,* 409–429.

Anderson, J. R. (1993). *Rules of the mind.* Hillsdale, NJ: Lawrence Erlbaum Associates.

Anderson, J. R. (1996). Implicit memory and metacognition: Why is the glass half-full? In L. M. Reder (Ed.), *Implicit memory and metacognition* (pp. 123–136). Mahwah, NJ: Lawrence Erlbaum Associates

Anderson, J. R., & Betz, J. (1997). Modeling categorization in ACT–R. *Proceedings of the Fourth Annual ACT–R Workshop.* Carnegie Mellon University, Pittsburgh, PA.

Anderson, J. R., Bothell, D., Lebiere, C., & Matessa, M. (in press). An integrated theory of list memory. *Journal of Memory and Language.*

Anderson, J. R., & Bower, G. H. (1972). Recognition and retrieval processes in free recall. *Psychological Review, 79,* 97–123.

461

Anderson, J. R., & Bower, G. H. (1973). Human associative memory. Mahwah, NJ: Lawrence Erlbaum Associates.

Anderson, J. R., & Bower, G. H. (1974). Interference in memory for multiple contexts. Memory and Cognition, 2, 509–514.

Anderson, J. R., Conrad, F. G., & Corbett, A. T. (1989). Skill acquisition and the LISP Tutor. Cognitive Science, 13, 467–506.

Anderson, J. R., Corbett, A. T., Koedinger, K., & Pelletier, R. (1995). Cognitive tutors: Lessons learned. Journal of Learning Sciences, 4, 167–207.

Anderson, J. R., Farrell, R., & Sauers, R. (1984). Learning to program in LISP. Cognitive Science, 8, 87–130.

Anderson, J. R., & Fincham, J. M. (1994). Acquisition of procedural skills from examples. Journal of Experimental Psychology: Learning, Memory, and Cognition, 20, 1322–1340.

Anderson, J. R., & Fincham, J. M. (1996). Categorization and sensitivity to correlation. Journal of Experimental Psychology: Learning, Memory, and Cognition, 22, 259–277.

Anderson, J. R., Fincham, J. M., & Douglass, S. (1997). The role of examples and rules in the acquisition of a cognitive skill. Journal of Experimental Psychology: Learning, Memory, and Cognition, 23, 932–945.

Anderson, J. R., John, B. E., Just, M. A., Carpenter, P. A., Kieras, D. E., & Meyer, D. E. (1995). Production system models of complex cognition. In Proceedings of the Seventeenth Annual Conference of the Cognitive Science Society (pp. 9–12). Hillsdale, NJ: Lawrence Erlbaum Associates.

Anderson, J. R., Kline, P. J., & Beasley, C. M. (1979). A general learning theory and its application to schema abstraction. In G. H. Bower (Ed.), The psychology of learning and motivation (pp. 277–318). New York: Academic Press.

Anderson, J. R., Kushmerick, N., & Lebiere, C. (1993). The Tower of Hanoi and goal structures. In J. R. Anderson (Ed.), Rules of the mind (pp. 121–142). Hillsdale, NJ: Lawrence Erlbaum Associates.

Anderson, J. R., & Matessa, M. (1992). Explorations of an incremental, Bayesian algorithm for categorization. Machine Learning, 9, 275–308.

Anderson, J. R., & Matessa, M. P. (1997). A production system theory of serial memory. Psychological Review, 104, 728–748.

Anderson, J. R., Matessa, M., & Douglass, S. (1995). The ACT–R theory and visual attention. In Proceedings of the Seventeenth Annual Conference of the Cognitive Science Society (pp. 61–65). Hillsdale, NJ: Lawrence Erlbaum Associates.

Anderson, J. R., Matessa, M. P., & Lebiere, C. (1997). ACT–R: A theory of higher-level cognition and its relation to visual attention. Human Computer Interaction, 12, 439–462.

Anderson, J. R., & Milson, R. (1989). Human memory: An adaptive perspective. Psychological Review, 96, 703–719.

Anderson, J. R., & Reder, L. M. (in press). The fan effect: New results and new theories. Journal of Experimental Psychology: General.

Anderson, J. R., & Schooler, L. J. (1991). Reflections of the environment in memory. Psychological Science, 2, 396–408.

Anderson, J. R., & Schunn, C. D. (in press). Implications of the ACT–R learning theory: No magic bullets. In R. Glaser, (Ed.), Advances in instructional psychology (Vol. 5).

Anderson, J. R., & Thompson, R. (1989). Use of analogy in a production system architecture. In S. Vosniadou & A. Ortony (Eds.), Similarity and Analogy, (pp. 367–397). New York: Cambridge University Press.

Anisfeld, M., & Knapp, M. (1968). Association, synonymity, and directionality in false recognition. Journal of Experimental Psychology, 77, 171–179.

Anzai, Y., & Simon, H. A. (1979). A theory of learning by doing. Psychological Review, 86, 124–140.

Ashcraft, M. H. (1987). Children's knowledge of simple arithmetic: A developmental model and simulation. In J. Bisanz, C. J. Brainerd, & R. Kail (Eds.), *Formal methods in developmental psychology: Progress in cognitive development research* (pp. 302–338). New York: Springer-Verlag.

Ashcraft, M. H. (1992). Cognitive arithmetic: A review of data and theory. *Cognition, 44*, 75–106.

Ashcraft, M. H. (1995). Cognitive psychology and simple arithmetic: A review and summary for new directions. *Mathematical Cognition, 1*, 3–34.

Ashcraft, M. H., & Christy, K. S. (1995). The frequency of arithmetic facts in elementary texts: Addition and multiplication in grades 1–6. *Journal for Research in Mathematics Education, 26*(5), 396–421.

Atkinson, R. C., & Shiffrin, R. M. (1968). Human memory: A proposed system and its control processes. In K. Spence & J. Spence (Eds.), *The psychology of learning and motivation* (Vol. 2, pp. 90–195). New York: Academic Press.

Baddeley, A. D. (1986). *Working memory.* London: Oxford University Press.

Baddeley, A. D., Thompson, N., & Buchanan, M. (1975). Word length and the structure of short-term memory. *Journal of Verbal Learning and Verbal Behavior, 14*, 575–589.

Baker, L., & Dunbar, K. (1996). Constraints on the experimental design process in real-world science. *Proceedings of the 18th Annual Conference of the Cognitive Science Society* (pp. 21–22). Hillsdale, NJ: Lawrence Erlbaum Associates.

Benford, F. (1938). The law of anomalous numbers. *Proceedings of American Philosophy Society, 78*, 551–572.

Berry, D. A., & Fristedt, B. (1985). *Bandit problems: Sequential allocation of experiments.* New York: Chapman and Hall.

Bjork, E. L., & Healy, A. F. (1974). Short-term order and item retention. *Journal of Verbal Learning and Verbal Behavior, 13*, 80–97.

Blessing, S., & Anderson, J. R. (1996). How people learn to skip steps. *Journal of Experimental Psychology: Learning, Memory, and Cognition, 22*, 576–598.

Bobrow, D. G. (1980). Special issue on non-monotonic logic. *Artificial Intelligence, 13*(1–2), 1–174.

Bobrow, D. G., & Winograd, T. (1977). An overview of KRL, a knowledge representation language. *Cognitive Science, 1*, 3–46.

Bovair, S., Kieras, D. E., & Polson, P. G. (1990). The acquisition and performance of text editing skill: A cognitive complexity analysis. *Human Computer Interaction, 5*, 1–48.

Bower, G. H. (1996). Reactivating a reactivation theory of implicit memory. *Consciousness and Cognition, 5*, 27–72.

Bower, G. H., & Winzenz, D. (1969). Group structure, coding, and memory for digit series. *Journal of Experimental Psychology Monograph, 80*, 1–17.

Braveman, N. S., & Fischer, G. J. (1968). Instructionally induced strategy and sequential information in probability learning. *Journal of Experimental Psychology, 76*, 674–676.

Briggs, G. E. (1974). On the predictor variable for choice reaction time. *Memory & Cognition, 2*, 575–580.

Broadbent, D. E., Fitzgerald, P., & Broadbent, M. H. P. (1986). Implicit and explicit knowledge in the control of complex systems. *British Journal of Psychology, 77*, 33–50.

Brusilovsky, P., Eklund, J., & Schwarz, E. (1997). Adaptive navigation support in educational hypermedia on the World Wide Web. In S. Howard, J. Hammond, & G. Lindgaard (Eds.), *Human-computer interaction* (Proceedings of INTERACT97, 6th IFIP World Conference on Human-Computer Interaction, Sydney, Australia, 14–18, July 1997, pp. 278–285). New York: Chapman & Hall.

Brusilovsky, P., Schwarz, E., & Weber, G. (1996) A tool for developing adaptive electronic textbooks on WWW. In *Proceedings of WebNet'96—World Conference of the Web Society*, 16–19, October 1996 (pp. 64–69). San Francisco, CA: AACE.

Burgess, N., & Hitch, G. J. (1992). Toward a network model of the articulatory loop. *Journal of Memory and Language, 31*, 429–460.

Burrows, D., & Okada, R. (1975). Memory retrieval from long and short lists. *Science, 188*, 1031–1033.

Busemeyer, J. R., & Myeung, I. J. (1992). An adaptive approach to human decision making: Learning theory, decision theory, and human performance. *Journal of Experimental Psychology: General, 121*, 177–194.

Campbell, J. I. D. (1991). Conditions of error priming in number-fact retrieval. *Memory & Cognition, 19*, 197–209.

Campbell, J. I. D. (1995). Mechanisms of simple addition and multiplication: A modified network-interference theory and simulation. *Mathematical Cognition, 1*, 121–164.

Campbell, J. I. D. (1997). On the relation between skilled performance of simple division and multiplication. *Journal of Experimental Psychology: Learning, Memory, and Cognition, 23*, 1140–1159.

Card, S., Moran, T., & Newell, A. (1983). *The psychology of human-computer interaction.* Hillsdale, NJ: Lawrence Erlbaum Associates.

Carrier, L. M., & Pashler, H. (1995). The attention demands of memory retrieval. *Journal of Experimental Psychology: Learning, Memory, and Cognition, 21*, 1339–1348.

Cheng, P. C.-H. (1990). *Modeling scientific discovery.* Unpublished doctoral dissertation, Open University, Milton Keynes.

Chi, M. T. H., Bassok, M., Lewis, M., Reimann, P., & Glaser, R. (1989). Self-explanations: How students study and use examples in learning to solve problems. *Cognitive Science, 13*, 145–182.

Chi, M. T. H., Feltovich, P. J., & Glaser, R. (1981). Categorization and representation of physics problems by experts and novices. *Cognitive Science, 5*, 121–152.

Cho, B., Rosenbloom, P. S., & Dolan, C. P. (1991). Neuro-Soar: A neural-network architecture for goal-oriented behavior. In *Proceedings of the Thirteenth Annual Conference of the Cognitive Science Society* (pp. 673–677). Hillsdale, NJ: Lawrence Erlbaum Associates.

Chong, R. S., & Laird, J. E. (1997). Identifying dual-task executive process knowledge using EPIC-Soar. In *Proceedings of the Nineteenth Annual Conference of the Cognitive Science Society* (pp. 107–112). Mahwah, NJ: Lawrence Erlbaum Associates.

Cohen, N. J., Eichenbaum, H., Deacedo, B. S., & Corkin, S. (1985). Different memory systems underlying acquisition of procedural and declarative knowledge. In D. S. Olton, E. Gamzu, & S. Corkin (Eds.), *Memory dysfunctions: An integration of animal and human research from preclinical and clinical perspectives. Annals of the New York Academy of Sciences, 444*, 54–71.

Conrad, R. (1964). Acoustic confusions in immediate memory. *British Journal of Psychology, 55*, 75–84.

Conrad, R. (1965). Order error in immediate recall of sequences. *Journal of Verbal Learning and Verbal Behavior, 4*, 161–169.

Corbett, A. T., & Anderson, J. R. (1992). The LISP intelligent tutoring system: Research in skill acquisition. In J. Larkin, R. Chabay, C., & Scheftic (Eds.), *Computer assisted instruction and intelligent tutoring systems: Establishing communication and collaboration* (pp. 73–110). Hillsdale, NJ: Lawrence Erlbaum Associates.

Corbett, A. T., Anderson, J. R., & O'Brien, A. T. (1995). Student modeling in the ACT Programming Tutor. In P. Nichols, S. Chipman, & B. Brennan (Eds.), *Cognitively diagnostic assessment* (pp. 19–41). Hillsdale, NJ: Lawrence Erlbaum Associates.

Covrigaru, A., & Kieras, D. E. (1987). *PPS: A parsimonious production system* (Tech. Rep. No. 26; TR–87/ONR–26). Ann Arbor, MI: University of Michigan, Technical Communication Program.

Cowan, N. (1992). Verbal memory span and the timing of spoken recall. *Journal of Memory and Language, 31,* 668–684.

Craik, F. I. M. (1970). The fate of primary memory items in free recall. *Journal of Verbal Learning and Verbal Behavior, 9,* 143–148.

Curran, T., & Keele, S. W. (1993). Attentional and non attentional forms of sequence learning. *Journal of Experimental Psychology: Learning, Memory, and Cognition, 19,* 189–202.

Davis, D. G. S., Staddon, J. E. R., Machado, A., & Palmer, R. G. (1993). The process of recurrent choice. *Psychological Review, 100,* 320–341.

Devenport, J. A., & Devenport, L. D. (1993). Time-dependent decisions in dogs (*Canis familiaris*). *Journal of Comparative Psychology, 107,* 169–173.

Devenport, L. D., & Devenport, J. A. (1994). Time-dependent averaging of foraging information in least chipmunks and golden-mantled ground squirrels. *Animal Behaviour, 47,* 787–802.

Devenport, L. D., Hill, T., & Ogden, E. (in press). Tracking and averaging in variable environments: A transition rule. *Journal of Experimental Psychology: Animal Behavior Processes.*

Dietterich, T. G. (1997). Four current directions in machine learning research. *AI Magazine, 18*(3).

Dolan, C. P., & Smolensky, P. (1989). Tensor Product Production System: A modular architecture and representation. *Connection Science 1,* 53–68.

Doorenbos, R. (1992). *The match cost of adding a new rule: A clash of views* (Rep. No. CS-92-158). Pittsburgh, PA: Carnegie Mellon University, School of Computer Science.

Doorenbos, R. (1995). *Production matching for large learning systems.* Unpublished doctoral thesis, Carnegie Mellon University, School of Computer Science, Pittsburgh, PA.

Duncker, K. (1945). On problem solving. *Psychological Monographs, 58,* 270.

Ebbinghaus, H. (1913). *Memory: A contribution to experimental psychology* (H. A. Ruger & C. E. Bussenues, Trans.). New York: Teachers College, Columbia University. (Original work published 1885).

Edwards, W. (1956). Reward probability, amount, and information as determiners of sequential two-alternative decisions. *Journal of Experimental Psychology, 52,* 177–188.

Egan, D. E., & Greeno, J. (1974). Theory of rule induction: Knowledge acquired in concept learning, serial pattern learning, and problem solving. In L. W. Gregg (Ed.), *Knowledge and cognition* (pp. 43–103) Hillsdale, NJ: Lawrence Erlbaum Associates.

Eliaser, N. M., Siegler, R. S., Campbell, J. I. D., & Lemaire, P. (1997). *The tie effect in simple arithmetic.* Unpublished manuscript.

Elkind, J. I., Card, S. K., Hochberg, J., & Huey, B. M. (1990). *Human performance models for computer-aided engineering.* Washington, DC: National Academy Press.

Elliot, S. W., & Anderson, J. R. (1995). Effect of memory decay on predictions from changing categories. *Journal of Experimental Psychology: Learning, Memory, and Cognition, 21,* 815–836.

Estes, W. K. (1964). All-or-none processes in learning and retention. *American Psychologist, 19,* 16–25.

Estes, W. K. (1964). Probability learning. In A. W. Melton (Ed.), *Categories of human learning* (pp. 89–128). New York: Academic Press.

Estes, W. K. (1973). Phonemic coding and rehearsal in short-term memory for letter strings. *Journal of Verbal Learning and Verbal Behavior, 12,* 360–372.

Estes, W. K. (1986). Array models for category learning. *Cognitive Psychology, 18,* 500–549.

Falkenhainer, B., Forbus, K. D., & Gentner, D. (1989). Structure-mapping engine. *Artificial Intelligence, 41*, 1–63.

Feldman, J. (1963). Simulation of behavior in the binary choice experiment. In E. A. Feigenbaum & J. Feldman (Eds.), *Computers and thought* (pp. 297–309). New York: McGraw-Hill.

Feustel, T. C., Shiffrin, R. M., & Salasoo, A. (1983). Episodic and lexical contributions to the repetition effect in word identification. *Journal of Experimental Psychology: General, 112*, 309–346.

Fitts, P. M. (1954). The information capacity of the human motor system in controlling the amplitude of movement. *Journal of Experimental Psychology, 47*, 381–391.

Flexser, A. J., & Tulving, E. (1978). Retrieval independence in recognition and recall. *Psychological Review, 85*, 153–171.

Forgy, C., & McDermott, J. (1977). OPS, a domain-independent production system. In *Proceedings of the Fifth International Joint Conference on Artificial Intelligence* (pp. 933–939).

Friedman, M. P., Burke, C. J., Cole, M., Keller, L., Millward, R. B., & Estes, W. K. (1964). Two-choice behavior under extended training with shifting probabilities of reinforcement. In R. C. Atkinson (Ed.), *Studies in mathematical psychology* (pp. 250–316). Stanford, CA: Stanford University Press.

Gallistel, C. R. (1993). *The organization of learning* (first paperback ed.). Cambridge, MA: MIT Press.

Gardiner, J. M., Thompson, C. P., & Maskarinec, A. S. (1974). Negative recency in initial free recall. *Journal of Experimental Psychology, 103*, 71–78.

Geary, D. C. (1996). The problem-size effect in mental addition: Developmental and cross-national trends. *Mathematical Cognition, 2*, 63–93.

Gentner, D. (1983). Structure-mapping: A theoretical framework for analogy. *Cognitive Science, 7*, 155–170.

Gentner, D. (1989). The mechanisms of analogical learning. In S. Vosniadou & A. Ortony (Eds.), *Similarity and analogical reasoning* (pp. 199–241). Cambridge, England: Cambridge University Press.

Gentner, D., & Forbus, K. D. (1991). MAC/FAC: A model of similarity-based retrieval. In *Proceedings of the Thirteenth Annual Conference of the Cognitive Science Society* (pp. 504–509). Hillsdale, NJ: Lawrence Erlbaum Associates.

Gentner, D., & Toupin, C. (1986). Systematicity and surface similarity in the development of analogy. *Cognitive Science, 10*, 277–300.

Gick, M. L., & Holyoak, K. J. (1980). Analogical problem solving. *Cognitive Psychology, 12*, 306–355.

Gick, M. L., & Holyoak, K. J. (1983). Schema induction in analogical transfer. *Cognitive Psychology, 15*, 1–38.

Glenberg, A. M., Bradley, M. M., Kraus, T. A., & Renzaglia, G. J. (1983). Studies of the long-term recency effect: Support for a contextually guided retrieval hypothesis. *Journal of Experimental Psychology: Learning, Memory, and Cognition, 9*, 231–255.

Glenberg, A. M., Bradley, M. M., Stevenson, J. A., Kraus, T. A., Tkachuk, M. J., Gretz, A. L., Fish, J. H., & Turpin, B. A. M. (1980). A two-process account of long-term serial position effects. *Journal of Experimental Psychology: Human Learning and Memory, 6*, 355–369.

Gluck, M. A., & Bower, G. H. (1988). From conditioning to category learning: An adaptive network model. *Journal of Experimental Psychology: General, 117*, 225–244.

Goldberg, D. E. (1990). Probability matching, the magnitude of reinforcement, and classifier system bidding. *Machine Learning, 5*(4), 407–425.

Goldman, S. R., Pellegrino, J. W., & Mertz, D. L. (1988). Extended practice of basic addition facts: strategy changes in learning-disabled students. *Cognition & Instruction, 5*, 223–265.

Graf, P., Squire, L. R., & Mandler, G. (1984). The information that amnesic patients do not forget. *Journal of Experimental Psychology: Learning, Memory, and Cognition, 10,* 164–178.

Gray, W. D. (in press). The nature, detection, & correction of errors in a rule-based task with a display-based control structure. *Cognitive Science.*

Gray, W. D., John, B. E., & Atwood, M. E. (1993). Project Ernestine: A validation of GOMS for prediction and explanation of real-world task performance. *Human-Computer Interaction, 8,* 237–309.

Griggs, R. A., & Ransdell, S. E. (1986). Scientists and the selection task. *Social Studies of Science, 16,* 319–330.

Groen, G. J., & Parkman, J. M. (1972). A chronometric analysis of simple addition. *Psychological Review, 79,* 329–343.

Grudin, J. (1980). Processes of verbal analogy solution. *Journal of Experimental Psychology: Human Perception and Performance, 6,* 67–74.

Haber, R. N. (1983). The impending demise of the icon: A critique of the concept of iconic storage in visual information processing. *Behavioral and Brain Sciences, 6,* 1–11.

Haider, H., & Frensch, P. A. (1996). The role of information reduction in skill acquisition. *Cognitive Psychology, 30,* 304–337.

Haider, H., & Frensch, P. A. (in press). Information reduction in skill acquisition: Is redundant task information no longer perceived? *Journal of Experimental Psychology: Learning, Memory, and Cognition.*

Hake, H. W., & Hyman, R. (1953). Perceptions of the statistical structure of a random series of binary symbols. *Journal of Experimental Psychology, 45,* 64–74.

Halliday, D., & Resnick, R. (1988). *Fundamentals of physics.* New York: Wiley.

Hamann, M. S., & Ashcraft, M. H. (1986). Textbook presentations of the basic addition facts. *Cognition & Instruction, 3,* 173–192.

Hayman, C. G., & Tulving, E. (1989). Is priming in fragment completion based on a "traceless" memory system? *Journal of Experimental Psychology: Learning, Memory, and Cognition, 15,* 941–956.

Healy, A. F., & McNamara, D. S. (1996). Verbal learning and memory: Does the modal model still work? In J. T. Spence, J. M. Darley, & D. J. Foss (Eds.), *Annual Review of Psychology, 47,* 143–172.

Heit, E. (1992). Categorization using chains of examples. *Cognitive Psychology, 24,* 341–380.

Henson, R. N. A., Norris, D. G., Page, M. P. A., & Baddeley, A. D. (1996). Unchained memory: Error patterns rule out chaining models of immediate serial recall. *Quarterly Journal of Experimental Psychology, 49A,* 80–115.

Herrnstein, R. J. (1961). Relative and absolute strength of response as a function of frequency of reinforcement. *Journal of Experimental Analysis of Behavior, 4,* 267–272.

Hinrichs, J. V. (1968). Prestimulus and poststimulus cueing of recall order in the memory span. *Psychonomic Science, 12,* 261–262.

Hinsley, D. A., Hayes, J. R., & Simon, H. A. (1977). From words to equations: Meaning and representation in algebra word problems. In M. A. Just & P. A. Carpenter (Eds.), *Cognitive processes in comprehension* (pp. 89–106). Hillsdale, NJ: Lawrence Erlbaum Associates.

Hinton, G. E., & Anderson, J. A. (1981). *Parallel models of associative memory.* Hillsdale, NJ: Lawrence Erlbaum Associates.

Hinton, G. E., & Sejnowsky, T. J. (1986). Learning and relearning in Boltzmann machines. In D. E. Rumelhart, J. L. McClelland, and the PDP Group, *Parallel distributed processing: Explorations in the microstructure of cognition. Volume 1: Foundations* (pp. 282–317), Cambridge, MA: MIT Press.

Hintzman, D. L. (1992). Mathematical constraints and the Tulving-Wiseman Law. *Psychological Review, 99,* 536–542.

Holyoak, K. J., & Thagard, P. R. (1989a). Analogical mapping by constraint satisfaction. *Cognitive Science, 13*, 295–355.

Holyoak, K. J., & Thagard, P. R. (1989b). A computational model of analogical problem solving. In S. Vosniadou & A. Ortony (Eds.), *Similarity and analogical reasoning* (pp. 243–266). Cambridge, England: Cambridge University Press.

Hopfield, J. J., (1982). Neural Networks and Physical Systems with Emergent Collective Computational Abilities. *Proceedings of the National Academy of Sciences, USA, 79*, 2554–2558.

Hopfield, J. J., (1984). Neurons with graded response have collective computational properties like those of two-state neurons. *Proceedings of the National Academy of Sciences, USA, 81*, 3088–3092.

Hornof, A. J., & Kieras, D. E. (1997). Cognitive modeling reveals menu search is both random and systematic. *Human factors in computing systems: Proceedings of CHI 97* (pp. 107–114). New York: ACM Press.

Hummel, J. E., & Holyoak, K. J. (1997). Distributed representations of structure: A theory of analogical access and mapping. *Psychological Review, 104*, 427–466.

Humphreys, L. G. (1939). Acquisition and extinction of verbal expectations in a situation analogous to conditioning. *Journal of Experimental Psychology, 25*, 294–301.

Jacoby, L. L., Toth, J. P., & Yonelinas, A. (1993). Separating conscious and unconscious influences of memory: Measuring recollection. *Journal of Experimental Psychology: General, 122*, 139–154.

Jarvik, M. E. (1951). Probability learning and negative recency effect in the serial anticipation of alternative symbols. *Journal of Experimental Psychology, 41*, 291–297.

Jensen, E. M., Reese, E. P., & Reese, T. W. (1950). The subitizing and counting of visually presenting fields of dots. *Journal of Psychology, 30*, 363–392.

John, B. E. (1996). TYPIST: A theory of performance in skilled typing. *Human-Computer Interaction, 11*, 321–355.

Johnson, G. J. (1991). A distinctiveness model of serial learning. *Psychological Review, 98*, 204–217.

Johnson, N. F. (1970). The role of chunking and organization in the process of recall. In G. H. Bower (Ed.), *The psychology of learning and motivation* (Vol. 4, pp. 171–247). New York: Academic Press.

Johnson, N. L., Kotz, S. & Balakrishhnan, N. (1995). *Continuous univariate distributions* (Vol. 2). New York: Wiley.

Johnson, T. R. (1997). Multistrategy learning and transfer in tic-tac-toe. *Proceedings of the Fourth Annual ACT–R Workshop*. Carnegie Mellon University, Pittsburgh, PA

Johnson, T. R. (1997a). Computation and retrieval in alphabet arithmetic. *Proceedings of the Fourth Annual ACT-R Workshop*. Carnegie Mellon University, Pittsburgh, PA.

Johnson, T. R. (1997b). Control in ACT–R and Soar. In *Proceedings of the Nineteenth Annual Conference of the Cognitive Science Society* (pp.343–348). Mahwah, NJ: Lawrence Erlbaum Associates.

Johnston, W. A., Dark, V., & Jacoby, L. L. (1985). Perceptual fluency and recognition judgments. *Journal of Experimental Psychology: Learning, Memory, & Cognition, 11*, 3–11.

Johnston, W. A., Hawley, K. J., & Elliott, J. M. G. (1991). Contributions of perceptual fluency to recognition judgments. *Journal of Experimental Psychology: Learning, Memory, & Cognition, 17*, 210–233.

Just, M. A., & Carpenter, P. N. (1992). A capacity theory of comprehension: Individual differences in working memory. *Psychological Review, 99*, 122–149.

Kahneman, D., & Tversky, A. (1984). Choices, values, and frames. *American Psychologist, 39*, 341–350.

Kamil, A. C., Lindstrom, F., & Peters, J. (1985). The detection of cryptic prey by blue jays (*Cyanocitta cristata*) I: The effects of travel time. *Animal Behaviour, 33,* 1068–1079.

Karat, J. (1982). A model of problem solving with incomplete constraint knowledge. *Cognitive Psychology, 14,* 538–559.

Karlin, L., & Kestenbaum, R. (1968). Effects of the number of alternatives on the psychological refractory period. *Quarterly Journal of Experimental Psychology, 20,* 67–178.

Keane, M. T., Ledgeway, T., & Duff, S. (1994). Constraints on analogical mapping: A comparison of three models. *Cognitive Science, 18,* 387–438.

Kendler, T. S., & Kendler, H. H. (1959). Reversal and nonreversal shifts in kindergarten children. *Journal of Experimental Psychology, 58,* 56–60.

Kern, L. H., Mirels, H. L., & Hinshaw, V. G. (1983). Scientists' understanding of propositional logic: An experimental investigation. *Social Studies of Science, 13,* 131–146.

Kessler, C. M. (1988). *Transfer of programming skills in novice LISP learners.* Unpublished doctoral dissertation, Carnegie Mellon University, Pittsburgh, PA.

Kieras, D. E., & Meyer, D. E. (1994). *The EPIC architecture for modeling human information-processing and performance: A brief introduction* (Rep. No. 1, TR-94/ONR-EPIC-1). Ann Arbor: University of Michigan.

Kieras, D. E., & Meyer, D. E. (1996). *The EPIC architecture: Principles of operation.* Unpublished manuscript from ftp://ftp.eecs.umich.edu/ people/kieras/EPICarch.ps.

Kieras, D. E., & Meyer, D. E. (1997). An overview of the EPIC architecture for cognition and performance with application to human-computer interaction. *Human-Computer Interaction, 12,* 391–438.

Kieras, D. E., & Polson, P. G. (1985). An approach to the formal analysis of user complexity. *International Journal of Man-Machine Studies, 22,* 365–394.

Kieras, D. E., Wood, S. D., & Meyer, D. E. (1995). *Predictive engineering models based on the EPIC architecture for a multimodal high-performance human-computer interaction task* (EPIC Tech. Rep. No. 4, TR-95/ONR-EPIC-4). Ann Arbor: University of Michigan, Department of Electrical Engineering and Computer Science.

Kieras, D. E., Wood, S. D., & Meyer, D. E. (1997). Predictive engineering models based on the EPIC architecture for a multimodal high-performance human-computer interaction task. *Transactions on Computer-Human Interaction, 4,* 230–275.

Kimberg, D. Y. (1994). *Executive functions, working memory, and frontal lobe function.* Unpublished dissertation, Carnegie Mellon University, Pittsburgh, PA.

Kimberg, D. Y., & Farah, M. J. (1993). A unified account of cognitive impairments following frontal lobe damage: The role of working memory in complex, organized behavior. *Journal of Experiment Psychology: General, 122,* 411–428.

Kintsch, W. (1992). A cognitive architecture for comprehension. In H. L. Pick, Jr., P. van den Broek, & D. C. Knill (Eds.), *Cognition: Conceptual and methodological issues* (pp. 143–164). Washington, DC: American Psychological Association.

Kirk, E. P., & Ashcraft, M. H. (1997). *Verbal reports on simple arithmetic: A demanding task.* Poster presented at the 38th Annual Meeting of the Psychonomic Society, November, Philadelphia.

Klahr, D., & Dunbar, K. (1988). Dual space search during scientific reasoning. *Cognitive Science, 12,* 1–48.

Klahr, D., Fay, A. L., & Dunbar, K. (1993). Heuristics for scientific experimentation: A developmental study. *Cognitive Psychology, 25*(1), 111–146.

Klahr, D., Langley, P., & Neches, R. (Eds.), (1987). *Production system models of learning and development.* Cambridge, MA: MIT Press.

Klein, R. (1988). Inhibitory tagging system facilitates visual search. *Nature, 334,* 430–431.

Knowlton, B. J., Mangels, J. A., & Squire, L. R. (1996). A neostriatal habit learning system in humans. *Science, 273,* 1399–1402.

Kuhn, D. (1989). Children and adults as intuitive scientists. *Psychological Review, 9*, 674–689.

Kuhn, T. S. (1970). *The structure of scientific revolutions* (2nd ed.). Chicago: University of Chicago Press.

Larkin, J. H. (1989). Display-based problem solving. In D. Klahr & K. Kotovsky (Eds.), *Complex information processing: The impact of Herbert A. Simon* (pp. 319–341). Hillsdale, NJ: Lawrence Erlbaum Associates.

Lebiere, C., & Anderson, J. R. (1993). A connectionist implementation of the ACT–R production system. In *Proceedings of the Fifteenth Annual Conference of the Cognitive Science Society* (pp. 635–640). Hillsdale, NJ: Lawrence Erlbaum Associates.

Lee, C. L., & Estes, W. K. (1981). Order and position in primary memory for letter strings. *Journal of Verbal Learning and Verbal Behavior, 16*, 395–418.

LeFevre, J.-A., Bisanz, J., Daley, K. E., Buffone, L., Greenham, S. L., & Sadesky, G. S. (1996b). Multiple routes to solution of single-digit multiplication problems. *Journal of Experiment Psychology: General, 125*(3), 284–306.

LeFevre, J.-A., Sadesky, G. S., & Bisanz, J. (1996a). Selection of procedures in mental addition: Reassessing the problem size effect in adults. *Journal of Experimental Psychology: Learning, Memory and Cognition, 22*(1), 216–230.

Lehman, J. F., Van Dyke, J., & Rubinoff, R. (1995). Natural language processing for IFORs: Comprehension and generation in the air combat domain. In *Proceedings of the Fifth Conference on Computer Generated Forces and Behavioral Representation* (pp. 115–123). Technical Report 1ST-TR-95-04, Florida Institute for Simulation and Training.

Lemaire, P., & Siegler, R. S. (1995) Four aspects of strategic change: Contributions to children's learning of multiplication. *Journal of Experimental Psychology: General, 124*, 83–97.

Lewandowsky, S., & Murdock, B. B., Jr. (1989). Memory for serial order. *Psychological Review, 96*, 25–57.

Lewicki, P., Hill, T., & Bizot, E. (1988). Acquisition of procedural knowledge about a pattern of stimuli that cannot be articulated. *Cognitive Psychology, 20*, 24–37.

Lewis, C. H. (1988). *Production system models of practice effects.* Unpublished doctoral dissertation, University of Michigan, Ann Arbor.

Li, S. C., & Lewandowsky, S. (1995). Forward and backward recall: Different retrieval processes. *Journal of Experimental Psychology: Learning, Memory, and Cognition, 21*, 837–847.

Logan, G. D. (1988). Toward an instance theory of automatization. *Psychological Review, 95*, 492–527.

Logan, G. D., & Klapp, S. T. (1991). Automatizing alphabet arithmetic: I. Is extended practice necessary to produce automaticity? *Journal of Experimental Psychology: Learning, Memory, and Cognition, 17*, 179–195.

Lovett, M. C. (1994). *The effects of history of experience and current context on problem solving.* Unpublished doctoral dissertation, Carnegie Mellon University, Pittsburgh, PA.

Lovett, M. C., & Anderson, J. R. (1995). Making heads or tails out of selecting problem-solving strategies. In *Proceedings of the Seventeenth Annual Conference of the Cognitive Science Society* (pp. 265–270). Hillsdale, NJ: Lawrence Erlbaum Associates.

Lovett, M. C., & Anderson, J. R. (1996). History of success and current context in problem solving: Combined influences on operator selection. *Cognitive Psychology, 31*, 168–217.

Lovett, M. C., Reder, L. M., & Lebiere, C. (in press). Modeling working memory in a unified architecture. In A. Miyake & P. Shah (Eds.), *Models of working memory: Mechanisms of active maintenance and executive control.* New York: Cambridge University Press.

Lovett, M. C., & Schunn, C. D. (in press). Task representations, strategy variability and base-rate neglect. *Journal of Experimental Psychology: General.*

Luce, R. D. (1959). *Individual choice behavior: A theoretical analysis.* New York: Wiley.

Luchins, A. S. (1942). Mechanization in problem solving. *Psychological Monographs, 54*, 248.

Luchins, A. S., & Luchins, E. H. (1959). *Rigidity of behavior*. Eugene, OR: University of Oregon Books.

Luria, A. R. (1965). Two kinds of motor perseveration in massive injury of the frontal lobes. *Brain, 88*, 1–10.

Mahoney, M. J., & DeMonbreun, B. G. (1977). Psychology of the scientist: An analysis of problem-solving bias. *Cognitive Therapy and Research, 3*, 229–238.

Mandler, G. (1967). Organization and memory. In K. W. Spence & J. T. Spence (Eds.), *The psychology of learning and motivation: Advances in research and theory* (Vol. 1, pp. 328–372). New York: Academic Press.

Mandler, G., & Shebo, B. J. (1982). Subitizing: An analysis of its component processes. *Journal of Experimental Psychology: General, 111*, 1–22.

Mark, T. A., & Gallistel C. R. (1994). Kinetics of matching. *Journal of Experimental Psychology: Animal Behavior Processes, 20*, 79–95.

Marr, D. (1982). *Vision*. San Francisco: W. H. Freeman.

McClelland, J. L., & Chappell, M. (1994). *Bayesian recognition*. Poster presented at the 35th Annual Meeting of the Psychonomic Society, St. Louis.

McClelland, J. L., & Rumelhart, D. E. (1981). An interactive model of context effects in letter perception: I. An account of basic findings. *Psychological Review, 88*, 375–407.

McClelland, J. L., & Rumelhart, D. E. (1986). *Parallel distributed processing: Explorations in the microstructure of cognition*. Cambridge, MA: Bradford Books.

McCloskey, M., & Lindemann, A. M. (1992). MATHNET: Preliminary results from a distributed model of arithmetic fact retrieval. In J. I. D. Campbell (Ed.), *The nature and origins of mathematicall skills*, (pp. 365–409). Amsterdam: Elsevier Science.

McKendree, J. E., & Anderson, J. R. (1987). Frequency and practice effects on the composition of knowledge in LISP evaluation. In J. M. Carroll (Ed.), *Cognitive aspects of human-computer interaction* (pp. 236–259). Cambridge, MA: MIT Press.

Metcalfe, J., & Sharpe, D. (1985). Ordering and reordering in the auditory and visual modalities. *Memory & Cognition, 13*, 435–441.

Meyer, D. E., & Kieras, D. E. (1997). A computational theory of executive cognitive processes and multiple-task performance: Part 1. Basic mechanisms. *Psychological Review, 104*, 3–65.

Miller, G. A. (1956). The magical number seven, plus or minus two: Some limits on our capacity for processing information. *Psychological Review, 63*, 81–97.

Miller, K., Perlmutter, M., & Keating, D. (1984). Cognitive arithmetic: Comparison of operations. *Journal of Experimental Psychology: Learning, Memory, and Cognition, 10*, 46–60.

Milner, B. (1963). Effects of different brain lesions on card sorting. *Archives of Neurology, 9*, 90–100.

Murdock, B. B. (1962). The serial position effect in free recall. *Journal of Experimental Psychology, 64*, 482–488.

Murdock, B. B. (1993). TODAM2: A model for the storage and retrieval of item, associative, and serial-order information. *Psychological Review, 100*, 183–203.

Myers, J. L., & Atkinson, R. C. (1964). Choice behavior and reward structure. *Journal of Mathematical Psychology, 1*, 170–203.

Myers, J. L., & Cruse, D. (1968). Two-choice discrimination learning as a function of stimulus and event probabilities. *Journal of Experimental Psychology, 77*, 453–359.

Myers, J. L., Fort, J. G., Katz, L., & Suydam, M. M. (1963). Differential monetary gains and losses and event probability in a two-choice situation. *Journal of Experimental Psychology, 66*, 521–522.

Nairne, J. S. (1992). The loss of positional certainty in long-term memory. *Psychological Science, 3*, 199–202.

Nelson, G. H., Lehman, J. F., & John, B. E. (1994). Integrating cognitive capabilities in a real-time task. *Proceedings of the Sixteenth Annual Conference of the Cognitive Science Society* (pp. 353–358). Hillsdale, NJ: Lawrence Erlbaum Associates.

Newcomb, S. (1881). Note on the frequency of use of the different digits in natural numbers. *American Journal of Mathematics, 4,* 39–40.

Newell, A. (1973a). You can't play 20 questions with nature and win: Projective comments on the papers of this symposium. In W. G. Chase (Ed.), *Visual information processing* (pp. 283–310). New York: Academic Press.

Newell, A. (1973b). Production systems: Models of control structures. In W. G. Chase (Ed.), *Visual information processing* (pp. 463–526). New York: Academic Press.

Newell, A. (1990). *Unified theories of cognition.* Cambridge, MA: Cambridge University Press.

Newell, A., & Rosenbloom, P. S. (1981). Mechanisms of skill acquisition and the law of practice. In J. R. Anderson (Ed.), *Cognitive skills and their acquisition* (pp. 1–56). Hillsdale, NJ: Lawrence Erlbaum Associates.

Nilsen, E. L. (1991). *Perceptual-motor control in human-computer interaction* (Tech. Rep. No. 37). Ann Arbor, MI: Cognitive Science and Machine Intelligence Laboratory, University of Michigan.

Nilsson, L.-G., & Gardiner, J. M. (1993). Identifying exceptions in a database of recognition failure studies from 1973 to 1992. *Memory & Cognition, 21,* 397–410.

Nissen, M. J., & Bullemeyer, P. (1987). Attentional requirements of learning: Evidence from performance measures. *Cognitive Psychology, 19,* 1–32.

Nissen, M. J., Knopman, D. S., & Schacter, D. L. (1987). Neuro-chemical dissociation of memory systems. *Neurology, 37,* 789–794.

Novick, L. R. (1988). Analogical transfer, problem similarity, and expertise. *Journal of Experimental Psychology: Learning, Memory, and Cognition, 14,* 510–520.

Novick, L. R. (1992). The role of expertise in solving arithmetic and algebra word problems by analogy. In J. I. D. Campbell (Ed.), *The nature and origins of mathematical skills* (pp. 155–188). New York: Elsevier.

Novick, L. R., & Holyoak, K. J. (1991). Mathematical problem solving by analogy. *Journal of Experimental Psychology: Learning, Memory, and Cognition, 17,* 398–415.

Pashler, H. (1994). Dual-task interference in simple tasks: Data and theory. *Psychological Bulletin, 116,* 220–244.

Pashler, H., & Johnston, J. C. (1989). Chronometric evidence for central postponement in temporally overlapping tasks. *Quarterly Journal of Experimental Psychology, 41A,* 19–45.

Payne, J. W. (1976). Task complexity and contingent processing in decision making: An information search and protocol analysis. *Organizational Behavior and Human Performance, 16,* 366–387.

Pennington, N., Nicolich, R., & Rahm, J. (1995). Transfer of training between cognitive subskills: Is knowledge really use specific? *Cognitive Psychology, 28,* 175–224.

Peterson, S., Morton, K., & Simon, T. J. (1997). Modeling a functional explanation of the subitizing limit. In *Proceedings of the Nineteenth Annual Conference of the Cognitive Science Society* (pp. 602–607). Mahwah, NJ: Lawrence Erlbaum Associates.

Pew, R. W., & Mavor, A. S. (1998). *Modeling human and organizational behavior: Application to military simulations.* Panel on Modeling Human Behavior and Command Decision Making: Representation for Military Simulations. Washington, DC: National Academy Press.

Phelps, E. A. (1989). *Cognitive skill learning in amnesics.* Unpublished doctoral dissertation, Princeton University, Princeton, NJ.

Piaget, J. (1952). *The origins of intelligence in children.* New York: International Universities Press.

Pirolli, P. L., & Anderson, J. R. (1985). The role of practice in fact retrieval. *Journal of Experimental Psychology: Learning, Memory, & Cognition, 11*, 136–153.

Poldrack, R. A., & Logan, G. D. (1997). Fluency and response speed in recognition judgments. *Memory & Cognition, 25*, 1–10.

Posner, M. I. (1980). Orienting of attention. *Quarterly Journal of Experimental Psychology, 32*, 3–25.

Qin, Y., & Simon, H. A. (1990). Laboratory replication of scientific discovery processes. *Cognitive Science, 14*, 281–312.

Raaijmakers, J. G. W., & Shiffrin, R. M. (1981). Search of associative memory. *Psychological Review, 88*, 93–134.

Raaijmakers, J. G. W., & Shiffrin, R. M. (1992). Models for recall and recognition. *Annual Review of Psychology, 43*, 205–234.

Rabinowitz, J. C., Mandler, G., & Barsalou, L. W. (1977). Recognition failure: Another case of retrieval failure. *Journal of Verbal Learning and Verbal Behavior, 16*, 639–663.

Rabinowitz, M., & Goldberg, N. (1995). Evaluating the structure-process hypothesis. In F. E. Weinert & W. Schneider (Eds.), *Memory performance and competencies: Issues in growth and development* (pp. 225–242). Hillsdale, NJ: Lawrence Erlbaum Associates.

Raeburn, V. P. (1974). Priorities in item recognition. *Memory & Cognition, 2*, 663–669.

Raimi, R. A. (1976). The first digit problem. *American Mathematics Monthly, 83*, 531–538.

Ratcliff, R., Clark, S., & Shiffrin, R. M. (1990). The list strength effect: I. Data and discussion. *Journal of Experimental Psychology: Learning, Memory, and Cognition, 16*, 163–178.

Ratcliff, R., McKoon, G., & Tindall, M. (1994). Empirical generality of data from recognition memory receiver-operating characteristic functions and implications for the global memory models. *Journal of Experimental Psychology: Learning, Memory, & Cognition, 20*, 763–785.

Reder, L. M. (1982). Plausibility judgments versus fact retrieval: Alternative strategies for sentence verification. *Psychological Review, 89*, 250–280.

Reder, L. M. (1987). Strategy selection in question answering. *Cognitive Psychology, 19*, 90–138.

Reder, L. M. (1988). Strategic control of retrieval strategies. In G. H. Bower (Ed.), *The psychology of learning and motivation* (Vol. 22, pp. 227–259). San Diego, CA: Academic Press.

Reder, L. M. (Ed.), (1996). *Implicit memory and metacognition.* Mahwah, NJ: Lawrence Erlbaum Associates.

Reder, L. M., & Gordon, J. S. (1996). Subliminal perception: Nothing special cognitively speaking. In J. Cohen & J. Schooler (Eds.), *Cognitive and neuropsychological approaches to the study of Consciousness* (pp. 125–134). Mahwah, N.J: Lawrence Erlbaum Associates.

Reder, L. M., Nhouyvansivong, A., Schunn, C. D., Ayers, M. S., Angstadt, P., & Hiraki, K. (1997). Modeling the mirror effect in a continuous remember/know paradigm. *Proceedings of the 19th Annual Cognitive Science Meetings* (pp. 644–649). Mahwah, NJ: Lawrence Erlbaum Associates.

Reder, L. M., & Ritter, F. (1992). What determines initial feeling of knowing? Familiarity with question terms, not with the answer. *Journal of Experimental Psychology: Learning, Memory, and Cognition, 18*, 435–451.

Reder, L. M., & Schunn, C. D. (1996). Metacognition does not imply awareness: Strategy choice is governed by implicit learning and memory. In L. M. Reder (Ed.), *Implicit memory and metacognition* (pp. 45–78). Mahwah, NJ: Lawrence Erlbaum Associates.

Reeves, L. M., & Weisberg, R. W. (1994). The role of content and abstract information in analogical transfer. *Psychological Bulletin, 115*, 381–400.

Rescorla, R. A., & Wagner, A. R. (1972). A theory of Pavlovian conditioning: Variations in the effectiveness of reinforcement and non-reinforcement. In A. H. Black & W. F. Prokasy

(Eds.), *Classical conditioning II: Current theory and research* (pp. 64–99). New York: Appleton-Century-Crofts.

Richman, H. B., Staszewski, J. J., & Simon, H. A. (1995). Simulation of expert memory using EPAM IV. *Psychological Review, 102,* 305–330.

Roberts, W. A. (1972). Free recall of word lists varying in length and rate of presentation: A test of total-time hypotheses. *Journal of Experimental Psychology, 92,* 365–372.

Rosenbaum, D. A. (1980). Human movement initiation: Specification of arm, direction, and extent. *Journal of Experimental Psychology: General, 190,* 475–495.

Ross, B. H. (1989). Distinguishing types of superficial similarities: Different effects on the access and use of earlier problems. *Journal of Experimental Psychology: Learning, Memory, and Cognition, 15,* 456–468.

Ross, B. H., & Kennedy, P. T. (1990). Generalizing from the use of earlier examples in problem solving. *Journal of Experimental Psychology: Learning, Memory, and Cognition, 16,* 42–55.

Rubin, D. C., & Wenzel, A. E. (1996). One hundred years of forgetting: A quantitative description of retention. *Psychological Review, 103,* 734–760.

Ruiz, D. (1987). Learning and problem solving: What is learned while solving the Tower of Hanoi (Doctoral Dissertation, Stanford University). *Dissertation Abstracts International, 42,* 3438B.

Rumelhart, D. E., & McClelland, J. L. (1986). *Parallel distributed processing: Explorations in the microstructure of cognition.* Cambridge, MA: Bradford Books.

Rumelhart, D. E., & Ortony, A. (1976). The representation of knowledge in memory. In R. C. Anderson, R. J. Spiro, & W. E. Montague (Eds.), *Semantic factors in cognition* (pp. 99–136). Hillsdale, NJ: Lawrence Erlbaum Associates.

Rumelhart, D. E., Smolensky, P., McClelland, J. L., & Hinton, G. E. (1986). Schematic and sequential thought processes in PDP models. In J. L. McClelland & D. E. Rumelhart (Eds.), *Parallel distributed processing* (Vol. 2, pp. 7–57). Cambridge, MA: MIT Press.

Runquist, W. N. (1983). Some effects of remembering on forgetting. *Memory & Cognition, 11,* 641–650.

Ryle, G. (1949). *The concept of mind.* London: Hutchinson.

Salthouse, T. A. (1991). *Theoretical perspectives on cognitive aging.* Hillsdale, NJ: Lawrence Erlbaum Associates.

Sauers, R., & Farrell, R. (1982). *GRAPES user's manual* (Tech. Rep.) Pittsburgh, PA: Department of Psychology, Carnegie Mellon University.

Schank, R. C., & Abelson, R. P. (1977). *Scripts, plans, goals, and understanding: An inquiry into human knowledge structures.* Hillsdale, NJ: Lawrence Erlbaum Associates.

Schauble, L. (1990). Belief revision in children: The role of prior knowledge and strategies for generating evidence. *Journal of Experimental Child Psychology, 49,* 31–57.

Schunn, C. D., & Anderson, J. R. (1997). General and specific expertise in scientific reasoning. In *Proceedings of the 19th Annual Conference of the Cognitive Science Society* (pp. 674–679). Mahwah, NJ: Lawrence Erlbaum Associates.

Schunn, C. D., & Klahr, D. (1995). A 4-space model of scientific discovery. In *Proceedings of the 17th Annual Conference of the Cognitive Science Society* (pp. 106–111). Hillsdale, NJ: Lawrence Erlbaum Associates.

Schunn, C. D., Reder, L. M., Nhouyvanisvong, A., Richards, D. R., & Stroffolino, P. J. (1997). To calculate or not calculate: A source activation confusion (SAC) model of problem-familiarity's role in strategy selection. *Journal of Experimental Psychology: Learning, Memory, & Cognition, 23,* 1–27.

Servan-Schreiber, E. (1991). *The competitive chunking theory: Models of perception, learning, and memory.* Unpublished doctoral dissertation, Carnegie Mellon University, Pittsburgh, PA.

Shiffrin, R. M., & Cook, J. R. (1978). A model for short-term item and order retention. *Journal of Verbal Learning and Verbal Behavior, 17,* 189–218.

Shiffrin, R. M., & Steyvers, M. (1997). A model for recognition memory: REM—Retrieving effectively from memory. *Psychonomic Bulletin & Review, 4,* 145–166.

Shiffrin, R. M., & Schneider, W. (1977). Controlled and automatic human information processing: I. Detection, search, and attention. *Psychological Review, 84,* 1–66.

Shraagen, J. M. (1993). How experts solve a novel problem in experimental design. *Cognitive Science, 17(2),* 285–309.

Shrager, J. C. (1985). *Instructionless learning: Discovery of the mental model of a complex device.* Unpublished doctoral dissertation, Carnegie Mellon University, Pittsburgh.

Shrager, J. C. (1987). Theory change via view application in instructionless learning. *Machine Learning, 2,* 247–276.

Shrager, J. (1990). Commonsense perception and the psychology of theory formation. In J. Shrager & P. Langley (Eds.), *Computational models of scientific discovery and theory formation* (pp. 437–469). San Mateo, CA: Morgan Kaufmann.

Siegel, S., & Goldstein, D. A. (1959). Decision-making behavior in a two-choice uncertain outcome situation. *Journal of Experimental Psychology, 57,* 37–42.

Siegler, R. S. (1987). The perils of averaging data over strategies: An example from children's addition. *Journal of Experimental Psychology: General, 116,* 250–264.

Siegler, R. S. (1988). Strategy choice procedures and the development of multiplication skill. *Journal of Experimental Psychology: General, 117,* 258–275.

Siegler, R. S. (1996). *Emerging minds: The process of change in children's thinking.* New York: Oxford University Press.

Siegler, R. S., & Shipley, C. (1995). Variation, selection and cognitive change. In G. Halford & T. Simon (Eds.), *Developing cognitive competence: New approaches to process modeling* (pp. 31–76). Hillsdale, NJ: Lawrence Erlbaum Associates.

Siegler, R. S., & Shrager, J. (1984). Strategy choices in addition and subtraction: How do children know what to do? In C. Sophian (Ed.), *Origins of cognitive skills* (pp. 229–293). Hillsdale, NJ: Lawrence Erlbaum Associates.

Simon, H. A. (1975). The functional equivalence of problem solving skills. *Cognitive Psychology, 7,* 268–288.

Simon, H. A. (1989). The scientist as a problem solver. In D. Klahr & K. Kotovsky (Eds.), *Complex information processing: The impact of Herbert Simon.* Hillsdale, NJ: Lawrence Erlbaum Associates.

Simon, H. A., & Ijiri, Y. (1977). *Skew distributions and the sizes of business firms.* New York: Elsevier/North Holland.

Simon, T., Cabrera, A., & Kliegl, R. (1994). A new approach to the study of subitizing as distinct enumeration processing. In *Proceedings of the Sixteenth Annual Conference of the Cognitive Science Society* (pp. 929–934). Hillsdale, NJ: Lawrence Erlbaum Associates.

Singley, M. K., & Anderson, J. R. (1989). *Transfer of cognitive skill.* Cambridge, MA: Harvard University Press.

Slamecka, N. (1967). Serial learning and order information. *Journal of Experimental Psychology, 74,* 62–66.

Spearman, C. (1904). The proof and measurement of association between two things. *American Journal of Psychology, 15,* 72–101.

Spellman, B. A., & Holyoak, K. J. (1993). An inhibitory mechanism for goal-directed analogical mapping. In *Proceedings of the Fifteenth Annual Conference of the Cognitive Science Society* (pp. 947–952). Hillsdale, NJ: Lawrence Erlbaum Associates.

Sperling, G. A. (1960). The information available in brief visual presentation [Special issue]. *Psychological Monographs, 74(498).*

Squire, L. R. (1992). Memory and the hippocampus: A synthesis from findings with rats, monkeys, and humans. *Psychological Review, 99,* 195–232.

Sternberg, R. J. (1977). Component processes in analogical reasoning. *Psychological Review, 84,* 353–378.

Sternberg, R. J., & Gardner, M. K. (1983). Unities in inductive reasoning. *Journal of Experimental Psychology: General, 112,* 80–116.

Sternberg, S. (1969). Memory scanning: Mental processes revealed by reaction time experiments. *American Scientist, 57,* 421–457.

Sternberg, S., Monsell, S., Knoll, R. L., & Wright, C. E. (1978). The latency and duration of rapid movement sequences: Comparisons of speech and typewriting. In G. E. Stelmach (Ed.), *Information processing in motor control and learning* (pp. 117–152). New York: Academic Press.

Stevens, S. S. (1946). On the theory of scales of measurement. *Science, 103,* 677–680.

Taatgen, N. (1997). A rational analysis of alternating search and reflection strategies in problem solving. In *Proceedings of the Nineteenth Annual Conference of the Cognitive Science Society* (pp. 727–732). Mahwah, NJ: Lawrence Erlbaum Associates.

Tambe, M., Newell, A., & Rosenbloom, P. S. (1990). The problem of expensive chunks and its solution by restricting expressiveness. *Machine Learning, 5,* 299–348.

Thagard, P., Holyoak, K. J., Nelson, G., & Gochfeld, D. (1990). Analogue retrieval by constraint satisfaction. *Artificial Intelligence, 46,* 259–310.

Thorndike, E. L. (1913). *Educational psychology: The psychology of learning* (Vol. 2, pp. 29, 31–37, 60). New York: Teachers College.

Thorndike, E. L. (1922). *The psychology of arithmetic.* New York: Macmillan.

Tipper, S. P., Driver, J., & Weaver, B. (1991). Object centered inhibition of return of visual attention. *Quarterly Journal of Experimental Psychology, 43A,* 289–298.

Toth, J. P., Reingold, E. M., & Jacoby, L. L. (1994). Toward a redefinition of implicit memory: Process dissociations following elaborative processing and self-generation. *Journal of Experimental Psychology: Learning, Memory, and Cognition, 20,* 290–303.

Treisman, A. M., & Gelade, G. (1980). A feature-integration theory of attention. *Cognitive Psychology, 12,* 97–136.

Treisman, A. M., & Sato, S. (1990). Conjunction search revisited. *Journal of Experimental Psychology: Human Perception and Performance, 16,* 459–478.

Tschirgi, J. E. (1980). Sensible reasoning: A hypothesis about hypotheses. *Child Development, 51,* 1–10.

Tulving, E., & Thomson, D. M. (1971). Retrieval processes in recognition memory: Effects of associative context. *Journal of Experimental Psychology, 87,* 116–124.

Tulving, E., & Wiseman, S. (1975). Relation between recognition and recognition failure of recallable words. *Bulletin of the Psychonomic Society, 6,* 79–82.

Underwood, B. J., & Freund, J. S. (1968). Effect of temporal separation of two tasks on proactive inhibition. *Journal of Experimental Psychology, 78,* 50–54.

Van Selst, M., & Jolicoeur, P. (1997). Decision and response in dual-task interference. *Cognitive Psychology, 33,* 266–307.

VanLehn, K., & Jones, R. M. (1993). Better learners use analogical problem solving sparingly. In *Machine learning: Proceedings of the Tenth International Conference* (pp. 338–345). San Mateo, CA: Morgan Kaufman.

Voss, J. F., Tyler, S. W., & Yengo, L. A. (1983). Individual differences in the solving of social science problems. In R. F. Dillon & R. R. Schmeck (Eds.), *Individual differences in cognition* (Vol. 1, pp. 205–232). New York: Academic.

Wallach, D. (1997). Modeling complex problem solving. *Proceedings of the Fourth Annual ACT-R Workshop,* Carnegie Mellon University, Pittsburgh, PA.

Wallach, D. P. (1998). *Kognitionswissenschaftliche Analyse komplexer Problemloeseprozesse.* Wiesbaden: Westdeutscher Verlag.

Watkins, M. J., & Gibson, J. M. (1988). On the relationship between perceptual priming and recognition memory. *Journal of Experimental Psychology: Learning, Memory and Cognition, 14,* 477–483.

West, B. J., & Salk, J. (1987). Complexity, organization and uncertainty. *European Journal of Operational Research 30,* 117–128.

Whalen, J. (1996). *The influence of the semantic representations of numerals on arithmetic fact retrieval.* Unpublished dissertation proposal. Baltimore, MD: Johns Hopkins University.

Whitely, S. E., & Barnes, G. M. (1979). The implications of processing event sequences for theories of analogical reasoning. *Memory & Cognition, 7,* 323–331.

Wickelgren, W. A. (1965a). Short-term memory for phonemically similar lists. *American Journal of Psychology, 78,* 567–574.

Wickelgren, W. A. (1965b). Short-term memory for repeated and non-repeated items. *Quarterly Journal of Experimental Psychology, 17,* 14–25.

Wiesmeyer, M. D. (1992). *An operator-based model of covert visual attention.* Unpublished doctoral thesis, University of Michigan, Ann Arbor.

Winkelman, J., & Schmidt, J. (1974). Associative confusions in mental arithmetic. *Journal of Experimental Psychology, 102,* 734–736.

Winograd, T. (1975). Frame representations and the declarative-procedural controversy. In D. Bobrow & A. Collins (Eds.), *Representations and understanding* (pp. 185–210). New York: Academic Press.

Wishaw, I. Q., & Dringenberg, H. C. (1991). How does the rat (*Rattus norvegicus*) adjust food-carrying responses to the influences of distance, effort, predatory odor, food size, and food availability? *Psychobiology, 19,* 251–261.

Wolfe, J. M. (1994). Guided search 2.0: A revised model of visual search. *Psychonomic Bulletin & Review, 1,* 202–238.

Wu, Q., & Anderson, J. R. (1993). Strategy choice and change in programming. *International Journal of Man-Machine Studies, 39,* 579–598.

Young, R. K. (1968). Serial learning. In T. R. Dixon & D. L. Horton (Eds.), *Verbal behavior and behavior theory* (pp. 122–148). Englewood Cliffs, NJ: Prentice Hall.

Zbrodoff, N. J. (1979). *Development of counting and remembering as strategies for performing simple arithmetic in elementary school children.* Unpublished master's thesis, University of Toronto.

Zbrodoff, N. J. (1995). Why is 9 + 7 harder than 2 + 3? Strength and interference as explanations of the problem-size effect. *Memory & Cognition, 6,* 689–700.

Author Index

Subject Index